275.-

PRAHA

PRAG • PRAGUE • PRAGUE • PRAGA

2. Panorama Pražského hradu ● Panorama der Prager Burg ● Prague Castle Panorama ● Le panorama du Château de Prague ● Il panorama

del Castello di Praga

Miroslav
KROB
& jr.
PRAHA
PRAG • PRAGUE
• PRAGUE • PRAGA
Marie MŽYKOVÁ

KVARTA 1992

KVARTA Praha 1992
ISBN 80-85570-10-6

3. F. Ženíšek: Libuše věští slávu Praze ● F. Ženíšek: Libussa, den Ruhm Prags prophezeiend ● František Ženíšek: Libussa Augurs Glory of Prague ● František Ženíšek: Libuše prédisant la gloire de Prague ● F. Ženíšek: Libussa (Libuše) predice la gloria a Praga

PRAHA

Malebné přírodní uspořádání, zvýrazněné citlivým vrstvením stavebních celků s kouzlem dochovaných památek, dovoluje přijmout tvrzení o Praze, že je nejkrásnějším městem střední Evropy. Strategicky výhodná poloha v samém srdci Evropy, a to na průsečíku dávných obchodních cest, vytvořila podmínky pro příznivý rozvoj města, rozloženého kolem toku Vltavy.

Ve vltavské kotlině došlo k osídlování již v mladší době kamenné. S příchodem Slovanů v 7. století nastalo souvislé budování sídel na levém břehu řeky, kde se posléze začali usazovat také Židé. Vyvýšený vltavský ostroh se později stal nejvýznamnějším místem kmene Čechů. Vládu na sebe strhl cílevědomý rod Přemyslovců, zakládající asi roku 884 první křesťanský kostel zasvěcený Panně Marii. Je příznačné, že záhy vybudované knížecí sídlo, i k podpoře svého rodu, využilo spojení s církví. Dříve než došlo v roce 973 k založení biskupství, v roce 921 byla zbudována románská bazilika sv. Jiří. V její blízkosti pak kníže Václav, před rokem 935, dal stavět první kamennou patrovou rotundu zasvěcenou sv. Vítu. V ní se roku 1085 konala první královská korunovace Vratislava II. z rodu Přemyslovců. (Za rozporů mezi Přemyslovci došlo po roce 1061 k vybudování druhého hradu na Vyšehradě, kde později začínaly korunovační obřady.)

Královské město nabývalo na politickém významu demonstrovaném i skrze výpravnost staveb. Tlumený rytmus, mohutnost a tíha románského slohu poznamenává architekturu, vznikající mezi léty 1100 až 1230. S přispěním královského vlivu dochází k soustavnému rozrůstání obchodně prosperujícího města. V letech 1232 až 1234 Václav I. na pravém břehu Vltavy zakládá Staré (Velké) Město, k jehož osadníkům patřili i němečtí kolonisté, záhy budující kostel sv. Mikuláše. Z podnětu Přemysla Otakara II. po roce 1257 došlo k založení Menšího Města pražského (Malé Strany), rovněž za přispění cizích osadníků. V blízkosti Hradu pak pražský purkrabí Berka z Dubé zakládá Hradčany. Karel IV., za jehož éry Praha dociluje lesku císařského rezidenčního města, zakládá roku 1348 Nové Město. Ve snaze o zvýšení prestiže a moci lucemburské dynastie dává tento panovník městu největší dar: Praha se stává plnohodnotným, sebevědomým partnerem nejvyspělejších evropských měst. Karel IV. důstojně zvelebuje panovnické sídlo, v jehož blízkosti je vybudována katedrála francouzského typu. K podpoře a vzdělanosti roku 1348 zakládá první středoevropskou univerzitu. Ke zvelebení Prahy, která je obehnána věncem hradeb, přispívá řada jeho stavebních počinů, z nichž k nejmarkantnějším patří stavba Karlova mostu. Nakupení rytmů ulic a uliček Karlovy středověké Prahy, s jejím židovským ghettem, výrazně předznamenalo další komunikativní uspořádání a výstavbu města, které po Karlově smrti ztrácí dynamičnost rozvoje.

Následná kapitola husitského revolučního dění architektonickému vývoji města neprospěla. Po dostavění Betlémské kaple v roce 1391, v níž kázal mistr Jan Hus, léta 1416—1437 vymezují údobí sociálních bouří a husitského obrazoboreckého hnutí, které v Praze postihlo mnohé historické památky.

Nová vlna stavebního podnikání za Jagellonců v letech 1471 až 1526 obohacuje zejména architekturu katedrály a Hradu. Po nástupu Ferdinanda I. prosazujícího protireformaci a zejména hájícího absolutistické zájmy Habsburků proti českým stavům, dochází k vyhrocenému konfliktu a vzpouře proti panovníkovi. Její porážka v roce 1547 vede k potlačení městských svobod. Nicméně další stavební úsilí katolicky orientovaných feudálních vrstev otvírá cesty především vlašským stavitelům a řemeslníkům, přinášejícím do Čech nové renesanční tvarosloví. V tomto duchu je rekonstruován částečně vyhořelý hrad, kolem nějž jsou zakládány a zvelebovány zahrady s královsky komfortními odpočinkovými stavbami. Nová obrysová arabeska ušlechtile souměrných staveb, pokrytých křehkým krajkovím sgrafit, se v druhé polovině 16. století vepsala do palácové výstavby Rožmberků, Pernštejnů či Lobkoviců, obohacujících a zjemňujících profil městského panoramatu. Reprezentativní výstavnost Prahy nabývá vyostření koncem 16. století, kdy císař Rudolf II. posiluje rezidenční význam města. Jeho císařský dvůr, přenesený opět do Prahy, učinil město centrem říše, přitažlivé pro umělce a vědce, řemeslníky i dobrodruhy z celé Evropy. Stopy rudolfínské éry a jejího cizokrajného ruchu se malebně vtiskují i do pitoreskně zhuštěné Zlaté uličky v areálu Hradu.

Výjimečná, avšak krátká kulturní perioda rudolfínské Prahy s pověstnými císařovými sbírkami předcházela tíživé době, v níž vyvrcholily rozpory mezi Habsburky a protestantskými stavy. Důsledkem potlačeného povstání české šlechty i měšťanů byly popravy a exekuce, po nichž docházelo k rozsáhlé emigraci nekatolických vrstev národa. Drastický průběh třicetileté války měl za následek hospodářský úpadek země. Praha, která již ztratila rezidenční význam, byla v roce 1648 oloupená švédskými vojsky o značnou část rudolfínských sbírek i o mnohé památky. Přesto se v tomto údobí válečných zvratů otvírá nová kapitola stavebního podnikání, která je provázena vzestupnou energií mezinárodního barokního slohu, přinášeného zejména Vlachy. Jména Spezza, Caratti, Orsini nebo Canevalle jsou spjata s výstavbou, či přestavbou řady pražských staveb. Smělost záměru a demonstraci síly vyjadřuje velkolepá stavba Valdštejnského paláce. Výrazovou mohutnost a plastickou skvělost dokládá Černínský palác na Hradčanech. Nejrozsáhlejší počet aristokratických sídel i měšťanských domů nabírá barokní zhudebnělý rytmus a kontrasty hmot, účinně uplatňovaných zejména v dynamické církevní architektuře obou Dienzenhoferů, Santiniho a posléze i F. M. Kaňky. K bohaté výzdobě chrámů přispívá vyspělá tvorba domácích mistrů malířů, jakými byli třeba K. Škréta, P. Brandl či V. V. Reiner, sochařů velikosti M. B. Brauna nebo F. M. Brokoffa. Architektonický profil doby baroka nejvýrazněji formuje podobu Prahy, která se svou výstavností opět ocitá na úrovni nejvyspělejších evropských měst. Melodický půvab vyspělých barokních staveb harmonicky dotvářejí nově zakládané zahrady a parky.

S nástupem vlády Marie Terezie a následně i Josefa II. dochází na újmu Prahy k důslednější vídeňské centralizaci, ale i národnostnímu útlaku. Přestože ze strany Vídně upadá zájem o Prahu, která už není sídelním městem, nastává rozsáhlá přestavba Hradu, spočívající v sjednocení palácových křídel a fasád. Práce započaté podle projektu N. Pacassiho v roce 1745 přesahují až do 70. let 18. století. V souvislosti s josefínskými reformami, zahrnujícími i rušení řady klášterů a kostelů, přichází Praha o četné památky. Na druhé straně jiné josefínské reformy, včetně zrušení nevolnictví, otevírají možnosti pro větší rozvoj města, mimo jiné i prostřednictvím svobodnějšího podnikání. V důsledku reforem dochází v roce 1784 k sjednocení čtyř historických pražských měst v c. k. magistrát. Praha pozvolna začíná ožívat svébytnějším kulturním děním. Tóny Mozartovy hudby v nově postaveném Nosticově divadle projasňují atmosféru provinčně ztichlého města. Průmyslová výstava v roce 1791 shrnula příznivé výsledky počátečního technického rozvoje. Vznikají vědecké společnosti k podpoře národní vzdělanosti a kultury.

S počínajícím novým věkem došlo prostřednictvím patrioticky orientované zemské šlechty k založení Národního muzea. V Praze nového civilního rázu, daného technickým pokrokem, jsou budovány nové komunikace i chodníky. Dochází k výstavbám nádraží a na konci století se zřizuje elektrická dráha. Do městského interiéru jsou včleňovány pomníky. Romantismus a vyspělejší sociální cítění vede ke zřizování veřejných parků, odvozených od parků anglického typu. Nastává prostor pro rovnoprávnější postavení Židů. Po staletí izolované ghetto Židovského Města je pod názvem Josefov roku 1850 připojeno k Praze, jako rovnoprávný pátý obvod. Na konci století pak špatné hygienické podmínky stísněné židovské čtvrti vedly k její asanaci a následnému vybudování reprezentativní Pařížské třídy se secesními a historizujícími stavbami. Do historizujícího stavebního hávu se odívají i monumenty národní kultury, především zhmotnělý výraz národního sebevědomí, Národní divadlo, budované prostřednictvím lidové sbírky a dále Rudolfinum, dům umělců. Stavby Ulmannovy, Zítkovy, Schulzovy, Barvitiovy či Wiehlovy novorenesančního nebo novobarokního charakteru pozměňují především centrum města.

Dne 28. října 1918, kdy došlo k vyhlášení samostatného Československa, se Praha stává jeho hlavním městem. Již v roce 1920 je k ní připojeno dalších 37 obcí (v r. 1968 dále 21 obcí, v r. 1974 30 obcí). Dochází k nové cílevědomé výstavbě. Moderní architektura je budována zejména v Dejvicích, Bubenči, Ořechovce, Bubnech a na Vinohradech. Příznivý rozvoj zmrazil rok 1939, přinášející okupaci a vyhlášení protektorátu

Čechy a Morava. Válka a poválečné formování politických poměrů zásadně změnily směr stavebního podnikání i jeho dobu. Ačkoliv památkový charakter městského centra byl v podstatě konzervován a v roce 1971 nařízením vlády došlo k vyhlášení pražské památkové rezervace, docházelo k překotné výstavbě nekvalitních sídlišť a řady výškových administrativních staveb, vesměs nepříznivě narušujících harmonii městského panoramatu. Pro realizaci nemnoha vskutku tvůrčích projektů nezbývalo mnoho příležitostí.

Praha řadící se svou historií, kulturním dědictvím, ale i nynějším počtem obyvatel (1 215 660) mezi evropská velkoměsta, znovu čeká na oživení bývalé slávy.

PRAG

Dank seiner malerischen Einbettung in die Landschaft, die durch eine feinfühlige Verteilung der verschiedenen Baukomplexe mit vielen Denkmälern noch unterstrichen wird, wird Prag mit Recht als die schönste Stadt Mitteleuropas gepriesen. Seine strategisch günstige Lage im Herzen Europas, im Kreuzpunkt alter Handelswege, schuf für die an den Ufern der Moldau gelegene Stadt besonders gute Entwicklungsbedingungen.

Im Moldaubecken ließen sich Menschen bereits in der jüngeren Steinzeit nieder. Nachdem sich hier im 7. Jahrhundert n. Chr. Slawen niedergelassen hatten, begann ein kontinuierlicher Aufbau der Siedlungen am linken Ufer, wo sich etwas später auch Juden dazugesellten. Der erhöhte Felsenvorsprung über dem Fluß wurde später zur bedeutendsten Stätte des Stammes der Tschechen, als das zielstrebige Geschlecht der Přemysliden die Regierungsmacht an sich riß. Sie waren es, die hier im Jahre 884 die erste christliche Kirche, der Jungfrau Maria geweiht, gründeten. Es ist bezeichnend, daß der bald daraufhin errichtete Fürstensitz zur Unterstützung seines Geschlechts auch die Verbindung mit der Kirche zu nutzen wußte. Bereits einige Jahrzehnte bevor das Bistum Prag gegründet wurde, gab es hier seit 921 die romanische St. Georgbasilika; in ihrer Nähe ließ dann Fürst Wenzel noch vor 935 die erste steinerne Rotunda erbauen und dem Hl. Veit weihen. Darin fand im Jahre 1085 die erste Krönung des Fürsten Vratislav II. aus dem Geschlecht der Přemysliden, zum König, statt.

Die königliche Stadt gewann allmählich an politischer Bedeutung, was sich auch am Reichtum seiner Bauten zeigte. Gedämpfter Rhytmus, Mächtigkeit und Schwere des romanischen Stils prägen die zwischen 1100 und 1230 entstehende Architektur. Mit Hilfe des königlichen Einflusses wurde die aufblühende Stadt ständig erweitert. In den Jahren 1232 bis 1234 gründete Wenzel I. am rechten Moldauufer die Alte (Große) Stadt, zu deren Ansiedlern auch deutsche Kolonisten gehörten, die bald daraufhin die St. Niklaskirche erbauten. Auf Veranlassung von Přemysl Ottokar II. kommt es nach 1257 zur Gründung der Kleineren Prager Stadt (Kleinseite), ebenfalls mit Unterstützung fremder Kolonisten. In der Nähe der Burg gründet schließlich der Prager Burggraf Berka von Dubé den Hradschin. Karl IV., während dessen Regierungszeit Prag den Glanz der kaiserlichen Residenzstadt erreicht, gründet 1348 die Neue Stadt. In seinem Bestreben, das Prestige und die Macht des Geschlechts der Luxemburger zu erhöhen, schenkt dieser Herrscher der Stadt ein neues Selbstbewußtsein: Prag entwickelt sich unter ihm von einem Provinznest zu einer der bedeutendsten Städte jener Zeit. Karl IV. bringt den Herrschersitz zu Ansehen, als er den Bau des heutigen Doms im Stile einer Kathedrale französischen Typus veranlaßt. Die ersten Architekten waren im 14. Jh. der Franzose Matthias von Arras und sein Nachfolger der süddeutsche Baumeister und Bildhauer Peter Parler, sowie dessen beide Söhne. Zur Unterstützung der allgemeinen Bildung gründet Karl IV. im Jahre 1348 die erste Universität Mitteleuropas, wodurch Prag zu einem einzigartigen Kulturzentrum aufsteigt.

Zur Förderung Prags, das mit einem Mauerkranz umschlossen wurde, trug eine ganze Reihe von Bautätigkeiten bei, unter denen die Karlsbrücke herausragt. Die Anhäufung von Rhythmen der Strassen und Gassen des mittelalterlichen Prags der Karlszeit mit seinem jüdischen Ghetto nahm die weitere Anordnung der Kommunikationsstränge und des Städtebaus maßgeblich vorweg, der nach Karls Tod an Dynamik verliert. Die nachfolgenden Glaubenskämpfe im Zuge der Hussitenrevolutionen brachten der baukünstlerischen Entwicklung der Stadt keinen Gewinn. Nach der Fertigstellung der Betlehemskapelle im Jahre 1391, in der Magister Jan Hus predigte und die Mißtände der katholischen Kirche anprangerte, kamen von 1416—1437 Jahre der sozialen Unruhen und der Bilderstürmerei, denen viele Baudenkmäler in Prag zum Opfer fielen.

Eine neue Welle der Bautätigkeit unter den polnischen Jagellonen von 1471—1526 bereicherte insbesondere die Architektur der Kathedrale und der Burg. Nach dem Regierungsantritt von Ferdinand I., der unter der Fahne der Gegenreformation für die absolutistischen Belange der Habsburger gegen den böhmischen Adel kämpfte, kam es zum offenen Konflikt und zum Aufstand gegen den Herrscher. Die Niederlage im Jahre 1547 führte zur Beschneidung der Stadtfreiheiten. Auf der anderen Seite öffneten die nachfolgenden baulichen Anstregungen des katholisch orientierten Adels für viele italienische Baumeister und Handwerker den Weg nach Prag, die neue der Renaissance verbundene Ausdrucksmittel nach Böhmen mitbrachten. In diesem Geist wird nun die zum Teil ausgebrannte Burg wiederaufgebaut und um sie herum Gärten mit königlich luxuriösen Gartenbauten angelegt. Neue baukünstlerische Umrisse, edle Bauharmonie, betont durch das zerbrechliche Spitzengewebe der Sgraffiti, bestimmten in der zweiten Hälfte des 16. Jh. den Grundton der Palais Rosenberg, Pernštejn oder Lobkowitz, die das Profil des städtischen Panoramas bereicherten und verfeinerten. Unter Kaiser Rudolf II., der 1583 seine Hauptstadt von Wien nach Prag verlegte, erlebten Kunst und Wissenschaft einen neuen Aufschwung. Der kaiserliche Hof machte aus Prag wiederum einen Anziehungspunkt für Künstler und Wissenschaftler, Handwerker und Abenteuerer aus ganz Europa. Die Spuren der rudolfinischen Ära und ihres fremdländischen Treibens sprechen uns heutzutage noch an in der pittoresken Form des Goldenen Gäßchen auf der Burg.

Der einmaligen, jedoch kurzen kulturellen Periode des rudolfinischen Prag mit seinen prächtigen Kunstsammlungen folgte nun eine schwierige Zeit, während der die Widersprüche zwischen den Habsburgern und den protestantischen Ständen ihren Gipfel fanden. Die böhmischen Stände erlitten in der vor den Toren Prags ausgetragenen Schlacht am Weißen Berg eine entscheidende Niederlage.

Der militante Katholik Ferdinand II. ließ die Anführer des Aufstandes hinrichten und den Katholizismus als einzige Religion wieder herstellen. Die Nichtkatholiken wurden zur Massenemmigration gezwungen. Das von den Kämpfen gezeichnete, von schwedischen Soldaten ausgeraubte und seiner Rolle als kaiserliche Hauptstadt beraubte Prag veränderte sein Antlitz. Und doch wird in dieser Zeit ein neues Kapitel der Baugeschichte eingeleitet, die von der aufsteigenden Energie des Barockstils getragen wird. Die Italiener dominieren: Namen wie Spezza, Caratti, Orsini oder Canevalle sind mit dem Auf- oder Umbau vieler Prager Bauwerke verbunden. Kühnheit des Vorhabens und Machtdemonstration sind die tragenden Ideen des grandiosen Wallenstein Palais. Das Palais Černín auf dem Hradschin zeugt von der Größe des Ausdrucks und der plastischen Originalität. Die meisten Sitze der Aristokratie und Patrizierhäuser unterwerfen sich dem Musik gewordenen Barockrhythmus und den Kontrasten der Materialien, die sich zu grosser Wirkung steigern, vor allem in der dynamischen Kirchenarchitektur der beiden Dienzenhofer, Santinis und später auch F. M. Kaňkas. Zu dem prunkvollen Innenschmuck der großen Kirchen trägt das künstlerische Schaffen der einheimischen Meister, der Maler wie vor allem K. Škréta, P. Brandl oder V. V. Reiner, aber auch der Bildhauer wie M. B. Braun oder F. M. Brokoff bei. Das architektonische Profil der Barockzeit prägt das Antlitz Prags am nachhaltigsten, das dank seiner neuen architektonischen Schönheit wiederum das Niveau der bedeutendsten Städte Europas erreicht. Neu angelegte Gärten und Parkanlagen harmonieren mit der melodischen Schönheit der Barockbauwerke.

Während der Regierungszeit Maria Theresias und Josefs II. kam es zum Nachteil von Prag zu einer konsequenten Wiener Zentralisierung, aber auch zur nationalen Unterdrückung. Obwohl von der Seite Wiens das Interesse an Prag sank, das nun keine Haptstadt mehr war, wurde ein umfangreicher Umbau der Burg in Angriff genommen, während dessen die Palastflügel und Fassaden einheitlich gestaltet werden sollten. Die nach dem Entwurf von N. Pacassi im Jahre 1745 begonnenen Arbeiten werden sich bis in die 70er Jahre des 18. Jahrhunderts hinziehen. Im Zusammenhang mit den Reformen Josefs II., die auch die Auflösung einer ganzen Reihe von Klöstern und Kirchen zur Folge hatten, wurde Prag um einige Denkmäler ärmer. Dafür eröffneten die Reformen, darunter auch die Aufhebung der Leibeigenschaft, neue Möglichkeiten für eine größere Entfaltung der Stadt, insbesondere durch das freie Unternehmertum. Infolge der Reformen kam es im Jahre 1784 zur Vereinigung der vier historischen Prager Städte in einen k. und k. Magistrat. Prag erwacht allmählich zu einem neuen eigenartigen kulturellen Leben. Mozarts Musik im neu erbauten Nostitztheater brachte Licht in die Atmosphäre der provinziell still gewordenen Stadt. Die industrielle Ausstellung im Jahre 1781 präsentierte die zukunftsweisenden Ergebnisse des beginnenden technischen Fortschritts. Neue wissenschaftliche Gesellschaften zur Förderung der nationalen Bildung und Kultur entstanden in jener Zeit.

Mit dem beginnenden neuen Zeitalter hing auch die Errichtung des Nationalmuseums durch den patriotisch gesinnten Landadel zusammen. In Prag, das durch den technischen Fortschritt einen nüchterneren Charakter bekam, wurden neue Straßen gebaut und Transportsysteme eingeführt. Es wurden Bahnhöfe gebaut und gegen das Ende des Jahrhunderts hielt die Elektrische siegreich Einzug in die Stadt. Das Stadtbild wurde um Denkmäler bereichert. Der Romantizismus und das wachsende soziale Empfinden führten zur Errichtung öffentlicher Parkanlagen, die sich am Beispiel des englischen Parks orientierten. Die Emanzipationsbestrebungen der Prager Juden führten im Jahre 1850 zur Eingliederung des jahrhundertelang isolierten Ghettos als fünfter gleichberechtigter Stadtbezirk, ab jetzt Josefstadt genannt, in das große Prag. Am Ende des Jahrhunderts wurde das Prager Judenviertel infolge der schlechten hygienischen Bedingungen abgerissen und an seiner Stelle entstand die repräsentative Pariser Straße mit ihren Jugendstil- und historisierenden Häusern. In das historisierende architektonische Gewand kleideten sich auch die Monumente der nationalen Kultur — an erster Stelle das Nationaltheater als Wirklichkeit gewordenes nationales Selbstbewußtsein, und das Rudolfinum, das Haus der Künstler. Die im Neurenaissance- und Neubarockstil ausgeführten Bauwerke von Ulmann, Zítek, Schulz, Barvitius oder Wiehl veränderten vor allem das Stadtbild im Stadtzentrum.

Am 28. Oktober 1918 wurde die selbständige Tschechoslowakei geboren und Prag wurde ihre

Hauptstadt. Bereits im Jahre 1920 wurden weitere 37 Ortschaften eingemeindet (1968 weitere 21, 1974 kamen noch weitere 30 dazu).

Überall wurde zielbewußt gebaut. Eine neue Architektur prägt die Stadtteile Dejvice, Bubeneč, Ořechovka, Bubny und Vinohrady. Diese positive bauliche Entwicklung wurde 1939 durch die Erklärung des Protektorats Böhmen und Mähren am Vorabend des zweiten Weltkrieges unterbrochen. Der Krieg und die Nachkreigszeit, in der die Weichen für die künftige politische Entwicklung gestellt wurden, veränderten gänzlich die Bauaktivitäten in Prag. Im Jahre 1971 wurde das historische Zentrum durch einen Regierungserlaß zum Stadtreservat erklärt. An den Stadträndern kam es zum vorschnellen Aufbau neuer Ballungsgebiete und neuer administrativer Hochhäuser, die die Harmonie des Stadtpanoramas ungünstig beeinflußten. Für die Verwirklichung der wenigen tatsächlich schöpferischen Projekten blieben nicht viele Gelegenheiten übrig.

Prag, das goldene, das hunderttürmige, die Mutter der Städte, das mit seinen 1,2 Mio. Einwohnern die Millionengrenze längst überschritten hat, nimmt dank seiner Geschichte und kulturellen Vergangenheit unter den europäischen Großstädten einen ehrenvollen Platz ein. Es wartet auf die Auferstehung des vergangenen Ruhmes.

PRAGUE

A picturesque variety of natural conditions amplified by a careful stratification of buildings and a magic of preserved monuments allow for a general adoption of the saying that Prague is the most beautiful Central European city. A strategic geographical position in the very heart of Europe on the crossroads of ancient trade corridors became a precondition of a favourable development of the town around the Vltava river.

The first settlements in the Vltava basin were in the Early Stone Age. Upon the arrival of the Slavs in the 7th century, a continuous building of settlements began on the left river bank. Later, Jews took up their residence in this area too. An elevated headland of the Vltava river became the most significant settlement of the Czech tribe, governed by the tenacious Premyslid dynasty. In 884, the first Christian church was established here, consecrated to the Virgin Mary. Interrelations with church were typical of the princes seat built up here, supporting the power of the ruling dynasty. Before a bishopric was established in 973, the Romanesque St. George's basilica as built in 921 and the first stone two-storey chapel was founded before 935 by Prince Wenceslas, consecrated to St. Vitus. Here, the first coronation of King Vratislav II of the Premyslid dynasty took place in 1085. (As a result of controversies between the members of the Premyslid dynasty, another castle was built on the Vyšehrad rock, where the following coronations started.)

The royal town of Prague started gaining political importance, which was reflected in its architecture. A soft rhythm, robustnesss and mass are characteristic of the architecture between 1100 and 1230. Promoted by the royal power, the commercially prospering town keeps spreading. In 1232—1234, the Old (Great) Town was founded on the right Vltava bank by Wenceslas I and populated on the right Vltava bank by Wenceslas I and populated also with German colonists, who built the St Nicholas cathedral. Initiated by Přemysl Otakar II, the Lesser Town was founded in 1257, with the support of foreign settlers. Then, the Hradčany Town was founded in the vicinity of the Prague Castle by a Prague burgrave Berka of Dubá. Charles IV, under whom Prague achieves the glory of the Kaiser's residential town, gives rise to the New Town in 1348. In order to multiply the prestige and the power of the Luxemburg dynasty, this emperor presents the town with the highest dignity: Prague becomes an equal and a self-confident partner to the most advanced European towns. Charles IV raises the king's seat to a higher level—a French-style cathedral is being finished near the castle. In 1348, the first Central European university is founded to promote culture and education. Prague is encircled with walls and enriched with such constructions as the Charles Bridge, for example. A further communicative arrangement and constructional expansion of Prague resulted from an accumulation of the rhythm of streets and lanes of the medieval town and the Jewish ghetto. After Charles' death, however, the town development slows down significantly.

What came during the Hussite revolutionary movement was rather detrimental to the architectural development of the town. In 1391, the Bethlehem Chapel was completed and witnessed John Huss preaching sermons. The 1416—1437 period was characterized by social uprisings and the iconoclastic movement, which inflicted great damage to Prague's historical monuments.

A new wave of constructing efforts in 1471—1526 during the reign of the Jagellon dynasty develops the architecture of the St. Vitus Cathedral and the Prague Castle in particular. Under Ferdinand I, enforcing the Counter-Reformation and advocating the absolutistic interests of the Habsburg dynasty against the Czech Estates, the contrasts culminated, and a rebellion against the monarch broke out. Its defeat in

1547 resulted in town franchises being suppressed. Nevertheless, further building efforts of the Catholic feudal class provide access of Italian architects and craftsmen to the Czech countries, who introduce here a new, Renaissance morphology. In this style, the partly burnt down Prague Castle was reconstructed and surrounded with new and renewed gardens with luxurious buildings intended for recreation. A new contour arabesque of gracefully symmetrical constructions surfaced with fragile lace of grafitti was a typical feature of the palaces of the Rožmberk, Pernštejn, and Lobkovic dynasties in the second half of the 16th century, enriching and sophisticating the profile of the town's panorama. The representative and imposing architecture of Prague reached its height in the late 16th century under Rudolph II, who augmented the residential importance of the town. Having been transferred back to Prague, the Kaiser's court elevated the town to the centre of the empire, attracting artists, scientists, craftsmen and adventurers from all over Europe. The impact of the Rudolph era and its exotic flavour can also be found in the picturesque compactness of the Golden Lane at the Prague Castle.

The extraordinary, yet very short period of the Rudolphian Prague with the Emperor's famous collections was followed by hard times, since the contrasts between the Habsburgs and the protestant Estates came to a head. The uprising of the Czech nobility and burghers was stifled, resulting in executions and a vast emigration wave of the non-Catholic population. The drastic course of the Thirty Year War events brought about an economic decline of the country. Prague, which had lost its residential significance, was robbed of the essential part of Rudolph's collections and many other valuable artifacts by Swedish troops. Despite this, a new architectural period began in this turbulent period, featuring the progressive power of the international Baroque style, brought by the Italians in particular. Such names as Spezza, Caratti, Orsini, and Canevallo are associated with the construction or reconstruction of a number of Prague's monuments. The magnificent Wallenstein Palace demonstrates courage and spirit of intention. The Černín Palace in the Hradčany Town witnesses an expressive robustness and splendour. Most aristocratic residences and burgher houses are given a melodious rhythm and mass contrasts of the Barogue style, applied, especially, with a great effect in the dynamic church architecture of the Dienzenhofers, Santini and later Kaňka. Churches are sumptuously decorated also by home artists, for example by such painters as Karel Škréta, Petr J. Brandl and Václav V. Reiner, and sculptors as Matyáš B. Braun and Ferdinand M. Brokoff. It was Baroque that shaped Prague's profile most distinctly, ranking once more among the most advanced European towns. The melodious charm of its Baroque buildings is harmonically complemented by newly established gardens and parks.

With Maria Theresa and later Joseph II ascending to the throne, a more perseverant centralization in Vienna and oppression of nationalities were experienced. Despite Vienna's lower interest in Prague, which is no longer a residential town, Prague Castle is being reconstructed by a regularization of palace wings and fronts. The activities based on Pacassi's project of 1745 last until 1770s. As a result of Joseph's reforms, abolishing many monasteries and churches among others, Prague loses many monuments. Other reforms, on the other hand, are positive in promoting the development of the town by allowing free undertaking, for example. As a result of the above mentioned reforms, four historical Prague towns were united in 1784 under the Central Municipal Board. Step by step, Prague is becoming a racier cultural centre. The tones of Mozart's music that can be heard in the newly built Nostic Theatre make the silent atmosphere of the town brighten. The Industrial Exhibiton in 1791 summarizes the assets of the beginnings of the technological development. New scientific associations are established to maintain education and culture of the nation.

The beginning of a new century was connected with the foundation of the National Museum enforced by the patriotic nobility. New communications and pavements are built, endowing Prague with a new, civil character based on the technological progress. Railway stations are built and, in the late 19th century, the electric tramway is introduced. Memorials become component parts of the urban interior. Romanticism and advanced social awareness give rise to public parks in the English style. Conditions are created for a more equal position of the Jews. The Jewish Town ghetto, isolated for centuries, is called Josefov and joined to Prague as its fifth town with equal rights in 1850. Due to poor hygienic conditions, the narrow Jewish quarter was demolished and replaced by a representative Pařížská (Paris) Avenue with Art Nouveau and historicizing buildings in the late 19th century. The monuments of the national culture also set clad in historicizing robes—particularly the National Theatre, a materialized expression of the national self-confidence, built by means of a public money collection, and Rudolphinum, the House of Artists. Ulmann's, Zítek's, Shulz', Barvitius' and Wiehl's buildings alter the face of the town centre.

On 28 October 1918, an independent Czechoslovakia was declared and Prague becomes its capital. Another 37 communities are joined to it in 1920 (a further 21 communities in 1968 and 30 communities in 1974). New, purposeful constructions come into being. Modern architecture can be found especially in the Dejvice, Bubeneč, Ořechovka, Bubny, and. Vinohrady quarters. This positive development was interrupted in 1939 by the Nazi occupation and the declaration of the Protectorate of Bohemia and Moravia. The war and the post-war political directions basically changed the trends of the architectural undertaking. Although the town center monuments remained preserved in principle and a conservation area of Prague was established by a governmental decree in 1971, bad quality housing estates and many multi-storey administrative buildings were built in haste, mostly impairing the harmony of the town's panorama. There were few opportunities indeed to carry out inventive and creative projects.

Thanks to its history, cultural heritage and the present-day population 1, 215, 660, Prague is one of Europe's major cities and looks forward to shining in its former glory.

PRAGUE 

La situation de la capitale tchécoslovaque aux alentours pittoresques se mariant à perfection aux styles architectoniques les plus divers et à la magie des monuments historiques conservés permet de soutenir l'opinion caractérisant Prague comme la plus belle ville de l'Europe centrale. Sa disposition favorable du point de vue stratégique, en plein cœur de l'Europe, au carrefour des voies de communication anciennes sillonnées par des commerçants, a créé des conditions favorables pour le développement de la ville, s'étendant le long du cours de la Vltava.

Le bassin de la Vltava est peuplé déjà à l'âge de la pierre polie. L'arrivée des tribus slaves au VIIe siècle se traduit par l'édification systématique des demeures sur le bord gauche de la rivière où également les Juifs ne tardent pas à s'installer. L'éperon rocheux devient le siège de première importance de la tribu des Tchèques à la tête desquels se trouve la famille ambitieuse des Přemyslides qui y fondent, en 884, la première église chrétienne du pays, consacrée à la Sainte Vierge. Il est significatif que les princes, après avoir érigé leur siège, se joignent à l'Eglise catholique pour renforcer la position incombant à leur dynastie. Encore avant la fondation de l'évêché en 973, la basilique Saint-Georges voit le jour en 921, à proximité de laquelle le prince Venceslas entame, avant l'an 935, la construction de la première rotonde en pierre à un étage, consacrée à saint Guy, devenue, en 1085, le lieu du premier couronnement — la couronne royale ceint Vratislav II, descendant de la famille des Přemyslides. Les différends ayant opposé après l'an 1061 les descendants des Přemyslides se traduisent par l'édification du second siège seigneurial, à Vyšehrad, où, plus tard, les cérémonies de couronnement se déroulent.

La ville royale n'arrête pas de consolider son influence politique, ce dont témoignent, entre autres, les édifices somptueux. Un rythme sobre, la puissance et la lourdeur du style roman caractérisent les œuvres architectoniques, érigées dans les années 1100—1230. La ville prospérante du point de vue commercial s'agrandit systématiquement, ceci avec le concours de l'autorité royale. Dans les années 1232—1233, Venceslas Ier fonde sur le bord droit de la Vltava la Vieille (Grande) Ville de Prague, peuplée non en dernier lieu par les colons allemands, édifiant bientôt l'église Saint-Nicolas. Sur l'initiative du roi Přemysl Otokar II, est fondée, après l'an 1257, la Cité mineure de Prague (l'actuelle Malá Strana) qui voit le jour également grâce au concours des colons étrangers. A proximité du Château, Berka de Dubá, burgrave de Prague, fonde le quartier de Hradčany, dominé par la résidence royale. Charles IV, sous le règne duquel Prague resplendit en tant que siège impérial, fonde, en 1348, la Nouvelle Ville de Prague. Ses efforts visant à renforcer le prestige et le pouvoir de la dynastie des Luxembourg ont pour conséquence le fait que grâce à cet empereur éclairé, Prague se transforme en un partenaire à part entière et plein d'assurance des villes européennes les plus prospérantes. Charles IV métamorphose le siège des souverains de Bohême; à sa proximité voit le jour une cathédrale de type français. Il concourt à l'instruction et l'érudition de la population et fonde, en 1348, la première Université en Europe centrale. Prague, à cette époque-là, entourée de fortifications, est le lieu d'activités architectoniques sans précédent. Parmi les ouvrages dus aux efforts de ce bâtisseur inlassable, mentionnons le pont Charles, construction la plus remarquable en son temps. L'entassement cadencé des rues et ruelles médiévales qui voient le jour à l'époque du règne de Charles IV détermine, ensemble avec le ghetto de Prague, la disposition du réseau routier et l'édification subséquente de la ville, dont le dynamisme et l'éclat disparaissent après la mort de Charles IV.

S'ensuit la période du mouvement hussite qui est loin de concourir à l'essor architectonique de la ville. Après l'achèvement de la Chapelle de Bethléem en 1391, où prêche le Maître Jan Hus, les années 1419 à 1437 peuvent être caractérisées comme une étape d'émeutes sociales et d'iconoclasme dont de nombreux monuments historiques pragois sont les victimes.

Une nouvelle vague d'entreprise de bâtiment sous les Jagellon, dans les années 1471—1526, ne tarde pas à marquer l'aspect architectonique de la cathédrale et du Château de Prague. A l'avènement au trône de Bohême de Ferdinand Ier, partisan fervent des tendances anti-réformatrices et playdoyeur passionné en faveur des intérêts absolutistes, opposant la dynastie des Habsbourgs aux états tchèques, nous sommes les témoins de l'insurrection contre le souverain par laquelle culminent les conflits aigüs de l'époque. La défaite des états tchèques en 1547 aboutit à la suppression des libertés dont bénéficièrent jusqu'alors les villes du royaume. Pourtant, les efforts des couches féodales orientées vers la religion catholique ouvrent un large champ d'action notamment aux architectes et artisans italiens, introduisant en Bohême de nouveaux éléments Renaissance. Ce style ne tarde pas à se faire remarquer, plus particulièrement pendant la reconstruction du Château partiellement incendié, aux abords duquel sont fondés et cultivés des jardins dominés par des édifices de plaisance magnifiques. Les lignes sublimes des édifices bien proportionnés affichant des sgraffites, faisant penser aux dentelles délicates, caractérisent les palais érigés dans la seconde moitié du XVIe siècle par les familles Rožmberk, Pernštejn ou Lobkowitz, enrichissant le panorama de la ville et lui conférant un aspect imprégné de douceur. Le caractère représentatif des complexes architectoniques s'étendant sur le territoire de Prague atteint son apogée à la fin du XVIe siècle quand l'empereur Rodolphe II concourt au renforcement de la position de Prague, qui voit s'attribuer une nouvelle importance en tant que ville résidentielle impériale. La cour réunie par l'empereur Rodolphe II et transférée à Prague, transforme cette ville en un centre plaisant aux artistes, hommes de science, artisans et aventuriers, originaires de l'Europe entière. Les traces de l'époque de Rodolphe II et de l'animation étrangère dont cette dernière fut le témoin, empreignent encore de nos jours la pittoresque ruelle Dorée, coincée dans l'enceinte du Château.

La période tout à fait exceptionnelle, mais, hélas, trop brève du règne de Rodolphe II, se caractérisant par un essor culturel, ce dont témoignent les fameuses collections réunies par cet amateur passionné des arts, est antérieure à une époque pénible au cours de laquelle les conflits opposant les Habsbourgs aux états tchèques battent le plein. L'insurrection de la noblesse et bourgeoisie tchèques est suivie par des peines capitales et des confiscations qui aboutissent à une forte émigration des couches non catholiques. Le déroulement dramatique de la guerre de Trente ans a pour conséquence un déclin économique du pays. Prague qui perdit son importance résidentielle, est pillée, en 1648, par la soldatesque suédoise qui s'empare de nombreuses collections réunies par Rodolphe II et fait disparaître de nombreux monuments historiques. Pourtant cette période, témoin d'événements bouleversants, ouvre une nouvelle étape de l'entreprise de bâtiment, qui s'accompagne par l'essor de l'art baroque, style architectonique se faisant valoir à l'échelle internationale, introduit en Bohême notamment par les Italiens. Les noms tels que Spezza, Caratti, Orsini ou Canevallo sont à jamais liés à l'édification ou reconstruction de nombreux bâtiments pragois. L'ardeur du dessein et la manifestation de la détermination sont exprimés par l'édifice majestueux du palais Wallenstein. La monumentalité expressive et la splendeur plastique, tels sont les attributs à conférer au palais Černín, situé dans l'enceinte du Château de Prague. Les résidences aristocratiques et bourgeoises de l'époque se caractérisent par la cadence baroque presque musicale et les effets dus au contraste des matériaux mis parfaitement en valeur notamment par les bâtisseurs des églises, affichant un dynamisme sans précédent, œuvres des deux Dienzenhofer, de Santini et plus tard de F. M. Kaňka. Les artistes du pays, plus particulièrement les peintres (K. Škréta, P. Brandl, V. V. Reiner) et les sculpteurs (M. B. Braun et F. M. Brokoff) ne tardent pas à apporter leur contribution aux riches décors des églises de l'époque. Les silhouettes des édifices baroques découpent vigoureusement le panorama de Prague qui, grâce à l'harmonie et la beauté extérieure égale les villes européennes les plus évoluées. La grâce mélodique des bâtiments baroques se marie harmonieusement au charme des jardins et parcs fondés en même temps.

Le règne de Marie-Thérèse et de son successeur Joseph II se caractérisent par une centralisation de la cour viennoise au détriment de Prague, accompagnée d'une oppression nationale sous laquelle gémissent les pays constituant jadis le royaume de Bohême. Même si Vienne est loin de manifester de l'intérêt pour Prague qui perdit son rôle de siège royal et impérial, on procède à une reconstruction de grande envergure du Château de Prague aboutissant à l'unification des ailes du palais et des façades. Les travaux, entamés selon le projet de N. Pacassi en 1745 ne se parachèvent que dans les années 70 du XVIIIe siècle. En conséquence des réformes apportées par Joseph II, se traduisant non en dernier lieu par l'abolition de nombreux monastères et églises, Prague voit disparaître plusieurs monuments historiques. Cependant, les réformes de Joseph II, plus particulièrement l'abolition du servage, se traduisant par une entreprise plus libre, ouvrant de nouvelles possibilités à l'essor ultérieur de la ville.

Par suite des réformes, l'an 1784 est le témoin de l'unification des quatre villes historiques de Prague constituant dorénavant la municipalité impériale et royale. Peu à peu, Prague reprend le souffle et s'anime d'événements culturels. Les sons de la musique de Mozart résonnant dans le théâtre Nostitz nouvellement bâti pénètrent les ténèbres dans lesquelles sombre la ville provinciale réduite au silence. L'exposition universelle organisée en 1791 est l'expression éloquente des débuts prometteurs du développement des branches techniques. En même temps, les sociétés savantes voient le jour afin d'encourager l'instruction et la culture nationales.

Au seuil des temps nouveaux est fondé, grâce au concours de l'aristocratie patriotique du pays, le Musée national. Prague, manifestant un aspect toujours plus civil, dû au progrès technique, voit apparaître de nouvelles voies de communication et des trottoirs. Les gares voient le jour et à la fin du XIXe siècle son territoire est sillonné par les premiers tramways. Les monuments s'intègrent à l'intérieur de la ville. Le romantisme et le sentiment envers les couches sociales moins fortunées amènent à l'aménagement des parcs publics à l'anglaise. Egalement la colonie juive connaît, peu à peu, une condition sociale plus égale. La Cité juive, représentant pendant de longs siècles un ghetto isolé, voit s'attribuer le nom de Josefov et en 1850, elle est intégrée à la Ville de Prague pour figurer désormais comme son cinquième arrondissement et donc partenaire à part entière. A la fin du XIXe siècle, le souci d'hygiène et les conditions insalubres caractérisant la Cité juive serrée et surpeuplée sont l'origine de l'assainissement de cette dernière; l'avenue de Paris représentative ne tarde pas à être bordée de nouveaux édifices affichant le goût de l'histoire ou bâtie dans le style de l'Art nouveau. Même des monuments représentant l'expression de la culture nationale sont marqués par le goût des styles architectoniques du passé — à titre d'exemple, mentionnons le Théâtre national, matérialisant l'assurance de la nation tchèque d'elle-même, car érigé grâce aux collectes populaires, et le Rudolfinum, appelé également Maison des artistes. Les édifices bâtis selon les projets dessinés par Ulmann, Zítek, Schulz, Barvitio et Wiehl, dans le style néo-Renaissance ou néo-gothique, transforment l'aspect surtout du centre de la ville.

Le 28 octobre 1918, la Tchécoslovaquie indépendante est proclamée dont Prague devient la capitale. Déjà en 1920, 37 nouvelles communes s'intègrent à l'agglomération de la métropole et sont suivies, en 1968, par 21 communes ultérieures ; enfin, en 1974, les faubourgs de Prague incluent 30 nouvelles communes. Des ouvrages architectoniques modernes sont implantés notamment dans les quartiers de Dejvice, Bubeneč, Ořechovka, Bubny et Vinohrady. Le développement prometteur est interrompu en 1939, année du début de l'occupation nazie et de la proclamation du Protectorat de Bohême-Moravie. La Seconde Guerre mondiale et la nouvelle situation politique enregistrée pendant l'après-guerre marquent d'une manière significative l'orientation de l'entreprise du bâtiment de même que l'étape qui suit. Malgré que le caractère du centre de la capitale, considéré comme cité classée et donc protégée, se soit plus ou moins conservé (en 1971 le centre de Prague est classé réserve de monuments historiques de première importance, on se précipite d'édifier de grands ensembles, des cités-satellites et des buildings, sièges administratifs des organismes les plus divers, déconcertant, pour la plupart, le panorama harmonieux de la ville. Les occasions de réaliser des projets ingénieux sont vraiment rares.

Prague appartenant, grâce à son riche passé, son legs culturel et non en dernier lieu le nombre d'habitants (1 215 660) aux grandes villes européennes, attend le moment de regagner son ancien éclat.

PRAGA 

La pittoresca composizione naturale con la sua stratificazione chiaramente sentita dei suoi complessi edili, con l'incanto dei monumenti conservati, avvalora la sentenza, che Praga è la più bella città dell'Europa Centrale. La sua posizione è vantaggiosa trovandosi nel cuore stesso dell'Europa, quindi, nel punto d'intersezione delle antiche strade commerciali; da qui sgorgano le condizioni per lo sviluppo favorevole della città estesa lungo il flusso della Moldava.

Nella valle della Moldava si registrano gli insediamenti già nel neolitico. Con la venuta degli Slavi nel VII secolo iniziano le costruzioni degli insediamenti sulla riva sinistra del fiume, dove più tardi vengono ad abitare anche gli Ebrei. Il promontorio rialzato sopra la Moldava diventa più tardi luogo più importante della stirpe dei Cechi: il potere fu conquistato dal casato dei Premyslidi noto per la sua tenacia di propositi, che qui nell' 884 aveva fondato la prima chiesa cristiana dedicata alla Vergine Maria. Caratteristico è il fatto, che poco dopo la sede del principe ormai edificata sfruttò la situazione affiancandosi alla Chiesa, anche per garantirsi i necessari appoggi a favore del casato. Prima che nel 973 venisse istituita la diocesi con a capo il vescovo, nel 921 fu costruita la basilica romanica di San Giorgio e nelle sue vicinanze il principe Venceslao, prima del 935, fece erigere la prima rotonda a piano in pietra, dedicata più tardi a San Vito. In essa nel 1085 avvenne la prima incoronazione del re Vratislao II dei Premyslidi. (Durante le liti sorte tra i Premyslidi, dopo il 1061, fu costruito il secondo castello, quello di Vyšehrad, dove più tardi iniziavano le cerimonie dell'incoronazione.)

La città regia stava acquisendo l'influsso politico che si rivela attraverso la spettacolarità delle costruzioni. Un ritmo attenuato, la grandiosità e il peso dello stile romanico, segnano l'architettura nascente tra gli anni 1100 e 1230. Con il contributo dell'influsso reale si giunge ad una costante estensione della città che dal punto di vista commerciale prospera. Negli anni 1232 e 1235 Venceslao I fonda, sulla riva destra della Moldava, la Città Vecchia (Grande), e tra i suoi abitanti figurano i colonizzatori tedeschi che qui costruiscono la chiesa di San Nicola. Su stimolo di Premysl Ottocaro II, dopo il 1257, si giunge alla fondazione della Città Minore (Malá Strana) di Praga, pure con un forte contributo degli abitanti dall'estero. Nelle vicinanze del Castello, quindi, il burgravio Berka di Dubé fonda il quartiere Hradčany. Carlo IV, all'epoca del quale Praga raggiunge lo splendore della città residenziale dell'imperatore, nel 1348 fonda la Città Nuova. Con l'intento di aumentare il prestigio e il potere della dinastia dei Lussemburgo, questo sovrano offre alla città il dono più grande: Praga diventa partner di pieno valore e consapevole delle città europee più avanzate. Carlo IV con dignità urbanizza la sede del sovrano, nelle cui vicinanze viene costruita la cattedrale di tipo francese. Per promuovere la cultura, nel 1348 egli fonda la prima università centroeuropea.

Per dare la prosperità a Praga, ormai circondata dalla cintura delle mura, egli promuove varie opere edili, tra cui la più importante è la costruzione del Ponte Carlo. Il raggruppamento del ritmo delle vie e delle viuzze della Praga medioevale di Carlo con il suo ghetto ebraico in modo marcato aveva predeterminato le comunicazioni posteriori e il piano urbano, che dopo la morte di Carlo perde il dinamismo del proprio sviluppo.

Il seguente capitolo comprendente gli avvenimenti rivoluzionari dell'ussitismo non giovò allo sviluppo della città. Dopo la costruzione della Cappella di Betlemme nel 1391, in cui aveva predicato il maestro Jan Hus, gli anni dal 1416 al 1437 delimitano il periodo di guerre sociali e di movimenti iconoclastici, che a Praga colpirono numerosi monumenti storici.

Una nuova ondata di impresa edile nel periodo degli Jagelloni, tra gli anni 1471 e 1526, arricchisce soprattutto l'architettura della cattedrale e del Castello. Dopo la venuta di Ferdinando I, il quale era promotore della controriforma e in particolare difendeva gli interessi assolutistici degli Asburgo contro gli Stati cechi, si giunge ad un acuito conflitto e alla ribellione contro il sovrano. La sua sconfitta nel 1547 sfocia nella reppressione delle libertà civiche. Ciononostante un ulteriore impegno edile delle fasce feudali orientate verso il cattolicesimo apre strada soprattutto ai costruttori e agli artigiani italiani, che portano in Boemia un nuovo stile, quello rinascimentale. In questo spirito è ricostruito il Castello, in parte distrutto da un incendio: tutt'attorno vengono fondati e abbelliti i giardini assieme alle costruzioni reali, con tutto il comfort, per fini di riposo. Il nuovo arabesco dei contorni delle costruzioni gentilmente simmetriche, riempite di fragili fasce di graffiti, nella seconda metà del XVI secolo rientra nelle costruzioni di palazzi di Rožmberk, Pernštejn o Lobkovic, che arricchiscono e rendono più fine il profilo del panorama cittadino. La monumentalità rappresentativa di Praga raggiunge l'apice verso la fine del XVI secolo, quando l'imperatore Rodolfo II si impegna a dare alla città l'importanza residenziale. La sua corte imperiale riportata nuovamente a Praga, trasformò la città in un centro dell'impero, capace di attirare gli artisti e i dotti, gli artigiani e gli avventurieri dell'intera Europa. Le tracce dell'epoca rodolfina e dei suoi movimenti esotici si imprimono in maniera pittoresca nel Castello di Praga dopo la costruzione meravigliosa della Viuzza dell'oro.

Il periodo culturale eccezionale, ma breve, della Praga rodolfina nota per le famose collezioni dell'imperatore, precedeva l'epoca più gravosa, in cui culminarono i dissensi tra gli Asburgo e gli Stati protestanti. Le conseguenze dell'insurrezione domata per opera della nobiltà e dei cittadini cechi furono le esecuzioni capitali con la successiva ampia emigrazione delle fasce non cattoliche della nazione. Gli svolgimenti drammatici della Guerra dei trent'anni ebbero come risultato il decadimento economico del paese. Praga, dopo aver perso l'importanza di una residenza imperiale, nel 1648 fu derubata di una parte notevole delle collezioni rodolfine e di numerosi cimeli, per opera degli eserciti svedesi. Nonostante questo, nel periodo degli sconvolgimenti bellici, si apre un nuovo capitolo delle imprese edili, che sono accompagnate dall'energia crescente dello stile barocco ormai internazionale, portato particolarmente qui dagli Italiani. I nomi come Spezza, Caratti, Orsini oppure Canevalle sono legati alla costruzione o alla ricostruzione di tutta una serie di edifici praghesi. Il coraggio di queste intenzioni e la dimostrazione di tale forza risaltano dalla costruzione del Palazzo Valdštejn. Un'imponenza di espressione nonché la bellezza plastica le documenta il Palazzo Černín a Hradčany. Il numero molto ampio delle sedi di aristocrazia e delle case dei cittadini assume un ritmo di musica barocca e di contrasti materiali, che sono applicati in particolare nella dinamica dell'architettura chiesastica di entrambi Dienzenhofer, Santini e, infine, di F. M. Kaňka. Alle decorazioni ricchissime delle chiese contribuisce l'opera matura dei maestri locali, dei pittori come sono per es. K. Škréta, P. Brandl, oppure V. V. Reiner, o degli scultori tipo M. B. Braun o F. M. Brokoff. Il profilo architettonico del periodo barocco forma l'aspetto di Praga, che con la sua monumentalità ritorna al livello delle città europee più avanzate. L'incanto melodico delle costruzioni barocche avanzate viene completato da nuovi giardini e parchi.

Con la venuta del governo di Maria Teresa e quindi di Giuseppe II si giunge ad una più decisa centralità di Vienna, ovviamente a scapito di Praga, e, purtroppo, anche alle reppressioni nazionali. Ma anche se da parte di Vienna l'interesse di Praga cala — infatti essa non è più la città residenziale degli imperatori — si inizia con un'ampia ristrutturazione del Castello, consistente nell'unificazione delle ali dei palazzi e delle facciate. I lavori iniziati su progetto di N. Pacassi nel 1745 proseguono fino agli anni 70 del XVIII secolo. In relazione alle riforme di Giuseppe II, che comprendono anche l'abolizione di numerosi conventi e chiese, Praga perde anche non pochi monumenti. Dall'altro lato altre riforme di Giuseppe II, compresa l'abolizione della servità della gleba, aprono nuove possibilità per lo sviluppo della città, tra l'altro per mezzo delle imprese più libere. In virtù delle riforme, nel 1784 si giunge all'unificazione di quattro città storiche praghesi in un municipio imperiale e regio. Praga man mano comincia a rivivere gli avvenimenti culturali più autonomi. I toni della musica di Mozart nel nuovo Teatro Nostic schiariscono l'atmosfera della città provinciale portata al silenzio. L'esposizione industriale avvenuta nel 1791, raccoglie i risultati favorevoli dello sviluppo tecnico iniziale. Nascono le società scientifiche che promuovono l'istruzione nazionale e la cultura.

Con la venuta della nuova epoca si giunse, per opera della nobiltà del paese orientata verso i sentimenti patriottici, alla fondazione del Museo Nazionale. A Praga, che assume una nuova espressione civica data dal progresso tecnico, vengono costruite nuove comunicazioni e marciapiedi. Viene costruita la stazione ferroviaria e verso la fine del secolo si realizza la linea tranviaria. Nell'interno cittadino sono inserite nuove statue. Il romanticismo nonché un sentimento sociale più maturo, portano alla costruzione di parchi pubblici, su stampo inglese. Si presenta lo spazio per una posizione più equa degli Ebrei. Il ghetto della Città Ebraica, isolato per interi secoli, nel 1850, sotto la denominazione Josefov, viene incorporato a Praga in quanto la sua quinta circoscrizione. Alla fine del secolo poi le condizioni igieniche disastrose portarono alla demolizione del quartiere ebraico angustiato in se stesso e alla successiva costruzione del Viale rappresentativo Pařížská třída, con edifici in stile liberty o storicizzanti. Nel manto edile storicizzante si vestono anche i monumenti della cultura nazionale — in particolare il Teatro Nazionale, espressione materializzata della coscienza nazionale, costruito con l'aiuto delle raccolte popolari, e il Rudolfinum, casa degli artisti. Le costruzioni di Ulmann, Zítek, Schulz, Barvitius oppure di Wiehl, di carattere neorinascimentale o neobarocco, trasformano soprattutto il centro cittadino.

Il 28 ottobre 1918, avvenuta la dichiarazione della Cecoslovacchia indipendente, Praga diventa la sua capitale. Già nel 1920 vi sono aggiunti altri 37 comuni (nel 1968 altri 21 comuni, nel 1974 infine 30 comuni). Comincia una nuova e risoluta edilizia urbanistica. L'architettura moderna è usata in particolare a Dejvice, a Ořechovka, a Bubny e a Vinohrady. Lo sviluppo favorevole fu congelato nel 1939 con l'occupazione e la dichiarazione del Protettorato di Boemia e Moravia. La guerra e la formazione della situazione politica nel dopoguerra, mutarono gli orientamenti dell'impresa edilizia e la sua epoca. Anche se il carattere monumentale del centro di Praga è stato in sostanza conservato e nel 1971, con un decreto governativo è stata dichiarata la zona monumentale di Praga, si proseguì nella costruzione frettolosa di quartieri popolari di poca qualità, e di tutta una serie di edifici tipo amministrativo molto alti, che in gran parte violano l'armonia naturale del panorama cittadino. Non c'erano troppe occasioni per la relizzazione di progetti veramente creativi.

Praga, che con la sua storia, la sua eredità culturale, ma anche con il numero attuale di abitanti (1 215 660), si inserisce tra le metropoli europee, attende nuovamente il ravvivamento della sua passata gloria.

4. Pohled ze Staroměstské radnice na Týnský chrám

● Blick vom Altstädter Rathaus auf die Teynkirche

● View of Týn Cathedral from Old Town Townhall

● Vue sur l'église Notre-Dame-du-Týn depuis l'Hôtel de ville de la Vieille Ville

● La veduta della chiesa di Týn dal Municipio della Città Vecchia

5. Pražské mosty ● Prager Brücken ● Prague's Bridges ● Les ponts de Prague ● I ponti di Praga

6

6. Letecký pohled na Pražský hrad ● Luftaufnahme der Prager Burg ● Aerial View of Prague Castle ● Le Château de Prague — vue à vol d'oiseau ● La veduta aerea del Castello di Praga

7

8

9

7.—9. Hradčanské náměstí ● Arcibiskupský palác ● Vstupní brána Pražského hradu

Hradschinplatz ● Erzbischöfliches Palais ● Eingangstor der Prager Burg

Hradčany Square ● Archbishops's Palace ● Prague Castle Entrance Gate

La place du Château (Hradčanské náměstí) ● Le palais archiépiscopal ● La porte d'entrée du Château de Prague

La piazza Hradčanské náměstí ● Il palazzo arcivescovile ● La porta d'ingresso nel Castello di Praga

10. Třetí nádvoří Pražského hradu ● Dritter Burghof der Prager Burg ● Prague Castle Third Courtyard ● La troisième cour du Château de Prague ● Il terzo cortile del Castello di Praga

11. Bazilika sv. Jiří ● Georgsbasilika ● St. George's Basilica ● La basilique Saint-Georges ● La basilica di San Giorgio

12. Hlavní loď katedrály sv. Víta

• Mittelschiff des Veitsdoms

• St. Vitus' Cathedral Nave

• La nef principale de la cathédrale Saint-Guy

• La navata centrale della cattedrale di San Vito

13. Svatováclavská kaple

• Wenzelskapelle

• St. Wenceslas Chapel

• La chapelle Saint-Venceslas

• La cappella di San Venceslao

14

14. Mistr Theodorik: Sv. Papež ● Meister Theodorik: Hl. Papst ● Master Theodorik: St. Pope ● Maître Théodoric: Saint Pape ● Maestro Teodorico: un papa santo

15.–17. Mistr Theodorik: Sv. Jeroným ● Sv. Augustýn ● Sv. Vít

Meister Theodorik: Hl. Hieronymus ● Hl. Augustin ● Hl. Veit

Master Theodorik: St. Jerome ● St. Augustine ● St. Vitus

Maître Théodoric : Saint Jérôme ● Saint Augustin ● Saint Guy

Maestro Teodorico: San Girolamo ● Sant'Agostino ● San Vito

15

16

17

19

20

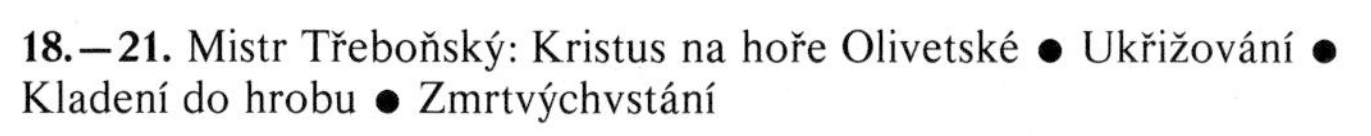

18.—21. Mistr Třeboňský: Kristus na hoře Olivetské • Ukřižování • Kladení do hrobu • Zmrtvýchvstání

Meister von Třeboň: Christus auf dem Ölberg • Kreuzigung • Grablegung • Auferstehung

Master of Třeboň: Christ on Mount of Olives • Crucifixion • Laying to Rest • Resurrection

Maître du retable de Třeboň : Christ sur le mont des Oliviers • La Crucifixion • La mise au tombeau • La Résurrection

Maestro di Třeboň: Cristo sul Monte degli Ulivi • La crocifissione • La deposizione nel sepolcro • La resurrezione

21

22

24

22.—23. Vladislavský sál • Stará sněmovna Pražského hradu

Wladislawsaal • Alte Landtagsstube der Prager Burg

Vladislav Hall • Prague Castle Old Parliament

La Salle Vladislas • L'ancienne Chambre du Château de Prague

La sala di Vladislao • La vecchia cancelleria del Castello di Praga

25

24.—25. Adriaen de Vries: Rudolf II. • Jezdecká socha sv. Jiří

Adriaen de Vries: Rudolf II • Reiterstandbild des hl. Georg

Adriaen de Vries: Rudolph II • Equestrian Statue of St. George

Adriaen de Vries : Rodolphe II • La statue équestre de Saint George

Adriaen de Vries: Rodolfo II • La statua equestre di San Giorgio

26

26. Tizian: Toaleta mladé ženy

- Tizian: Toilette einer jungen Frau
- Titian: Young Woman's Toilet
- Titien : La toilette d'une jeune femme
- Tiziano: La toilette della giovane donna

27. P. P. Rubens: Shromáždění olympských bohů (detail) ● P. P. Rubens: Versammlung der Olympgötter (Detail) ● Peter Paul Rubens: Meeting of Olympian Gods (Detail) ● P. P. Rubens : La réunion des dieux à l'Olympe — détail ● P. P. Rubens: La riunione degli dei di Olimpo / dettaglio

28

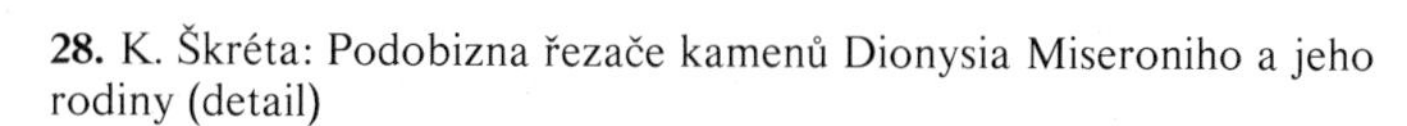

28. K. Škréta: Podobizna řezače kamenů Dionysia Miseroniho a jeho rodiny (detail)

• K. Škréta: Bildnis des Edelsteinschneiders Dionysius Miseroni und seiner Familie (Detail)

• Karel Škréta: Portrait of Diamond-Cutter Dionysius Miseroni and His Family (Detail)

• Karel Škréta : Le portrait du tailleur de pierres Dionisio Miseroni et de sa famille — détail

• K. Škréta: Il ritratto del tagliatore di pietra Dionisio Miseroni e della sua famiglia / dettaglio

29

29. J. Kupecký: Alegorie malířství

• J. Kupecký: Allegorie der Malerei

• Jan Kupecký: Allegory of Painting

• Jan Kupecký : L'allégorie de la peinture

• J. Kupecký: Allegoria della pittura

30

31

30. P. Brandl: Apoštol Pavel
- P. Brandl: Apostel Paulus
- Peter Brandl: Apostle Paul
- Petr Brandl : L'apôtre Paul
- P. Brandl: L'apostolo Paolo

31. P. Brandl: Vlastní podobizna (Lobkovická)
- P. Brandl: Selbstbildnis (Lobkowitz-Sammlungen)
- Peter Brandl: Own Portrait (Lobkovic Collections)
- Petr Brandl : L'autoportrait (variante dite de Lobkowitz)
- P. Brandl: Autoritratto (Lobkovická)

32

32. P. Veronese: Sv. Kateřina s andělem
- P. Veronese: Hl. Katharina mit dem Engel
- Paolo Veronese: St. Catherine with Angel
- P. Veronese : Sainte Catherine avec l'ange
- P. Veronese: Santa Caterina con l'angelo

33.–34. Lobkovický palác a Černá věž ● Panorama Prahy z Lobkovického paláce

Palais Lobkowitz und Schwarzer Turm ● Panorama Prags vom Palais Lobkowitz

Lobkovic Palace and Black Tower ● Prague Viewed from Lobkovic Palace

Le palais Lobkowitz et la tour Noire ● Le panorama de Prague depuis le palais Lobkowitz

Il palazzo Lobkovic e la Torre Nera ● Panorama di Praga dal palazzo Lobkovic

33

35

35.–36. Kolowratská zahrada ● Královská zahrada
Kolowratt-Garten ● Königlicher Garten
Kolowrat Garden ● Royal Garden
Le jardin des seigneurs de Kolowrat ● Le jardin royal
Il giardino Kolowrat ● Il giardino reale

36

37

37. Hartigovská zahrada
● Hartig-Garten
● Hartig Garden
● Le jardin Hartigovský
● Il giardino Hartig

38

38. Zpívající fontána (detail)

● Singende Fontäne (Detail)

● Singing Fountain (Detail)

● La Fontaine chantante — détail

● La fontana cantante / dettaglio

39

40

39.—40. Velká míčovna ● M. B. Braun, dílna: Noc

● Großes Ballhaus ● M. B. Braun, Werkstatt: Nacht

● Great Ball-Game Hall ● Matthias B. Braun's Workshop: Night

● La Grande salle du jeu de paume ● L'atelier de M. B. Braun : La Nuit

● La Grande Sala della palla ● M. B. Braun, bottega: La notte

41. Královský letohrádek (Belveder) ● Königliches Lustschloß (Belvedere) ● Royal Summer Residence (Belveder) ● Le pavillon d'été royal (Belvédère) ● Il Belvedere Reale

42

42. Zlatá ulička • Goldenes Gäßchen
• Golden Lane • La ruelle Dorée
• Il Vicolo dell'oro

43. Malostranský chrám sv. Mikuláše
• St. Niklaskirche auf der Kleinseite
• Lesser Town St. Nicholas' Church
• L'église Saint-Nicolas à Malá Strana
• La chiesa di San Nicola a Malá Strana

44. Katedrála sv. Víta noční
• St. Veitsdom in der Nacht
• St. Vitus' Cathedral at Night
• La cathédrale Saint-Guy la nuit
• La cattedrale di San Vito di notte

43

45

45. Loreta • Loreto • Loretto • Notre-Dame-de-Lorette • La chiesa di Loreto

46. Pražský hrad s Jelením příkopem
• Prager Burg mit dem Hirschgraben
• Prague Castle with Stag Moat
• Le Château de Prague et le fossé dit du Cerf
• Il Castello di Praga con il Fossato dei Cervi

47

48

47.–48. Petřínská rozhledna ● Hvězdárna na Petříně

Aussichtsturm auf dem Laurenziberg ● Sternwarte auf dem Laurenziberg

Petřín Look-Out Tower ● Petřín Observatory

La tour de Petřín ● L'observatoire sur la butte de Petřín

La Torre di Petřín ● L'osservatorio astronomico di Petřín

49.–50. Pohled z Petřína ● Jaro v jižních zahradách Pražského hradu

Blick vom Laurenziberg ● Frühling in den Südgärten der Prager Burg

View from Petřín ● Spring in Prague Castle Southern Gardens

La vue depuis la butte de Petřín ● Les jardins sud du château de Prague au printemps

La veduta da Petřín ● La primavera nei giardini meridionali del Castello di Praga

49

50

51

52

51.–52. Strahovský klášter • Kostel p. Marie

Kloster Strahov • Kirche der Jungfrau Maria

Strahov Monastery • Church of Virgin Mary

Le Monastère de Strahov • Notre-Dame

Il monastero di Strahov • La chiesa della Vergine Maria

53

53.—54. Teologický sál a Filozofický sál Strahovské knihovny

● Theologie-Saal und Philosophie-Saal in der Strahover Bibliothek

● Strahov Library Theological Hall and Philosophical Hall

● Les salles Théologique et Philosophique de la Bibliothèque de Strahov

● La Sala teologica e la Sala filosofica della biblioteca di Strahov

54

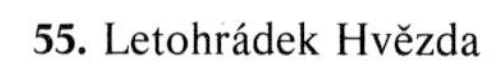

55

55. Letohrádek Hvězda
- Lustschloß Hvězda (Stern)
- Hvězda Summer Residence
- Le pavillon d'été Hvězda (L'Etoile)
- Il belvedere Hvězda

56.—57. Břevnovský klášter s kostelem sv. Markéty
- Kloster Břevnov mit der Margaretenkirche
- Břevnov Monastery with St. Margaret's Church
- Le Monastère de Břevnov avec l'église Sainte-Margueritte
- Il monastero di Břevnov con la chiesa di Santa Margherita

56

57

58

59

58.–60. Malá Strana s chrámem sv. Mikuláše • Interiér chrámu se sousoším I. F. Platzera st.

Kleinseite mit der St. Niklaskirche • Kircheninneres mit der Statuengruppe I. F. Platzers d. Ä.

Lesser Town with St. Nicholas' Church • Church Interior with Platzer's Group

Vue sur Malá Strana et l'église Saint-Nicolas • L'intérieur du temple Saint-Nicolas avec le groupe de statues par I. F. Platzer l'Aîné

Malá Strana con la chiesa di San Nicola • L'interno della chiesa con il gruppo di statue di I. F. Platzer seniore

ALEXANDRI

61

62

61.–65. Večer na Klárově a Malé Straně s chrámem sv. Mikuláše a Petřínskou rozhlednou

● Abend im Klárov-Viertel ● Abend auf der Kleinseite mit der St. Niklaskirche und dem Aussichtsturm auf dem Laurenziberg

● Evening above Klárov a Lesser Town with St. Nicholas' Church and Petřín Look-Out Tower

● Klárov et Malá Strana avec l'église Saint-Nicolas dominés par la tour de Petřín le soir

● A Klárov e a Malá Strana di sera, con la chiesa di San Nicola e con la torre di Petřín

63

64

65

66. Letecký pohled na Valdštejnský palác

• Luftaufnahme des Palais Wallenstein

• Aerial View of Wallenstein Palace

• Le palais Wallenstein à vue d'oiseau

• La veduta aerea del palazzo Valdštejn

67

68

69

70

67.–70. Valdštejnský palác ● Rytířský sál ● Kožený sál ● Valdštejnova pracovna

Palais Wallenstein ● Rittersaal ● Ledersaal ● Wallensteins Arbeitszimmer

Wallenstein Palace ● Knights'Hall ● Leather Hall ● Wallenstein's Workroom

Le palais Wallenstein ● La Salle des Chevaliers ● La Salle dite en Cuir ● Le cabinet de travail de Wallenstein

Palazzo Valdštejn ● La Sala dei Cavalieri ● La Sala di Cuoio ● Lo Studio di Valdštejn

71

71. Kolowratský palác a palác Pálffyův

● Palais Kolowratt und Palais Palffy

● Kolowrat Palace and Pálffy Palace

● Les palais Kolowrat et Palffy

● Palazzo Kolowrat e Palazzo Pálffy

72. Letecký pohled na Valdštejnskou zahradu

- Wallenstein-Garten aus der Vogelperspektive
- Aerial View of Wallenstein Garden
- Le jardin Wallenstein à vol d'oiseau
- Veduta aerea del giardino Valdštejn

72

73

74

73.–74. Salla terrena Valdštejnského paláce a Valdštejnská zahrada

• Salla terrena des Palais Wallenstein • Wallenstein-Garten

• Wallenstein Palace Salla Terrena and Wallenstein Garden

• La salla terrena et le jardin du palais Wallenstein

• La Sala terrena del Palazzo Valdštejn e il giardino Valdštejn

76

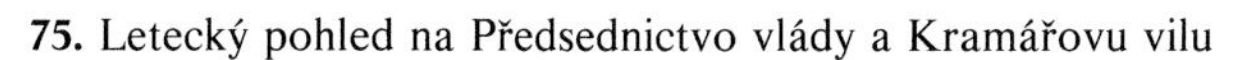

75. Letecký pohled na Předsednictvo vlády a Kramářovu vilu

● Luftaufnahme der Residenz des Regierungspräsidiums und der Kramář-Villa

● Aerial View of Presidium and Kramář's Villa

● Le siège de la présidence de gouvernement et la villa Kramář

● Veduta aerea dell'edificio della Presidenza del Governo e della villa Kramář

76.–77. Karlův most a Staré Město

● Karlsbrücke und Altstadt

● Charles Bridge and Old Town

● Le pont Charles et la Vieille Ville de Prague

● Il Ponte Carlo e la Città Vecchia

77

78

78. Hanavský pavilón ● Hanauer Pavillon ● Hanavský Pavilion ● Le pavillon Hanavský ● Il padiglione Hanavský

79. Vltava a Pražský hrad ● Moldau und Prager Burg ● Vltava and Prague Castle ● La Vltava et le Château de Prague ● La Moldava e il Castello di Praga

80. Karlův most a Smetanovo muzeum (letecký pohled)

• Karlsbrücke und Smetana-Museum

• Charles Bridge and Smetana Museum (Aerial View)

• Le pont Charles et le Musée Smetana (vue à vol d'oiseau)

• Il Ponte Carlo e il Museo Smetana / veduta aerea

81

82

81.–82. Karlův most a Hradčany • Sousoší Kalvárie z Karlova mostu
Karlsbrücke und Hradschin • Statuengruppe Kalvarie auf der Karlsbrücke
Charles Bridge and Hradčany Town • Calvary Group on Charles Bridge
Le pont Charles et le Château de Prague • Le groupe de statues Le Calvaire décorant le pont Charles
Il Ponte Carlo e Hradčany • Gruppo scultoreo Il Calvario sul Ponte Carlo

83

83. Pohled z Malostranské mostecké věže
● Blick vom Kleinseitner Brückenturm
● View from Lesser Town Bridge Tower
● Vue depuis la tour du pont Charles située du côté de Malá Strana
● Veduta dalla torre di Malá Strana

84

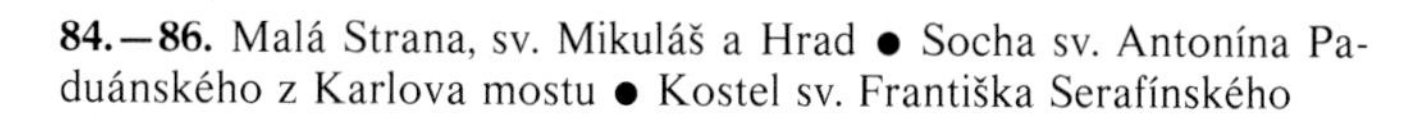

84.—86. Malá Strana, sv. Mikuláš a Hrad ● Socha sv. Antonína Paduánského z Karlova mostu ● Kostel sv. Františka Serafínského

Kleinseite, St. Niklaskirche und Burg ● Statue des hl. Antonius von Padua auf der Karlsbrücke ● Kreuzherrenkirche

Lesser Town, St. Nicholas' Church and Prague Castle ● Statue of St. Anthony of Padua on Charles Bridge ● St. Franciscus-Seraph's Church

Malá Strana, l'église Saint-Nicolas et le Château de Prague ● La statue de saint Antoine de Padoue agrémentant le pont Charles ● L'église Saint-François de Séraphin

Malá Strana, San Nicola e il Castello ● La statua di Sant' Antonio di Padova sul Ponte Carlo ● La chiesa di San Francesco Serafico

85

86

87.–90. Karlův most a jeho barokní výzdoba

- Karlsbrücke und ihr Statuenschmuck
- Charles Bridge and Its Baroque Statues
- Le pont Charles et ses décorations baroques
- Il Ponte Carlo e la sua decorazione barocca

87

89

90

91. Karlův most a Staré Město (letecký pohled)

• Karlsbrücke und Altstadt (Luftaufnahme)

• Charles Bridge and Old Town (Aerial View)

• Le pont Charles et la Vieille Ville (vue à vol d'oiseau)

• Il Ponte Carlo e la Città Vecchia / veduta aerea

92

93

94

92.–94. Hradčany a Karlův most ● Labutě na Vltavě ● Kostel sv. Františka Serafínského s pomníkem Karla IV.
Hradschin und Karlsbrücke ● Schwäne auf der Moldau ● Kreuzherrenkirche mit dem Denkmal Karls IV.
Hradčany and Charles Bridge ● Swans on Vltava ● St. Franciscus-Seraph's Church with Charles IV Memorial
Le Château de Prague et le pont Charles ● Les cygnes sur le miroir de la Vltava ● L'église Saint-François de Séraphin avec le monument érigé en l'honneur de Charles IV.
Hradčany e il Ponte Carlo ● I cigni sulla Moldava ● La chiesa di San Francesco Serafico con il monumento di Carlo IV

95

96

97

95.—97. Staroměstská mostecká věž • Výzdoba Staroměstské mostecké věže • Socha Karla IV.
Altstädter Brückenturm • Schmuck am Altstädter Brückenturm • Statue Karls IV.
Old Town Bridge Tower • Old Town Bridge Tower Decorations • Charles IV Statue
La tour terminant le pont Charles du côté de la Vieille Ville • Les décors de la tour de la Vieille Ville • La statue de Charles IV
La torre della Città Vecchia — La decorazione della torre della Città Vecchia • La statua di Carlo IV

98. Vltavské mosty ● Brücken über die Moldau ● Vltava Bridges ● Les ponts surplombant la Vltava ● I ponti sulla Moldava

99

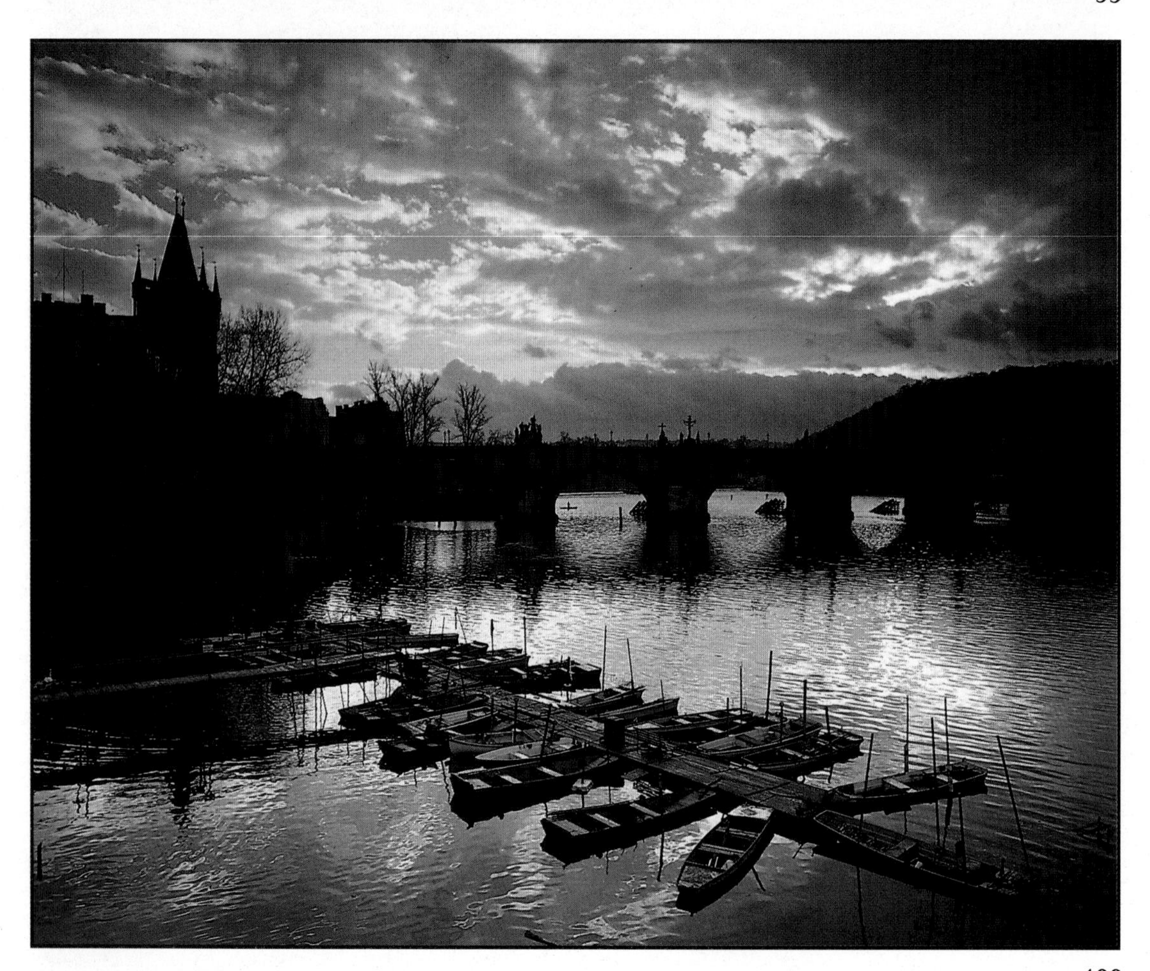

100

99.–100. Pražský hrad • Vltava a Karlův most
Prager Burg • Moldau und Karlsbrücke
Prague Castle • Vltava and Charles Bridge
Le Château de Prague • La Vltava et le pont Charles
Il Castello di Praga • La Moldava e il Ponte Carlo

101. Karlův most a Pražský hrad
- Karlsbrücke und Prager Burg
- Charles Bridge and Prague Castle
- Le pont Charles et le Château de Prague
- Il Ponte Carlo e il Castello di Praga

102

102. Pomník mistra Jana Husa (detail)

- Magister-Jan-Hus-Denkmal (Detail)
- Master John Huss Memorial (Detail)
- Le monument à Jan Hus — détail
- Il monumento al maestro Jan Hus / dettaglio

103. Letecký pohled na Staroměstské náměstí

- Luftaufnahme des Altstädter Rings
- Aerial View of Old Town Square
- La place de la Vieille Ville vue à vol d'oiseau
- Veduta aerea della Piazza della Città Vecchia

104. Staroměstské náměstí a Týnský chrám ● Altstädter Ring und Teynkirche ● Old Town Square and Týn Cathedral ● La place de la Vieille Ville et Notre-Dame-du Týn ● La Piazza della Città Vecchia e la chiesa della Madonna di Týn

105

105. Gotický arkýř kaple Staroměstské radnice
● Gotischer Erker der Kapelle des Altstädter Rathauses
● Old Town Townhall Chapel Gothic Bay
● L'encorbellement gothique de l'Hôtel de ville de la Vieille Ville
● Il balcone chiuso gotico della cappella del Municipio della Città Vecchia

106

106. Dům U minuty ● Haus Zur Minute ● "At the Minute" House ● La maison « A la minute » ● La casa Al Minuto

107

107. Okno Staroměstské radnice
● Fenster am Altstädter Rathaus
● Old Town Townhall Window
● La fenêtre de l'Hotel de ville
● La finestra del Municipio della Città Vecchia

108

108. Staroměstský orloj
● Altstädter astronomische Uhr
● The Astronomical Clock of the Old Town
● L'horloge de l'Hôtel de Ville de la Vieille Ville
● L'Orologio della Città Vecchia

109

110

111

112

113

109.–115. Výzdoba Staroměstského orloje ● J. Mánes: Leden ● Apoštolové sv. Tomáš, sv. Filip, sv. Petr ● U orloje ● Staroměstská radnice

Ausschmückung der Altstädter astronomischen Uhr ● J. Mánes: Januar ● Apostel hl. Thomas, hl. Philipp, hl. Petrus ● An der astronomischen Uhr ● Altstädter Rathaus

The Astronomical Clock of the Old Town Decorations ● Josef Mánes: January ● St. Thomas, St. Philip, St. Peter Apostles ● At Horologe ● Old Town Townhall

Les décors de l'horloge de la Vieille Ville de Prague ● Les apôtres St-Thomas, St-Philippe, St-Pierre ● Près de l'horloge de la Vieille Ville de Prague ● L'Hôtel de Ville de la Vieille Ville

● La decorazione dell'Orologio della Città Vecchia ● J. Mánes: Gennaio ● Gli apostoli: San Tommaso, San Filippo, San Pietro ● Presso l'Orologio ● Il Municipio della Città Vecchia

114

116

117

118

119

116.—120. Staroměstská radnice — Stará radní síň ● M. Aleš: Hold Slovanstva městu Praze ● V. Brožík: Hus před koncilem ● V. Brožík: Volba Jiřího z Poděbrad za českého krále (detail)

Altstädter Rathaus — Alter Rathaussaal ● M. Aleš: Ehrung der Stadt Prag durch das Slawentum ● V. Brožík: Hus vor dem Konzil ● V. Brožík: Wahl des Georg von Podiebrad zum böhmischen König (Detail)

Old Town Townhal—Old Council Hall ● Mikoláš Aleš: Tribute of Slavs to Prague ● Václav Brožík: Huss at Council ● Václav Brožík: Electing George of Poděbrady King of Bohemia (Detail)

L'Hôtel de Ville de la Vieille Ville — la salle de réunions Ancienne ● Mikoláš Aleš : L'hommage rendu par les Slaves à la ville de Prague ● Václav Brožík : Jan Hus devant le concile ● Václav Brožík : L'élection de Georges de Poděbrady roi de Bohême — détail

Il Municipio della Città Vecchia — Antica Sala della Giunta municipale ● M. Aleš: Omaggio del Mondo Slavo alla città di Praga ● V. Brožík: Hus davanti al Concilio ● V. Brožík: L'elezione di Giorgio di Poděbrady a re di Boemia /dettaglio

120

121

121.—123. Pohled z věže Staroměstské radnice

- Blick aus dem Rathausturm
- View from Old Town Townhall Tower
- Vue depuis la tour de l'Hôtel de ville de la Vieille Ville
- Veduta dalla torre del Municipio della Città Vecchia

122

124

125

124.–125. Chrám sv. Mikuláše na Starém Městě ● Kočáry na Staroměstském náměstí

St. Niklaskirche in der Altstadt ● Kutschen auf dem Altstädter Ring

Old Town St. Nicholas Church ● Coaches on Old Town Square

L'église Saint-Nicolas de la Vieille Ville ● Les calèches stationnant sur la place de la Vieille Ville

La chiesa di San Nicola nella Città Vecchia ● Le carrozze in Piazza della Città Vecchia

126

127

128

126.—128. Palác Golz-Kinských a dům U zvonu ● Východní strana Staroměstského náměstí ● Štorchův dům

Palais Golz-Kinský und Haus Zur Glocke ● Ostseite des Altstädter Rings ● Storch-Haus

Golz-Kinský Palace and "At the Bell" House ● Eastern Side of Old Town Square ● Štorch's House

Le palais Golz-Kinsky et la maison « A la cloche »● Le côté est de la place de la Vieille Ville ● La maison Štorch

Il Palazzo Golz-Kinsky e la casa Alla Campana ● Il lato est della Piazza della Città Vecchia ● La casa Štorch

129. Staroměstské náměstí ● Altstädter Ring ● Old Town Square ● La place de la Vieille Ville ● La Piazza della Città Vecchia

130. Staroměstská radnice ● Altstädter Rathaus ● Old Town Townhall ● L'Hôtel de ville de la Vieille Ville ● Il Municipio della Città Vecchia

131. Chrám sv. Mikuláše ● St. Niklaskirche ● St. Nicholas' Church ● L'église Saint-Nicolas ● La chiesa di San Nicola

132

133

132.—133. Gotický arkýř Karolina • Arkýřová kaple Karolina

Gotischer Erker am Carolinum • Erkerkapelle des Carolinum

Carolinum Gothic Bay • Carolinum Bay Chapel

L'encorbellement gothique du Carolinum • La chapelle du Carolinum

Il balcone chiuso gotico del Karolinum • La cappella con il balcone chiuso del Karolinum

134

134. Pečeť Karlovy univerzity

• Siegel der Karlsuniversität

• Charles University Seal

• Le sceau de l'Université Charles

• Il sigillo dell'Università Carlo

135

135. Stavovské divadlo ● Ständetheater ● Theatre of the Estates ● Le Théâtre des états ● Il Teatro degli Stati

136

137

138

139

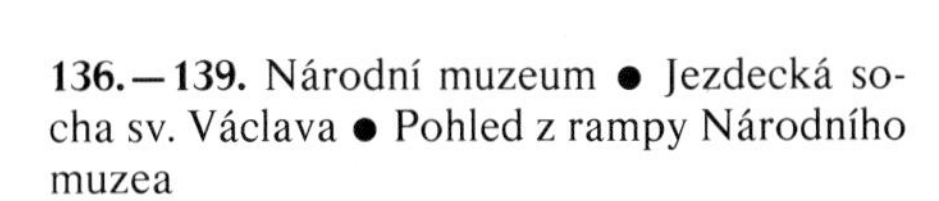

136.—139. Národní muzeum ● Jezdecká socha sv. Václava ● Pohled z rampy Národního muzea

Nationalmuseum ● Reiterstandbild des hl. Wenzel ● Blick von der Rampe des Nationalmuseums

National Museum ● Equestrian Statue of St. Wenceslas ● View From National Museum Platform

Le Musée national ● La statue équestre de saint Venceslas ● Vue depuis la rampe du Musée national

Il Museo Nazionale ● Statua equestre di San Venceslao ● Veduta dalla rampa del Museo Nazionale

140

140. Jungmannovo náměstí ● Jungmannplatz ● Jungmann Square ● Le place Jungmann ● La piazza Jungmann

142

141.—143. Pantheon Národního muzea ● Schodiště ● V. Brožík: J. A. Komenský v Amsterodamu

Pantheon im Nationalmuseum ● Treppenaufgang ● V. Brožík: Comenius in Amsterdam

National Museum Pantheon ● Staircase ● Václav Brožík: Comenius in Amsterdam

Le Panthéon du Musée national ● L'escalier du Musée national ● V. Brožík : Jan Amos Comenius à Amsterdam

Il Pantheon del Museo Nazionale ● La scalinata ● V. Brožík: Jan Amos Comenius ad Amsterdam

143

144

144. Příkopy — pěší zóna ● Am Graben — Fußgängerzone ● Příkopy Traffic-Free Zone ● La rue Na příkopech — la zone piétonnière ● Příkopy — zona pedonale

145. Václavské náměstí • Wenzelsplatz • Wenceslas Square • La place Venceslas • Piazza San Venceslao

146.–148. Prašná brána ● Pohled na Staré Město z Prašné brány ● Letecký pohled na náměstí Republiky

Pulverturm ● Blick auf die Altstadt vom Pulverturm ● Platz der Republik (Luftaufnahme)

Powder Tower Gate ● View of Old Town from Powder Tower ● Aerial View of Square of Republic

La Tour Poudrière ● Vue sur la Vieille Ville depuis la Tour Poudrière● La place de la République vue à vol d'oiseau

La Torre delle Polveri ● Veduta sulla Città Vecchia dalla Torre delle Polveri ● Veduta aerea sulla piazza della Repubblica

147

148

149

149.—150. Obecní dům hlavního města Prahy ● A. Mucha: J. A. Komenský (z výzdoby Primátorského sálu)

Repräsentationshaus der Hauptstadt Prag ● A. Mucha: Comenius

Municipal House of Capital of Prague ● Alfons Mucha: Comenius (exhibited in Mayor's Hall)

La Maison municipale ● A. Mucha : Jan Amos Comenius (peinture décorant la salle de Maires)

La Casa comunale della capitale Praga ● A. Mucha: Jan Amos Comenius (dalla decorazione della Sala del primo sindaco)

ZDAR TOBĚ PRAHO
JAK ODOLALA VĚKY BOUŘIM

152

153

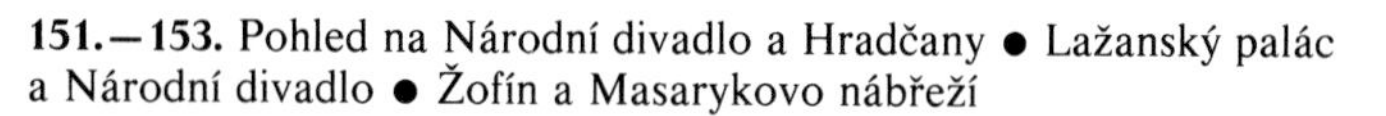

151.–153. Pohled na Národní divadlo a Hradčany ● Lažanský palác a Národní divadlo ● Žofín a Masarykovo nábřeží

Blick auf das Nationaltheater und den Hradschin ● Palais Lažanský und Nationaltheater ● Sophiensinsel (Žofín) und Masarykkai

View of National Theatre and Hradčany ● Lažan Palace and National Theatre ● Žofín Island and Masaryk Embankment

Vue sur le Théâtre national et le Château de Prague ● Le palais Lažanský et le Théâtre national ● L'île de Žofín et le quai Masaryk

Veduta sul Teatro Nazionale e su Hradčany ● Il palazzo Lažanský e il Teatro Nazionale ● Žofín e il lungofiume Masaryk

151

154

155

154.—155. Národní divadlo ● Střelecký ostrov

Nationaltheater ● Schützeninsel

National Theatre ● Střelecký Island

Le Théâtre national ● L'île Střelecký (l'ancien champ de tir)

Il Teatro Nazionale ● L'isola Střelecký ostrov

156. Pražské mosty s Vyšehradem ● Prager Brücken mit Vyšehrad ● Prague's Bridges with Vyšehrad ● Les ponts de Prague avec Vyšehrad

au second plan ● I ponti di Praga con Vyšehrad

158

157.–158. Socha B. Smetany před Smetanovým muzeem ● Smetanovo muzeum a Novotného lávka

Bedřich-Smetana-Denkmal vor dem Smetana-Museum ● Smetana-Museum und Novotný-Brücke

Bedřich Smetana Statue in Front of Smetana Museum ● Smetana Museum and Novotný Footbridge

La statue de Bedřich Smetana, compositeur tchèque du XIXe siècle, devant le Musée Smetana ● Le Musée Smetana et la passerelle Novotný

Statua di B. Smetana davanti al Museo Smetana ● Il Museo Smetana e la passerella Novotný

159

160

159.–160. Dům U zlaté studně ● Domovní znamení na Starém Městě

Haus Zum goldenen Brunnen ● Hauszeichen in der Altstadt

"At the Golden Well" House ● Old Town House Signs

La maison « Au puit d'or » ● Les emblèmes marquant les devants des maisons situées dans la Vieille Ville

La casa Al Pozzo d'oro ● Il segno di casa nella Città Vecchia

162

163

161

164

161.—165. Starý židovský hřbitov ● Bývalá obřadní síň ● Staronová synagóga ● K. Hladík: Franz Kafka

Alter jüdischer Friedhof ● Ehemaliger Zeremoniesaal ● Altneusynagoge ● K. Hladík: Franz Kafka

Old Jewish Cemetery ● Former Ceremony Hall ● Old-New Synagogue ● K. Hladík: Franz Kafka

Le Vieux cimetière juif ● L'ancienne salle de cérémonies ● La Synagogue Vieille-Nouvelle ● K. Hladík : Franz Kafka

Il Cimitero Ebraico ● L'ex sala di cerimonie ● La sinagoga Vecchia-nuova ● K. Hladík: Franz Kafka

165

166

167

168

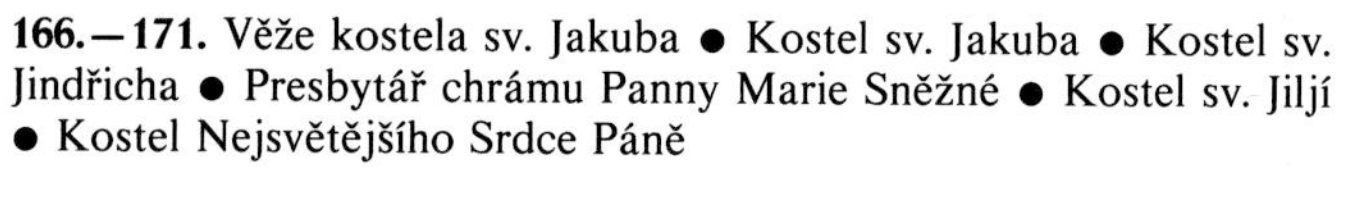

166.—171. Věže kostela sv. Jakuba ● Kostel sv. Jakuba ● Kostel sv. Jindřicha ● Presbytář chrámu Panny Marie Sněžné ● Kostel sv. Jiljí ● Kostel Nejsvětějšího Srdce Páně

Türme der Jakobskirche ● Jakobskirche ● Heinrichskirche ● Presbyterium der Maria Schnee Kirche ● Ägidiuskirche ● Kirche des Allerheiligsten Gottesherzens

St. James' Church Towers ● St. James' Church ● St. Henry's and St. Cunigund's Churches ● Presbytary of Church of Our Lady of Snow ● St. Giles' Church ● Church of Holiest Heart of Lord

Les tours dominant l'église Saint-Jacques ● L'église Saint-Jacques ● L'église Saint-Georges et Sainte-Cunégonde ● Le presbytère de Notre-Dame-des-Neiges ● L'église Saint-Gilles ● L'église du Sacro-Saint-Cœur-du-Seigneur

Le torri della chiesa di San Giacomo ● La chiesa di San Giacomo ● La chiesa di Sant'Enrico e di Santa Cunegonda ● Il presbiterio della chiesa della Vergine Maria delle Nevi ● La chiesa di Sant'Egidio ● La chiesa del Cuore Santissimo del Signore

169

170

171

172

173

174

172.—174. Vila Amerika ● Busta A. Dvořáka z rodného domu v Nelahozevsi ● Zkouška orchestru České filharmonie v Dvořákově síni Rudolfina
Villa Amerika ● Büste Antonín Dvořáks aus dem Geburtshaus in Nelahozeves ● Probe des Orchesters der Tschechischen Philharmonie im Dvořák-Saal im Rudolfinum
Villa America ● Antonín Dvořák's bust from Dvořák's Native House in Nelahozeves ● Czech Philharmony Orchestra Rehearsal in Dvořák Hall in Rudolphinum
La villa nommée l'Amérique ● Le buste d'Antonín Dvořák, compositeur tchèque, disposée à l'heure actuelle dans sa maison natale à Nelahozeves ● La répétition de la Philharmonie tchèque dans la salle Dvořák du Rudolphinum
Villa Amerika ● Il busto di A. Dvořák proveniente dalla sua casa natia di Nelahozeves ● La prova dell'orchestra della Filarmonica ceca

175

176

175.—176. Zrcadlová síň Klementina ● Památník W. A. Mozarta v Bertramce
Spiegelsaal im Klementinum ● W.-A.-Mozart-Denkmal in der Villa Bertramka
Clementinum Mirror Hall ● Wolfgang A. Mozart Memorial at Bertramka Manor
La salle des Glaces du Clementinum ● Le monument à Wolfgang Amadeus Mozart à Bertramka
La Sala degli Specchi del Clementinum ● Il Museo W. A. Mozart a Bertramka

177. Podvečer na Bertramce ● Früher Abend in der Bertramka ● Early Evening at Bertramka ● La tombée de la nuit à Bertramka

● Il Crepuscolo a Bertramka

178

178. Vltavské mosty se sochou Viktorie
- Brücken über die Moldau mit der Statue der Viktoria
- Vltava Bridges with Victory Statue
- Les ponts surplombant la Vltava avec la statue de la Victoire
- I ponti sulla Moldava e la statua di Vittoria

179

180

179.—180. Smetanovo nábřeží a Pražský hrad
- Smetanakai und Prager Burg
- Smetana Embankment and Prague Castle
- Le quai Smetana et le Château de Prague
- Il lungofiume Smetana e il Castello di Praga

181

181.—185. Pařížská třída a Staré Město ● Hotel Atrium ● Hotel Intercontinental ● Pražské mosty ● Závod surfů na Vltavě

Pariser Straße und Altstadt ● Hotel Atrium ● Hotel Intercontinental ● Prager Brücken ● Surfrennen auf der Moldau

Pařížská Avenue and Old Town ● Atrium Hotel ● Intercontinental Hotel ● Prague's Bridges ● Windsurfing Competition on Vltava

L'avenue Pařížská et la Vieille Ville de Prague ● L'hôtel Atrium ● L'hôtel Intercontinental ● Les ponts de Prague ● Le concours de planches à voile sur la surface de la Vltava

Il viale Pařížská e la Città Vecchia ● L'albergo Atrium ● L'albergo Intercontinental ● I fiumi di Praga ● La gara di surf sulla Moldava

182

183

184

185

186. Vltava v noci ● Moldau in der Nacht ● Vltava at Night ● Lą Vltava la nuit ● La Moldava di notte

187. Vltava s Vyšehradem

- Moldau mit Vyšehrad
- Vltava with Vyšehrad
- La Vltava dominée par Vyšehrad
- La Moldava con Vyšehrad

188

189

190

188.—191. Klášter na Slovanech (Emauzy) ● Vyšehrad ● Letecký pohled na Vyšehrad ● Vyšehradský hřbitov s kostelem sv. Petra a Pavla

Emmauskloster ● Vyšehrad ● Vyšehrad (Luftaufnahme) ● Friedhof auf dem Vyšehrad mit Peterskirche

“Na Slovanech” Monaster (Emaus) ● Vyšehrad ● Aerial View of Vyšehrad ● Vyšehrad Cemetery with St. Peter and Paul’s Church

Le monastère d’Emmaüs ● Vyšehrad ● Vyšehrad vu à vol d’oiseau ● Le cimetière de Vyšehrad avec l’église Saint-Pierre-et-Paul

Il monastero Na Slovanech (Emmaus) ● Vyšehrad e la veduta aerea su Vyšehrad ● Il cimitero di Vyšehrad con la chiesa dei Santi Pietro e Paolo

191

192

193

192.—196. Pohled z Vyšehradu ● Myslbekovo sousoší Záboje a Slavoje na Vyšehradě ● Letecký pohled na Vyšehrad ● Slavín ● Rotunda sv. Martina

Blick vom Vyšehrad ● J. V. Myslbek: Záboj und Slavoj ● Vyšehrad (Luftaufnahme) ● Slavín ● Rotunde des hl. Martin

View from Vyšehrad Hill ● Myslbek's Group "Záboj and Slavoj" at Vyšehrad ● Aerial View of Vyšehrad ● Slavín Burial Grounds ● St. Martin's Rotunda

Vue depuis le Vyšehrad ● Le groupe de statues de Záboj et Slavoj à Vyšehrad par Myslbek ● Vyšehrad — vue à vol d'oiseau ● Le Panthéon Slavín ● La rotonde Saint-Martin

Veduta da Vyšehrad ● Gruppo scultoreo di Myslbek: Záboj e Slavoj a Vyšehrad ● Veduta aerea su Vyšehrad ● Il cimitero Slavín — La rotonda di San Martino

194

195

196

197. Pohled na Prahu z Vyšehradu ● Blick vom Vyšehrad auf Prag ● View of Prague from Vyšehrad ● Vue sur Prague depuis Vyšehrad

● Veduta di Praga da Vyšehrad

198

198.—199. Nuselský most • Palác kultury a hotel Forum

Nusler Brücke • Kulturpalast und Hotel Forum

Nusle Bridge • Palace of Culture and Forum Hotel

Le pont de Nusle • Le Palais de la culture et l'hôtel Forum

Il Ponte di Nusle • Il palazzo della Cultura e l'albergo Forum

FORUM
FORUM

200. Ohňostroj pod Petřínem • Feuerwerk unter dem Laurenziberg • Fireworks below Petřín • Le feu d'artifice organisé au pied de la butte

de Petřín ● I fuochi artificiali sotto la collina di Petřín

1791
1891
1991

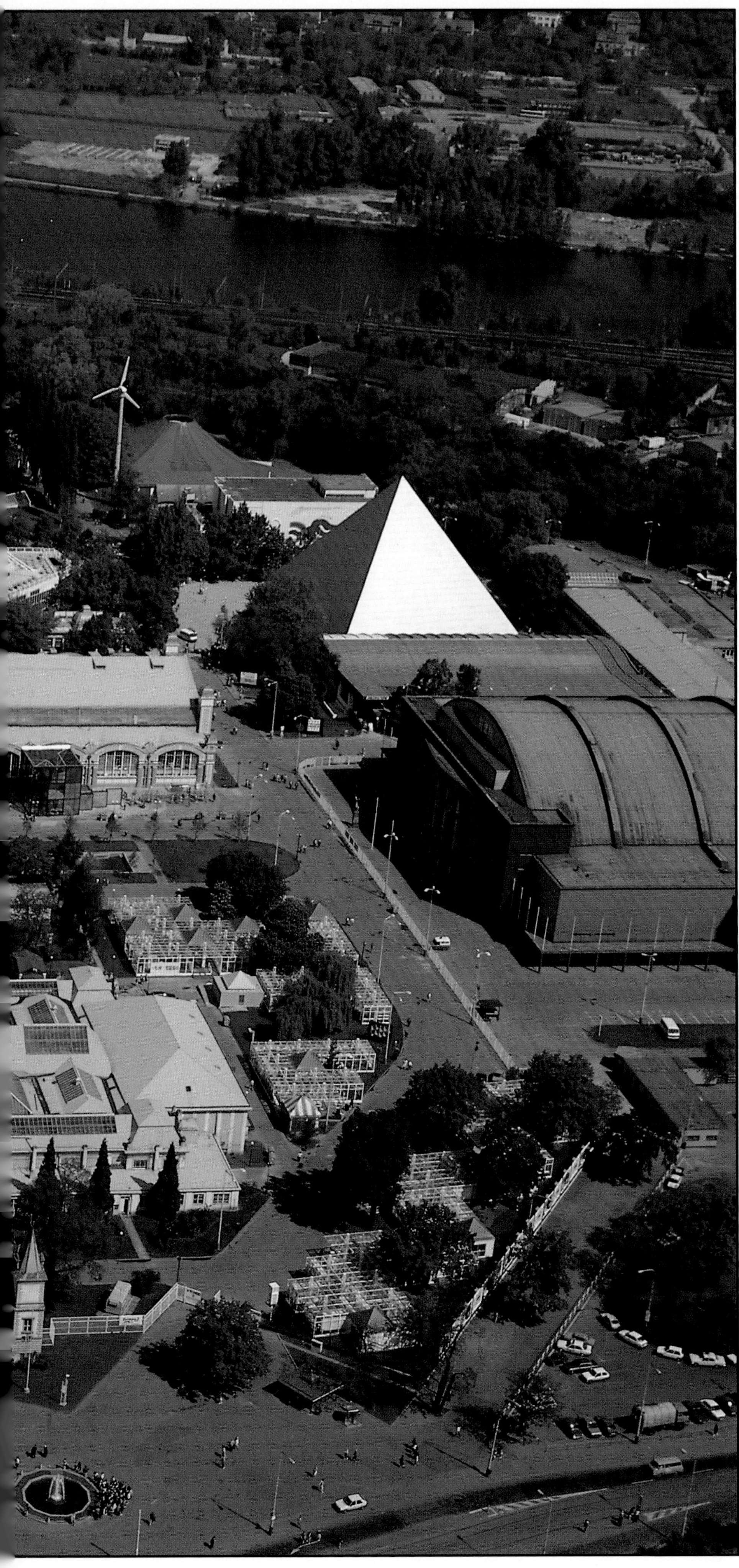

201. Pražské výstaviště

- Prager Ausstellungsgelände
- Prague Exhibition Area
- Le parc des expositions à Prague
- Le esposizioni di Praga

202. Křižíkova fontána na výstavišti

• Křižík-Fontäne auf dem Ausstellungsgelände

• Křižík's Fountain in Exhibition Area

• La fontaine Křižík située dans le parc des expositions

• La fontana Křižík alle Esposizioni

203. Zámek Trója ● Schloß Troja ● Trója Mansion ● Le Château de Trója ● La Villa di Trója

204

205

204.—206. Zámek Zbraslav ● B. Schnirch: Triga ● Štursův sál na Zbraslavi

Schloß Zbraslav ● B. Schnirch: Triga ● Štursa-Saal im Schloß Zbraslav

Zbraslav Mansion ● Bohuslav Schnirch: Triga ● Štursa Hall at Zbraslav

Le château de Zbraslav ● Bohuslav Schnirch : Le Trige ● La salle du château de Zbraslav abritant les sculptures par Jan Štursa

La villa di Zbraslav ● B. Schnirch: Triga ● La sala Štursa a Zbraslav

207

207.—208. J. V. Myslbek: Hudba (detail) ● Myslbekův sál na Zbraslavi

J. V. Myslbek: Musik (Detail) ● Myslbek-Saal im Schloß Zbraslav

Josef V. Myslbek: Music (Detail) ● Myslbek Hall at Zbraslav

Josef Václav Myslbek : La Musique — détail ● La salle Myslbek au château le Zbraslav

J. V. Myslbek: La musica / dettaglio ● La sala Myslbek a Zbraslav

209. Zámek Zbraslav ● Schloß Zbraslav ● Zbraslav Mansion ● Le château de Zbraslav ● La villa di Zbraslav

PRAHA

VLTAVA 1, 185 — pramenící v šumavských hvozdech (dlouhá 430,2 km, povodí 28 090 km) představuje levostranný přítok řeky Labe u Mělníka. Ač velikostí druhá, svým významem násobeným národní mytologií se řadí na první místo v Čechách. V Praze dosahuje značné šířky a hloubky (š. 316, hl. až 3,8 m). Člení se na čtyři nádrže a rozdělena v ramena utváří několik ostrovů (např. Žofínský, Střelecký, Rohanský, Císařský). Výrazně se podílí na malebnosti pražského exteriéru.

PRAŽSKÝ HRAD 2, 6, 46, 99, 180 — byl založen na hradčanském ostrohu v blízkosti toku Vltavy po r. 880, kdy sem bylo z Levého Hradce přeneseno sídlo českých knížat. Formující se centrum českého přemyslovského státu se stávalo i střediskem církevního dění. První křesťanský kostel Panny Marie byl zde postaven před koncem 9. století; v 2. polovině 10. století v blízkosti knížecího paláce byla vybudována rotunda sv. Víta s biskupským palácem a kostel sv. Jiří. Palác, od 13. století královský, plnil rezidenční funkci panovníkova sídla, jehož vrcholný vzestup nastal za vlády císaře Karla IV., horlivého a kultivovaného stavebníka. Reprezentativnost císařského sídla podpořila zejména rozsáhlá výstavba katedrály sv. Víta započatá r. 1344 v duchu francouzských vzorů. Výrazná stavební aktivita nastala koncem 15. století, kdy král Vladislav Jagellonský rozšířil palác s Vladislavským sálem. Za jeho vlády jako součást pozdně gotického opevnění hradu byla podle návrhu B. Rieda vybudována pověstná věž Daliborka, nazývaná podle rytíře Dalibora z Kozojed, jenž si zde odpykával vězení. Jeho romantický příběh se stal námětem Smetanovy opery Dalibor. K opevnění z této doby patřila rovněž Bílá věž, sloužící od r. 1584 jako státní vězení.

Po zasypání dvojího příkopu v druhé čtvrtině 16. století došlo k výstavbě druhého nádvoří Hradu, postupně dobudovaného a dále přestavěného podle projektu N. Pacassiho do r. 1775. Severní křídlo zahrnuje Španělský sál s Rudolfovou galerií. Přízemní část západního křídla spolu s konírnami byla v r. 1965 upravena v Obrazárnu Hradu. V jihovýchodním rohu nádvoří je kaple sv. Kříže, původně stavěná podle návrhu A. Luraga. Po úpravách sem byla v r. 1963 instalovaná svatovítská klenotnice.

Třetí hradní nádvoří, tvořící jádro hradního areálu, zahrnuje renesanční palác císaře Rudolfa II., Maxmiliána II. a raně barokní palác královnin, mající jednotnou úpravu fasád provedenou podle návrhu N. Pacassiho v třetí čtvrtině 18. století. Zde se nacházejí úřadovny Kanceláře prezidenta republiky. Reprezentativní vchod s balkónem je zdoben sochami I. F. Platzera z l. 1760—61. Toto náměstí je obepínáno královským palácem i katedrálou sv. Víta a napojuje se na náměstí u sv. Jiří. Z opačné strany se k němu napojuje Vikářská ulice s bývalým kapitulním domem děkana a s novým vikářstvím, v němž je dnes proslulá restaurace Na Vikárce, spjatá s literárním dílem Sv. Čecha.

K areálu Pražského hradu náleží tzv. Prašná věž z konce 15. století, jinak zvaná Mihulka, rovněž vybudovaná B. Riedem. V této původně dělostřelecké věži je expozice věnovaná vědě a kultuře pěstované na Hradě v 16. a 17. století, nechybí ani model alchymistické dílny.

Pražský hrad obklopují jižní hradní zahrady, Rajská zahrada a zahrada Na valech, nabízející mimo jiné jedinečné výhledy na pražské panoráma.

FRANTIŠEK ŽENÍŠEK (1849—1916), LIBUŠE VĚŠTÍ SLÁVU PRAHY; 3 — dílo příslušníka první generace Národního divadla se upíná k legendární postavě českých bájí, kněžce Libuši, a jejímu prorockému vidění slávy města — Prahy.

STAROMĚSTSKÁ RADNICE 4, 105, 107, 114—120, 123 — jejíž efektní torzo se malebně zvedá po straně Staroměstského náměstí, je dokladem existence významné městské samosprávy, sahající až k roku 1338. Jádrem mnohokrát přebudované stavby byl gotický dům Wolflina od Kamene vykoupený měšťany, kteří k němu do r. 1346 přistavěli čtyřbokou věž s kaplí (vysvěcenou r. 1381) s krásným zdobeným arkýřem. M. Rejskovi z Prostějova bývá připisován ozdobný portál hlavního vchodu osazený v l. 1470—80. Do průčelí radnice v prvním poschodí pod radní síní na rozšířenou část domu bylo po r. 1520 umístěno okno s nápisem Praga caput regni (Praha, hlava království) a znakem Starého Města z r. 1475. Za autora této raně renesanční přestavby bývá považován proslavený B. Ried. K rozšiřování a přestavbám radnice docházelo až po 19. století. Den před skončením druhé světové války, 8. května 1945, došlo k těžkému poškození a požáru novogotické severní části objektu budovaného P. Nobilem. Po stržení zbytku stavby docházelo k snahám o rekonstrukci či novostavbu tohoto křídla, na něž byly vypsány neúspěšné konkursy.

Ve vestibulu radnice je mozaiková výzdoba klasika českého umění konce 19. a počátku 20. století, M. Alše, představující Hold Slovanstva Praze (1904). Je výtvarnou replikou promluvy K. Sladkovského při slavnostním položení základního kamene Národního divadla. Představuje Libušino prorocké vidění města, „jehož sláva hvězd se dotýká". Z historických interiérů radnice se k nejpamátnějším řadí stará radní síň dochovaná v původní podobě z r. 1470. Vnitřek zdobí převážně obrazy V. Brožíka upínajícího se k dějinným aktům, výrazně ovlivňujícím i formování národního sebevědomí.

PRAŽSKÉ MOSTY 5, 98, 156, 178, 184 — mají vedle technického a funkčního zřetele dobře vnímatelný estetický charakter, vyplývající nejen ze stavební a výzdobné složky, ale i ze souhry s malebností toku řeky, jejími reflexy a přírodními náladami.

HRADČANSKÉ NÁMĚSTÍ 7 — skýtá pohled na první, nejmladší nádvoří Pražského hradu se vstupní branou. Nádvoří bylo vybudováno v duchu italsko-vídeňského neoklasicismu v l. 1759—69 podle projektu architekta N. Pacassiho. Na atiku budov byly umístěny vojenské emblémy a sochy I. F. Platzera. Úpravu nádvoří prováděl v letech 1920—22 P. Janák, k rozsáhlé adaptaci došlo v l. 1979—80.

Proti bráně prvního nádvoří stojí Matyášova brána budovaná patrně G. M. Filippim na způsob italských pevnostních staveb, neboť původně tvořila součást opevnění nad hradním příkopem.

ARCIBISKUPSKÝ PALÁC 8 — uzavírající Hradčanské náměstí před průčelím Pražského hradu, představuje reprezentativní zbarokizovanou stavbu s dominujícím znakem arcibiskupa Antonína Příchovského. Základem paláce byl někdejší Gryspekovský dům, který koupil Ferdinand I. pro sídlo obnoveného pražského arcibiskupství.

V l. 1562—64 došlo k přestavbě O. Aostalise. Novou výraznou přestavbu provedl v l. 1669—79 chráněnec arcibiskupa J. B. z Valdštejna J. B. Mathey, vynikající architekt francouzského původu. Závěrečný rokokový ráz vtiskl stavbě v l. 1764—65 J. J. Wirch, vůdčí představitel vídeňsky orientovaného slohu. Palác zdobí sochy Víry a Naděje od T. Seidana z 80. let 19. století, zbytek plastické dekorace od I. F. Platzera, jehož sochařská výzdoba je dochována i v interiéru schodiště. Palác zahrnuje i unikátní sbírkový soubor. V kapli z r. 1599, vyzdobené nástropními malbami D. Adama z Květné, vynikají zlacené bysty sv. Petra a Pavla z doby kolem r. 1413. V trůnním sálu je cenný soubor osmi tapisérií s exotickým námětem Nové Indie zhotovených v Neilsonově ateliéru v Paříži podle kartónů A. Desportesa. Ve sbírce obrazů jsou zahrnuta díla J. J. Heinsche, M. V. Halwachse, F. Dallingera a dalších. Jedinečný je sled portrétů pražských arcibiskupů. V souboru uměleckého řemesla vyniká kolekce českého řezaného skla, bohatá je sbírka vídeňského porcelánu. Vybavení paláce mohou návštěvníci zhlédnout každoročně na Zelený čtvrtek.

VSTUPNÍ BRÁNA PRAŽSKÉHO HRADU 9 — z Hradčanského náměstí je tvořena monumentálními mřížovými vraty vsazenými mezi rokokové zábradlí z doby Marie Terezie. Výzdobu tvoří skupiny Zápasících gigantů, dále vázy a putti vytvořené v r. 1769 I. F. Platzerem. Chátrající pískovcové skulptury byly však v r. 1912 nahrazeny kopiemi pořízenými Č. Vosmíkem a A. Procházkou.

V pozadí dominuje předbarokní kamenná brána, zbudovaná za vlády císaře Matyáše v r. 1614. Vedle označení císařových hodností jsou po stranách znaky jednotlivých zemí císařství.

TŘETÍ NÁDVOŘÍ PRAŽSKÉHO HRADU 10 — bylo postupně budováno po velkém požáru v r. 1551, po němž došlo k zasypání zbytků středověké zástavby. Po 1. světové válce J. Plečnik nad archeologickými nálezy vyprojekoval betonovou konstrukci a žulovou dlažbu.

Severní stranu třetího nádvoří uzavírá jižní část svatovítského chrámu s velkou chrámovou věží založenou P. Parléřem r. 1396. Její pozdější renesanční věž byla nově přebudována r. 1770 podle návrhu N. Pacassiho. Ve věži, dosahující 99,6 m, jsou čtyři renesanční zvony, mezi nimiž výškou 203 cm vyniká Zikmund. Toto největší zvonařské dílo v Čechách vytvořil T. Jaroš r. 1549.

Vpravo pod věží je arkádový portikus, tzv. Zlatá brána, nesoucí komoru, v níž jsou uloženy korunovační klenoty Království českého. Na jejím průčelí je mozaika Poslední soud vytvořená v l. 1370—71 benátskými mistry z českého skla.

Budova Starého proboštství za mrákotínským monolitem má podobu ze 17. století. Na jejím místě stával románský biskupský palác.

BAZILIKA SV. JIŘÍ 11 — tvořící východní stranu svatojiřského náměstí je nejdochovanější románskou stavbou v Praze. Kostel byl založen v r. 921 knížetem Vratislavem, podoba trojlodní baziliky však spadá do doby abatyše Berty, tj. před r. 1142, kdy došlo k požáru Hradu. Hlavní průčelí bylo barokizováno — patrně F. Carattim — v letech 1677—78. Vedle něj F. M. Kaňka v l. 1718—22 přistavěl kapli sv. Jana Nepomuckého, dotvořenou nad vchodem sousoším od F. M. Brokoffa. K jižní věži baziliky z poloviny 12. století byla ve 14. stol. připojena kaple sv. Ludmily. Na jižním boku baziliky upoutává renesanční sloupový portál, vytesaný hutí B. Rieda z Pístova kolem r. 1500. Gotický reliéf drakobijce sv. Jiří byl v r. 1934 nahrazen kopií. Pod jižní věží ve zbytcích kaple Panny Marie je dochována románská výmalba z první poloviny 13. století. Uvnitř baziliky, románsky upravené na přelomu 19. a 20. století, jsou mimo jiné náhrobky knížat Boleslava II. a Oldřicha i tumba knížete Vratislava.

Součástí přiléhajícího stavebního komplexu je první ženský klášter v Čechách řehole sv. Benedikta, založený sestrou knížete Boleslava II. blahoslavenou Mladou. Vícekrát přestavovaný klášter byl zrušen r. 1782 a záhy se zčásti proměnil v kasárna. V l. 1962—74 byl předán Národní galerii v Praze a po dokončené adaptaci v něm byla vytvořena expozice českého umění doby gotiky, renesance, manýrismu a baroka.

KATEDRÁLA SV. VÍTA 12, 44 — je největším a nejdůležitějším pražským chrámem, kde jsou uloženy korunovační klenoty Českého království. Spočívají zde také ostatky českých panovníků. Katedrála výrazně dotvářející siluetu Hradčan byla založena Karlem IV. v r. 1344 na místě románské trojlodní baziliky a předchozí rotundy, zbudované sv. Václavem, patronem České země, před r. 935. Trojlodní katedrála s příčnou lodí, ochozem a věncem kaplí začala být stavěna podle návrhu Francouze Matyáše z Arrasu, po jehož smrti se r. 1356 stavby ujal P. Parléř, pocházející ze švábského Gmündu. Jeho nástupci se stali jeho synové Václav a Jan. Po dobudování chóru s kaplemi a rozestavění hlavní věže do r. 1420 je významná renesanční perioda, v níž byl v r. 1564 B. Wohlmutem vystavěn ochoz na věži a helmice. Barokní cibulová střecha byla dokončena v r. 1770 N. Pacassim. Katedrála dostavěná až v r. 1929 zaznamenala rovněž novogotickou stavební etapu započatou v r. 1873. Z této doby pochází novogotický oltář, před nímž je královské mauzoleum vytesané v mramoru A. Colinem v. l. 1566—89. V chrámovém triforiu je 21 portrétních bust z let 1374—85 zobrazujících Karla IV. a panovnickou rodinu, arcibiskupy i stavitele chrámu. V jeho podzemí, kde jsou dochovány zbytky románské rotundy, je královská hrobka. Významným místem je komora s korunovačními klenoty, uzamčená sedmi zámky. Za nejvzácnější z korunovačních pokladů je považována svatováclavská koruna z r. 1346. V kaplích katedrálního ochozu jsou tumby českých panovníků vytvořené v Parléřově huti v l. 1370—75. V době vlády Vladislava Jagellonského došlo v r. 1493 k výstavbě královské oratoře s naturalistickým ornamentem v podobě propletených větví a znaky zemí. Renesanční epochu dokládá Wohlmutova varhanní kruchta, přemístěná do příčné lodi v r. 1924. Z barokní výzdoby chrámu upoutá zejména náhrobek hraběte L. Šlika vytvořený společně J. E. Fischerem z Erlachu, F. M. Kaňkou a M. Brandlem v r. 1723. K vynikajícím dílům z nové doby patří socha klečícího kardinála B. Schwarzenberga ztvárněná J. V. Myslbekem v l. 1892—95. Z první třetiny 20. století pochází řada barevných oken jednotlivých kaplí provedených podle kartónů A. Muchy, F. Kysely, C. Boudy a dalších. Chrám je pokladnicí uměleckých děl v rozsahu od románské doby (např. porýnský, tzv. jeruzalémský svícen) až po artefakty z 20. století.

SVATOVÁCLAVSKÁ KAPLE 13 — jejíž stavbu započal Matyáš z Arrasu, byla pojatá jako protějšek kaple sv. Kříže na Karlštejně. Byla dobudována P. Parléřem v l. 1362—66, a to na místě původního světcova hrobu z r. 935, tj. při jižní části přední lodi. Kaple, náležející k nejpřednějším klenotům vrcholné české gotiky, má spodní část obloženou 1345 jaspisy a ametysty. Malířskou výzdobu prvořadé úrovně tvoří Pašijový cyklus od neznámého mistra z l. 1372—73, v horní části malby od Mistra litoměřického z let 1506—09 zobrazují legendu sv. Václava. Oltář kaple má gotickou tumbu ze 14. století, opuková socha sv. Václava byla vytvořena P. Parléřem v r. 1373. Drobné malby nad oltářem představují Karla IV. a jeho čtvrtou manželku Elišku z Pomořan, dále jsou zde zachyceny postavy Václava IV. a Jany Bavorské. Dominující postavy namalované nad sochou sv. Václava představují patrně Vladislava Jagellonského a jeho choť Annu de Foi-Candale. Liturgické předměty na oltáři, právě tak jako zlacený tabernákl a lustr z let 1912—13 (prováděl F. Anýž podle návrhů K. Hilberta, S. Suchardy a J. Kryšpína) doplňují sled gotických a renesančních artefaktů. Pod oknem kaple je portálek vedoucí ke schodišti do korunovační komory, kde je bezpečně uložen soubor korunovačních klenotů.

MISTR THEODORIK, SV. PAPEŽ, SV. JERONÝM, SV. AUGUSTÝN, SV. VÍT 14—17 — deskové malby císařského malíře a představeného malířského cechu pražského byly vytvořeny v 70. letech 14. století pro dvorní kapli Karla IV. na Karlštejně. Myšlenku univerzální jednoty světa nebeského a pozemského odráží 130 obrazů umístěných ve třech pásech táflovaných stěn. Tento polyptych má přísně hieratické uspořádání. Monumentálně cítěné nadživotní postavy strážců císařského pokladu jsou jedinečným příkladem feudálního řádu, za nějž odpovídala osobnost panovníka respektujícího Vítěznou církev. Malby představující nebeské vojsko Kristovo jsou i dokladem středověkého kultu světců — mučedníků, jejichž relikvie byly vsazeny do rámu každého obrazu.

Theodorikova měkce malebná forma s naturalistickým obměňováním jednoho fyziognomického typu je dokladem pokročilé tvůrčí orientace císařem preferovaného mistra. Znalost byzantské právě tak jako západní, jmenovitě benátské a boloňské tvorby zdá se být průkazná.

MISTR TŘEBOŇSKÝ, KRISTUS NA HOŘE OLIVETSKÉ, UKŘIŽOVÁNÍ, KLADENÍ DO HROBU, ZMRTVÝCHVSTÁNÍ 18—21 — díla zastoupená ve sbírkách Národní galerie v Praze pocházejí z oltáře augustiniánského kostela sv. Jiljí v Třeboni, deska Ukřižování je z kaple sv. Barbory u Třeboně. Tyto deskové malby vytvořil anonymní mistr světové úrovně kolem r. 1380. Složitá kompozice se zjemnělou arabeskou tvarů a sytý barevný kontrast umocňují výtvarný idealismus a zvláštní mystické vytržení. Díla lyrického dosahu předjímají umění krásného slohu z doby kolem r. 1400.

VLADISLAVSKÝ SÁL 22 — zaujímá rozlohu celého druhého patra Starého paláce Pražského hradu. Představuje nejdůstojnější prostoru Hradu, neboť se zde tradičně odehrávají nejdůležitější státní akty. Byl vybudován za Vladislava Jagellonského v l. 1492—1502 poté, kdy došlo k přenesení sídla královského dvora ze Starého Města na Hrad. Stavbu na místě tří gotických síní z doby Karla IV. projektoval královský stavitel B. Ried. Byl vybudován největší a nejreprezentativnější světský prostor středoevropské pozdní gotiky (délka 62 m, šířka 16 m, výška 13 m). Konaly se v něm korunovace i stavovské sněmy, ale také rytířské turnaje, jimž sloužily i přilehlé Jezdecké schody. Po přesídlení panovnické rezidence do Vídně sloužil sál častěji za společenské shromaždiště, v němž se konaly i trhy dvorských kramářů. Sál byl pietně renovován po 1. světové válce, kdy došlo k odstranění pozdních výmaleb.

Z Vladislavského sálu je přístup do bočního křídla Hradu, tzv. Ludvíkova paláce z počátku 16. století.

STARÁ SNĚMOVNA PRAŽSKÉHO HRADU 23 — v níž až do r. 1847 zasedal nejvyšší soud zemský a rovněž zde sněmovali zástupci českých stavů, byla zbudována v l. 1559—65 císařským stavitelem B. Wohlmutem. Reprezentativní prostora se síťovou krouženou klenbou byla do r. 1857 využívána i stavovskými sněmy k volbě králů. V nové době zde dochází k podpisování ústavních listin prezidentem, mimořádně zde probíhají slavnostní zasedání České národní rady.

ADRIAEN DE VRIES (1546—1626), RUDOLF II. 24 — jedna ze tří Vriesových podobizen císaře (z r. 1603), jehož teoretik a malíř Van Mander nazval „největším a prvním přítelem umění na světě“, pochází z unikátních rudolfínských sbírek, jejichž torzo je vystaveno v Obrazárně Pražského hradu. Nizozemec de Vries byl největší sochařskou osobností rudolfínského dvora. Rozsáhlé množství jeho děl se stalo předmětem švédské kořisti za obléhání Prahy v r. 1648.

SV. JIŘÍ 25 — bronzová jezdecká socha bájného drakobijce je kopií díla mistrů Jiřího a Martina z Kluže (Klausenburgu), vytvořeného v r. 1373. Původně byla umístěna v jižní části hradního nádvoří před tzv. Maxmiliánovými kuchyněmi. Figury koně a draka byly později zčásti přelité a po poškození v r. 1562 opravené kovolitcem T. Jarošem. Podstavec sochy zároveň při vydláždění III. nádvoří v r. 1928 navrhl J. Plečnik, který rovněž projektoval 18 m vysoký monolit z mrákotínské žuly. Byl vztyčen k výročí desetiletého trvání republiky a na paměť obětem 1. světové války.

TIZIANO VECELLIO (asi 1480/90–1576), TOALETA MLADÉ ŽENY 26 — toto dílo největšího představitele benátské malby 16. století bylo doloženo v obrazárně Hradu v r. 1685. Rusovlasá mladá žena s toaletními potřebami, jíž obdivně přisluhuje mladík v turbanu, se typově blíží vídeňskému obrazu cikánské madony (kol. 1510) vzniklému v době Tizianova plného obdivu k Giorgionovi. Pražská malba, vytvořená kolem r. 1512–15, byla asi po polovině 18. století zmenšena snad pro táflování (na 83×79 cm). Přesná renesanční kopie malby (o rozměru 109,2×91,3 cm) byla dražebním domem Christie v Londýně (27. 11. 1957) prodána do soukromé sbírky. Jiné, méně kvalitní barokní kopie byly J. Neumannem zaznamenány v dalších soukromých sbírkách (např. v Toulouse).

Téma Toaleta mladé ženy se objevuje i v dalších verzích, z nichž nejznámější je Tizianovo dílo z Louvru pocházející ze sbírky anglického krále Karla I. Originalita pražské malby byla v minulosti zpochybňována. Již v r. 1832 bylo dílo připisováno Tizianovu synovi Oraziovi, později bylo považováno za kopii.

PETRUS PAULUS RUBENS (1577–1640), SHROMÁŽDĚNÍ OLYMPSKÝCH BOHŮ (detail) 27 — již toto rané dílo hlavního představitele flámského baroka nastiňuje mohutnost energie, smyslnost a symfonický proud mnohovrstevných dějů, jimiž později překypuje Rubensova tvorba. Malba vznikla patrně kolem r. 1602, kdy se Rubens stal dvorním malířem mantovského vévody Vinzenza Gonzagy. Obraz zachycuje shromáždění Olympanů v čele s Jupiterem, kdy strážkyně pevných manželských svazků Héra — Junona přednáší svou stížnost na lehkomyslnou, leč triumfující bohyni lásky Venuši — Afrodité, korunovanou amoretty.

Tato malba, nesoucí pečeť vlivu G. Romana, je ve sbírkách Hradu poprvé doložena r. 1685, a to jako dílo anonymního mistra, v l. 1718–37 je spojována se jménem Raffaelovým. Rubensovo autorství bylo krátce zmiňováno v r. 1797, originalitu jeho tvorby stvrdil po r. 1962 J. Neumann.

KAREL ŠKRÉTA (1610–1674), PODOBIZNA ŘEZAČE DRAHOKAMŮ DIONYSIA MISERONIHO A JEHO RODINY (detail) 28 — dílo zakladatelské osobnosti české barokní malby, vytvořené patrně r. 1653, zachycuje vedoucího brusičské dílny a správce hradních uměleckých sbírek v kruhu rodiny. Právě Dionysius Miseroni v r. 1648 zabraňoval Švédům ve vstupu do proslulých sbírek rudolfínské kunstkomory. Jeho otec Octavio Miseroni byl v r. 1588 povolán z Milána ke dvoru Rudolfa II., kde byl jmenován dvorním řezačem drahokamů, a v r. 1608 získal šlechtický predikát.

JAN KUPECKÝ (KUPEZKY JOHANNES, 1667–1740), ALEGORIE MALÍŘSTVÍ 29 — dílo českého exulanta, který se zapsal mezi přední evropské portrétisty počátku 18. století, je protějškovým obrazem k Alegorii sochařství ze sbírek Národní galerie v Praze. Personifikace malby jako mladé ženy v barokním oděvu, s vavřínovým věncem slávy na bohatých plavých vlasech je vřazována do druhého desetiletí 18. století, kdy působil především ve Vídni.

PETR BRANDL (1668–1735), VLASTNÍ PODOBIZNA 31 — z lobkovických sbírek, zapůjčená do Národní galerie v Praze, byla vytvořena v r. 1697. Věrohodně dokládá charakterizační i koloristické mistrovství největšího malíře vrcholného baroku v Čechách, který vstoupil do povědomí nejen jako portrétista, ale zejména jako tvůrce světelně dynamických oltářních obrazů i děl s mytologickou a žánrovou tematikou.

PAOLO CALIARI, ZVANÝ VERONESE (1528–1588), SV. KATEŘINA S ANDĚLEM 32 — dílo jednoho z největších představitelů benátské malby 16. století vytvořené kolem r. 1580, je doloženo v II. galerii Pražského hradu již r. 1685 s názvem Pokušení světice. Nesprávný výklad obrazu byl patrně dovozován z důvěrného gesta anděla. Podle J. Neumanna alexandrijská světice je však zobrazena jako Kristova nevěsta ve chvíli, kdy jí nebeský posel vyjevuje její osud, mučednickou smrt, jak o tom vypovídá palmová ratolest a meč v ruce anděla.

LOBKOVICKÝ PALÁC A ČERNÁ VĚŽ 33 — jsou přístupné od Starých zámeckých schodů ve východním obvodu Hradu. Černá věž, vybudovaná na starším základě v druhé čtvrti 12. století, byla součástí románského opevnění z doby knížete Soběslava. Její degradace po požáru z r. 1538, kdy musela být snížena o jedno patro, se promítla i v názvu. Dříve byla totiž věž označována jako „Zlatá" — podle střechy, pobité za Karla IV. pozlaceným olověným plechem. Věž byla využívána i jako vězení pro dlužníky. Původně sloužila jako východní brána hradu. Za Václava I. po r. 1230 byla pod ní vybudována nová vstupní brána. Přiléhá k Lobkovickému, původně Pernštejnskému paláci, vystavěném Jaroslavem a Vratislavem z Pernštejna v l. 1555–62 a 1570–76. Stavba byla v r. 1625 poškozena požárem. K nové přestavbě paláce došlo zejména v l. 1651–68 za Lobkoviců, v jejichž majetku byl palác od r. 1626. Václav Eusebius z Lobkovic zadal projekt C. Luragovi, vlašští kameníci G. Galli a G. Pozzo prováděli kamenické práce, štukatér D. Galli vyzdobil strop hlavního sálu, do nějž F. V. Hárovník vsadil olejomalby. Výzdobu dotvářeli domácí řemeslníci. K dílčím přestavbám docházelo i v dalších dobách, zejména v r. 1810 a v l. 1861–62. V r. 1976 začaly rekonstrukce paláce, do nějž byla umístěna expozice historicko-archeologického oddělení Národního muzea. V rámci restitucí v r. 1992 je palác znovu navrácen roudnické větvi rodu Lobkoviců.

PANORAMA PRAHY Z LOBKOVICKÉHO PALÁCE 34 — zachycuje jedinečný pohled na rozlehlou malostranskou enklávu Valdštejnského paláce, zbudovaného na ploše 23 domů s dvory a zahradami, cihelny a městské brány. Za ním se tyčí kostel sv. Tomáše, založený spolu s klášterem Václavem II. r. 1285 pro augustiniány-poustevníky. Autorem dochované barokní přestavby z let 1723–31 byl vynikající architekt K. I. Dienzenhofer. Honosnou výzdobu kostela vytvářeli přední čeští představitelé doby baroka, pro hlavní oltář však byla objednána dvě díla P. P. Rubense, doložená dnes kopiemi (originály přeneseny do Národní galerie).

KOLOWRATSKÁ ZAHRADA 35 — projektovaná v l. 1769–89 I. J. Palliardim se rozprostírá za hlavní budovou Kolowratského paláce a menším Černínským palácem, vybudovaným v r. 1770 místo někdejšího domu Popela z Lobkovic. Rokoková terasovitá zahrada s nádechem orientální exotiky a malebnosti zahrnuje altány a schodiště s balustrádami vedoucí k trojdílné sale terreně.

KRÁLOVSKÁ ZAHRADA 36 — upravená dnes v anglickém stylu byla založena r. 1535 Ferdinandem I. v duchu italských renesančních zahrad na ploše mezi Prašným mostem a Jelením příkopem. Byla osázena také exotickými rostlinami, ale i vinnou révou, bylo založeno nizozemské giardinetto. Došlo k vybudování četných staveb, ptáčnice a oranžérie, vznikaly vodní nádrže, fontány a vodotrysky, bludiště. K zásadní úpravě podle návrhu K. I. Dienzenhofera došlo v l. 1725–34, kdy květinový parter francouzského stylu byl doplněn skulpturami lvů, váz a alegorií z dílny M. B. Brauna.

HARTIGOVSKÁ ZAHRADA 37, 50 — se rozkládá na jižním úbočí Pražského hradu mezi dalšími zahradami jedinečné krásy a malebnosti. Vedle procházek spojených s překrásným výhledem na panorama Prahy nabízely se zde i působivé kulturní produkce, jako tomu bylo v hudebním pavilónu Hartigovské zahrady. Stavba z první čtvrti 18. století, připisovaná G. B. Alliprandimu, má horní sál dekorován malbami zřícenin a štukaturami. Před pavilón byly umístěny skulptury antických božstev z dílny A. Brauna, vzniklé kolem r. 1735, jež byly na Pražský hrad po r. 1945 přemístěny ze zahrad štiřínského zámku.

ZPÍVAJÍCÍ FONTÁNA 38 — nacházející se před Královským letohrádkem byla ulita 1564–68 brněnským kovolitcem T. Jarošem, a to podle návrhu vlašského mistra F. Terzia. Fontána je umístěna uprostřed obnoveného giardinetta, vytvořeného podle vzorníku nizozemského architekta a dekoratéra V. de Vriese. Její název je odvozen od zvuku vodních kapek, dopadajících z dvoupatrové nádrže zdobené loveckými motivy. Fontána je řazena k nejkrásnějším renesančním dílům svého druhu severně od Alp.

VELKÁ MÍČOVNA. MATYÁŠ BERNARD BRAUN — DÍLNA, NOC 39, 40 — Velká míčovna byla postavena v Královské zahradě nad Jelením příkopem B. Wohlmutem a O. Aostalisem v l. 1567–69 původně pro módu míčových her. Ušlechtilá sálová stavba (dlouhá 60 m) s palladiánskými sloupy je pokryta křehkými sgrafity, jež jsou alegoriemi Ctností, Věd a Živlů. Opuštěný objekt byl však r. 1723 proměněn v konírny, později ve vojenské skladiště. Ještě v r. 1734 ale byla před jeho průčelí umístěna sousoší z dílny M. B. Brauna, vytvořená jeho synovcem A. Braunem, alegorie Noci a Dne. Toto druhé dílo bylo zničeno za bombardování Hradu Prusy v r. 1757.

V r. 1945 Míčovna vyhořela, byla však v r. 1952 opravena a v l. 1971–73 znovu adaptována. V současné době slouží reprezentačním účelům, pro něž jsou zde instalovány bruselské tapiserie J. van Leefdaela ze 17. století na téma Antonius a Kleopatra.

KRÁLOVSKÝ LETOHRÁDEK (BELVEDER) 41 — vybudovaný v blízkosti Pražského hradu nad údolím Brusnice v l. 1538—63 je skvělou ukázkou vlivu italské renesance v českých zemích. Stavba z podnětu Ferdinanda I. probíhala podle návrhu vlašského kameníka a architekta P. della Stelly, dále pak H. Tirola a dvorního stavitele B. Wohlmuta, O. Aostalise; stavebním dozorem byl pověřen sekretář České komory F. z Griesbachu. Bohatou kamenickou výzdobu prováděla dílna P. della Stelly (do r. 1538) a poté další vlašští mistři. Letohrádek měl sloužit i k odpočinku a zábavě královny Anny. Vznikla v něm bohatá galerie, byl vybudován taneční sál, místnosti měly nákladné vybavení. Švédský vpád v r. 1648 poznamenal i Belveder a jeho sbírky. Za Josefa II. byl objekt znehodnocen proměnou v laboratoř (do r. 1836). V l. 1851—65 na stěnách prvního patra byl vymalován cyklus témat z českých dějin podle kartónů ředitele pražské Akademie K. Rubena. V současné době letohrádek, restaurovaný P. Janákem, slouží k výstavním účelům.

ZLATÁ ULIČKA 42 — vede za hradním purkrabstvím nad Jelením příkopem. Dnešní pestře natřené miniaturní domky nestejného stáří začaly být koncem 16. století vestavovány do oblouků hradního opevnění z doby jagellonské. Do r. 1597 v nich pobývali hradní střelci, drobní řemeslníci a zlatotepci Rudolfa II. Podle názvu uličky „Zlatnická“ užívaného od sedmdesátých let 17. století vznikla později pověst, že zde bývali rudolfínští alchymisté. V l. 1952—55 byly domky adaptovány právě tak jako krytá chodba spojující tři věže, kudy bývali převáděni vězni. V obnovených domcích byla zřízena expozice o dějinách této populární části Hradu, dále pak prodejny knih a suvenýrů.

MALOSTRANSKÝ CHRÁM SV. MIKULÁŠE 43, 59—60, 62, 64, 65 — Uprostřed Malostranského náměstí, kde dříve stával gotický dům a v jeho blízkosti byly masné krámy, se nachází dominanta pražské architektury doby baroka, přiléhající na jižní straně k bývalé jezuitské koleji. Stavba chrámu sv. Mikuláše byla prováděna v l. 1704—11 K. Dienzenhoferem, přišlým do Prahy přes Waldsassy; jeho syn K. I. Dienzenhofer dobudoval v l. 1732—52 kněžiště a kopuli. Dienzenhoferův švagr A. Lurago přistavoval v l. 1751—56 štíhlou rokokovou zvonici, původní jádro sporu s malostranskou obcí, jež oddálila započetí stavby chrámového komplexu. Průčelí chrámu, dobudované r. 1710, je dokladem vlivu římského baroka iluzívního směru. Vedle znaku Fr. Liebštejnského z Kolowrat jsou zde umístěny sochy církevních otců a dále alegorie Teologie, ztvárněné sochařem A. Braunem před r. 1735.

Vnitřní prostor chrámu je nejpompéznějším příkladem vrcholného baroka v Praze. Na freskové výmalbě se zde podíleli J. L. Kracker a J. Heger, monumentální kapli o rozměru 75 m^2 vyzdobil F. X. Palko. Čtyři nadživotní dřevěné štukované sochy církevních světců pod kopulí vytvořil v l. 1752—55 I. F. Platzer, autor měděné sochy sv. Mikuláše na hlavním oltáři a dalších plastik. Součástí honosné výzdoby chrámu jsou obrazy K. Škréty, I. Raaba, J. L. Krackera. Na varhanech postavených v l. 1745—46 T. Schwarzem hrával za svých pražských pobytů W. A. Mozart.

Po zrušení jezuitského řádu papežem Klimentem XIV. v r. 1773 se sv. Mikuláš stal farním kostelem malostranským.

LORETA 45 — postavená nákladem rodu Lobkoviců proti monumentální kulise Černínského paláce na Hradčanech v l. 1626—1750 byla poutním místem přiléhajícím k prvnímu kapucínskému klášteru v Čechách z r. 1601. Průčelí Lorety vybudoval v l. 1621—23 K. I. Dienzenhofer, sochařskou výzdobu, nahrazenou dnes kopiemi, provedli O. F. Quittainer a J. B. Kohl. Průčelí je převýšeno věží z r. 1693 se zvonkohrou hodináře P. Neumanna. Podmanivé mariánské písňové variace, oživující malebné hradčanské prostranství, vytváří složitý mechanismus zvonků, ulitých v Amsterodamu. Uprostřed nádvoří Lorety je vlastní Santa casa, Svatá chýše, zbudovaná stavitelem G. B. Orsim r. 1631 a pokrytá nápadnými štukovými reliéfy od vlašských mistrů z r. 1664. Jde o připomenutí legendy o domku Panny Marie v Nazaretu, jenž měl být ve 13. století přenesen anděly do italské Lorety. Proto uvnitř chýše jsou obrazy ze života Panny Marie a její cedrová socha. Při ambitech východní strany stavby je kostel Narození Páně, vybudovaný v l. 1734—35 podle plánů J. J. Aichbauera, s nástropními freskami V. V. Reinera.

Loreta, navrácená dnes kapucínskému klášteru, skýtá jedinečné sbírkové bohatství. V klenotnici s poklady nedozírné ceny jsou uloženy zejména zlatnické práce, mezi nimiž je nejcennější diamantová monstrance z r. 1699 (s 6 222 diamanty).

PETŘÍNSKÁ ROZHLEDNA 47 — vysoká 60 m se tyčí na skalnatém svahu (odtud název — petri — skála), který se zvedá do výše 318 m západně nad malostranskou kotlinou. K vybudování rozhledny jako zmenšené kopie pařížské Eiffelovky došlo z popudu Klubu turistů v souvislosti s přípravou Zemské jubilejní výstavy v r. 1891.

HVĚZDÁRNA NA PETŘÍNĚ 48 — na konci Růžového sadu byla vybudována v l. 1925—30 z obecního domu nákladem České astronomické společnosti (projektant J. Veselík). Podnes slouží pro potřeby amatérské hvězdářské činnosti, zároveň je zde umístěna stálá astronomická expozice.

STRAHOVSKÝ KLÁŠTER 51 — založený knížetem Vladislavem II. r. 1140 na popud olomouckého biskupa Jindřicha Zdíka byl osazen řeholními kanovníky premonstrátského řádu, zabývajícího se výchovou a šířením vzdělanosti. Rozlehlý klášterní komplex nad Prahou na petřínském svahu zahrnuje dva kostely, klášter, klášterní prelaturu, knihovny a hospodářské dvory. Jednotlivé objekty prošly složitými proměnami a stavebními zvraty zejména v době husitského hnutí a za útoků francouzských nebo pruských vojsk v 18. století. Jádrem celého areálu je klášter s knihovnou, kde byl r. 1953 umístěn Památník národního písemnictví. Hlavní vstup do areálu vede branou z Pohořelce, vybudovanou r. 1742 A. Luragem. Kostelík sv. Rocha po levé straně byl zřízen na náklad Rudolfa II. jako poděkování za odvrácení moru. A. Lurago se podílel i na přestavbách opatského chrámu Nanebevzetí Panny Marie, v jehož jádře je zahrnuta původní románská bazilika z 12. století. Na hlavním nádvoří se rozprostírá budova prelatury z druhé poloviny 16. století, upravená v l. 1680—99 podle projektu J. B. Matheye a M. A. Canevalla. Nástropní fresky zde maloval premonstrát S. Nosecký. Čtyřkřídlá konventní budova románského základu (po r.1142) byla přebudována v raném i vrcholném baroku. Připojeným schodištěm je přístup do klášterní budovy vystavěné za opata V. Mayera architektem I. P. Palliardim v l. 1782—84. Chloubou tohoto objektu je Filozofický a Teologický sál s bohatou výzdobou a připomínkami jedinečného historického sbírkového bohatství. Součástí klášterního areálu je architektonicky upravená zahrada pod jižním křídlem. Klášter byl v r. 1991 navrácen řádu premonstrátů, který obnovuje přervanou činnost a přejímá torza svých historických a uměleckých fondů.

KOSTEL NANEBEVZETÍ P. MARIE 52 — zahrnující zbytky románské rotundy, dobudované r. 1182 a mnohokrát dostavované, dnes ukazuje výstavbu podle A. Luraga z l. 1745—52. Interiér chrámu má zachovanou původní trojlodní románskou dispozici v barokní úpravě, se štukami K. A. Palliardiho a obrazy na téma mariánské legendy nebo oslavy sv. Norberta od J. Kramolína, I. Raaba, V. Neunherze, F. X. Palka, J. K. Lišky, M. Willmanna, se sochařskými díly J. A. Quittainera a dalších. Na nástropní výmalbě kaplí se podílel strahovský řeholník a malíř S. Nosecký. V kapli sv. Voršily jsou na oltáři umístěny ostatky sv. Norberta, zakladatele řádu premonstrátů. Ke kulturním zajímavostem patří barokní varhany v chrámu, na něž hrával W. A. Mozart.

TEOLOGICKÝ SÁL 53 — zbudovaný v l. 1671—79 architektem G. D. Orsim, sloužil původně jako knihovní sál. Odtud je v barokních skříních dochována teologická literatura, včetně úseku zakázaných knih („libri prohibiti“). Ve vitrínách jsou uloženy vzácné iluminované rukopisy, z nichž nejstarší, Strahovský evangeliář, pochází z 9. století. V prostoru sálu, vyzdobeného štukami a nástěnnými malbami na téma knihovnictví od malíře a premonstráta S. Noseckého, jsou umístěny astrologické glóby ze 17. století, dokládající vědecké zájmy členů řádu.

FILOZOFICKÝ SÁL 54 — pocházející z doby výstavby klášterních budov I. J. Palliardim v l. 1782—84 patří k nejpozoruhodnějším prostorám kláštera. V r. 1794 byl vyzdoben jedinečnou nástropní malbou Dějiny lidstva od vůdčího představitele vídeňského rokoka, F. Maulbertsche. Ořechové barokní skříně vyrobené truhlářem J. Lachhovenem sem byly přeneseny z moravského premonstrátského kláštera v Louce u Znojma. Ve vitríně je umístěna mramorová bysta císaře Františka I. od F. X. Lederera, ve skříních jsou dochovány knižní dary klášteru od Napoleonovy choti Marie Louisy.

LETOHRÁDEK HVĚZDA 55 — byl vybudován na jihozápadním konci stejnojmenné obory v Horní Liboci, kde byl dříve les náležející od 10. století břevnovskému klášteru. Obora, založená císařem Ferdinandem I. v r. 1534, byla v 16. století místem královských kratochvílí a střeleckých slavností. Autorem projektu neobvyklého letohrádku hvězdicového půdorysu (o průměru 40 m) se stal císařův vzdělaný syn, arcivévoda Ferdinand, zvaný Tyrolský, císařský místrodržící v Čechách. Výstavbu letohrádku v l. 1555—65 prováděli stavitelé pražského královského dvora G. M. Aostalis a G. Lucchese pod dohledem H. Tirola a později B. Wohlmuta. Bohatá a jemná výzdoba na téma řecké mytologie, řeckých a římských dějin vznikala za účasti A. del Pambia, G. Campiona a dalších italských mistrů, uplatňujících tak v l. 1556—63 poprvé v Čechách štukatury, a to jedinečné úrovně. Výjimečnost celé stavby a její výzdoby byla dána i stavebníkovým záměrem — uvést sem svou tajnou choť Filipinu Welserovou, která nesměla pobývat na Hradě.

Než došlo k dalším fázím, tentokrát malířské výzdoby z 2. poloviny 17. století, obora Hvězda, ležící pod Bílou horou, se stala místem pohnutých národních dějin. V r. 1620 se zde odehrála krvavá porážka stavovských vojsk katolickou ligou a císařskou armádou. Obora i s letohrádkem začaly od této bělohorské bitvy pustnout, zvláště když se zde v dalších dobách stávala tábořiští nepřátelských armád. Za Josefa II. v opuštěném letohrádku byla zřízena prachárna. K rekonstrukcím stavby došlo po r. 1918 a v l. 1949—51, kdy podle projektu P. Janáka byl objekt adaptován pro muzejní účely. V r. 1951 zde vznikl památník spisovatele historických románů A. Jiráska (1851—1930). V r. 1964 zahájilo činnost muzeum významného českého malíře M. Alše (1852—1913).

BŘEVNOVSKÝ KLÁŠTER S KOSTELEM SV. MARKÉTY 56, 57 — představuje jedinečný stavební komplex vybudovaný v l. 1708—45 nákladem opatů O. Zinkeho a B. Loebla podle návrhu K. Dienzenhofera a jeho syna K. I. Dienzenhofera. K této výstavbě došlo na místě předchozího, husity zničeného a ochromeného kláštera benediktinů založeného pražským biskupem Vojtěchem a knížetem Boleslavem II. r. 993 jako první mužský klášter v Čechách.

Klášterní chrám představuje klenot českého stavitelství s rovnocennou vnitřní výzdobou — na pozadí nástropních maleb J. J. Steinfelse z let 1719—21, a s působivou iluzívní malbou J. Hagera z r. 1761. K ní je přistavěna benátská práce z počátku 14. století, náhrobní deska benediktinského poustevníka bl. Vintíře. Mezi uměleckými díly vynikají obrazy P. Brandla, sochy M. V. Jäckla a R. Prachnera. Pod chórem chrámu byla odkryta nejcennější památka předrománské architektury v Čechách, krypta z druhé čtvrtiny 11. století.

Budova konventu a prelatury, sloužící do nedávného navrácení objektu benediktinskému řádu jako depozitáře Státního ústředního archívu, má bohatou freskovou výzdobu. Pozoruhodný je zejména tzv. Tereziánský sál s výmalbou od bavorského malíře K. D. Asama z r. 1727.

Za klášterem je barokní zahrada s opatským letohrádkem Vojtěškou, budovaným podle projektu K. I. Dienzenhofera, s kaplí a studánkou. Salu terrenu v polovině 16. století vyzdobil sochař R. Prachner.

NOČNÍ POHLED Z NERUDOVY ULICE 63 — dokládá kulturně nejzajímavější malostranskou komunikaci klesající od Pražského hradu k Malostranskému náměstí. Ulice s převážně barokními fasádami, označenými půvabnými domovními znameními, byla pojmenována podle básníka a novináře J. Nerudy, který zde bydlil v domech U tří černých orlů a U dvou slunců.

VALDŠTEJNSKÝ PALÁC 66—70, 72—74 — na nebývale rozsáhlé ploše (30 306 m^2) pod svahem Hradčan představuje první monumentální stavbu raného baroka v Čechách. Toto velkolepé sídlo Albrechta z Valdštejna odpovídalo excentrické ctižádosti „generála moře Baltského a Oceánského", jenž v průběhu třicetileté války jako generalissimus císařských vojsk napřáhl i ruku po královské koruně, a záhy prozrazen, byl z příkazu císaře násilně odstraněn.

Stavbu z let 1624—30 s čtyřmi víceúčelovými nádvořími projektoval Lombarďan A. Spezza, po něm N. Sebregondi a od r. 1626 pevnostní inženýr a architekt G. Pieroni. Na stavbě se podíleli vlašští i domácí řemeslníci. V průčelí paláce zůstal zachován obraz Madony z Val D'Urazzo jako součást vestavěného Trčkovského paláce. Dvěma patry severní části stavby prostupuje reprezentativní Rytířský sál s mramorovým ostěním, přeneseným v r. 1853 z Černínského paláce. Nástropní fresku zobrazující Apoteózu Valdštejna jako boha války Marta provedl Vlach B. del Bianco. K sálu kolmo přiléhají tři místnosti, tzv. Kožený sál s nástropní malbou Pallas Athenae od P. Maixnera z r. 1866, sál Zrcadlový a údajná Valdštejnova pracovna.

Palác obklopuje výstavná zahrada s rybníkem, fontánami, voliérou pro vzácné ptactvo, krápníkovými grotami a slavnostní lodžií se štukami vlašských mistrů a malbami B. del Bianca na námět Vergiliovy Aeneidy (2. zpěv o válce trojské). Sochařská výzdoba od rudolfínského mistra A. del Vriese, uloupená v r. 1648 Švédy a umístěná v zahradách zámku Drootningholmu, byla nahrazena kopiemi.

Palác je dnes využit převážně pro účely ministerstva kultury.

KOLOWRATSKÝ PALÁC A PALÁC PÁLFFYŮV 71 — ležící protilehle k Valdštejnskému paláci ve Valdštejnské ulici jsou spojeny nádhernými rokokovými, terasově utvářenými zahradami, stoupajícími k hradčanskému svahu. Kolowratský palác, dnes sídlo ministerstva kultury, bylo již v l. 1918—38 sídlem předsednictva vlády Československa. Z tohoto důvodu se zde odehrála tíživá jednání týkající se Mnichova a nástupu protektorátu. Vlastní palácová stavba N. Palliardiho vznikala po r. 1784 na objednávku Černínů. V 19. století, než palác koupili Kolowratové, bylo zde sídlo A. Windischgrätze.

Sousedící palác náležel v l. 1660—89 temné postavě utlačovatele Chodů, jenž vstoupil do legend, Lomikarovi — V. M. z Lamingeru. K rozšíření stavby a jejímu přebudování došlo r. 1712 za nového majitele, J. J. z Valdštejna. Jeho rod zde vystřídali Fürstenbergové, z nichž Karel Egon v paláci v r. 1775 připravil první zasedání Učené společnosti nauk. V 19. století došlo k nové novorokokové úpravě vnitřku paláce, jenž získal název Pálffyovský po posledních majitelích (do r. 1945).

LETECKÝ POHLED NA PŘEDSEDNICTVO VLÁDY A KRAMÁŘOVU VILU 75 — zachycuje závěr Letenských sadů, budovaných v l. 1859—60, kde byla v l. 1908—11 postavena pseudobarokní státní vila pro dr. K. Kramáře podle návrhu B. Ohmanna, a dále rozlehlou stavbu bývalé Strakovy akademie. V této stavbě s výraznou kupolí z doby přestavby z let 1893—96 podle návrhu V. Roštapila bývalo učiliště pro šlechtické syny, založené r. 1710 z nadace J. P. hraběte Straky. Dnes je v této budově Úřad předsednictva vlády.

KARLŮV MOST 76, 77, 79—81 87—93, 100, 101 — spojující Staré Město a Malou Stranu je nejstarším dochovaným pražským mostem. Původně se nazýval Pražský nebo Kamenný, r. 1870 dostal název Karlův, neboť byl založen Karlem IV. v r. 1357 na místě zříceného Juditina mostu vybudovaného již v r. 1165. Most z pískovcových kvádrů, položený na šestnácti obloucích, má délku 520 m, šířku 10 m. Jeho stavbu řídil sedmadvacetiletý stavitel P. Parléř; k jejímu dokončení došlo až počátkem 15. století. Most, přes nějž vedla královská cesta, byl i místem pohnutých dějů, zejména v r. 1648, když přes něj Švédové útočili na Prahu a zčásti poškodili jeho výzdobu.

Na mostě bylo v r. 1723 instalováno olejové osvětlení, v r. 1866 sem bylo zavedeno osvětlení plynové s využitím litinových gotizujících kandelábrů z Komárovských sléváren.

Na mostě je vždy imponující jeho výzdoba, tvořená nejen jeho věžemi, ale hlavně souborem 33 soch a sousoší, postupně dosazovaných na zábradlí. Tato díla podléhající nepříznivým vnějším vlivům jsou nahrazována kopiemi, originály jsou přemísťovány do lapidárií Národního muzea nebo Muzea hl. města Prahy.

Sochařská díla jsou skvělou galerií, dokládající tvorbu významných představitelů české kultury zejména z let 1683—1714: M. B. Brauna, J. Brokoffa, F. M. Brokoffa, M. V. Jäckela, J. B. Kohla nebo J. O. Mayera a dalších.

Při Karlově mostě stojí socha Bruncvíka od L. Šimka z r. 1884, připomínající výsadní práva Staroměstských k mostu.

HANAVSKÝ PAVILÓN 78 — vytvořený původně jako výstavní litinový objekt sléváren V. knížete Hanavského pro Zemskou jubilejní výstavu v r. 1891 podle Heiserova a Hercíkova projektu, byl v r. 1898 darován pražské obci a smontován na Letné. Dnes je v této efektně umístěné novobarokní litinové stavbě zřízena výběrová restaurace.

SOUSOŠÍ KALVÁRIE Z KARLOVA MOSTU (detail) 82 — je na místě, kde od 14. století stával gotický kříž. V r. 1657 byl zde umístěn zlacený bronzový korpus od N. Brohna, odlitý v Drážďanech. Z hebrejského nápisu kolem kříže vyplývá, že byl pořízen z pokuty zaplacené Židem, jenž se kříži posmíval. Sochy Panny Marie a sv. Jana Evangelisty vytesal v r. 1861 E. Max.

MALÁ STRANA 83, 84 — z větší části přehlédnutelná z Malostranské věže, budované po r. 1411, se původně nazývala Nové, později

Menší Město pražské. K jeho založení došlo v r. 1257 z podnětu Přemysla Otakara II. V úzkém sousedství s Hradem došlo k velkému rozmachu této čtvrti za Karla IV., který ji rozšířil a opevnil hradbami. Blízkost Hradu měla i negativní politické důsledky. V r. 1419 za bojů Pražanů s královskými vojsky Malá Strana téměř celá vyhořela. Rovněž požár z r. 1541, jenž poškodil i Hrad, nepříznivě zbrzdil znovu se vzmáhající rozvoj čtvrti. K jejímu největšímu rozkvětu došlo v době baroka, což dokládají i zachované monumentální památky — chrám sv. Mikuláše, paláce Valdštejnský, Fürstenberský, Lichtenštejnský, Nostický, Michnovský, Buquoyský a další. Přesto se hlavní kouzlo Malé Strany neobráží jen v těchto monumentech, ale spíše v malebné konstelaci této čtvrti s jejími půvabnými zákoutími, danými i přírodními podmínkami.

KOSTEL SV. FRANTIŠKA SERAFINSKÉHO S POMNÍKEM KARLA IV. 86, 94, 97 — na urbanisticky působivě řešeném náměstí, uzavřeném jezuitským kostelem sv. Salvátora a Colloredo-Mansfeldským palácem, jsou umístěny na komunikačně nejživější trase vedoucí ke Karlovu mostu. Kostel byl vybudován na gotickém základě D. Canevallem v l. 1679—89 podle plánů burgundského architekta J. B. Matheye pro křížovníky s červenou hvězdou. Tento jediný český církevní řád, ustavený v polovině 13. století, sídlil v přilehlém klášteře. V nádherné kopuli chrámu je freska V. V. Reinera Poslední soud, vnitřek chrámu dotvářejí nástěnné i závěsné malby J. K. Lišky, M. Willmanna a M. Pirnera, právě tak jako sochařská díla M. V. Jäckla a štukové postavy světců od drážďanských sochařů J. a K. Süssnerů. Průčelí kostela zdobí sochy R. Prachnera z r. 1758 a dalších českých autorů. K němu je při nároží přistaven tzv. vinařský sloup z r. 1846 se sochou sv. Václava vytvořenou J. Bendlem v r. 1676.

V prostoru jedinečného Křižovnického náměstí po dokončení jeho terénu firmou bratří Kleinů z Vízmberka byl r. 1849 nákladem Pražské univerzity zřízen novogotický pomník císaře Karla IV. s alegoriemi čtyř univerzitních fakult. Byl vytvořen v dílně norimberského kovolitce D. J. Burgschmidta podle modelu drážďanského sochaře A. Hähnela.

STAROMĚSTSKÁ MOSTECKÁ VĚŽ 95, 96 — jíž vrcholí památkový význam Křižovnického náměstí, byla zbudována na prvním pilíři Karlova mostu podle návrhu P. Parléře. Věž, řazená mezi nejkrásnější mostní díla v Evropě, byla dostavěná kolem r. 1391 nejen jako součást mostu, ale také jako součást opevnění Starého Města pražského. Před jejím dokončením kolem r. 1380 vznikala její jedinečná sochařská výzdoba, řazená k vrcholným dílům středoevropského sochařství. Dílna P. Parléře se v ní soustředila na panovnické osobnosti a budovatele mostu, Karla IV. a Václava IV. v ochraně patronů země české se znaky zemí. V r. 1978 byly sochy nahrazeny kopiemi, originály jsou umístěny v Národní galerii. V r. 1621 byly na věži vystaveny hlavy dvanácti popravených českých pánů, účastníků stavovského odboje, a setrvaly zde celých deset let. Sochařská výzdoba věže na západní straně utrpěla újmu v r. 1648, kdy zde došlo k dobývání Prahy Švédy. K podstatné obnově a dostavbě střechy došlo v l. 1874—78.

LADISLAV ŠALOUN (1870—1946), POMNÍK MISTRA JANA HUSA (detail) 102 — byl odhalen v den 500. výročí upálení českého kazatele a reformátora v Kostnici, 6. července 1915. Monumentální rozloha mnohafigurálního, kamenného a bronzového pomníku, vytvořeného jedním z hlavních představitelů českého secesního sochařství, byla předmětem řady diskusí. Dotýkaly se kompozice a umístění díla v historickém prostředí Staroměstského náměstí před palácem Golz-Kinských.

STAROMĚSTSKÉ NÁMĚSTÍ 103, 104, 121, 122, 125, 127, 129 — které svůj název získalo v r. 1895 (od 14. století Tržiště, Velké Tržiště, Rynk, Velký rynk), se vedle Pražského hradu řadí k místům nejpohnutějších historických událostí v Praze. Již na přelomu 11. a 12. století zde křižovatka obchodních cest formovala rozlehlé tržiště přibližně o dnešní rozloze náměstí (asi 9 000 m^2). Náležela k němu celnice, dnešní Ungelt, kde bylo vykládáno zboží přivážené do Čech. Náměstí s radnicí se stalo i tradičním shromaždištěm při politickém a revolučním dění, při reprezentativních aktech i při represích. V r. 1422 byl na dvoře radnice popraven husitský radikání kazatel J. Želivský, na náměstí byl v r. 1437 popraven poslední husitský hejtman Jan Roháč z Dubé. Popravu 27 českých pánů a měšťanů, účastnících se stavovského odboje připomínají i kříže v mozaice dlažby před východním křídlem radnice. V její radní síni byl v r. 1458 volen český král Jiří z Poděbrad. V roce 1918 se zde konala důležitá manifestace ke zřízení samostatné republiky, jiná manifestace iniciovaná komunisty se zde odehrála v únoru r. 1948.

K reprezentativnosti náměstí s původními gotickými a přebudovávanými domy, s rokokovým palácem Golz-Kinských přispěla i novodobá výstavba, jakou nejlépe dokládá secesní barokizující stavba bývalé Pražské městské pojišťovny od architekta O. Polívky, dnes ministerstvo obchodu a cestovního ruchu, zdobená sochařskou tvorbou L. Šalouna, F. Procházky a B. Schnircha, před níž je rozložen mohutný pomník mistra J. Husa.

Staroměstské náměstí a skrze něj vedoucí Královská cesta patří k turisticky nejvyhledávanějším částem Prahy.

DŮM U MINUTY 106 — kolmo přiléhající k staroměstskému radnímu domu, má gotické jádro z počátku 15. století. Jeho renesanční přestavba proběhla po r. 1564, renesanční sgrafita provedená podle rytin M. Raimondiho a H. S. Behama vznikla po r. 1603 a 1610. Koncem 18. století, kdy zde byla lékárna, byla na nároží osazena kamenná socha lva. K odkrytí později obnovovaných sgrafit znovu došlo až r. 1905. V domě jsou dnes umístěny úřadovny magistrátu.

STAROMĚSTSKÝ ORLOJ 108—113 — Orloj ve své původní podobě byl sestaven kolem r. 1410 hodinářem Mikulášem z Kadaně, jeho přestavbu v souvislosti s honosnějšími stavebními úpravami radnice provedl Mistr Hanuš zvaný z Růže. Hodinářský mechanismus byl zdokonalen v l. 1553—60; k zhotovení plastik došlo v r. 1659, dále v 18. století a v r. 1864. Výmalbu kalendářní desky orloje s alegoriemi Měsíců vytvořil v r. 1865 hlavní představitel českého národního umění 19. století, J. Mánes (1820—1871). Originál této malby byl již r. 1885 převeden do sbírek Muzea hl. města Prahy a nahrazen kopií, která shořela i s částí řezbářské výzdoby v r. 1945. V r. 1962 byla nahrazena kopií B. Číly, řezby apoštolů už v r. 1948 vytvořil sochař V. Sucharda (1884—1972).

Orloj patří k největším turistickým atrakcím Starého Města: každou celou hodinu je uveden do chodu mechanismus pohybujících se figur, majících alegorické, náboženské a historické souvislosti (memento mori, aluze na turecké výboje atd.).

CHRÁM SV. MIKULÁŠE NA STARÉM MĚSTĚ 124 — byl zbudován při benediktinském klášteře podle projektu K. I. Dienzenhofera v l. 1732—35.

PALÁC GOLZ-KINSKÝCH A DŮM U ZVONU 126 — na Staroměstském náměstí jsou nejkrásnější stavby představené před chrámem Panny Marie před Týnem. Po odkrytí novobarokní omítky domu U kamenného zvonu bylo odkryto jedinečné zachované gotické průčelí z doby kolem r. 1350 s dekorativní kamenickou výzdobou. Při stavebním průzkumu vnitřku domu byla zjištěna kaple s gotickými nástěnnými malbami z poloviny 14. století. V interiérech rekonstruovaného domu Galerie hl. města Prahy pořádá výstavy soudobého umění.

Sousedící rokoková stavba paláce Golz-Kinských, náležející již v r. 1635 knížeti R. Kinskému, byla do své graciézní a efektní podoby přestavěna v l. 1755—65 A. Luragem podle plánů K. I. Dienzenhofera. Palác vyrůstající na místě starší, románské zástavby využívá Národní galerie v Praze pro své výstavy.

ŠTORCHŮV DŮM 128 z působivé řady domů na východní straně Staroměstského náměstí byl vybudován v r. 1897 podle návrhu architektů B. Ohmanna a R. Krieghammera. Novorenesanční dům Štorchova nakladatelství upoutává figurální výmalbou L. Nováka podle kartónů M. Alše, zachycující postavu sv. Václava a Tři krále. Malby, které byly poškozeny v květnu r. 1945, obnovil malíř F. Sembtner.

POHLED Z VĚŽE TÝNSKÉHO CHRÁMU 130—131 — vynikající gotické trojlodní stavby, založené r. 1365, představuje výhled z osmdesátimetrové výše věží, dostavěných až počátkem 16. století.

KAROLINUM 132—134 — v Železné ulici, ústící na Staroměstské náměstí, představuje ústřední budovu Karlovy univerzity, kterou 7. dubna 1348 založil Karel IV. původně jako jednu z univerzitních kolejí. Šlo o první vysokou školu ve střední Evropě, mající povznést zdejší vzdělanost na nejvyspělejší úroveň. Základem stavebního komplexu Karolina byl Rothlevův dům, který získal Václav IV. a daroval jej r. 1383 Karlově koleji, do té doby umístěné v domě u kostela sv. Mikuláše. Vnější podoba Karolina pochází zejména z barokní přestavby dokončené r. 1718 F. M. Kaňkou. V průčelí do Železné ulice je barokní okno z r. 1687 a prosklené loubí s gotickou žebrovou klenbou. Přístavba z doby kolem r. 1358 směrem k Stavovskému divadlu má dochovanou cennou arkýřovou kapli s bohatou vnější výzdobou. Její obnovu provedl v r. 1881 J. Mocker; k dalším adaptacím a úpravám došlo v l. 1946—75 podle projektu J. Frágnera a za účasti sochařů V. Makovského, K. Lidického, J. Laudy a K. Pokorného.

Jádrem budovy je upravená velká aula vybudovaná již po r. 1383. K ní byla připojena arkýřová kaple. V čele auly je umístěna tapisérie M. Teinitzerové z r. 1947 vycházející z námětu pečetidla Karlovy univerzity provedeného sochařem V. Sychrou, na němž je postava Karla IV. klečícího před sv. Václavem.

STAVOVSKÉ DIVADLO 135 — dříve nazývané Tylovo a původně Nosticovo — představuje novoklasicistní budovu, postavenou na náklad hraběte F. A. Nostice v r. 1781 podle návrhu A. Haffeneckera a za odborné součinnosti hraběte K. H. Khünigla. V l. 1859, 1881 a 1892 postupně docházelo k úpravám a přestavbám objektu, jehož rozsáhlá generální obnova byla ukončena v r. 1991. Součástí rekonstrukce je provozní napojení na protilehlý Kolowratův palác.

V divadle se původně hrálo německy a italsky. V r. 1787 zde byla uskutečněna premiéra Mozartovy opery Don Giovanni. V l. 1813—16 byl šéfem opery skladatel C. M. von Weber. Dne 21. prosince 1834 zde byla provedena Tylova hra Fidlovačka s hudbou F. Škroupa. V této premiéře poprve zazněla píseň Kde domov můj, která se od r. 1918 stala československou státní hymnou.

NÁRODNÍ MUZEUM 136, 138, 139, 141, 142 — stojící na místě někdejší Koňské brány představuje přes 100 m dlouhou budovu, impozantně uzavírající horní část Václavského náměstí. Stavba byla provedena v l. 1885—90 podle projektu prof. J. Schulze pro účely muzea, založeného v r. 1818 na principu zemského patriotismu šlechtici sledujícími kulturní a vědecké cíle.

Novorenesanční nákladná stavba má čtyři křídla se dvěma dvory. Reprezentativní vstup je veden po rampě s fontánou a alegorickými sochami A. Wagnera z l. 1891—94 představujícími alegorie Čechie, Moravy a Slezska, řek Labe a Vltavy. Sochařská výzdoba celé stavby je přehlednou galerií tohoto druhu české výtvarné tvorby konce 19. století, v konkurenci s dílem mnichovského sochaře L. Schwanthalera. Jeho bronzové sochy Libuše, Přemysla, Václava a Přemysla II. původně objednané do souboru 24 plastik pro Český Slavín do Tupadel u Liběchova našly umístění ve vstupní sloupové hale, na niž navazuje reprezentativní schodiště v rozloze téměř celého středního křídla budovy. Je dotvářeno sochami A. Poppa a B. Schnircha z let 1897—99 představujícími 16 popsí mužů, kteří se zasloužili o muzeum, a 32 medailóny českých králů.

Svatyní českých národních tužeb a projeveným sebevědomím je čtvercová stavba Pantheonu, završeného kopulí s 48 bystami a sochami velikánů českého národa. Historicky zaměřené obrazy vytvořili přední malíři generace Národního divadla V. Brožík a F. Ženíšek; alegorické dekorativní výplně pod kopulí jsou dílem francouzsky orientovaného malíře této generace V. Hynaise.

V budově muzea jsou historicky a přírodovědně zaměřená oddělení a cenná knihovna, zahrnující zhruba milionový fond s unikátními středověkými rukopisy.

JOSEF VÁCLAV MYSLBEK (1848—1922), JEZDECKÁ SOCHA SV. VÁCLAVA 137 — patrona české země, je i symbolem svébytnosti a záštitou samostatnosti národa. K umístění díla v horní části Václavského náměstí došlo v l. 1912—13 na architektonickém podkladu A. Dryáka a s ornamentální výzdobou C. Kloučka. S rozpracováním tématu Myslbek začal v r. 1887, sádrový model konečného díla byl hotov v r. 1904. Ušlechtilé, novorenesačně pojaté dílo tvoří celek se sochami sv. Prokopa, sv. Anežky a sv. Ludmily. V r. 1924 došlo k osazení poslední, Myslbekem již nedokončené sochy sv. Vojtěcha, která byla ulita v dílně B. Maška. Klasicky cítěné dílo se zvnitřnělými výrazy jednotlivých postav prozrazuje orientaci na předchozí francouzskou tvorbu.

JUNGMANNOVO NÁMĚSTÍ 140 — v jehož nevelkém prostoru je s urbanistickou citlivostí umístěna socha spisovatele a předního představitele českého literárního obrození J. Jungmanna, se nachází v těsné blízkosti Václavského náměstí. Sochařské dílo L. Šimka z r. 1872 podle staršího náčrtu V. Levého bylo umístěno na mramorový podstavec podle návrhu A. Barvitia v r. 1878.

PŘÍKOPY 144 — představují jednu z nejrušnějších obchodních částí Prahy navazující na dolní konec Václavského náměstí a Můstek s postmoderní stavbou A. Šrámkové pro ČKD. V novodobé zástavbě Příkopů zaujme konstruktivistická stavba Dětského domu z r. 1928. Na pravé straně se nachází nejstarší obchodní dům v Praze, vybudovaný proslaveným vídeňským architektem Th. Hansenem v l. 1869—71. Zjemnělou aristokratickou kulturu doby rokoka dokládá palác Sylva-Tarouccovský (pův. Piccolominiovský), postavený v l. 1743—51 K. I. Dienzenhoferem a A. Luragem. Střídmou empírovou stavbu kostela sv. Kříže, vytvořenou v l. 1816—24, navrhoval J. Fischer. Slovanský dům, původně barokní palác Příchovských, byl upraven F. Hegerem v r. 1798. Z řady bank, umístěných na Příkopech, je nejvýpravnější Investiční banka, postavená v duchu novorenesance O. Polívkou v l. 1894—96, zdobená Alšovými mozaikami a reliéfy C. Kloučka a S. Suchardy.

VÁCLAVSKÉ NÁMĚSTÍ 145 — původně nazývané Koňský trh, bývalo hlavním tržištěm Nového Města, v jehož středu stávala socha sv. Václava od J. J. Bendla z r. 1680 (přemístěná r. 1879 na Vyšehrad). Náměstí v délce 750 m představuje nejvýznamnější společenský a obchodní bulvár s reprezentativními hotely. Horní část náměstí kolmo uzavírá dominantní stavba Národního muzea (J. Schulz, 1885—90), která je holdem vědění a poznání, jemuž budova má sloužit. Výrazem národního sebevědomí i útěchy je Myslbekův monumentální pomník s jezdeckou sochou sv. Václava. Na protější dolní části náměstí stávalo v l. 1786—89 dřevěné divadlo Bouda, kde byla první česká scéna. Na obou stranách i ve středu náměstí jsou vchody do stanic metra.

PRAŠNÁ BRÁNA 146—148 — budovaná k uctění krále Vladislava Jagellonského v r. 1475 je dílem M. Rejska z Prostějova, stavěným na místě starší brány opevnění. V jejím sousedství Václav IV. dal postavit Králův dvůr jako panovnickou rezidenci. Po jejím vyklizení r. 1483 začal význam místa upadat. Samotná věž řazená k nejhodnotnějším památkám pozdní gotiky již koncem 17. století sloužila za skladiště prachu. Za pruského obléhání byla stavba poškozena. Její novogotická úprava je dílem architekta J. Mockera z r. 1875—76, jenž přistavěl ještě ochoz a střechu. Z věže se nabízí výhled na nejstarší městskou čtvrť, Staré Město, i na jedno z rušných míst Prahy, náměstí Republiky s budovou bývalé hlavní celnice (kol. r. 1810) — domem U hybernů, kapucínským kostelem sv. Josefa a moderní stavbou banky z r. 1938.

OBECNÍ DŮM HLAVNÍHO MĚSTA PRAHY 149, 150 — vybudován na místě Králova dvora v l. 1906—11 podle plánů A. Balšánka a O. Polívky. Tam, kde bývalo sídlo českých králů, zejména Jiřího z Poděbrad, svolávajícího sem nejen české sněmy, ale vyzývajícího odtud evropské panovníky k míru a sjednocení, je dnes reprezentativní společenské a kulturní centrum. Jsou zde pořádány koncerty, plesy, výstavy, je zde kavárna, restaurace, vinárna. Vnitřní prostory mají bohatou malířskou a sochařskou výzdobu od předních českých umělců z počátku 20. století: v Primátorském sále jsou malby A. Muchy, v sále Palackého malby J. Preislera, Grégrův sál je vyzdoben malbami F. Ženíška. Přízemí a restauraci zdobí obrazy M. Alše a J. Obrovského. Sochaři J. V. Myslbek, K. Novák a L. Šaloun jsou zastoupeni ve Smetanově síni a v Riegrově salónku.

NÁRODNÍ DIVADLO 151—154 — bylo vybudováno z národních sbírek v l. 1868—81 podle plánu architekta J. Zítka. Hodnotná novorenesanční stavba byla hned po dokončení zachvácena požárem. Její obnova a dostavba, prováděná architektem J. Schulzem, byla dokončena r. 1883 i s novou vnitřní výzdobou a oponou, provedenou V. Hynaisem. Na vnější výzdobě lodžie se podílel malíř J. Tulka, sochařská díla pocházejí především od A. Wagnera, J. V. Myslbeka a B. Schnircha. Reprezentačnímu foyeru divadla dominují lunetové obrazy M. Alše a F. Ženíška, který je také autorem nástropních maleb hlediště. Královskou, nyní prezidentskou lóži zdobí malby V. Hynaise, V. Brožíka a J. Mařáka. Četná sochařská díla ve foyeru zachycují popsí velikánů české kultury.

Při rozsáhlé rekonstrukci divadla v l. 1977—83 spojené s modernizací technického provozu došlo k dostavbě proluky mezi divadlem a voršilským klášterem. Nová sedmiposchoďová budova i Nová scéna Národního divadla byla dokončena r. 1983 podle projektu architekta K. Pragra s využitím skleněných obkladů S. Libenského.

V protějšku historického Národního divadla je bývalý palác Lažanských s kavárnou Slavií, budovaný ve stylu francouzské renesance v l. 1861—63. V prvním patře hraběcího paláce bydlel do r. 1869 přední český hudební skladatel B. Smetana.

Boční strana Národního divadla vede po Masarykově nábřeží s reprezentativní řadou činžovních domů s historizujícími fasádami a s výhledem na Vltavu a Slovanský ostrov, nazývaný do r. 1925 Žofín.

STŘELECKÝ OSTROV 155 — název ostrova není náhodný. Poté, co v r. 1472 připadl Starému a Novému Městu, stal se cvičištěm pražských střelců. V 16. století se na něm konaly oblíbené střelecké hry Pražanů, nazývané „střílení ku ptáku". Koncem 19. století se zde odehrávaly tábory lidu. V r. 1882 se zde uskutečnil 1. sokolský slet.

SOCHA BEDŘICHA SMETANY (1824—1884), SMETANOVO MUZEUM A NOVOTNÉHO LÁVKA 157—158, 179 — Smetanovo nábřeží je dokladem nejstaršího pražského urbanistického řešení tohoto druhu, které provedla firma V. Lanny v l. 1841—45 podle návrhu B. Gruebera. Hlavní výstavbu činžovních domů vyprojektoval stavební ředitel Strobach již v r. 1836. Na místě dřívějšího mlýna byla postavena novogotická budova Karlových lázní, v nichž v r. 1848 žil přední český básník a novinář K. H. Borovský. Před lázněmi z nábřeží vybočuje Novotného lávka z r. 1879, pojmenovaná podle potomka starobylé mlynářské rodiny. Budovy staroměstských mlýnů mají novorenesanční charakter ve slohu I. Ulmanna, zdobeny jsou sochami puttů od J. V. Myslbeka. Vypíná se zde Vodárenská věž, vybudovaná r. 1489 a mnohokrát přestavovaná, naposled po požáru r. 1885. Mostní lávku uzavírá budova Smetanova muzea dokládající tzv. českou renesanci z r. 1883, projektovanou architektem A. Wiehlem, původně pro vodárnu města Prahy. Průčelí stavby je pokryto sgrafitem Boj se Švédy na Karlově mostě r. 1648 podle kartónů F. Ženíška, ve výklencích jsou zobrazeny postavy osob, jež se zasloužily o záchranu Prahy před Švédy, jak je provedl J. Šubič podle návrhů M. Alše a J. Kouly. Muzeum založila Společnost B. Smetany v r. 1936 a soustředila zde doklady o životě a tvorbě tohoto předního českého hudebního skladatele, jehož socha od J. Malejovského byla v r. 1984 umístěna před budovou.

DŮM U ZLATÉ STUDNĚ 159 — představuje rožní budovu, jež je výraznou komunikační tepnou vedoucí od Starého Města ke Karlovu mostu. Na tomto renesančním, barokně upravovaném domě upoutávají štukové reliéfy ochránců před morem, sv. Šebestián a sv. Roch, jak je vytvořil sochař J. O. Mayer asi po r. 1700 po morové epidemii.

DOMOVNÍ ZNAMENÍ NA STARÉM MĚSTĚ 160 — v Týnské ulici č. 10 označuje dům, jenž měl v 17. století název V pekle. Později dům patrně patřil hraběcímu rodu Kinských, majících ve znaku tři vlčí drápy nebo spíše tři kančí zuby. Po přestavbě domu v 18. století architektem F. Hegerem byl znak přemalován ve tři pštrosí pera.

Význam domovních znamení, souvisejících i s tradicí vývěsních štítů, kromě účelu identifikačního, reprezentačního i orientačního míval i zjevný smysl symbolický. Půvabná domovní znamení vypovídají staropražské příběhy nejen na Starém Městě, ale také v malebných zákoutích Malé Strany, na Hradčanech aj.

STARÝ ŽIDOVSKÝ HŘBITOV. STARONOVÁ SYNAGÓGA 161—164 — představují doklady židovského osídlení, které bylo zaznamenáno v pražském podhradí již v 10. století. Židovská obec představovala v Praze na počátku 18. století téměř třetinu všeho obyvatelstva. Přesto zde byla zaznamenána řada pogromů a omezení, která nutila Židy téměř bezvýhradně pobývat v uzavřeném ghettu. Po osvobozujících dekretech císaře Josefa II. se pražské Židovské Město začalo nazývat Josefov, jenž se až po r. 1848 stal rovnoprávnou pátou pražskou čtvrtí. Její stísněné nehygienické podmínky vedly k stavební asanaci kolem r. 1900.

Na dlouhá staletí pražské židovské historie upomíná starý židovský hřbitov, kde nejstarší dochovaný náhrobní kámen pochází z r. 1439. Elegické kouzlo tohoto hřbitova se zhruba 11 tisíci kamenných náhrobků (pod nimiž je až 12 hřbitovních vrstev) má jedinečnou historickou vypovídací cenu. Náhrobky zaznamenávají nejen jména a data zemřelých, ale i jejich zařazení ve společnosti, se symboly tradičních rodů tvořících odedávna kněžskou hierarchii. Jména zemřelých bývají často označena zástupným symbolem majícím zvláštní poetizační výraz. Mezi náhrobky je dochována tumba vlivného starosty a primase Židovského Města M. Mordechaje Maisla († 1601), po němž je nazvána ulice uprostřed bývalého ghetta, ale i jedna ze synagog. Se sugestivní legendou je spjato jméno na jiném vyhledávaném náhrobku, patřícím J. Löwovi ben Bezalelovi. Z dílny tohoto proslulého rabbiho Löwa pode pověsti vyšel umělý člověk, kterého vytvořil — Golem.

Z Židovského Města se dochovala nejstarší synagóga v Evropě, zvaná Staronová. Byla zbudována kolem r. 1280 jako dvoulodní síň. Cihlový štít má ze 14. století, kdy došlo k přistavění předsíně. Protože hlavní prostor byl určen pouze pro muže, v 18. století byl na severní straně dobudován přístavek pro ženy. Vnitřek synagógy dokládá cenné památky židovské kultury zejména od 16. do 19. století.

U Starého židovského hřbitova je bývalá obřadní síň, která dnes slouží pro expozici Dětské kresby z Terezína. Jako výstavní prostora je využita tzv. Vysoká synagóga, kde jsou doloženy synagogální textilie. Pinkasova synagóga je památníkem obětí nacismu, v Maiselově synagóze je vystavena unikátní sbírka stříbrných a jiných kovových předmětů. Esoterické kouzlo památek Židovského Města dotváří Židovská radnice s věží a hodinami s hebrejským ciferníkem.

KAREL HLADÍK (1912—1967), FRANZ KAFKA 165 — bysta na budově postavené v r. 1902 O. Polívkou, kde předtím stávala prelatura bývalého kláštera benediktinů, připomíná, že se zde r. 1883 narodil geniální spisovatel židovského původu. Dílo vytvořil představitel domácí klasické realistické tvorby, vyrovnávající se zejména s podněty soudobé italské plastiky.

KOSTEL SV. JAKUBA 166—167 — v Malé Štupartské ulici šikmo proti východu z Ungeltu byl spolu s klášterem založen Václavem I. v r. 1232. Průčelí zdobí výrazné štukatérské dílo vlašského sochaře O. Mosta z r. 1695, vytvořené při barokizaci chrámu po požáru v r. 1689. V interiéru chrámu s 21 oltáři působí bohatým dojmem nástropní malby F. M. Vogela, vzniklé při dokončení přestavby v l. 1736—39. Součástí vynikající výzdoby jsou obrazy P. Brandla, V. V. Reinera a dalších. Kvalitním dílem je náhrobek nejvyššího kancléře J. V. hraběte Vratislava z Mitrovic, který je dílem J. B. Fischera z Erlachu z l. 1714—16.

KOSTEL SV. JINDŘICHA 168 — v Jindřišské ulici na Novém Městě představuje gotickou stavbu založenou v druhé polovině 14. století, s renesanční předsíní, s barokními přístavbami i barokními úpravami vnitřku. Na vnější stranu chrámu byla přemístěna řada náhrobníků ze zrušeného hřbitova. V l. 1875—79 došlo k Mockerově regotizaci kostela, jehož bohaté vnitřní vybavení zahrnuje památky od dob gotiky (např. tabulový obraz Madony svatoštěpánské z 15. století, socha sv. Jindřicha atd.) přes řadu barokních uměleckých děl hlavně od českých malířů a sochařů — až po tvorbu z 19. století (např. malovaná okna z r. 1891 podle návrhu F. Sequense).

Regotizovaná zvonice v blízkosti chrámu byla postavena již kolem r. 1475. Gotického původu je fara, založená r. 1386.

PRESBYTÁŘ CHRÁMU PANNY MARIE SNĚŽNÉ 169 — za budovou františkánské fary na Jungmannově náměstí se vypíná nejvyšší chrámová stavba v Praze, nikdy nedokončená. Byla založena Karlem IV. r. 1347 jako korunovační kostel zároveň sloužící klášternímu řádu karmelitánů. Zachovaná stavba kněžiště pochází z let 1379—97, neboť původní vyšší klenba se předtím zřítila. Následné husitské revoluční hnutí výrazně zasáhlo do dějin chrámu. Vůdce pražské chudiny kazatel J. Želivský vyburcoval v r. 1419 před chrámem, jehož se později zmocnil, pochod na Novoměstskou radnici, kde došlo k defenestraci konšelů. V kostele kázal až do své popravy v r. 1422. V r. 1606 pražský arcibiskup daroval chrám s klášterem františkánům, jejichž působení zde mělo tragickou epizodu. V r. 1611 při vpádu pasovských vojsk do Prahy chudina, podezírající mnichy, že ukryli prchající pasovské vojáky, vtrhla do kláštera a všechny františkány povraždila.

V interiéru kostela upoutá raně barokní oltář, nejvyšší v Praze, zbudovaný při novém osazení františkány v l. 1649—61. K cennému vnitřnímu vybavení kostela, kde je při stěnách rozestaveno deset soch františkánských světců z doby kolem r. 1625, patří např. obraz Zvěstování Panny Marie od V. V. Reinera z r. 1724, umístěný na bočním oltáři, nebo cínová křtitelnice z r. 1449.

KOSTEL SV. JILJÍ 170 — umístěný mezi dnešní Jilskou a Husovou ulicí na Starém Městě byl budován v l. 1339—71 biskupem Janem z Dražic a pak arcibiskupem Arnoštem z Pardubic jako trojlodní kapitulní kostel. V r. 1364 v něm česky kázal J. Milíč z Kroměříže. V duchu této tradice kostel v r. 1420 sloužil husitům. Naproti tomu císař Ferdinand II. jej r. 1626 daroval dominikánům, kteří zde přistavěli rozlehlý klášter. V r. 1731 provedli barokizaci kostela, na němž se podílel stavitel F. M. Kaňka. Malby na klenbách a obraz sv. Václava vytvořil V. V. Reiner, hlavní sochařskou výzdobu provedl J. A. Quittainer a v l. 1839—45 mnichovský profesor L. Schwanthaler; řezbářské práce jsou převážně od F. I. Weise z l. 1734—38.

KOSTEL NEJSVĚTĚJŠÍHO SRDCE PÁNĚ 171 — byl postaven v l. 1928—32 podle návrhu J. Plečnika na způsob starokřesťanského chrámu, umístěného ve středu prostorného náměstí Jiřího z Poděbrad na Vinohradech. Originální transformace antikizujícího umění se promítá opět ve výzdobě, v plastikách B. Stefana nad třemi portály chrámu i ve ztvárnění hlavního mramorového oltáře a vnitřní sochařské výzdobě od D. Pešana.

VILA AMERIKA 172 — původně označovaná Michnovský letohrádek, je první stavbou nejpřednějšího z tvůrců barokní architektury v Čechách K. I. Dienzenhofera. Půvabná stavba v dnešní ulici Ke Karlovu na Novém Městě, snoubící vliv vídeňské monumentální tvorby L. Hildebrandta a s tím i francouzskou eleganci a uměřenost, kterou tento stavitel sledoval, byla vybudována v l. 1712—20 na náklady hraběte J. V. Michny z Vacínova. Hlavní sál byl r. 1720 vyzdoben nástěnnými malbami J. F. Schora na téma mytologických bájí. Letohrádek obklopovala zahrada dekorovaná vázami a skupinami Ročních dob z dílny A. Brauna. V této zahradě se od konce 18. století konaly dobytčí trhy. V r. 1932 letohrádek zakoupila Společnost A. Dvořáka. Podnes je zde muzeum tohoto světoznámého skladatele, instalované Společností.

Vila Amerika, jejíž název vznikl v 19. století podle označení nedaleké hospody, je oddělen od ulice kopií barokních mříží. Půvabné umístění stavby dnes zaniká v převyšující okolní zástavbě.

DVOŘÁKOVA SÍŇ RUDOLFINA 174 — nejvýznamnější novorenesanční stavba po Národním divadle od architekta J. Zítka, J. Schulze a V. Vejrycha z l. 1876—84 slouží jako sídlo České filharmonie koncertům a společensky významným událostem. Budova dostala název na počest korunního prince Rudolfa.

ZRCADLOVÁ SÍŇ KLEMENTINA 175 — dobudovaná r. 1724 F. M. Kaňkou jako součást bývalé jezuitské koleje je nádherně zdobenou prostorou, kde jsou pořádány koncerty a výstavy. Bohaté štuky, do nichž jsou zasazeny zrcadlové výplně, tvoří rámec k nástropním malbám ze života Panny Marie provedené patrně J. Hieblem. Obrazy světců pocházejí od V. V. Reinera. Ke zrušení kaple došlo r. 1784, v r. 1816 byla krátce obnovena. Dnes je součástí Národní knihovny.

PAMÁTNÍK WOLFGANGA AMADEA MOZARTA (1756—1791) V BERTRAMCE 176, 177 — Bertramka, představující předměstskou usedlost původně ze 17. století, naposled přestavovanou r. 1873, se zapsala do kulturních dějin Prahy jako místo, kde pobýval jeden z nejpřednějších hudebních géniů W. A. Mozart. Poté, co r. 1784 Bertramku koupil skladatel Fr. X. Dušek se svou ženou Josefinou, znamenitou pěvkyní, stával se Mozart při pražských pobytech jejich hostem. V r. 1787 zde složil svou nejznámější operu Don Giovanni, jejíž první uvedení v Nosticově divadle mělo mimořádný úspěch.

PAŘÍŽSKÁ TŘÍDA 181, 182 — spojující Staroměstské náměstí s mostem Sv. Čecha je zároveň přístupovou částí k torzu bývalého Židovského Města, zbořeného při asanaci. Tato široká třída, která se dříve nazývala Mikulášská, je tvořena reprezentativními činžovními domy, budovanými převážně v l. 1901—1906. Za nejvýznamnější památkou bývalého Židovského Města, jakou představuje Staronová synagóga, je parková proluka, na níž je umístěna bronzová socha Mojžíše od F. Bílka z r. 1905. V závěru ulice je budova Právnické fakulty Karlovy univerzity, vybudovaná v l. 1924—27 podle projektu J. Kotěry z r. 1914. Šikmo v jejím protějšku byl v l. 1970—74 postaven rozlehlý komplex hotelu Intercontinental podle projektu K. Filsaka, K. Bubeníčka a Švece.

HOTEL ATRIUM 182 — Francova, Nováčkova a Fenclova stavba dokončená za 23 měsíce v červnu 1990 představuje nejširší hotelovou stavbu ve střední Evropě. Stavba atriového typu má 788 pokojů s kapacitou 1 568 lůžek. Restaurace připravuje jídla mezinárodní kuchyně, ale má i specificky český jídelníček.

VYŠEHRAD 187, 189—191 — pověstné sídlo nejstarších českých knížat, Libuše a Přemyslovců, bylo založeno nad Vltavou na vyšehradské skále po Pražském hradu, asi v 10. století. Za vlády knížete Vratislava II. (1061—92, r. 1085 korunován na krále) sem bylo dokonce přeneseno panovníkovo sídlo, při němž byla r. 1070 založena církevní kapitula. Zároveň došlo k přestavbě dřevěného hradu v kamenný, při němž byly založeny nové kostely, pobořené za husitského revolučního hnutí.

Dnešní Vyšehrad je obehnán barokními hradbami a bastiony, vybudovanými italskými pevnostními staviteli a upravenými v r. 1882. Hradby obklopují kapitulní kostel sv. Petra a Pavla románského původu, přestavovaného v době gotiky i baroka a novogoticky upraveného v l. 1885—87. V blízkosti kostela jsou pozůstatky románského mostu, jenž byl patrně součástí opevnění paláce. V protějšku kostela je kaplička sv. Ludmily. Mezi vyšehradskými památkami zůstala zachována původní románská rotunda sv. Martina, k níž se přichází vstupní branou z ulice V pevnosti.

Proti průčelí svatopetrského kostela je hlavní brána hřbitova, budovaného kolem r. 1890 A. Wiehlem jako pohřebiště zasloužilých synů národa. Tento projekt prosazovaný proboštem V. Štulcem byl uskutečněn na místě farního hřbitova z r. 1660. Středem východní strany hřbitova byl v l. 1889—93 a 1903 podle Wiehla budován Slavín, důstojné pohřebiště národních velikánů.

Na travnatých plochách na místě vyhořelé zbrojnice byla v r. 1948 umístěna tři Myslbekova sousoší z poškozeného Palackého mostu, v r. 1978 sem bylo včleněno poslední rekonstruované sousoší, Přemysl a Libuše. Myslbekovy rekovné postavy byly vytvořeny na dobově aktuální národně-mytologické téma Královédvorského rukopisu. Lumír s Písní byl vytvořen v r. 1888, Přemysl a Libuše r. 1892, Záboj se Slavojem, navracející se z vítězného boje, r. 1895 a Ctirad a Šárka r. 1897. Opojné, poetické představy o slavné minulosti Slovanstva našly na Vyšehradě své opodstatnění.

KLÁŠTER NA SLOVANECH (EMAUZY) 188 — byl založen Karlem IV. r. 1347 pro slovanské benediktiny, kteří zde vytvořili jedinečné středisko vzdělanosti a umění. Zde r. 1395 vznikla hlaholská část tzv. Remešského evangelia, na které po r. 1546 francouzští králové skládali při korunovaci přísahu. V průběhu husitských válek zde byl ustaven jediný český kališnický klášter.

Postupně přestavovaný klášterní areál s kostelem Panny Marie byl v r. 1945 vážně poškozen bombardováním. V následných letech probíhaly rekonstrukce, r. 1967 byla dokončena novodobá dostavba průčelí a věží podle projektu F. M. Černého.

BRÁNA SLAVÍNA 195 — dominantou vyšehradského hřbitova je na východní straně Slavín, společná hrobka nejzasloužilejších představitelů národa. Výstavba proběhla v l. 1889—90 podle projektu arch. A. Wiehla, sochařskou výzdobu představující Génia vlasti, Vlast jásající a Vlast truchlící provedl v l. 1892—93 J. Maudr. Jako první byl na Slavíně pohřben v r. 1901 básník J. Zeyer a po něm 53 významných osobností (mimo jiné J. V. Myslbek, V. Hynais, E. Destinnová, A. Mucha, J. Kubelík, V. Špála). Náhrobky na tomto hřbitově prováděli přední čeští sochaři a architekti.

ROTUNDA SV. MARTINA 196 — nejstarší dochovaná vyšehradská památka pocházející z druhé poloviny 11. století. Její význam degradoval po vytvoření vyšehradské pevnosti, kdy byla kaple proměněna v prachárnu. V 19. století byla využívána jako skladiště. V r. 1878 však vyšehradská kapitula tuto cennou stavbu koupila a v r. 1878 ji dala obnovit podle projektu arch. A. Bauma. Interiér byl doplněn nástěnnými malbami A. Königa a J. Heřmana. Oltářní obraz namaloval F. Sequens. Stavba byla opět renovována r. 1915 a v l. 1969—70.

PALÁC KULTURY A HOTEL FÓRUM 198, 199 — potřeba širšího společenského a kulturního centra s možností pořádání konferencí, sympozií a sjezdů vedla v r. 1975 k rozhodnutí o vybudování Paláce kultury. Obrovský monoblok Paláce kultury na půdorysu nepravidelného sedmiúhelníku byl v r. 1980 dostavěn podle projektu kolektivu autorů Vojenského projektového ústavu (J. Mayer, V. Ustohal, A. Vaňek, J. Karlík). Na protějším jižním předmostí Nuselského mostu se tyčí polygonální věžová budova hotelu Forum. Stavba o 27 podlažích byla dokončena r. 1988 podle projektu J. Trávníčka.

PRAŽSKÉ VÝSTAVIŠTĚ 201, 202 — má svou dominantu ve Sjezdovém paláci, novobarokní železné stavbě B. Münzbergera z r. 1891, nově upravené v l. 1952—54. Plocha výstaviště zaujímá část někdejší Královské obory, v níž bývala lovná zvěř. V r. 1891 se zde na ploše 300 000 m^2 dobudovalo výstaviště (projekt A. Wiehla) pro Zemskou jubilejní výstavu. Památkou na ni je původní výstavní síň umělecké a retrospektivní výstavy po levé straně, kde je dnes Akademie výtvarných umění. Po pravé straně vstupní části je pavilón hl. města Prahy, sloužící dnes za lapidárium Národního muzea. Na rozsáhlé ploše výstaviště je řada atraktivních pavilónů (např. pro Maroldovo monumentální panoráma bitvy u Lipan, z r. 1898) i atraktivit (např. obnovená fontána vynálezce Fr. Křižíka).

ZÁMEK TRÓJA 203 — ve viniční oblasti na severním okraji pražské kotliny byl zbudován koncem 17. století V. V. ze Šternberka na způsob italských předměstských vil. Na projektu a provedení stavby se podíleli D. Orsi de Orsini, S. Carloni, ale také vynikající burgundský architekt J. B. Mathey. Mimořádně bohatou výmalbu vnitřních prostor s alegoriemi a kryptoportréty Šternberků prováděli F. a G. F. Marchetiové, malby hlavního sálu, které jsou poctou habsburskému rodu, vytvořil v l. 1691—97 malíř nizozemského původu A. Godyn. Ctižádostivý stavebník sledoval přímočaře kariéru dvorského úředníka. Jeho komfortní venkovské sídlo mělo posloužit i při očekávané panovníkově návštěvě jako místo odpočinku po lovu. Promyšlená byla i kompozice zámku: z podesty velkolepě pojatého vnějšího schodiště se sochami Gigantomachie, díla drážďanských J. J. a P. Heermannů, je v přímé ose patrná silueta Pražského hradu.

V nově rekonstruované budově zámku — s replikou původní historické zahrady — Galerie hl. města Prahy r. 1989 instalovala obrazové sbírky z 19. století.

ZÁMEK ZBRASLAV 204—209 — reprezentativně se vyjímající po levém břehu řeky Vltavy, po níž se výletníci mohou dopravovat z Prahy parníkem, sloužil za prelaturu cisterciáckého opatství. Stavba z r. 1739 s freskami V. V. Reinera byla v l. 1911—12 přestavěna na zámek náležející rodu Bartoňů z Dobenína.

Zbraslavský klášter založil Václav II. již v r. 1291. V opatském chrámu Panny Marie byl pohřben jeho zakladatel a po něm Václav III. a Eliška Přemyslovna. Dílem zdejších opatů je proslulá Zbraslavská kronika sahající až k r. 1337.

Konventní budova opatství byla před r. 1709 přestavěna podle návrhu J. Santiniho a v l. 1724—32 dokončena podle F. M. Kaňky. Štukovou výzdobu provedl T. Soldati, V. V. Reiner a F. X. Palko dotvořili kvalitní freskové malby. V r. 1785 byl klášter zrušen a posléze upadal. V éře Bartoňů z Dobenína byly interiéry zámku i konventu nově upraveny D. Jurkovičem a A. Čenským. V současné době jsou v konventní budově instalovány sochařské sbírky 19. a 20. století Národní galerie v Praze.

Významný díl tvoří kapitola věnovaná generaci Národního divadla: připomenut je např. původní návrh B. Schnircha, Trigy z r. 1873 pro pylony Národního divadla, jejichž osazení bylo provedeno v l. 1910—11 podle přepracovaného návrhu E. Hallmanna, S. Rouse a L. Šalouna. Zvláštní důraz je kladen na tvorbu nejvýznamnějšího představitele této generace, J. V. Myslbeka, jemuž je věnován samostatný sál, právě tak jako přední sochařské osobnosti tvořící v první čtvrti 20. století, J. Štursovi.

PRAG

DIE MOLDAU 1, 185 — entspringt auf den Höhen des Böhmerwaldes (430,2 km lang, das Einzugsgebiet der Quellen beträgt 28 000 km^2). Sie ist der linke Zufluß der Elbe bei Mělník. Obwohl sie hinsichtlich der Größe erst an zweiter Stelle steht, kommt ihr in Böhmen von der Bedeutung her bestimmt der erste Rang zu. In Prag erreicht sie eine erhebliche Breite und Tiefe (B. 316 m, T. bis 3,8 m). Auf dem Fluß befinden sich vier Stauseen und mit seinen Flußarmen bildet er mehrere Inseln. Sie ist ein markantes Zeichen des malerischen Prager Stadtbildes.

DIE PRAGER BURG 2, 6, 16, 99, 180 — wurde nach dem Jahre 880 auf dem Felsvorsprung des Hradschin in der Nähe der Moldau gegründet, als der Sitz der böhmischen Fürsten aus Levý Hradec hierher verlegt wurde. Das sich formende Zentrum des böhmischen Přemyslidenstaates wurde allmählich der Mittelpunkt des kirchlichen Geschehens. Die erste christliche, der Jungfrau Maria geweihte Kirche wurde vor Ende des 9. Jahrhunderts erbaut. In der 2. Hälfte des 10. Jahrhunderts wurde dann in der Nähe des Fürstenpalastes die St.-Veits-Rotunde mit dem Bischofssitz und der Georgsbasilika errichtet. Vom 13. Jh. an residierten Könige in dem Palast. Seinen größten Aufschwung erlebte er während der Regierungszeit Kaisers Karl IV., eines sehr gebildeten und aktiven Bauherrn.

Insbesondere der umfangreiche Ausbau der St.-Veitskathedrale, der im Jahre 1344 nach französischem Vorbild begann, unterstrich den repräsentativen Charakter der Burg. Eine ausgeprägte Bauaktivität begann gegen Ende des 15. Jh., als König Wladislaw Jagello das Schloß mit dem Wladislawsaal ausbauen ließ. Während seiner Regierungszeit wurde der berühmte Turm Daliborka nach Entwurf von Benedikt Ried als Bestandteil spätgotischer Befestigungsanlagen gebaut. Der Turm trägt den Namen des Ritters Dalibor von Kozojedy, welcher hier seine Gefängnisstrafe abbüste. Seine romantische Geschichte wurde Thema des Dalibor, einer der Opern von Bedřich Smetana. Zu den Befestigungsanlagen aus dieser Zeit gehörte ebenfalls der Weiße Turm, der ab 1584 als Staatsgefängnis diente.

Nachdem der doppelte Graben im 2. Viertel des 16. Jh. verschüttet wurde, kam es zum Ausbau des zweiten Burghofes, der bis zum Jahre 1775 schrittweise aus- und umgebaut wurde (nach dem Projekt von N. Pacassi). Der Nordflügel umfaßt den Spanischen Saal mit Rudolfs Galerie. Das Erdgeschoß des Westflügels wurde zusammen mit dem Marstall im Jahre 1965 zur Galerie der Prager Burg hergerichtet. In der südöstlichen Ecke des Hofes befindet sich die Heiligkreuzkapelle, ursprünglich nach dem Entwurf A. Luragos gebaut. Nach dem Umbau der Kapelle ist hier seit 1963 die Schatzkammer des Veitsdoms untergebracht.

Der dritte Burghof bildet den Kern des Burgareals und umfaßt das Renaissanceschloß des Kaisers Rudolf II., Maxmilian II. und den Frühbarockpalast der Königin. Beide haben eine einheitliche Fassade nach dem Entwurf N. Pacassis aus der 2. Hälfte des 18. Jh. Hier befinden sich die Amtsräume der Präsidialkanzlei. Der repräsentative Eingang mit dem Balkon ist mit Statuen von I. F. Platzer aus den Jahren 1760—61 geschmückt. Dieser Platz, dessen Seiten vom königlichen Palais und der St.-Veitskathedrale gesäumt werden, mündet in den Platz vor der Georgsbasilika. Von der anderen Seite kommt man durch die Vikářská auf diesen Platz.

Darin befindet sich das ehemalige Kapitelhaus des Dekans und das neue Vikariat, wo das berühmte Restaurant „Na Vikárce" seine Heimat fand.

Zum Areal der Prager Burg gehört auch der sogenannte Pulverturm vom Ende des 15. Jh., gleichfalls von Benedikt Ried erbaut. In diesem ursprünglichen Kanonenturm befindet sich eine Ausstellung, die Wissenschaft und Kultur der Burg im 16. und 17. Jahrhundert darstellt. Auch das Modell einer Alchimistenwerkstatt fehlt nicht.

Die Burg ist von den südlichen Burggärten, dem Paradiesgarten und dem Wallgarten umgeben. Von hier bietet sich dem Betrachter ein einzigartiger Blick auf das Panorama von Prag.

FRANTIŠEK ŽENÍŠEK (1849—1916), Libussa, den Ruhm Prags prophezeiend 3 — das Werk des Künstlers, der der ersten Generation des Nationaltheaters angehörte, bezieht sich auf die legendäre Gestalt der böhmischen Sagen, die Fürstin Libussa und auf ihre Prophezeiung der Größe und des Ruhmes der Stadt Prag.

DAS ALTSTÄDTER RATHAUS 4, 105, 107, 114—120, 123 — dessen wirkungsvolles Torso sich malerisch an der Seite des Altstätder Rings erhebt, ist ein Beweis für die Existenz der bedeutsamen städtischen Selbstverwaltung, deren Anfänge bis ins Jahr 1338 reichen. Den Kern des mehrmals umgebauten Bauwerks bildete das gotische Haus Wolflins zum Stein. An dieses Haus bauten die Patrizier bis 1364 den vierseitigen Turm mit einer 1381 eingeweihten Kapelle an, die von einem wunderschön gearbeiteten Erker geschmückt ist. Die Urheberschaft des schmuckverzierten Portals des Haupteingangs aus den Jahren 1470—80 wird M. Rejsek aus Prostějov zugeschrieben. In die Stirnwand des Rathauses wurde nach 1520 im ersten Stockwerk unter dem Rathaussaal ein Fenster mit der Aufschrift Praga caput regni (Prag, Hauptstadt des Königreichs) und dem Wappen der Altstadt aus dem Jahre 1475 angebracht. Für den Urheber dieses Frührenaissanceumbaus wird der berühmte B. Ried gehalten. Zu Aus- und Umbauten des Rathauses kam es mehrmals bis ins 19. Jh. Einen Tag, bevor der zweite Weltkrieg zu Ende ging, am 8. Mai 1945 wurde der neugotische, von P. Nobil gebaute Nordflügel des Bauwerkes schwer beschädigt und er brannte aus. Nachdem des ausgebrannte Gemäuer abgetragen worden war, kam es wiederholt zu Versuchen, den Nordflügel zu rekonstruieren oder neu zu gestalten, die allerdings bis jetzt ohne Erfolg blieben.

Im Vestibül des Rathauses befindet sich der Mosaikschmuck vom Klassiker der tschechischen bildenden Kunst der Jahrhundertwende M. Aleš, der die Ehrung Prags durch das Slawentum darstellt (1904). Das Kunstwerk ist eine bildliche Nachbildung der Rede K. Sladkovskýs anläßlich der feierlichen Grundsteinlegung des Nationaltheaters. Es stellt Libussas Prophezeihung der großen Zukunft einer Stadt dar, „deren Ruhm die Sterne berühren wird". Von den historischen Interieurs des Rathauses gehört der alte Zeremoniesaal zu den bedeutsamsten, der in seiner ursprünglichen Gestalt aus dem Jahre

1470 erhalten blieb. Das Innere ist vor allem mit großen historischen Gemälden von J. Brožík geschmückt, die es versuchen, wichtige historische Handlungen in der Geschichte der Formung des nationalen Selbstbewußtseins festzuhalten.

DIE PRAGER BRÜCKEN 5, 98, 156, 178, 184 — haben neben ihrem technischen und funktionalen Aspekt einen leicht wahrzunehmenden ästhetischen Wert, der sich nicht nur aus der Komposition von Bau und Dekor ergibt, sondern auch aus der Harmonie mit dem malerisch gelegenen Fluß, dessen Fluten die ihn umgebende Landschaft launenhaft widerspiegeln.

DER HRADSCHINPLATZ 7 — bietet den Blick auf den ersten, den jüngsten Burghof der Prager Burg mit dem Eingangstor. Der Burghof wurde nach einem Entwurf von N. Pacassis in den Jahren 1759—69 im Geiste des italienisch-wienerischen Neuklassizismus gestaltet. Auf der Attika der Gebäude wurden militärische Symbole und Statuen von I. F. Platzer angebracht. Den Burghof gestaltete von 1920—22 der bedeutende tschechische Architekt P. Janák aufs Neue, die letzten Veränderungen wurden 1979—80 vorgenommen.

Gegenüber dem Eingangstor in den ersten Burghof befindet sich das Matthiastor, höchstwahrscheinlich von G. M. Filippi im Stil der italienischen Befestigungsbauten errichtet, denn ursprünglich bildete es einen Bestandteil der Befestigung über dem Burggraben.

DAS ERZBISCHÖFLICHE PALAIS 8 — das sich auf dem Hradschinplatz rechts vor dem Eingangstor der Prager Burg befindet, ist ein repräsentatives barokisiertes Bauwerk, das vom Wappen des Erzbischofs Antonín Příchovský beherrscht wird. Das Palais nutzte für den umfangreichen Umbau die Bausubstanz des ehemaligen Gryspek-Hauses, das von Ferdinand I. aufgekauft und zum neuen Sitz des Prager Erzbistums bestimmt worden war.

In den Jahren 1562—64 baute es O. Aostalis um. Einen neuen markanten Umbau führte in den Jahren 1669—79 J. B. Mathey durch, ein Architekt französischer Herkunft und Schützling des Erzbischofs J. B. von Waldstein. Das endgültige Rokokoantlitz prägte dem Bau J. Wirch ein (1764—65), der führende Vertreter des an Wien orientierten Stils. Das Palais schmücken die Statuen der Hoffnung und des Glaubens von T. Seidan aus den 80er Jahren des 19. Jh. Die übrige Dekoration stammt von I. F. Platzer, dessen Statuenschmuck auch am Treppengang im Hausinneren erhalten geblieben ist. Das Palais verbirgt auch einmalige Kunstsammlungen. In der Kapelle aus dem Jahre 1598, die mit Deckengemälden von D. Adam aus Květná geschmückt ist, ragen vor allem vergoldete Büsten der Hl. Peter und Paul heraus. Sie stammen aus der Zeit um 1413. Im Thronsaal befindet sich eine wertvolle Kollektion von acht kostbaren Tapisserien mit exotischen Motiven aus Neuindien, die im Atelier Neilson in Paris nach den Kartons von A. Desportes angefertigt wurden. Die Gemäldegalerie umfaßt Werke von J. J. Heinsch, M. V. Halwachs, F. Dallinger u. a. Einmalig ist die Folge der Bildnisse von Prager Erzbischöfen. In der Sammlung des Kunsthandwerks ragt die Kollektion des böhmischen geschnittenen Glases hervor, wertvoll ist auch die Sammlung des Wiener Porzellans. Die Innenräume des erzbischöflichen Palais sind den Besuchern alljährlich am Grünen Donnerstag frei zugänglich.

DAS EINGANGSTOR DER PRAGER BURG 9 — vom Hradschinplatz wird von einer monumentalen Pforte gebildet, die zwischen zwei Rokokogeländern aus der Zeit Maria Theresias eingesetzt ist. Das Tor ist mit bedrohlichen Gestalten der Kämpfenden Giganten und mit Vasen und Putti geschmückt, die 1769 von I. F. Platzer geschaffen wurden. Die ursprünglichen Sandsteinskulpturen wurden jedoch 1912 infolge ihres schlechten Zustandes mit Kopien von C. Vosmík und A. Procházka ersetzt.

Der Hintergrund wird vom Steintor beherrscht, das während der Regierungszeit des Kaisers Matthias 1614 errichtet wurde. Neben der Kennzeichnung der Würden des Kaisers befinden sich auf beiden Seiten die Wappen der einzelnen Länder des Kaiserreichs.

DER DRITTE BURGHOF 10 — wurde schrittweise nach einem grossen Brand im Jahre 1551 gestaltet, nach dem die Überreste der mittelalterlichen Bebauung verschüttet wurden. Nach dem 1. Weltkrieg gestaltete J. Plečnik über den archeologischen Funden eine Betonkonstruktion und Granitpflaster.

Die Nordseite des dritten Burghofs wird von der Südfront des Veitsdoms mit dem großen, von P. Parler 1396 gegründeten Kirchenturm abgeschlossen. Der spätere Renaissanceturm wurde 1770 nach einem Entwurf N. Pacassis umgebaut. Im Turm, der eine Gesamthöhe von 99,6 m erreicht, befinden sich vier Renaissanceglocken, unter denen Zikmund mit ihren 203 cm herausragt. Dieses größte Werk der böhmischen Glockengießerei schuf 1549 T. Jaroš.

Rechts unter dem Turm befindet sich ein Arkadenportikus, die sog. Goldene Pforte, die die Kronkammer trägt, in der die Krönungskleinodien des Königreichs Böhmen aufbewahrt werden. Auf ihrer Stirnwand befindet sich ein oft restauriertes Mosaik des Jüngsten Gerichts aus böhmischem Glas, das 1370—71 von venezianischen Meistern geschaffen wurde.

Das Gebäude der Alten Propstei hinter dem Mrákotíner Monolith stammt aus dem 17. Jh. An ihrer Stelle stand früher das romanische Bischofspalais.

ST. GEORGSBASILIKA 11 — bildet die Ostseite des St. Georgsplatzes und ist das am besten erhaltene romanische Bauwerk in Prag. Die Kirche wurde im Jahre 921 vom Fürsten Wratislaw gestiftet, ihre dreischiffige Baugestalt fällt jedoch in die Zeit der Äbtissin Berta, d. h. vor das Jahr 1142, als die Burg ausbrannte. Das Hauptportal wurde barokisiert — wahrscheinlich von F. Caratti — in den Jahren 1677—78. An das Portal baute F. M. Kaňka in den Jahren 1718—22 die Kapelle des hl. Johann von Nepomuk an. Die Statuengruppe über dem Eingang von F. M. Brokoff gab der Kapelle ihre endgültige Gestalt. An den Südturm der Basilika aus der Mitte des 12. Jh. wurde im 14. Jh. die Kapelle der hl. Ludmila angebaut. An der Südseite der Basilika fesselt das Renaissancesäulenportal den Blick, das aus der Steinmetzhütte von B. Ried aus Pístov um 1500 stammt. Das gotische Relief des Drachenbezwingers St. Georg wurde im Jahre 1934 durch eine Kopie ersetzt. Unter dem Südturm blieb in den bäulichen Überresten der Kapelle der hl. Maria romanische Wandbemalung aus der ersten Hälfte des 13. Jh. erhalten. Innerhalb der Basilika, die um die Jahrhundertwende vom 19. zum 20. Jh. romanisch neugestaltet wurde, befinden sich unter anderem Grabmäler der Fürsten Boleslav II. und Oldřich sowie die Tumba des Fürsten Wratislaw.

Bestandteil des angeschlossenen Baukomplexes ist das erste Frauenkloster in Böhmen, das dem Benediktinerorden gehörte und von der Schwester des Fürsten Boleslav II., der seligen Mlada, gestiftet wurde. Das mehrmals umgebaute Kloster wurde 1782 aufgelöst und bald darauf verwandelte es sich zum Teil in eine Kaserne. In den Jahren 1962—74 wurde es der Nationalgalerie übergeben und nach erfolgter Adaptierung wurde hier die ständige Ausstellung der böhmischen Kunst der Gotik, Renaissance und des Manierismus untergebracht.

DER ST. VEITSDOM 12, 44 — ist die größte und wichtigste Prager Kirche. Hier werden die Krönungskleinodien des böhmischen Königsreiches aufbewahrt. Hier ruhen auch die böhmischen Herrscher. Hier ließ Herzog Wenzel, der Patron Böhmens, vor 935 das ursprüngliche Gotteshaus, eine dreischiffige romanische Basilika, errichten. Die Arbeiten am heutigen Dom begannen unter Karl IV. im Jahre 1344. Der französische Meister Matthias von Arras begann mit dem Bau der dreischiffigen Kathedrale, bestehend aus einem Querschiff, einem Ambitus und einem Kranz von Kapellen. Seine Nachfolger waren der süddeutsche Baumeister und Bildhauer Peter Parler aus dem schwäbischen Gmünd, sowie dessen Söhne Václav (Wenzl) und Jan (Hans). Nachdem bereits das Triforium errichtet und der Bau des Hauptturmes begonnen worden war, mußten die Arbeiten wegen der Hussitenkriege unterbrochen werden. Ein bedeutender Einschnitt in der Baugeschichte war das Renaissancejahr 1564. Damals wurde nämlich vom Architekten B. Wohlmut der Turmambitus samt Helm errichtet. Erst im Jahre 1929 war die Kathedrale ganz fertiggestellt. Dadurch repräsentiert sie auch die schon im Jahre 1873 begonnene neugotische Stilperiode der Prager Architektur. Aus dieser Zeit stammt der neugotische Altar vor dem Königsmausoleum, ein Werk des niederländischen Bildhauers A. Collin aus den Jahren 1374—85. Eine Treppe führt in die Gruft hinab, wo einige der berühmtesten Könige ruhen und Baureste der Vorgängerkirchen aus dem 10. und 11. Jahrhundert zu sehen sind. Im Triforium befindet sich eine Galerie von Porträt-Plastiken, die im Sinne der künstlerischen und historischen Intentionen Karls IV. die Bildnisse von Mitgliedern der Herrscherfamilie und jener Persönlichkeiten darstellen, die sich um den Bau des Doms verdient gemacht hatten. Ein bedeutender Platz des Domes ist die Kammer mit den Krönungskleinodien, die mit sieben Schlössern verschlossen ist. Für das wertvollste Stück des ganzen Kronschatzes wird die St. Wenzel Krone aus dem Jahre 1346 gehalten. In den Kapellen des Ambitus befinden sich Grabbilder böhmischer Herrscher, die in der Hütte P. Parlers in den Jahren 1370—75 geschaffen wurden. Während der Regierungszeit von Wladislaw Jagello kam es im Jahre 1493 zum Ausbau des königlichen Oratoriums mit naturalistischen Ornamenten, welche die Gestalt verflochtener Äste und Wappen haben. Die Renaissanceepoche wird vom Orgelsockel repräsentiert, der im Jahre 1924 ins Querschiff verlegt wurde. Von der barocken Ausschmückung zieht namentlich der Grabstein des Grafen L. Šlik die Aufmerksamkeit auf sich. Er wurde im Jahre 1723 gemeinsam von J. E. Fischer von Erlach, F. M. Kaňka und M. Brandl geschaffen.

Zu den hervorragenden Werken der Neuzeit gehört die kniende Statue des Kardinals B. S. Schwarzenberg, ein Werk von V. Myslbek aus den Jahren 1892—95. Aus dem ersten Drittel des 20. Jahrhunderts stammt die Reihe bunter Fenster in den einzelnen Kapellen. Sie wurden nach Zeichnungen von A. Mucha, F. Kysela, C. Bouda und anderen angefertigt. Der Dom ist eine Schatzkammer künstlerischer Werke von der romanischen Zeit (der Jerusalemleuchter aus dem Rheinland) bis zu den Artefakten des 20. Jahrhunderts.

DIE WENZELSKAPELLE 13 — deren Bau Matthias von Arras begann, wurde als das Gegenstück zu der Heiligkreuzkapelle auf der Burg Karlstein aufgefaßt. Sie wurde in den Jahren 1362—66 von Peter Parler fertiggestellt, und zwar an der Stelle des ursprünglichen Grabes des Heiligen aus dem Jahre 935, d. h. im Südteil des vorderen Schiffes. Der untere Teil der Wände in der Kapelle, die zu den größten Kleinodien der Hochgotik in Böhmen gehört, ist mit 1345 Jaspisen und Ametysten ausgelegt. Die kostbare Ausmalung stellt ein Kunstwerk ersten Ranges dar. Sie besteht aus dem Passionszyklus eines unbekannten Meisters aus den Jahren 1372—73 und aus Gemälden der Wenzelslegende vom Meister des Leitmeritzer Altars aus den Jahren 1506—09. Das Altar in der Kapelle hat eine gotische Tumba aus dem 14. Jh., die Statue des hl. Wenzel von 1373 aus Pläuerkalkstein ist ein unikates Werk aus der Werkstatt Peter Parlers. Die kleinen Gemälde über dem Altar stellen Karl IV. und seine vierte Gemahlin Elisabeth von Pommern, des weiteren sind hier Gestalten des Wenzel IV. und der Jana von Bayern abgebildet. Die beiden Gestalten über der Statue des hl. Wenzel sollen den Wladislaw Jagello und seine Gemahlin Anna de Fois-Candale darstellen. Liturgische Gegenstände auf dem Altar genauso wie das vergoldete Tabernakel und Luster aus den Jahren 1912—13 (eine Arbeit von F. Anýž nach den Entwürfen von K. Hilbert, S. Sucharda und J. Kryšpín) ergänzen die gotischen und Renaissancekunstgegenstände. Unter dem Fenster der Kapelle befindet sich ein kleines Portal, das zum Treppenaufgang zur Kronkammer führt, wo die Krönungskleinodien in Sicherheit aufbewahrt werden.

MEISTER THEODORIK, Hl. PAPST, Hl. HIERONYMUS, Hl. AUGUSTIN, Hl. VEIT 14—17 — die Plattengemälde des kaiserlichen Malers und Vorgesetzten der Prager Malerzunft wurden in den 70er Jahren des 14. Jh. für die Hofkapelle Karls IV. auf dem Karlstein geschaffen. Die Idee der universellen Einheit der himmlischen und der irdischen Welt wird in 130 Gemälden widerspiegelt, die in drei Reihen an getafelten Wänden angebracht sind. Dieses Polyptychon hat eine stark hieratische Anordnung. Die als monumental empfundenen Gestalten der Wächter des kaiserlichen Schatzes in Überlebensgröße liefern ein einzigartiges Beispiel der Feudalordnung, für die die Herscherpersönlichkeit verantwortlich war, natürlich der Siegreichen Kirche Respekt zollend. Gemälde, die das himmlische Heer Christi darstellen, sind ein Nachweis des mittelalterlichen Kults der Heiligen — Märtyrer, deren Reliquien in den Rahmen eines jeden Bildes eingesetzt wurden.

Die sanft malerische Form Theodoriks mit naturalistischer Abwandlung eines physiognomischen Typus beweisen die ausgereifte künstlerische und schöpferische Orientierung dieses vom Kaiser favorisierten Künstlers. Seine Kenntnis sowohl des byzantinischen, als auch des westlichen, namentlich venezianischen und bolognesischen Kunstschaffens scheint außer allen Zweifel zu sein.

MEISTER VON TŘEBOŇ, CHRISTUS AUF DEM ÖLBERG, KREUZIGUNG, GRABLEGUNG, AUFERSTEHUNG 18—21 — Werke, die in den Sammlungen der Nationalgalerie in Prag ausgestellt werden, stammen vom Alter der St. Ägidiuskirche in Třeboň (Südböhmen), das Plattengemälde Kreuzigung stammt aus der Kapelle der hl. Barbora aus der Nähe Třeboňs. Diese Plattengemälde wurden um 1380 von einem anonymen Meister vom Weltrang geschaffen. Die komplizierte Komposition mit einer subtilen Arabesque der Formen sowie der satte Farbenkontrast steigern noch den malerischen Idealismus und die seltsame mystische Entzückung. Werke mit lyrischer Wirkung nehmen die Kunst des schönen Stils aus der Zeit um 1400 vorweg.

DER WLADISLAWSAAL 22 — nimmt den ganzen zweiten Stock des Alten Palastes der Prager Burg ein. Er stellt den ehrenwürdigsten Raum der Burg dar, denn hier werden traditionsgemäß die wichtigsten Staatshandlungen ausgetragen. Er wurde während der Regierungszeit des Wladislaw Jagello in den Jahren 1492—1502 danach erbaut, als der Sitz der Residenz aus der Altstadt auf die Burg verlegt worden war. Den Bau des Saales an Stelle von drei gotischen Sälen aus der Zeit Karls IV. entwarf der königliche Baumeister B. Ried. Es wurde der größte und repräsentativste profane Raum der mitteleuropäischen Spätgotik erbaut (62 m lang, 16 m breit und 13 m hoch). Es fanden hier Krönungsfeste und Landtage statt, aber auch Turniere, zu deren Zwecken auch die anliegende Reittreppe diente. Nach der Verlegung des Herrschersitzes nach Wien diente der Saal öfters als gesellschaftlicher Versammlungsplatz, wo auch Märkte der Hofkrämer stattfanden. Der Saal wurde nach dem 1. Weltkrieg pietätsvoll restauriert, wobei die späten Malereien entfernt wurden.

Vom Wladislawsaal aus gibt es Zugang in den Seitenflügel der Burg, in das sog. Ludwigpalais aus dem Anfang des 16. Jh.

DIE ALTE LANDTAGSSTUBE DER PRAGER BURG 23 — in der bis 1847 das Oberste Landgericht tagte und wo die Vertreter der böhmischen Stände tagten, wurde in den Jahren 1559—65 vom kaiserlichen Baumeister B. Wohlmut erbaut. Der repräsentative Raum mit dem spätgotischen Netzgewölbe wurde bis 1857 von den Landtagen auch zur Königswahl benutzt. In der neuen Zeit werden hier Verfassungsgesetze unterzeichnet, es finden hier auch außerordentliche festliche Sitzungen des Tschechischen Nationalrates statt.

ADRIAEN DE VRIES (1546—1626), RUDOLF II 24 — eines der drei Bildnisse des Kaisers (aus dem Jahre 1603), den der Kunsttheoretiker und Maler Van Mander „... den größten und ersten Kunstfreund der Welt“ nannte, stammt aus den ehemaligen rudolfinischen Sammlungen, deren Torso in der Bildergalerie der Prager Burg ausgestellt ist. Der Niederländer de Vries war die größte Bildhauerpersönlichkeit am Hofe Rudolfs II. Viele seiner Werke fielen als Beute in die Hände der Schweden während der Belagerung Prags im Jahre 1648.

HL. GEORG 25 — das bronzene Reiterstandbild des sagenhaften Drachenbezwingers ist eine Kopie des Werkes der Meister Georg und Martin aus Klausenburg aus dem Jahre 1373. Ursprünglich befand sich das Standbild im südlichen Teil des Burghofs vor den sog. Maximilians Küchen. Die Figuren der Pferde und des Drachen wurden später zum Teil neu gegossen und nach ihrer Beschädigung im Jahre 1562 vom Metallgießer T. Jaroš restauriert. Den Sockel entwarf während der Bepflasterung des III. Burghofs im Jahre 1928 J. Plečnik. Er projektierte auch den 18 m hohen Monolith aus dem Mrákotíner Granit. Er wurde anläßlich des zehnjährigen Jubiläums der Tschechoslowakischen Republik und als Denkmal für die Opfer des 1. Weltkrieges aufgestellt.

TIZIANO VECELIO (um 1480/90—1576), TOILETTE EINER JUNGEN FRAU 26 — dieses Werk des größten Vertreters der venezianischen Malerei des 16. Jh. ist in der Gemäldegalerie der Prager Burg bereits 1685 belegt. Das Bild der rothaarigen jungen Frau mit ihren Toilettenutensilien, der ein Jüngling in voller Bewunderung zu Diensten ist, nähert sich dem Wiener Gemälde der Zigeunermadonna (um 1510), das in der Zeit geschaffen wurde, als Tizian voller Bewunderung zu Giorgione aufsah. Das Prager Gemälde, geschaffen etwa 1512—15, wurde nach etwa der Mitte des 18 Jh. wahrscheinlich wegen der Tafelung verkleinert (auf 83×79 cm). Eine genaue Renaissancekopie des Gemäldes (109,2×91,3 cm) wurde durch das Versteigerungshaus Christie in London am 27. 11. 1957 in eine Privatsammlung verkauft.

Das Thema, Toilette einer jungen Frau, taucht auch in weiteren Fassungen auf, unter denen das Tiziangemälde im Louvre am bekanntesten ist. Dieses stammt aus der Sammlung des englischen Königs Karl I. Die Authentizität des Prager Gemäldes wurde in der Vergangenheit angezweifelt. Bereits 1832 wurde das Bild Orazio, dem Sohn Tizians, zugeschrieben, später wurde es für eine Kopie gehalten.

PETER PAUL RUBENS (1577–1640) VERSAMMLUNG DER OLYMPGÖTTER (DETAIL) 27 – bereits dieses frühe Werk des Hauptvertreters des flämischen Barocks zeichnet sich aus durch die Kraft, Sinnlichkeit und symphonische Einheit von vielschichtigen Geschehnissen, die das spätere Werk Rubens so überwältigend dominiert. Das Gemälde entstand etwa um 1602, als Rubens zum Hofmaler des Herzogs von Mantua, Vincenzo Conzaga, geworden war. Das Gemälde stellt die Versammlung der olympischen Götter mit Jupiter an der Spitze dar, als die Schutzgöttin der festen ehelichen Bande Héra-Juno ihre Klage gegen die leichtsinnige, aber triumphierende Liebesgöttin Venus-Aphrodite vorträgt.

Dieses Gemälde, das unter dem Einfluss von G. Roman steht, wurde in der Gemäldesammlung der Burg zum erstenmal im Jahre 1685 belegt, und zwar als ein Werk eines unbekannten Meisters, in der Zeit von 1718–1737 wurde es mit dem Namen Raffaels in Verbindung gebracht. Die Urheberschaft Rubens' wurde im Jahre 1797 kurz erwähnt; die Authentizität des Kunstwerks wurde nach 1962 von J. Neumann bestätigt.

KAREL ŠKRÉTA (1610–1674), BILDNIS DES EDELSTEINSCHNEIDERS DIONYSUS MISERONI UND SEINER FAMILIE (DETAIL) 28 – das Kunstwerk des Mitbegründers der böhmischen Barockmalerei, gemalt um 1653, stellt den Leiter der Schleiferwerkstatt und den Kunstsammlungsverwalter der Burg im Familienkreise dar. Gerade Eionysius Miseroni versuchte im Jahre 1648, die Schweden am Betreten der Kunstkammer Rudolfs II. zu hindern. Sein Vater Octavio Miseroni war 1588 aus Mailand zum Hofe Rudolfs II. berufen worden, wo er zum Hofedelsteinschneider ernannt wurde und 1608 das Adelsprädikat errang.

JAN KUPECKÝ (KUPEZKY JOHANNES, 1667–1740), ALLEGORIE DER MALEREI 29 – das Kunstwerk des tschechischen überwiegend im Ausland tätigen Künstlers, der unter den herausragenden europäischen Bildnismalern der ersten Hälfte des 18. Jh. einen Ehrenplatz einnimmt, das ein Gegenstück zu seinem Gemälde Allegorie der Bildhauerkunst aus den Sammlungen der Nationalgalerie in Prag bildet. Personifizierung der Malerei als junge Frau im Barockgewand, mit Lorbeerruhmeskranz im dichten, blonden Haar, kann zeitlich ins 2. Jahrzehnt des 18. Jh. eingeordnet werden, als der Maler überwiegend in Wien weilte.

PETR BRANDL (1668–1735), SELBSTBILDNIS 31 – eine Leihgabe aus der Lobkowitz-Sammlung, das Bildnis wurde 1697 geschaffen. Es belegt über jeden Zweifel die überzeugende Meisterschaft des größten Malers des Hochbarocks in Böhmen, menschliche Charaktere zu erfassen. Brandl wurde insbesondere als Meister von lichtspielerischen dynamischen Altargemälden und von Werken mit mythologischer und Genrethematik berühmt.

PAOLO CALIARI GENANNT VERONESE (1528–1588), DIE HEILIGE KATHARINA MIT DEM ENGEL 32 – das Gemälde von einem der größtem Darsteller der venezianischen Malerei des 16 Jh., geschaffen um 1580, wurde in der II. Gemäldegalerie der Prager Burg unter dem Titel Versuchung einer Heiligen bereits 1685 belegt. Die falsche Deutung des Bildes wurde anscheinend auf die vertrauliche Geste des Engels zurückgeführt. Nach J. Neumann ist die Heilige jedoch als Christus Braut in jenem Augenblick abgebildet, wo sie von dem Himmelsboten ihren Schicksal eröffnet bekommt, den Märtyrertod, wie der Palmenzweig und der Schwert in der Engelshand bezeugen.

PALAIS LOBKOWITZ UND DER SCHWARZE TURM 33 – sind von der alten Schloßtreppe im östlichen Areal der Burg her zugänglich. Der Schwarze Turm wurde auf älterem Grundbau in der 2. Hälfte des 12. Jahrhunderts errichtet und war ein Bestandteil der romanischen Befestigungsanlage aus der Zeit des Fürsten Soběslav. Nach dem Brand im Jahre 1538 mußte er um ein Stockwerk gekürzt werden, was sich in seinem Namen widerspiegelte. Früher wurde der Turm nämlich als „Golden" bezeichnet, weil sein Dach unter Karl IV. mit vergoldetem Blech beschlagen war. Der Turm wurde als Gefängnis für Schuldner genutzt. Ursprünglich diente er als östliches Burgtor. In der Zeit Wenzels I. wurde nach 1230 unter ihm ein neues Eingangstor gebaut. Das an dieses Tor anliegende Palais Lobkowitz, früher Palais Pernstein genannt, ließen Jaroslav und Vratislav von Pernstein in den Jahren 1535–1562 und 1570–1576 errichten. Der Bau wurde 1625 bei einem Brand beschädigt. Zu einem erneuten Umbau des Palastes kam es in den Jahren 1651–1668, nachdem der Palast im Jahre 1626 in den Besitz der Lobkowitzer gelangt war. Wenzel Eusebius von Lobkowitz vergab den Auftrag an C. L. Lurago. Die italienischen Steinmetzen G. Galli und G. Pozzo führten die Steinarbeiten durch, der Stukkateur D. Galli verzierte die Decke des Hauptsaales, in die F. V. Hárovník seine Ölmalereien einsetzte.

Zu Teilumbauten kam es auch in späteren Jahren, vor allem 1810 und 1861–62. Im Jahre 1976 begann die Renovierung des Palastes, in dem sich heutzutage die historisch-archeologische Ausstellung des Nationalmuseums befindet. Im Rahmen der Rückübertragung von Eigentum wurde der Palast im Jahre 1992 an das Lobkowitzer Geschlecht zurückgegeben.

DAS PANORAMA VON PRAG VOM PALAIS LOBKOWITZ AUS, 34 – erfaßt den einzigartigen Blick auf die Kleinstädtner Enklave des Palais Wallenstein, welches auf der Fläche von 23 Häusern mit Höfen und Gärten, einer Ziegelbrennerei und eines Stadttores errichtet wurde. Hinter dem Palais ragt die St. Thomaskirche empor, die zusammen mit dem Kloster von Wenzel II. im Jahre 1285 für die Augustinereremiten gegründet wurde. Der Autor des barocken Umbaus in den Jahren 1723–31 ist der hervorragende Architekt K. I. Dienzenhofer. Die prächtige Kirchenverzierung stammt von den besten böhmischen Barockkünstlern, für den Hauptaltar wurden jedoch zwei Werke von P. P. Rubens bestellt, die heute durch zwei Kopien ersetzt sind. Die Originale wurden der Nationalgalerie übergeben.

DER KOLOWRATT-GARTEN 35 – in den Jahren 1769–89 von I. J. Palliardi entworfen, dehnt sich hinter dem Hauptgebäude des Palais Kolowratt und dem kleineren Palais Czernin (Černín) aus. Das letztere wurde im Jahre 1740 an Stelle des ehemaligen Hauses des Herrn Popel von Lobkowitz erbaut. Der Rokokoterassengarten mit einem pittoresken Hauch orientaler Exotik umfaßt Pavillons und zur dreiteiligen Salla terrena führende Treppen mit Balustraden.

DER KÖNIGLICHE GARTEN 36 – heutzutage im englischen Stil angelegt, wurde er im Jahre 1535 von Ferdinand I. in Anlehnung an italienische Renaissancegärten auf der Fläche zwischen der Pulverbrücke und dem Hirschgraben errichtet. Er wurde mit exotischen Pflanzen, aber auch mit Weinreben „bepflanzt" und daneben wurde das niederländische Giardinetto gegründet. Es kam zur Errichtung zahlreicher Gebäude, Volieren und Orangerien, es entstanden Bassins, Fontänen, Springbrunnen und Labyrinte. Eine grundlegende Umgestaltung erfolgte nach Entwürfen K. J. Dienzenhofers in den Jahren 1725–34, als der im französischen Stil angelegte Blumengarten durch Löwen-, Vasen- und Allegorieskulpturen aus der Werkstatt H. B. Brauns ergänzt wurde.

DER HARTIG-GARTEN 37, 50 – breitet sich neben anderen Gärten von einmaliger malerischer Anmut auf dem südlichen Hang der Prager Burg aus. Außer an den Spaziergängen, auf denen man den herrlichen Blick auf das Panorama von Prag genoß, konnte man sich hier an eindrucksvollen Ereignissen des kulturellen Lebens erfreuen, z. B. im Musikpavillon des Hartig-Gartens. Das Bauwerk aus der ersten Hälfte des 18. Jahrhunderts, G. B. Alliprandi zugeschrieben, hat einen mit Stuck und Gemälden von Burgruinen dekorierten oberen Saal. Vor dem Pavillon wurden Skulpturen antiker Gottheiten aus der Werkstatt A. Brauns aufgestellt. Sie entstanden um das Jahr 1735 und wurden im Jahre 1945 aus den Gärten des Schlosses Štiřín auf die Prager Burg gebracht.

DIE SINGENDE FONTÄNE 38 – befindet sich vor dem königlichen Lustschloß. Sie wurde in den Jahren 1564–68 von dem Brünner Glockengießer Tomáš Jaroš nach einem Entwurf des italienischen Meisters F. Terzio gegossen. Die Fontäne befindet sich inmitten des erneuerten Giardinettos, das nach dem Entwurf des niederländischen Architekten und Dekorateurs V. de Vries angefertigt wurde. Der Klang der Wassertropfen, die von dem zweistöckigen, mit Jagdmotiven geschmückten Becken fallen, verhalf der Fontäne zu ihrem Namen. Die Fontäne zählt in ihrer Art zu den schönsten Renaissancewerken nördlich der Alpen.

DAS BALLHAUS DER PRAGER BURG, MATTHIAS BERNARD BRAUN-WERKSTATT, NACHT 39, 40 – das große Ballhaus wurde in den Jahren 1567–69 von B. Wohlmut und O. Aostalis in den königlichen Gärten über dem Hirschgraben errichtet. Der edle Saalbau (60 m lang) mit plastischen Halbsäulen wurde mit zarten Sgraffitos besetzt, welche Allegorien der Tugenden, Wissenschaften und Elemente darstellen. Das verlassene Gebäude wurde jedoch 1723 in einen Marstall umgewandelt, später in ein Militärdepot. Noch im Jahre 1734 wurden vor seinem Portal zwei Statuen, Allegorien der Nacht und des Tages aufgestellt, Werke von A. Braun, des Neffen M. B. Brauns. Das zweite Werk, der Tag, wurde bei einem preußischen Bombardement Prags im Jahre 1757 vernichtet.

Im Jahre 1945 brannte das Ballhaus nieder, es wurde jedoch im Jahre 1952 wiederaufgebaut und in den Jahren 1971—73 renoviert. Zur Zeit dient es repräsentativen Zwecken. Aus diesem Grund wurden hier auch die Brüsseler Tapisserien von J. van Leefdaelen aufgehängt. Sie stammen aus dem 17. Jh. und zeigen das Motiv von Antonius und Kleopatra.

DAS KÖNIGLICHE LUSTSCHLOSS (BELVEDERE) 41 — erbaut von 1538—63 in der Nähe der Prager Burg über dem Brusnice-Tal, ist ein herrliches Beispiel des Einflusses der italienischen Rennaissance in den böhmischen Kronländern. Der Bau erfolgte auf Veranlassung von Ferdinand I. nach einem Entwurf der italienischen Baumeister und Steinmetze P. della Stella und H. Tiroli sowie des Hofbaumeister B. Wohlmut, die Bauaufsicht führte der Sekretär der Böhmischen Kammer F. von Griesbach. Die Arbeiten an der reichen Steinmetzausschmückung übernahm die Werkstatt P. della Stella (bis 1538), später kamen weitere italienische Steinmetzmeister hinzu. Das Lustschloß sollte der Königin Anna zur Erholung und Unterhaltung dienen. Darin entstand eine reiche und wertvolle Bildergalerie, ein Tanzsaal wurde hergerichtet, die Räumlichkeiten mit kostspieligem Schmuck und Mobiliar ausgestattet. Die schwedische Invasion im Jahre 1648 war folgenschwer auch für das Belvedere und seine Kunstsammlungen. Während der Regierungszeit von Josef II. wurde das Bauwerk schwer beschädigt durch seine Umwandlung in ein Labor (bis 1836). Von 1851—65 wurde an den Wänden des ersten Stockwerks ein Zyklus aus der tschechischen Geschichte gemalt. Die Kartonentwürfe stammten vom des Leiter der Prager Akademie der bildenden Künste K. Ruben. Gegenwärtig dient das von P. Janák restaurierte Lustschloß Ausstellungszwecken.

DAS GOLDENE GÄSSCHEN 42 — in der Jagello-Zeit gegen Ende des 16. Jh. begann man damit, die pastellfarbenen Miniaturhäuschen, die heutigen stammen aus den verschiedensten Epochen, in die Bögen der Burgbefestigung einzubauen. Bis zum Jahre 1597 wohnten hier Burgschützen und kleine Handwerker, darunter auch die Goldschmiede Rudolf II. Nach dem seit den 70er Jahren des 17. Jh. verwendeten Namen „Goldschmiedergäßchen" entstand Sage von den Alchimisten der Rudolfzeit.

In den Jahren 1952—53 wurden die Häuschen renoviert, genauso wie der geschützte, drei Türme verbindende Gang, durch den die Gefangenen überführt wurden. In den renovierten Häuschen wurden geschichtliche Ausstellungen über diesen Burgteil und Buch- und Souvenirläden eingerichtet.

DIE KLEINSEITNER ST. NIKLASKIRCHE 43, 59, 60, 62, 64, 65 — Inmitten des Kleinseitner Ringes, an der Stelle eines früheren gotischen Hauses befindet sich die expressiv wirkende Dominante des Prager Barocks, die an der Südseite mit dem Jesuiteninternat verbunden ist. Die Kirche, entstanden in den Jahren 1704—11, ist vermutlich ein Werk von C. Dienzenhofer. Sein Sohn K. I. Dienzenhofer erbaute in den Jahren 1732—52 das Presbytarium und die Kuppel. Den schlanken Glockenturm aus den Jahren 1751—56, der Kern der Streitigkeiten mit der Kleinseitner Gemeinde war, welche den Beginn der Bauarbeiten des ganzen Komplexes zu verschieben versuchte, errichtete Dienzenhofers Schwager A. Lurago.

Die mächtige gewellte Steinwand, eines der großartigsten Werke des Hochbarocks aus dem Jahre 1710 findet ihre Ergänzung in den Plastiken aus der Werkstatt von A. Braun. Neben dem Wappen von Fr. Liebstein von Kolowrat befinden sich Statuen der Kirchenväter und die Allegorie der Theologie. Dem ganzen Bauwerk kann man den Einfluß des illusionistischen römischen Barocks ansehen.

Das Interieur der Kirche zählt zu den prunkvollsten Schöpfungen des Prager Hochbarocks. An den Fresken beteiligten sich J. L. Krakker und J. Heger, die monumentale 75 m^2 große Kapelle schmückte F. X. Palko. Die vier Heiligenstatuen unter der Kuppel in Überlebensgröße schuf in den Jahren 1752—55 I. F. Platzer, der Autor der bronzenen St. Niklasstatue auf dem Hauptaltar und weiterer Plastiken.

Weitere Bestandteile der Ausschmückung sind die Gemälde von K. Škréta, I. Raab, J. K. Kracker. Auf der Orgel, gebaut von T. Schwarz in den Jahren 1745—46, spielte W. A. Mozart in der Zeit seiner Prager Aufenthälte.

Nachdem im Jahre 1773 der Jesuitenorden von Papst Klemens aufgelöst worden war, wurde die St. Niklauskirche zur Pfarrerkirche.

DIE LORETO-KIRCHE 45 — auf Kosten der Familie Lobkowitz als ein Gegenstück zum monumentalen Palais Czernin (Černín) auf dem Hradschin von 1626—1750 erbaut, war sie eine Wallfahrtsstätte, die an das erste Kapuzinerkloster in Böhmen aus dem Jahre 1601 angeschlossen war. Die kunstvolle Fassade entwarf der aus Bayern stammende Christian Dienzenhofer, ausgeführt wurde sie von seinem Sohn Kilian Ignaz. Der Statuenschmuck, heute durch Kopien ersetzt, sammt von O. F. Quittainer und J. B. Kohl. Über der Stirnwand erhebt sich ein Kirchenturm aus dem Jahre 1693, dessen 27 in Amsterdam gegossene Glocken stündlich ihre Melodie, eine rührende marianische Liedervariation, erklingen lassen. Der Entwurf des Glockenspiels stammt vom Uhrmacher P. Naumann (1694). In der Mitte eines grünen, von einem doppelgeschossigen Kreuzgang eingefaßten Hofes steht die Santa Casa, die Heilige Hütte, erbaut 1631 von G. B. Orsi und mit Stuckreliefs verschiedener italienischer Meister aus dem Jahre 1664 geschmückt. Sie ist eine Nachbildung des Häuschens der Jungfrau Maria in Nazareth, das Engel im 13. Jh. nach Loreto in Italien gebracht haben sollen. Daher befinden sich im Inneren des Häuschens Bilder mit Ausschnitten aus dem Leben der Jungfrau Maria und ihre Statue aus Zederholz. Eine weitere Sehenswürdigkeit innerhalb der Wallfahrtsstätte ist die 1734—35 nach Plänen von J. J. Aichbauer erbaute Christgeburtskirche mit glanzvollen Deckenfresken V. V. Reiners. Die Loreto-Kirche, nun wieder Besitz des Kapuzinerklosters, verbirgt in ihren Wänden einmaligen Reichtum an Sammlungen. In der Schatzkammer im oberen Teil des Umganges glitzern kostbare Reliquienschreine, Monstranzen, Kelche und Bischofsmützen. Das wertvollste Stück der Sammlung ist eine Wiener Monstranz aus dem Jahre 1699 mit ihren 6222 strahlenden und funkelnden Diamanten.

DER AUSSICHTSTURM AUF DEM LAURENZIBERG 47 — der 60 m hohe Turm ragt vom Felshang über dem Kleinseitner Kessel empor.

DIE STERNWARTE AUF DEM LAURENZIBERG 48 — wurde im Jahre 1925—30 aus einem Gemeindehaus auf Kosten der tschechischen astronomischen Gesellschaft errichtet (nach dem Projekt von J. Veselík) und befindet sich am Ende des Rosengartens. Es dient bis zur heutigen Zeit astronomischen Zwecken, gleichzeitig ist hier eine ständige astronomische Ausstellung untergebracht.

DAS KLOSTER STRAHOV 51 — vom Fürsten Vladislav II. auf Veranlassung des Olmützer Bischofs Jindřich Zdík im Jahre 1140 gegründet, wurde mit Ordensbrüdern des Prämonstratenserordens belegt, der sich den erzieherischen Aufgaben und der Bildungsverbreitung widmete. Der umfangreiche Klosterkomplex über Prag am Hange des Laurenziberges (Petřín) umfaßt zwei Kirchen, Kloster, Klosterprälatur, Bibliotheken und Wirtschaftsgebäude. Die einzelnen Objekte wurden von komplizierten Veränderungen und architektonischen Umwandlung insbesondere in der Zeit Hussitenbewegung und unter den Agriffen der französischen und preußischen Armeen im 18. Jh. geprägt. Den Kern des gesamten Areals bildet das Kloster mit der Bibliothek, wo 1953 die Gedenkstätte des nationalen Schrifttums untergebracht wurde. Der Klosterhaupteingang führt durch das im Jahre 1742 von A. Lurago gebaute Pohořelecer Tor. Die kleine St. Rochuskirche wurde auf Kosten Rudolfs II. als Danksagung für die Pestabwendung errichtet. A. Lurago beteiligte sich auch an den Umbauten der Abteikirche (Himmelfahrt der Jungfrau Maria), in deren Bausubstanz die ursprüngliche romanische Basilika aus dem 12. Jh. mit einbezogen ist. Auf dem Hauptklosterhof befindet sich das Gebäude der Prälatur aus der 2. Hälfte des 16. Jh., umgebaut von 1680—99 nach dem Projekt von J. B. Mathey und M. A. Canevallo. Die Deckenfresken wurden vom Prämonstratenser S. Nosecký gemalt. Das ursprünglich romanische Konventgebäude (nach 1142) wurde in der Barockzeit ebenso umgebaut. Die angeschlossene Treppe führt in das Klostergebäude, das von 1782—84 von I. P. Palliardi erbaut wurde. Der Stolz des Hauses sind der Philosophie- und Theologiesaal mit reichem Schmuck und einmaligen historischen Sammlungen. Zum Kloster gehört ebenso ein schöner Garten unter dem Südflügel. Das Kloster wurde 1991 dem Prämonstratenserorden zurückgegeben, der hier seine unterbrochenen Aktivitäten aufs neue aufnimmt.

DIE KIRCHE DER MARIÄHIMMELFAHRT 52 — welche die Baureste einer im Jahre 1182 gebauten und mehrmals baulich veränderten romanischen Rotunde einschließt, zeigt heute den Stand nach dem in den Jahren 1745—52 von A. Lurago durchgeführten Umbau. Das Kircheninnere läßt die ursprüngliche romanische dreischiffige Baudisposition erkennen, allerdings in der Barockumgestaltung. Es ist reichlich mit Stuckarbeiten K. A. Palliardis verziert und mit Gemälden von J. Kramolín, I. Raab, V. Neunherz, F. X. Palko, J. K. Liška und M. Willmann über Motive der marianischen Legende bzw. der Lobpreisung des Hl. Norbert geschmückt. Der Statuenschmuck ist überwiegend ein Werk von J. A. Quittainer. An den Deckengemälden in den Kapellen beteiligte sich der Strahover Klosterbruder und Maler S. Nosecký. In der Kapelle der Hl. Ursula befinden sich auf dem Altar Reliquien des Hl. Norbert, des Stifters des Prämonstratenserordens. Zu den kulturellen Besonderheiten gehört die Barockorgel in der Kirche, auf der W. A. Mozart spielte.

DER THEOLOGIESAAL 53 — wurde in der Jahren 1671—1679 vom Architekten G. D. Orsi errichtet. Er diente ursprünglich als Bücherei. Von da an enthalten seine Barockschränke theologische Literatur, unter der man auch die verbotenen Bücher, die sog. „libri prohibiti", finden kann. In den Vitrinen werden wertvolle illustrierte Handschriften aufbewahrt, von denen die älteste das Strahover Evangeliar aus dem 9. Jahrhundert ist. Im Saal, der mit Stukkaturen und Wandmalereien zum Thema Bibliothekswesen des Malers S. Nosecký verziert wurde, sind astrologische Globen aus dem 17. Jahrhundert aufgestellt, welche die wissenschaftlichen Interessen der Ordensmitglieder belegen.

DER PHILOSOPHIESAAL 54 — in den Jahren 1782—84 wurde nach dem Entwurf von I. J. Palliardi im Kloster ein neues Gebäude errichtet, in dem die reichhaltige Klosterbücherei Unterbringung fand. Die gewölbte Decke der Bibliothek schmückte der führende Vertreter des Wiener Rokokos, der Maler A. F. Maulbertsch im Jahre 1794 mit einer Wandmalerei genannt „Die Geschichte der Menschheit" aus. Die kostbaren Bücherschränke aus Nußholz, ein Werk des Schreiners und Schnitzers Johann Lachhoven, wurden nach Aufhebung des Prämonstratenserklosters in südmährischen Ort Louka bei Znaim nach Strahov überführt. In der Vitrine ist Marmorbüste des Kaisers Franz I. von F. X. Lederer aufbewahrt. In den Schränken sind Büchergaben von Napoleons Gemahlin Marie-Louise erhalten geblieben.

DAS LUSTSCHLOSS HVĚZDA (STERN) AM WEISSEN BERG 55 — es wurde am südöstlichen Ende des gleichnamigen Wildgartens in Horní Liboc erbaut, welcher vom 10. Jahrhundert dem Kloster Břevnov gehörte. Der Wildgarten wurde von Ferdinand I. im Jahre 1534 angelegt und war zum Schauplatz königlichen Vergnügens und Wettbewerbe im Schießen geworden.

Das Schloß, dessen ungewöhnlicher Grundriß ein sechszackiger Stern bildet (Durchmesser 40 m), entwarf der gebildete kaiserliche Sohn, des Erherzog Ferdinand von Tirol, der kaiserliche Statthalter Böhmens. Den Ausbau von 1555—65 führten die Baumeister des Prager Königshofes G. M. Aostalis und G. Lucchese unter der Aufsicht von H. Tirol, später von B. Wohlmut durch. Die reiche und zarte Verzierung mit Motiven aus der griechischen Mythologie, sowie der griechische und römischer Geschichte stammt von A. del Pambio, G. Campione und weiteren italienischen Meistern. In den Jahren 1556—63 wurden so zum erstenmal in Böhmen Stukkaturen von einzigartigem Niveau zur Geltung gebracht.

Die Außerordentlichkeit des ganzen Baus und dessen Verzierung, war schon durch die Absicht des Bauleiters bedingt, seine heimliche Gemahlin Philipine Welser hierher zu bringen, da sie sich nicht auf der Burg aufhalten durfte.

Bevor es um die Mitte des 17. Jh. zur weiteren Ausgestaltung des Inneren mit Gemälden kam, wurde der Wildgarten Hvězda Zeuge bewegter Ereignisse in der Nationalgeschichte. Im Jahre 1620 spielte sich hier die Schlacht der Armee der böhmischen und mährischen Stände gegen die katholische Liga und das kaiserliche Heer ab, die mit der blutigen Niederlage der Stände endete.

Der Wildgarten und das Lustschloß verwahrlosten von dieser Schlacht an, vor allem nachdem hier Heere, die gegen Prag zu Felde zogen, mehrmals ihre Lager aufgeschlagen hatten.

Unter Josef II. diente das Schloß als Pulverlager. Zu baulichen Veränderungen kam es nach dem Jahre 1918 und in den Jahren 1949—51, als das Objekt nach Entwürfen von P. Janák zu Museumzwecken umgebaut wurde. Heute beherbergt das Schloß das Museum des Schriftstellers A. Jirásek (1851—1930). Im Jahre 1964 wurde hier auch das Museum des tschechischen Malers M. Aleš (1852—1913) eröffnet.

DAS KLOSTER BŘEVNOV MIT DER KIRCHE DER HEILIGEN MARGARETE 56, 57 — stellt einen einzigartigen Baukomplex aus den Jahren 1708—45 dar, das auf Kosten der Äbte O. Zinke und B. Loeble von K. Dienzenhofer und seinem Sohn K. I. Dienzenhofer erbaut wurde. Der Bau wurde an Stelle eines von den Hussiten zerstörten Benediktinerklosters errichtet, welches der Prager Bischof Vojtěch (Adalbert) und der Fürst Soběslav II. im Jahre 993 stifteten. Es war das erste Männerkloster in Böhmen.

Die Klosterkirche stellt ein Schmuckstück der böhmischen Baukunst dar. Die Innengestaltung ist ebenfalls wertvoll. An der Deckenmalerei arbeitete J. J. Steinfels in den Jahre 1719—21 und an der wirkungsvollen illusionistischen Wandbemalung J. Hager im Jahr 1761. Eine Grabplatte für den Benediktiner Eremiten Vintíř wurde in sie eingebaut. Es ist die Arbeit eines venezianischen Künstlers aus dem 14 Jh. Unter vielen künstlerischen Werken ragen die Bilder von P. Brandl und die Statuen von M. J. Jäckl und R. Prachner hervor. Vor dem Kirchenchor wurde die wertvollste präromanische Sehenswürdigkeit entdeckt: eine Krypta aus der ersten Hälfte des 11. Jahrhunderts.

Das Gebäude des Konvents und der Prälatur, das bis zu der kürzlichen Rückgabe des Objektes an den Benediktinerorden als Depositar des zentralen Staatsarchives diente, zeigt eine reichliche Freskenverzierung. Sehenswert ist der sogenannte Theresianische Saal, der mit Malereien des bayrischen Künstlers K. D. Asam aus dem Jahr 1727 geschmückt ist.

Hinter dem Kloster befindet sich ein barocker Garten mit dem Lustschloß des Abtes Vojtěška, zu dem eine Kapelle und ein Brunnen gehören. Erbaut wurde es von K. I. Dienzenhofer, die Salla Terrena verzierte im 18. Jahrhundert der Bildhauer R. Prachner.

DER NÄCHTLICHE BLICK VON DER NERUDAGASSE 63 — Von der bis zur Burg steigenden Gasse kann man den kulturell interessantesten Teil Prags bewundern. Die Straße ist voll von Häusern mit Barockfassaden, die von reizenden Hauszeichen geschmückt werden. Sie trägt den Namen des Dichters und Journalisten J. Neruda, der hier in den Häusern ‚Zu den drei schwarzen Adlern' und ‚Zu den zwei Sonnen' wohnte.

DAS PALAIS WALLENSTEIN 66—70, 72—74 — unter dem Berghang des Hradschins auf ungewöhnlich großer Fläche erbaut (30306 m^2) stellt dieses Palais das erste monumentale Bauwerk des Frühbarocks in Böhmen dar. Diese einmalige Residenz von Albrecht von Wallenstein (Valdštejn) entsprach den Ambitionen und dem Ehrgeiz des kaiserlichen Generalissimus und berühmten Heerführers. Als jedoch Wallenstein, eine der umstrittensten Gestalten zur Zeit des Dreißigjährigen Krieges, es wagte, sogar nach der böhmischen Krone zu trachten, ließ ihn Ferdinand II. des Hochverrats beschuldigen und 1634 in Eger ermorden.

Den Bau aus den Jahren 1624—30 mit vier Mehrzweckhöfen entwarfen A. Spezza aus der Lombardei, B. Sebregondi und nach 1626 der Spezialist im Festungsbau G. Pieroni. Am Bau beteiligten sich italienische und einheimische Handwerker. In der Stirnwand des Palais blieb das Bild der Madonna aus Val D'Urazzo als Teil des eingebauten Palais Trčka erhalten. Zwei Stockwerke im Nordflügel des Palais werden vom repräsentativen Rittersaal mit der Marmorwandbekleidung dominiert, die man 1853 hierher aus dem Palais Czernin (Černín) brachte. Das Deckenfresko, das Wallenstein als Kriegsgott Mars darstellt, stammt vom Italiener B. del Bianco. An den Saal grenzen drei Räume, der sog. Ledersall mit dem Deckengemälde der Pallas Athena von P. Maixner (1866), der Spiegelsaal und das angebliche Arbeitszimmer Wallensteins.

Das Palais ist umgeben von einem prachtvollen Garten mit Teich, Fontänen, einer Voliere für seltenes Vogelvolk, Tropfsteinhöhlen und -grotten mit der festlichen Loggia mit Stuckverzierungen italienischer Meister und Gemälden von B. del Bianco über Themen aus Vergils Aeneis (Trojakrieg). Der ursprüngliche Statuenschmuck von A. de Vries, einem herausragenden Meister der Rudolfzeit, wurde 1648 von Schweden geraubt und in den Gärten des Schlosses Drootningholm aufgestellt. Die heute zu besichtigenden Statuen sind Kopien.

Der weitläufige Palast ist heute Sitz des Kulturministeriums.

DAS PALAIS KOLOWRATT UND DAS PALAIS PALFFY 71 — die gegenüber dem Palais Wallenstein in der Valdštejnská Straße liegen, sind durch prachtvolle, terassenartige Rokokogärten verbunden, die bis zum Hradschinhang hinaufsteigen. Das Palais Kolowratt, heute ein Teil des Kulturministeriums, war bereits 1918—38 Sitz der Regierung der Tschechoslowakischen Republik. Aus diesem Grunde spielten sich hier die Verhandlungen ab, die mit dem Münchner Abkommen von 1938 und der Entstehung des Protektorats Böhmen und Mähren zusammenhingen. Das Palais entstand nach 1784 nach einem Entwurf von N. Palliardi auf Wunsch der Familie Czernin (Černín). Im 19. Jh., bevor das Palais von der Familie Kolowratt gekauft wurde, residierte hier der österreichische General A. Windischgrätz.

Das Nachbarpalais gehörte 1660 bis 1689 der dunklen Gestalt des Chodenunterdrückers V. M. Laminger, der schließlich Legende geworden ist. Der neue Besitzer J. J. von Waldstein ließ das Palais 1712 erweitern und umbauen. Nach dieser Familie kam die Familie Fürstenberg, von denen Karl Egon 1775 in diesem Palais die erste Tagung der Gelehrten Gesellschaft der Wissenschaften vorbereitete. Im 19. Jh wurde noch einmal in Neurokokostil umgebaut und das Palais trug bis 1945 den Namen Palffy nach seinen letzten Besitzern.

DIE LUFTAUFNAHME DER RESIDENZ DES REGIERUNGSPRÄSIDIUMS UND DER KRAMÁŘ-VILLA 75 — zeigt die abschließende Partie der 1859—60 gestalteten Letná-Parkanlage, in der 1908—11 eine Staatsvilla im Pseudobarockstil nach Entwurf von B. Ohmann für den bedeutenden tschechischen Politiker und den ersten Ministerpäsidenten Dr. K. Kramář erbaut wurde. Daneben befindet sich der umfangreiche Baukomplex der ehemaligen Straka-Akademie. In diesem Bau mit der charakteristischen Kuppel aus der Zeit des Umbaus von 1893—96 nach dem Entwurf von V. Roštapil hatte die Lehranstalt für adelige Söhne ihren Sitz, die 1710 vom Grafen Straka gestiftet wurde. Heute ist das Gebäude Sitz des Amtes des Regierungspräsidiums.

DIE KARLSBRÜCKE 76, 77, 79,—81, 87—93, 100, 101 — die älteste Brücke Prags verbindet die Altstadt mit der Kleinseite. Sie wurde als Ersatz für die im Jahre 1342 eingestürzte einzige Brücke in Prag — die Judithbrücke aus dem Jahre 1165 — errichtet. Während der Jahrhunderte einfach Prager Brücke oder Steinerne Brücke genannt, wurde sie 1870 zu Ehren des kaiserlichen Bauherrn in Karlsbrücke umgetauft. Das auf 14 mächtigen Pfeilern ruhende, vom damals 24jährigen Baumeister P. Parler entworfene Bauwerk ist fast 520 m Lang, 10 m breit und leicht gekrümmt. Der Bau begann im Jahre 1357, wurde jedoch erst zu Beginn des 15. Jahrhunderts beendet. Über die Brücke führt der Königsweg, der Schauplatz bewegter historischer Ereignisse. Als die Schweden im Jahre 1648 über die Brücke zogen und Prag angriffen, wurde ein großer Teil der Ausschmückung beschädigt.

Im Jahre 1723 wurde Ölbeleuchtung auf der Brücke installiert, später, im Jahre 1866, wurde diese durch Gasbeleuchtung ersetzt.

Nicht nur die beiden Brückentürme zieren die Brücke, sondern vor allem 33 Statuen und Statuengruppen, mit denen nach und nach die Geländer besetzt wurden. Die kostbaren Werke unterliegen ungünstigen Umwelteinflüssen; deshalb wurden viele von ihnen durch Kopien ersetzt und die Originale im Lapidarium des Nationalmuseums oder des Museums der Hauptstadt Prag untergebracht. Die Skulpturen sind Beweise der ausgezeichneten bildhaurischen Leistungen bedeutender Vertreter der böhmischen Kultur aus den Jahren 1683—1714: M. B. Braun, J. Brokoff, F. M. Brokoff, M. V. Jäckel, J. B. Kohl oder J. O. Mauer.

Bei der Karlsbrücke steht auch die an Vorrechte der Altstädter Brücken erinnernde *Bruncvík*-Statue von L. Šimek aus dem Jahr 1884.

DAS HANAUER PAVILLON 78 — wurde ursprünglich als ein aus den Gießereien des Fürsten von Hanau stammendes Ausstellungsstück aus Gußeisen nach einem Projekt von Heiser und Hercík für die Jubiläumslandesausstellung im Jahre 1891 geschaffen. Im Jahre 1898 wurde es der Prager Gemeinde geschenkt und auf der Letná zusammenmontiert. Heute befindet sich in diesem wunderschön gelegenen Gußeisenbau im Stile des Neubarocks ein luxuriöses Restaurant.

DIE STATUENGRUPPE DES KALVARIENBERGES VON DER KARLSBRÜCKE (DETAIL) 82 — befindet sich an der Stelle, wo seit dem 14. Jahrhundert ein gotisches Kreuz gestanden hat. Im Jahre 1657 wurde hierher ein bronzener vergoldeter Korpus von N. Brohn gebracht, der in Dresden gegossen wurde.

Aus der hebräischen Aufschrift um das Kreuz herum ergibt sich, das es vom Strafgeld eines Juden angefertigt vurde, der das Kreuz auslachte. Die Statuen der Jungfrau Maria und des heiligen Evangelisten Johannes sind Werke des Bildhauers E. Max aus dem Jahr 1861.

DIE KLEINSEITE 83, 84 — dieses Prager Viertel kann man größtenteils vom Kleinseitner Turm überblicken. Mit dem Ausbau des Viertels begann man nach dem Jahr 1411, ursprünglich hieß es Neustadt, danach sogar Kleine Prager Stadt. Zur Gründung kam es schon im Jahre 1257 aufgrund einer Initiative Otokars II. Unter Karl IV. erlebte die an der Prager Burg liegenden Kleinseite eine Blütezeit, sie wurde erweitert und befestigt. Die Nähe der Burg hatte aber auch negative politische Konsequenzen. Während des Aufstandes im Jahre 1419 war in den Kämpfen der Prager mit dem königlichen Heer fast die ganze Kleinseite abgebrannt. Durch einen Brand aus dem Jahre 1541, der auch einen Teil der Burg beschädigte, wurde die zunehmende Entwicklung des Viertels erneut gebremst. Die höchste Blüte erlebte es im Barockzeitalter, was die Vielfalt an Sehenswürdigkeiten belegt. Es entstanden Prunkpaläste (Liechtenstein, Fürstenberg, Nostitz, Münchner, Buquoy und andere), anmutige Plätze, friedliche Gärten und eindrucksvolle Kirchen (z. B. die St. Niklauskirche). Trotz allem liegt der ganze Zauber der Kleinseite nicht nur in ihren Bauten. Wichtig ist die malerische Konstellation der Gebäude im Viertel mit seinen zahlreichen reizenden Schlupfwinkeln. Hierher gehören romantische Plätze und Parkanlagen am Moldauufer, Terassengärten unter den Hängen des Hradschins. Zum Glück blieb der ganze Reiz dieser Gegend von dem Einfluß neuzeitlicher Bauunternehmer unberührt.

DIE KREUZHERRNKIRCHE MIT DEM DENKMAL KARLS IV. 86, 94, 97 — befindet sich auf einem städtebaulich eindrucksvoll gestalteten Platz, der von der Jesuitenkirche St. Salvator und dem Palais Colloredo-Mansfeld umgeben ist. Der Platz ist sehr belebt, da von ihm aus der Weg zur Karlsbrücke führt. Die Kirche wurde auf gotischer Baugrundlage von D. Canevall in den Jahren 1679—89 errichtet. Die Pläne schuf der Burgunder Architekt J. B. Mathey für die Kreuzherrn mit dem roten Stern. Dieser einzige böhmische kirchliche Orden, um die Mitte des 13. Jahrhunderts gegründet, hatte im benachbarten Kloster seinen Sitz. Das Fresko „Das Jüngste Gericht" von V. V. Reiner ziert die prächtige Kuppel der Kirche. Gemälde von J. K. Liška, M. Willmann und M. Pirner prägen das Interieur wie auch Bildhauerwerke von M. J. Jäckl und Stuckfiguren von Heiligen, die von den Dresdnern Bildhauern J. und K. Süssner stammen. Das Portal der Kirche wird von Statuen R. Prachners aus dem Jahre 1758 und weiterer tschechischer Künstler geziert. An der Ecke des Baus findet man die sog. Winzersäule aus dem Jahre 1846, die sich neben der Statue des Hl. Wenzel befindet, geschaffen von J. Bendl im Jahre 1676.

Auf dem einzigartigen Platz, den die Gebruder Klein von Wiesenberg zu Ende bauten, wurde im Jahr 1849 auf Kosten der Prager Universität ein neogotisches Denkmal des Kaisers Karl IV. mit den Allegorien von vier Fakultäten errichtet. Es wurde in der Werkstatt des Nürnberger Metallgießers D. J. Burgschmidt nach einem Modell des Dresdner Bildhauers A. Hähnel gegossen.

DER ALTSTÄDTER BRÜCKENTURM 95, 96 — wurde zusammen mit der Brücke gebaut und um des Jahr 1391 vollendet. Das wohlausgeglichene Kunstwerk der Hochgotik ging aus der Bau- und Bildhauerhütte Peter Parlers hervor. Ein Teil der Brücke diente auch als Bestandteil der Befestigungsanlage der Altstadt. Im Jahre 1380 entstand die bildhauerische Ausschmückung mit den realistisch aufgefaßten Figuren Karls IV. und Wenzels IV., die zu den kostbarsten Denkwürdigkeiten der böhmischen gotischen Bildhauerkunst gehören. Im Jahre 1978 wurden die Skulpturen durch Kopien etsetzt; die Originale befinden sich in der Nationalgalerie. Nach dem Ständeaufstand im Jahre 1621 wurden hier die Köpfe von zwölf hingerichteten Herren für 10 Jahre zur Schau gestellt. Die bildhauerische Ausschmückung an der Westseite erlitt im Jahre 1648 Schaden, als Prag von den Schweden erobert wurde. In den Jahren 1874—1878 wurde das Bauwerk grundlegend erneuert und die Bedachung ihrer Vollendung zugeführt.

LADISLAV ŠALOUN (1870—1946), JAN-HUS-DENKMAL 102 — Es wurde am 6. 7. 1915 zum 500. Todestag des wegen Ketzerei in Konstanz verbrannten tschechischen Predigers und Reformators eingeweiht. Die riesigen Ausmaße des an Figuren reichen Stein- und Bronzendenkmals, angefertigt von einem führenden Vertreter des tschechischen Jugendstils, wurden zum Gegenstand zahlreicher Diskussionen. Diese betrafen die Komposition und Aufstellung des Werkes im historischen Kern Prags, auf dem Altstädter Ring vor dem Palais Golz-Kinský.

DER ALTSTÄDTER RING 103, 104, 121, 122, 125, 127, 129 — bekam seinen Namen im Jahr 1895 (er stammt aber aus dem 14. Jh. und wurde früher als Marktplatz, Großer Marktplatz, Ring, Großer Ring bekannt).

Neben der Prager Burg gehört der Altstädter Ring zu den Orten in Prag, die Zeugen bewegter historischer Ereignisse gewesen sind. Schon um die Wende vom 11. zum 12. Jh. formte sich der Platz zu seiner heutigen Größe (ungefähr 9000 m^2), als hier eine Marktkreuzung entstand. Zu ihr gehörte auch ein Zollhaus, das heutige Ungelt, wo die nach Böhmen gebrachte Ware ausgeladen wurde.

Der Ring mit dem Rathaus wurde zum traditionellen Versammlungsort bei politischen und revolutionären Ereignissen sowie deren Repressionen oder bei repräsentativen Anlässen. Im Jahre 1422 wurde im Rathaushof der radikale hussitische Prediger Jan Želivský hingerichtet.

Im Jahre 1437 folgte ihm auf dem Ring der letzte Hussitenhauptmann Jan Roháč z Dubé in den Tod.

Die ins Pflastermosaik eingefügten Kreuze, die sich vor dem Ostflügel des Rathauses befinden, erinnern an die Enthauptung von 27 böhmischen Herren und Bürgern der Stadt, die am Ständeaufstand im Jahre 1620—21 beteiligt waren. Im Rathaussaal wurde im Jahre 1548 Georg von Poděbrady zum böhmischen König gewählt.

Im Jahre 1918 fand hier eine wichtige Demonstration für die Unabhängigkeit einer selbstständigen Republik statt. Eine Demonstration ganz anderer Art inszenierten hier im Februar 1948 die kommunistischen Putschisten.

Auf dem repräsentativen Ring befinden sich Häuser aus den verschiedensten Epochen: Gotik, Barock, das Palais Golz-Kinský im Rokokostil, aber auch Bauten der Neuzeit, wie z. B. der barokisierende Bau der ehemaligen Prager Stadtversicherung. Er stammt vom Architekten O. Polívka und dient heute als Ministerium für Handel und Fremdenverkehr. Geschmückt wird es von Skulpturen der Bildhauer L. Šaloun, F. Procházka und B. Schnirch.

Der Altstädter Ring und der durch ihn führende Königsweg gehören zu den von den Touristen am meisten aufgesuchten Sehenswürdigkeiten.

DAS HAUS ZUR MINUTE 106 — das an das altstädtische Rathausgebäude anliegt, hat einen gotischen Kern aus dem 15. Jh. Der Renaissanceumbau erfolgte im Jahr 1564. In den Jahren nach 1603 und 1610 wurde die Stirnwand mit Sgrafittos nach Gravierungen von M. Raimondi und H. S. Beham ausgeschmückt. Von einer Ecknische der ehemaligen Apotheke überblickt ein Steinlöwe aus dem 18. Jh. den Platz. Die Sgrafittos wurden erst im Jahre 1905 wiederentdeckt und seit dem mehrmals wiederaufgefrischt. Zur Zeit befinden sich im Gebäude die Amtsräume des Stadtmagistrats.

DIE ALTSTÄDTER ASTRONOMISCHE UHR 108—113 — Die berühmte Aposteluhr wurde im Jahre 1410 von dem Uhrmacher Mikuláš von Kadaň konstruiert und im Jahre 1490 von Meister Hanuš, genannt von Růže zusammen mit einem erheblichen Teil des Rathauses renoviert.

In den Jahren 1553—60 wurde das Uhrenwerk vervollkomnet und 1659 kamen noch Plastiken hinzu. Die im Jahre 1865 von dem großen tschechischen Maler Josef Mánes (1820—71) geschaffene schöne Tafel mit dem Kalendarium wurde 1882 durch eine Kopie von B. Čìla ersetzt. Das Original der Kalenderscheibe befindet sich schon seit 1882 in der Sammlung des Nationalmuseums von Prag. Im Verlaufe des Prager Aufstandes 1945 erlitt die Uhr durch ein Feuer schweren Schaden. Sie wurde von dem Bildhauer V. Sucharda (1884—1972) repariert, der auch neue Plastiken für sie schuf.

Die Astronomische Uhr gehört zu den größten Touristenattraktionen der Altstadt: Zu jeder vollen Stunde wird ein Mechanismus von Figuren in Bewegung gesetzt, die allegorische, historische und religiöse Beziehungen ausdrücken.

DIE ST. NIKLASKIRCHE IN DER ALTSTADT 124 an der Nordwestecke des Altstädter Rings — wurde am Benediktinerkloster in den Jahren 1732—35 nach einem Entwurf von K. I. Dienzenhofer erbaut.

DAS PALAIS GOLZ-KINSKÝ UND DAS HAUS ZUR GLOKKE 126 — auf dem Altstädter Ring sind die schönsten Bauwerke vor der Teynkirche. Während der Restaurierungsarbeiten, nachdem man den Barockputz am Haus Zur Glocke abgetragen hatte, wurde eine einmalig erhalten gebliebene gotische Stirnwand aus der Zeit um 1350 mit dekorativem Steinmetzschmuck entdeckt. Während der Nachforschungen im Hausinneren wurde eine Kapelle mit gotischen Wandmalereien aus der gleichen Zeit entdeckt. In den Interieurs des rekonstruierten Hauses veranstaltet die Galerie der Hauptstadt Prag Ausstellungen der gegenwärtigen Kunst.

Das benachbarte Bauwerk, das Rokokopalais Golz-Kinský, das bereits 1635 Besitztum des Fürsten Kinský war, erhielt seine graziöse und wirkungsvolle Gestalt durch den Umbau von 1755—65 von A. Lurago nach einem Bauplan K. I. Dienzenhofers.

Heute befindet sich hier die Grafische Sammlung der Nationalgalerie.

DAS STORCH-HAUS 128 in der effektvollen Häuserreihe auf der Ostseite des Altstädter Rings wurde 1897 nach einem Entwurf von B. Ohmann und R. Krieghammer erbaut. Das ehemalige Verlagshaus ŠTORCH, im Stil der Neurenaissance gestaltet, fesselt mit figuralen Gemälden L. Nováks nach Kartonsvorlagen von M. Aleš, die die Gestalten des Hl. Wenzel und der Drei Könige darstellen. Die Gemälde, die im Mai 1945 beschädigt wurden, erneuerte der Maler F. Sembtner.

DER BLICK VOM TURM DER TEYNKIRCHE 130—131 zeigt die Aussicht aus der 80 m Höhe der erst Anfang des 16. Jh. fertiggebauten Türme dieses herausragenden gotischen dreischiffigen Kirchenbaus, der 1365 begonnen wurde.

DAS KAROLINUM 134 steht in der Eisengasse (Železná), einer weiteren historischen Hauptachse, die vom Altstädter Ring ausführt. Ursprünglich war es eines der Internate der am 7. April 1348 von Karl IV. gegründeten Karlsuniversität. Sie war die erste in Mitteleuropa und sollte die damalige Bildung auf das höchste Niveau bringen. Der Grundbau des ganzen Komplexes war das Rothlev-Haus, das Wenzel IV. erwarb und im Jahre 1383 dem Studentenwohnheim der Karlsuniversität schenkte, das bis zu der Zeit bei der St. Niklauskirche untergebracht war. Der barocke Umbau wurde im Jahre 1718 von F. M. Kaňka beendet. Im Portal zur Eisengasse befindet sich ein Barockfenster aus dem Jahr 1687 und verglaste Arkaden mit gotischem Rippengewölbe. Der Anbau in Richtung Ständetheater aus dem Jahre 1385 hat eine erhalten gebliebene, wertvolle Erkerkapelle mit reichem Außenschmuck. Ihre Erneuerung vollführte im Jahre 1881 J. Mocker; zu weiteren Umbauten kam es in den Jahren 1946—75 nach dem Entwurf von J. Fragner und unter Beteiligung der Bildhauer K. Lidický, J. Landa und K. Pokorný.

Den Kern des Gebäudes bildet die große Aula, errichtet schon nach dem Jahre 1383. An diese wurde die Erkerkapelle angebaut, in deren Vordergrund eine Tapisserie von M. Teinitzer aus dem Jahr 1941 aufgehängt wurde. Die Künstlerin ging vom Motiv des Universitätssiegels aus, das V. Sychra angefertigt hat. Auf ihm ist Karl IV. kniend vor dem Heiligen Wenzel dargestellt.

DAS STÄNDETHEATER 135 — das mächtige neuklassizistische Gebäude wurde in den Jahren 1781—83 vom Architekten A. Haffenecker erbaut. Die Kosten trug Graf Nostitz-Rieneck, daher wurde es auch Nostitztheater genannt. In den Jahren 1859, 1881 und 1892 nahm man Verbesserungen und Umbauten des Objektes vor, dessen umfangreiche Generalerneuerung im Jahre 1991 abgeschlossen wurde. Ein Bestandteil der Renovierung war der betriebstechnische Anschluß an das gegenüberliegende Palais Kolowratt.

Im Theater wurde ursprünglich nur Deutsch und Italienisch gespielt. Im Jahre 1787 fand hier die Uraufführung von Mozarts Don Giovanni statt. In den Jahren 1813—16 wirkte hier C. M. von Weber als Opernchef und Komponist. Am 21. Dezember 1837 bei der Uraufführung der Fidlovačka (Frühlingsfest) erklang zum erstenmale das Lied „Kde domov můj?" (Wo ist meine Heimat), das 1918 zur Staatshymne wurde, Die Musik zum Text komponierte F. Škroup.

DAS NATIONALMUSEUM 136, 138, 139, 141, 142 An der Stelle, wo bis zum 19. Jahrhundert das Pferdetor die Neustadt begrenzte, wurde 1885—1919 das über 100 Meter lange Gebäude des Nationalmuseums nach dem Entwurf von Prof. J. Schulz errichtet. Das Museum wurde im Jahre 1818 von patriotischen Adeligen, die kulturelle und wissenschaftliche Ziele verfolgten, gegründet.

Der Neurenaissancebau hat vier Flügel und zwei Höfe; ihm ist eine Rampe mit der bekannten Fontäne vorgelagert, über der sich die von A. Wagner in den Jahren 1891—1914 geschaffenen allegorischen Plastiken, Böhmen, Mähren und Schlesien und die der Flüsse Elbe und Moldau befinden. Die Ausschmückung des Gebäudes stellt eine Galerie tschechischer Bildhauerkunst des 19. Jahrhunderts dar, die in Konkurrenz stehen zum Münchener Bildhauer L. Schwanthaler. Seine

Bronzestatuen „Libuša, Přemysl, Wenzel und Otakar II“ waren ursprünglich für Kollektion von 24 Plastiken für Český Slavín in Tupadla bei Liběchov bestellt, fanden jedoch ihren Platz im Säulenfoyer. An das Foyer schließt der repräsentative Treppenaufgang an, der fast den ganzen Mittelflügel des Gebäudes einnimmt. Er ist mit 32 Medaillons böhmischer Könige und 16 Büsten von Männern, die sich am Bau verdient gemacht haben, geschmückt, einem Werk von A. Popp und B. Schnirch aus den Jahren 1897—99.

Zum Tempel der tschechischen nationalen Sehnsucht und zum Ausdruck eines neuen Selbstbewußtseins wurde das Pantheon mit der prächtigen Kuppel. Die 48 Plastiken neben ihr stammen von B. Schnirch und stellen große Persönlichkeiten der tschechischen Nation dar. Die historisch orientierten Gemälde schufen V. Brožík und F. Ženíšek, führende Maler der sog. Generation des Nationaltheaters; die allegorischen Dekorationen, welche die Kuppel ausfüllen, sind das Werk von V. Hynais, eines an der französischen Maler orientierten Maler dieser Generation.

Im Museumsbegäude befinden sich historische und naturwissenschaftliche Abteilungen und eine wertvolle Bibliothek, die ungefähr eine Million Bände umfaßt, unter denen auch Unikate mittelalterlicher Handschriften sind.

JOSEF VÁCLAV MYSLBEK (1848—1922). DAS REITERSTANDBILD DES HEILIGEN WENZEL — des Patrons Böhmens, ist auch zum Symbol der nationalen Unabhängigkeit und ihres Schutzes geworden. Das Denkmal wurde in den Jahren 1912—13 im oberen Teil des Wenzelsplatzes auf dem mit Ornamenten geschmückten Sockel von A. Dryák errichtet. Mit der Themenausarbeitung begann Myslbek schon im Jahre 1887, das Gipsmodell des Werkes war schon im Jahre 1094 fertig. An den Ecken des Sockels stehen Wache: Prokop, Adalbert, Ludmila und Agnes, vier weitere Landespatronen. Sie bilden zusammen mit dem Reiterstandbild eine edle Einheit des im Neurenaissancestil ausgeführten Werkes. Im Jahre 1924 wurde die letzte von Myslbek nicht mehr vollendete Statue des heiligen Adalbert aufgestellt. Sie war in der Werkstatt von B. Mašek gegossen worden. Das dem klassizistischen Stil verwandte Werk mit verinnerlichten Gesichtsausdrücken der einzelnen Gestalten verrät die Orientierung des Künstlers auf die französische Kunst hin.

DER JUNGMANNPLATZ 140 — auf dessen kleiner Fläche mit städtebaulichem Feingefühl die Statue des Schriftstellers und führenden Vertreters der tschechischen Aufklärung J. Jungmann aufgestellt wurde, befindet sich in unmittelbarer Nähe des Wenzelsplatzes. Das bildhauerische Werk L. Šimeks aus dem Jahr 1872, angefertigt nach der Skizze von V. Levý, wurde im Jahre 1878 auf den Marmorsockel von A. Barvitius gesetzt.

AM GRABEN (NA PŘÍKOPĚ) 144 — ein Straßenzug am unteren Ende des Wenzelsplatzes, der die Alt- von der Neustadt trennt. Er entstand Ende des 18. Jh. durch Aufschüttung des Wallgrabens — heute ist er Prags lebhafteste Fußgängerzone. In der neuzeitlichen Bebauung fesselt der konstruktivistische Bau des Kinderhauses (Dětský dům) aus dem Jahre 1928 den Blick. Auf der rechten Seite befindet sich das älteste Kaufhaus Prags, erbaut vom berühmten Wiener Architekten Th. Hansen von 1869—71. Den feinen Geschmack der Aristokratie in der Rokokozeit belegt das Palais Sylva-Taroucca (vormals Palais Piccolomini), das von 1743—51 von K. I. Dienzenhofer und A. Lurago erbaut wurde. Den schüchternen Empirebau der Kirche des Hl. Kreuzes aus den Jahren 1816—24 entwarf J. Fischer. Das Slawische Haus (Slovanský dům), ursprünglich das Barockpalais Příchovský, erhielt 1798 seine jetzige Gestalt. Vor einer ganzen Reihe von Bankgebäuden, die sich Am Graben befinden, ist die Investitionsbank am dekorativsten. Das im Geiste der Neorenaissance von O. Polívka in den Jahren 1894—96 erbaute Gebäude ist mit Mosaiken von M. Aleš und mit Reliefs C. Kloučeks und S. Suchardas verziert.

DER WENZELSPLATZ (VÁCLAVSKÉ NÁMĚSTÍ) 145 — ursprünglich Pferdemarkt genannt pflegte der Hauptmarkt der Neustadt zu sein. In seiner Mitte stand eine Statue des Hl. Wenzels von J. J. Bendl aus dem Jahre 1680, die 1879 auf den Vyšehrad gebracht wurde. Der Platz in der Gesamtlänge von 750 m ist der bedeutendste Geschäftsboulevard mit repräsentativen Hotels. Der obere Teil des Platzes wird von dem dominanten Bau des Nationalmuseums (J. Schulz, 1885—90) abgeschlossen. Eine weitere Dominante des Platzes bildet das Reiterstandbild des Hl. Wenzel, das gemeinsame Werk des Bildhauers J. V. Myslbek, der die Statue schuf, und Alois Dryáks, von dem der Sockel stammt. Am unteren Ende des Platzes stand 1786—89 ein Holztheater, genannt Baude, die erste tschechische Theaterbühne. An beiden Seiten und in der Mitte des Platzes befinden sich Eingänge in die Metro.

DER PULVERTURM 146—148 — zu Ehren des Königs Wladislaw Jagello im Jahre 1475 an Stelle eines befestigten Tores der Altstadt erbaut, ist er ein Werk von M. Rejsek aus Prostějov. In seiner unmittelbaren Nähe befand sich der um das Jahr 1380 vom Wenzel IV. erbaute Königshof. Als nach 1483 die Residenz verlassen wurde, verlor der Ort an Bedeutung. Der eigentliche Turm, der zu den kostbarsten Baudenkmälern der Spätgotik gerechnet wird, diente bereits am Ende des 17. Jh. der Lagerung vom Schießpulver, dem er seinen heutigen Namen verdankt. Während der preußischen Belagerung Prags durch Friedrich den Großen im Jahre 1757 erlitt er erheblichen Schaden. Seine neugotische Gestaltung aus den Jahren 1875—76 stammt vom Architekten J. Mocker der den Umgang und das Dach angebaut hat. Vom Pulverturm aus bietet sich ein schöner Blick auf das älteste Stadtviertel Prags, die Altstadt, sowie auf eine lebhafte Stelle Prags, den Platz der Republik mit dem Gebäude des ehemaligen Hauptzollamtes (um 1810), dem Hiberner-Haus, der Kapuzinerkirche St. Joseph und dem modernen Bankgebäude aus dem Jahre 1938 an.

DAS REPRÄSENTATIONSHAUS DER HAUPTSTADT PRAG 149, 150 — wurde von 1906—1911 nach Plänen von A. Balšánek und O. Polívka an der Stelle erbaut, wo einst der Königshof stand, der im 14. und 15. Jh. den böhmischen Königen u. a. auch Georg von Poděbrady, der von hier die europäischen Herrscher zum Frieden und Einigung aufforderte. Das Repräsentationshaus von heute dient als gesellschaftlicher und kultureller Sammelpunkt der Stadt. Das Veranstaltungsprogramm reicht von Bällen über Ausstellungen bis zu Sinfoniekonzerten; im Hause findet man ein Café, Gaststätten, Weinstuben.

Die Innenräume prahlen mit wertvoller künstlerischer Ausschmükkung von nahmhaften tschechischen Künstlern vom Anfang des 20. Jh.: den Oberbürgermeistersaal schmücken Gemälde von A. Mucha, den Palacký-Saal Gemälde von J. Preisler, den Grégr-Saal Gemälde von F. Ženíšek. Das Parterre und die Gaststätte sind mit Bildern von M. Aleš und J. Obsovský verziert. Werke der Bildhauer J. V. Myslbek, K. Novák und L. Šaloun sind im Smetana-Saal und im Rieger-Salon anzutreffen.

DAS NATIONALTHEATER 151—154 — wurde allein aus den Geldspenden des Volkes in den Jahren 1868—81 nach dem Entwurf des Architekten J. Zítek erbaut. Das wertvolle Bauwerk im Stil der norditalienischen Spätrenaissance fiel jedoch unmittelbar nach seiner Fertigstellung einem Brand zum Opfer. Der Wiederaufbau unter der Leitung von J. Schulz wurde samt der neuen Innendekoration und dem von V. Hynais ausgeführten Vorhang im Jahre 1883 beendet. Die künstlerische Ausschmückung des Nationaltheaters ist ein repräsentatives Beispiel der tschechischen Kunst jener Zeit. An der Außenverzierung der Loggia beteiligte sich J. Tulka. Der Statuenschmuck stammt vor allem von A. Wagner, J. V. Myslbek und B. Schnirch. Das prachtvolle Repräsentationsfoyer des Theaters wird von Lünettenbildern M. Aleš und F. Ženíšeks beherrscht, wobei der letztere ebenso als Autor der Deckengemälde im Zuschauerraum zeichnet. Die Königliche, nun Präsidentenloge, ist mit Gemälden von V. Hynais, V. Brožík und J. Mařák geschmückt. Zahlreiche Büsten im Foyer stellen die großen Persönlichkeiten der tschechischen Kultur dar.

Während der umfangreichen Rekonstruktion des Theaters in den Jahren 1977—83, bei der auch der gesamte technische Betrieb modernisiert wurde, wurde auch die Baulücke zwischen dem Theater und dem Ursulinenkloster geschlossen. Ein neues siebengeschossiges Gebäude und die Neue Bühne (Nová scéna) nach dem Projekt von K. Prager unter der Verwendung von Glasbausteinen nach S. Libenský wurden 1983 fertiggestellt.

Gegenüber dem historischen Nationaltheater befindet sich das ehemalige Palais Lažanský mit dem Café Slavia, das 1861—63 im Stile der französischen Renaissance erbaut wurde. Im ersten Stock des Grafenpalais wohnte bis 1869 der bedeutende tschechische Komponist B. Smetana.

Die Nebenseite des Nationaltheaters führt zum Masarykkai mit einer Reihe repräsentativer Mietshäuser mit historizisierenden Fassaden und dem Ausblick auf die Moldau und die Slawische Insel (Slovanský ostrov), die bis 1925 den Namen Sophiensinsel (Žofín) führte.

DIE SCHÜTZENINSEL 155 — Der Name der Insel ist kein Zufall. Nachdem die Insel im Jahre 1472 der Prager Alt- und Neustadt anheimgefallen war, wurde sie Übungsplatz der Prager Schützen. Im 16. Jh. fanden hier beliebte Schießspiele der Prager statt, die man „Schießen auf den Vogel" nannte. Am Ende des 19. Jh. wurden hier große nationale Versammlungen abgehalten. Im Jahre 1882 fand hier auch der 1. Sokolkongreß statt.

DAS BEDŘICH-SMETANA (1824—1884) — DENKMAL, DAS SMETANA-MUSEUM UND DIE NOVOTNÝ-BRÜCKE 157—158, 179 — Smetanakai ist das älteste Prager Beispiel für die Lösung einer städtebaulichen Aufgabe dieser Art, welche die Firma Lanna in den Jahren 1841—45 nach dem Entwurf von B. Grueber bewältigte. Bauleiter Strobach plante den Ausbau der Zinshäuser großenteils schon im Jahre 1836. An der Stelle der ehemaligen Mühle wurde das neugotische Gebäude des Karlsbads errichtet, in welchem der tschechische Denker und Journalist K. H. Borovský im Jahre 1848 wohnte. Vom Smetanakai biegt gerade vor dem Bad die Novotný-Brücke ab; sie stammt aus dem Jahre 1879 und trägt den Namen eines Nachkommen der alteingesessenen Müllers Familie. Die Gebäude der Altstädter Mühlen haben einen renaissanceartigen Charakter im Stil von F. Ulmann, geschmückt sind sie mit Puttenskulpturen von J. V. Myslbek.

Hier ragt auch der Wasserturm in die Höhe, der im Jahre 1483 errichtet und mehrere Male umgebaut wurde, das letzte Mal nach dem Feuer m Jahre 1885.

Am Ende der Brücke befindet sich das Gebäude des Smetana-Museums, das im Jahre 1883 von Antonín Wiehl im Stil der böhmischen Neurenaissance gebaut wurde (ursprünglich war es als Wasserturm für Prag gedacht).

Sein Portal bedeckt das Sgraffito „Kampf gegen die Schweden auf der Karlsbrücke im Jahre 1648" nach Zeichnungen von Fr. Ženíšek. Die in den Nischen abgebildeten Figuren sollen Persönlichkeiten darstellen, die einen Verdienst an der Rettung Prags vor den Schweden hatten. Geschaffen hat sie der Künstler J. Šubič nach den Entwürfen von M. Aleš und J. Kouba. Die Smetana-Gesellschaft gründete im Jahr 1936 das Museum und trug hier wichtige Dokumente über das Leben und Werk des hervorragenden Komponisten zusammen. Das Smetana-Denkmal vor dem Gebäude entstand im Jahre 1984 unter den Händen von J. Malejovský.

DAS HAUS ZUM GOLDENEN BRUNNEN 159 — Eckgebäude Lilien/Karlsstraße. Die letztere ist eine bedeutende Verkehrsader, die aus der Altstadt zur Karlsbrücke führt. An diesem Renaissancehaus, das später Stilelemente des Barocks erhielt, werden die Reliefe von zwei Beschützern vor der Pest, des Hl. Sebastian und des Hl. Rochus, das Auge des Betrachters fesseln. Beide wurden nach einer Pestepidemie im Jahre 1700 vom Bildhauer J. O. Mayer geschaffen.

HAUSZEICHEN IN DER ALTSTADT 160 — die Nummer 10 in der Teynstrasse bezeichnet ein Haus, das im 17. Jahrhundert die Benennung ‚In der Hölle' trug. Später gehörte das Haus wahrscheinlich dem gräflichen Geschlecht der Kinský, die in ihrem Wappen drei Wolfskrallen oder eher drei Eberzähne haben. Nach dem Umbau des Hauses im 18. Jahrhundert durch den Architekten F. Heger wurde das Hauszeichen auf Drei Strausfedern umgeändert.

Die Bedeutung der Hauszeichen hängt mit der Tradition von Aushängeschildern zusammen. Außer dem Zweck der Identifikation, dienten sie auch repräsentativen Zwecken oder der Orientierung; unverkennbar ist auch ihr symbolischer Sinn. Die reizenden Hauszeichen sagen viel über alte Prager Geschichten aus und das nicht nur in der Altstadt, sondern auch in den malerischen Winkeln der Kleinseite, des Hradschins und in anderen Vierteln.

DER ALTE JÜDISCHE FRIEDHOF, DIE ALTNEUSYNAGOGE 161—164 — das Viertel zeugt von der jüdischen Besiedlung Prags bereits im 10. Jahrhundert. In der jüdischen Gemeinschaft lebten am Anfang des 18. Jahrhunderts ein Drittel der Bevölkerung Prags. Trotzdem kam es zu einer ganzen Reihe von Pogromen. Einschränkungen zwangen die Juden dazu, sich fast auschließlich im geschlossenen Ghetto aufzuhalten. Nach den Befreiungsdekreten des Kaisers Josef II. benannte man die Prager jüdische Stadt zu Ehren des Kaisers Josefstadt. Erst nach dem Jahre 1848 wurde dieses Viertel zum fünften gleichberechtigten Prager Bezirk. Die eingeengten unhygienischen Verhältnisse führten im Jahre 1900 zum Abreißen der Gebäude.

An die jahrhundertelange Geschichte der Prager Juden erinnert der alte jüdische Friedhof, dessen ältester Grabstein aus dem Jahre 1439 stammt. Der elegische Zauber dieses Friedhofs mit ungefähr 11 000 Grabsteinen, unter denen sich bis zu 12 Friedhofschichten befinden, hat einen einzigartigen historischen Wert. Die Grabsteine vermerken nicht nur die Namen und Daten der Verstorbenen, sondern auch ihre gesellschaftliche Einordnung mit den Symbolen traditioneller Geschlechter, welche von jeher eine priesterliche Hierarchie bildeten. Die Namen der Verstorbenen sind oft auch mit Symbolen vertreten, die einen eigenartigen poetisierenden Ausdruck haben. Unter den Grabsteinen ist auch die Tumba des einflußreichen Bürgermeisters und Primas der Jüdischen Stadt M. Mordechaj Maisel († 1601) erhalten geblieben. Seinen Namen trägt eine Straße inmitten des ehemaligen Ghettos und sogar eine von den Synagogen. Mit dem Namen J. Löw ben Bezalel ist eine suggestive Legende verbunden. Aus der Werkstatt des berühmten Rabbi Löw kam der Sage nach Golem — ein künstlicher Mensch hervor.

Die älteste erhalten gebliebene Synagoge Europas, die Altneusynagoge, gehört mit fünf anderen zum staatlichen jüdischen Museum. Sie ist zweischiffig und wurde um das Jahr 1280 erbaut. Das Ziegelschild stammt aus dem 17. Jahrhundert, als man den Anbau der Vorhalle hinzufügte. Die Haupträume waren nur für Männer zugänglich, erst im 18. Jahrhundert wurde an der Nordseite ein kleiner Anbau für Frauen fertiggestellt. Im Inneren der Synagoge werden wertvolle Denkwürdigkeiten der jüdischen Kultur, vor allem aus der Zeit vom 16. bis 19. Jahrhundert, aufbewahrt.

Neben dem alten jüdischen Friedhof ist ein alter Zeremoniesaal, der heute als Ausstellungsraum der Theresienstädter Kinderzeichnungen dient. In der sogenannten Hohen Synagoge sind alte synagogale Textilien ausgestellt. Die Pinkassynagoge wurde zur Gedenkstätte der Opfer des Faschismus, in Maiselssynagoge befindet sich eine Sammlung silberner und anderer Metallgegenstände. Den esoterischen Zauber der Jüdischen Stadt prägt das barocke jüdische Rathaus, welches von einem hölzernen Uhrturm gekrönt wird. Darunter befindet sich eine zweite große Uhr mit hebräischen Ziffern, deren Zeiger linksherum laufen.

KAREL HLADÍK (1912—1967), FRANZ KAFKA 165 — die Büste an dem 1902 von O. Polívka an Stelle der Prälatur des ehemaligen Benediktinerklosters erbauten Gebäude, erinnert daran, daß hier der geniale Schriftsteller jüdischer Herkunft geboren wurde. Karel Hladík war Repräsentant der klassischen tschechischen realistischen Bildhauerkunst, inspiriert insbesondere durch die zeitgenössische italienische Plastik.

DIE JAKOBSKIRCHE 166—167 — in der Kleinen Štupartská Gasse schräg genüber dem Ausgang aus dem Ungelt wurde sie vom Wenzel I zusammen mit dem Kloster im Jahre 1232 gestiftet. Die Fassade ist mit der eindrucksvollen Stukkatur des italienischen Bildhauers O. Most aus dem Jahre 1695 geschmückt. Sie entstand während des umfangreichen Barockumbaus, der dem Brand von 1689 folgte. Im Kircheninneren mit 21 Altaren beeindrucken die prunkvollen Dekkengemälde F. M. Fogels, die 1736—39 ausgeführt wurden, als der Umbau beendet wurde. Zu den kostbarsten Kirchenschätzen gehören Gemälde von P. Brandl und V. V. Reiner, sowie das Grabdenkmal des Obersten Kanzlers S. M. des Grafen Vratislav von Mitrovice, ein Werk J. B. Fischers von Erlach aus den Jahren 1714—16.

DIE ST. HEINRICHKIRCHE 168 — in der Heinrichstrasse (Jindřišská) in der Neustadt befindet sich der gotische, in der 2. Hälfte des 14. Jahrhunderts gegründete Bau mit der Renaissancevorhalle, mit barocken Anbauten und barocker Innengestaltung. An der Außenseite der Kirche wurde eine Reihe von Grabsteinen von deren aufgelöstem Friedhof befestigt. In den Jahren 1875—79 führte Mocker eine „Regotisierung" der Kirche durch, deren reiche Innenausstattung Denkwürdigkeiten aus der Zeit der Gotik (Tafelbild der St. Stefans-Madonna aus dem 15. Jahrhundert, Statue des Hl. Heinrich u. s.) enthält sowie eine Reihe von barocken Kunstwerken vor allem tschechischer Meister, außer dem Werke des 19. Jahrhunderts (z. B. die gemalten Fenster, im Jahr 1891 nach dem Entwurf von F. Sequens entstanden). Der ‚regotisierte' Glockenturm in der Nähe der Kirche wurde um das Jahr 1475 errichtet. Gotischen Ursprungs ist auch das im Jahr 1386 gegründete Pfarrhaus.

DAS PRESBYTERIUM DER MARIA SCHNEE KIRCHE 169 — hinter dem Gebäude der Franziskanerpfarre auf dem Jungmannplatz ragt der höchste Kirchenbau Prags empor, heute bloß Presbyterium einer unvollendeten Domkirche. Die von Karl IV. im Jahre 1347 gegründete Krönungskirche dient gleichzeitig dem Klosterorden der

Karmeliter. Der erhaltengebliebene Bau des Presbytariums stammt aus den Jahren 1379—97, da das ursprünglich höhere Gewölbe eingestürzt ist. Die darauf folgende hussitische Revolution griff bedeutend in die Geschichte der Kirche ein. Der Führer der Prager Armeen, der Prediger J. Želivský, rief vor der Kirche im Jahre 1419 zu einem Umzug zum Neustädter Rathaus auf. Da kam es zum Fenstersturz der Konsule. In der Kirche predigte J. Želivský bis zu seiner Hinrichtung im Jahre 1422. Im Jahre 1606 schenkte der Prager Erzbischof die Kirche mit dem Kloster dem Franziskanenorden, in der Zeit seines Wirkens hier, ist es zu einer Tragödie gekommen. Im Jahre 1611 nach dem Einfall der Passauer Armee in Prag ist der städtische Pöbel ins Kloster eingedrungen und ermorderte alle Franziskaner, weil er glaubte, die Mönche hätten die fliehenden Passauer Soldaten verborgen.

Im Interieur der Kirche zieht der frühbarocker Altar, der höchste in Prag, die Aufmerksamkeit auf sich. Er wurde in den Jahren 1649—61 bei einer Neuansiedlung der Franziskaner errichtet. Zur wertvollen Innenausstattung der Kirche gehört das Gemälde Mariä Verkündigung von V. V. Reiner aus dem Jahre 1724, welches sich auf einem Seitenaltar befindet. Weiter stehen an den Seitenwänden zehn Statuen der Heiligen aus dem Franziskanerorden. Sie wurden um das Jahr 1625 geschaffen. Bemerkenswert ist auch das Taufbecken aus Zinn aus dem Jahre 1449.

ST. ÄGIDIUSKIRCHE 170 — befindet sich zwischen der Jilská und der Husova in der Altstadt. Am Ausbau beteiligten sich in den Jahren 1339—71 der Bischof Johann von Dražice und später Erzbischof Arnošt von Pardubice. Es ist eine dreischiffige Kapitelkirche, im Jahre 1364 prädigte hier J. Milíč von Kroměříž über die Notwendigkeit einer Kirchenreform. Seit 1420 diente sie den Hussiten. Im Jahre 1626 schenkte Kaiser Ferdinand II. die Kirche dem Dominikanerorden, der neben ihr noch ein Kloster errichten ließ. Im Jahre 1731 wurde eine Barokisierung der Kirche durchgeführt, an der sich der Baumeister F. M. Kaňka beteiligte. Die Gewölbemalereien und das Bild des heiligen Wenzel schuf V. V. Reiner, die Skulpturverzierung J. A. Quittainer und in den Jahren 1839—45 der Münchener Professor L. Schwanthaler. Die Schnitzarbeiten sind überwiegend von F. I. Weiss aus den Jahren 1734—38.

DIE KIRCHE DES ALLERHEILIGSTEN GOTTESHERZENS 171 — wurde in den Jahren 1928—32 nach dem Entwurf von J. Plečnik in der Art einer altchristlichen Kirche erbaut und befindet sich in der Mitte des Platzes Georg von Poděbrady im Prager Viertel Vinohrady. Die originelle Transformation der antikisierenden Kunst spiegelt sich in der Ausschmückung, in den Plastiken von B. Stefan über drei Portalen der Kirche, in der Gestaltung des Marmoraltars ebenso wie in der Skulpturenverzierung von D. Pešan wieder.

DIE VILLA AMERIKA 172 — er ist der erste Bau von K. I. Dienzenhofer, dem herausragenden Schöpfer der Barockarchitektur in Böhmen. Der reizende Bau findet sich in der Straße Zum Karlshof (Ke Karlovu) in der Neustadt, man sieht ihm die Vereinigung des Wiener Monumentalstiles von L. Hildebrandt und der französischen Eleganz und Proportionalität an. Erbaut wurde er in den Jahren 1712—20 auf Kosten des Grafen J. V. Michna von Vacínov. Der Hauptsaal wurde im Jahre 1720 von J. F. Schor mit Wandmalereien, die mythologische Motive zeigen, ausgeschmückt. Ein Garten, der mit Vasen und Skulpturen der Jahreszeiten aus der Werkstatt A. Brauns dekoriert war, umgab das Lustschloß. In diesem Garten fanden vom Ende des 18. Jahrhunderts an Viehmärkte statt. Im Jahre 1932 kaufte die Antonín-Dvořák-Gesellschaft das Lustschloß und errichtete hier das Museum des weltberühmten Komponisten.

Die Villa Amerika, deren Bezeichnung im 19. Jahrhundert nach dem gleichnamigen unweit gelegenen Gasthaus entstand, wird von der Straße mit einer Imitation barocker Gitter getrennt.

Die früher so anmutige Lage des Baus geht in der hohen Umgebung der Bebauung unter.

DER DVOŘÁK-SAAL IM RUDOLFINUM 174 — dient als Sitz der Tschechischen Philharmonie für Sinfoniekonzerte und bedeutende gesellschaftliche Ereignisse. Das Rudolfinum ist nach dem Nationaltheater der zweitbedeutendste Bau der Neurenaissance in Prag. Das Gebäude, zu Ehren des Kronprinzen Rudolf benannt, wurde von 1876—84 nach den Plänen von J. Zítek, J. Schulz und V. Vejrych gebaut.

DER SPIEGELSAAL IM KLEMENTINUM 175 — 1724 von F. M. Kaňka als Bestandteil des ehemaligen Jesuitenkollegs fertiggestellt, ist ein prachtvoll verzierter Raum, wo Konzerte und Ausstellungen veranstaltet werden. Reiche Stukkatur, in die die Spiegel eingesetzt sind, bildet den Rahmen für die Deckengemälde aus dem Leben der Jungfrau Maria, die anscheinend von J. Hiebel ausgeführt wurden. Die Bilder der Heiligen stammen von V. V. Reiner. Zur Auflösung der Kapelle kam es 1784, im Jahre 1816 wurde sie kurzfristig erneuert. Heutzutage ist sie Bestandteil der Nationalen Bibliothek.

WOLFGANG-AMADEUS-MOZART (1756—1791) — GEDENKSTÄTTE IN DER VILLA BERTRAMKA 176, 177 — die Bertramka stellt eine vorstädtische Niederlassung aus dem 17. Jahrhundert dar. Zuletzt wurde sie im Jahre 1873 umgebaut. Sie hat sich in die Kulturgeschichte Prags als ein Platz eingeschrieben, wo sich das Musikgenie W. A. Mozart aufhielt. Nachdem der Komponist F. X. Dušek und seine Frau Josephine, die eine ausgezeichnete Sängerin war, im Jahre 1784 die Villa Bertramka gekauft hatten, war Mozart hier bei seinem Prager Aufenthalt zu Gast. Im Jahre 1787 komponierte er hier seine bekannte Oper Don Giovanni, deren Uraufführung im Nostitztheater riesigen Erfolg erntete.

DIE PARISER STRASSE (PAŘÍŽSKÁ) 181, 183 — sie verbindet den Altstädter Ring mit der Sv.-Čech-Brücke und ist gleichzeitig der Zugang zum ehemaligen jüdischen Viertel, welches bei einer Sanierung größtenteils zerstört wurde. Diese breite Straße, früher Nikolasstraße genannt, wird von repräsentativen Zinshäusern gebildet, die vor allem in den Jahren 1901—1906 erbaut wurden. Hinter der bedeutendsten Sehenswürdikeit des jüdischen Viertels, der Altneusynagoge, befindet sich ein Park, in dem man die Bronzestatue von Moses, angefertigt von F. Bílek im Jahre 1905, bewundern kann. Am Ende der Straße steht das Gebäude der Juristischen Fakultät der Karlsuniversität. Es wurde in den Jahren 1924—27 nach dem Entwurf von J. Kotěra erbaut. Schräg gegenüber wurde in den Jahren 1970—1974 der umfangreiche Komplex des Hotels Intercontinental nach den Plänen von K. Filsak, K. Bubeníček und Šuld errichtet.

DAS HOTEL ATRIUM 182 — im Juni 1990 nach 23 Monaten Bauaktivitäten nach einem Entwurf von Franc, Nováček und Fencl fertiggestellt, stellt den breitesten Hotelbau in Mitteleuropa dar. Das atriumartige Gebäude bietet 788 Zimmer mit 1568 Betten. Das Hotelrestaurant bietet Speisen der internationalen Küche an, allerdings erweitert um Gerichte der tschechischen Küche.

WISCHEHRAD (VYŠEHRAD) 187, 189—191 — der legendäre Sitz der ältesten böhmischen Fürsten, der sagenumwobenenen Fürstin Libussa und der Přemysliden, wurde cca. im 10. Jh auf einem Felsen hoch über der Moldau gegründet. Während der Regierungszeit des Fürsten Wratislaw II. (1061—92, 1085 zum König gekrönt) wurde hierher sogar der Herrschersitz verlegt, dabei wurde 1070 die Kapitelkirche gegründet. Zu gleicher Zeit erfolgte der Umbau der hölzernen Burg in eine steinerne, an der neue Kirchen gestaiftet wurden, die während der Husssitenbewegung zerstört wurden.

Der heutige Vyšehrad (wörtlich Hochburg) ist von Festungsmauern und Basteien umgeben, die, begonnen unter der Herrschaft Karls IV., von italienischen Befestigungsbaumeistern vollendet wurden. Die Festungsmauern umgeben die Kapitelkirche der Hl. Peter und Paul, ursprünglich romanisch, später gotisch und barock umgebaut und schließlich von 1885—87 neugotisch gestaltet. In der Nähe der Kirche befinden sich Reste einer romanischen Brücke, die wahrscheinlich Bestandteil der Befestigungsanlage des Fürstenpalais war. Gegenüber der Kirche befindet sich eine kleine Ludmilakapelle. Unter den erhalten gebliebenen Bauwerken ist ebenso die ursprüngliche romanische Rotunde des Hl. Martin zu finden, die man durch das Eingangstor von der Straße V pevnosti erreicht.

Gegenüber der Stirnwand der Peterskirche befindet sich das Haupteingangstor des Friedhofs, um 1890 von A. Wiehl als Beisetzungsstätte der großen Söhne der Nation angelegt. Dieses vom Propst V. Štulc unterstützte Projekt wurde anstelle des Pfarrfriedhofs aus dem Jahre 1660 verwierklicht. An der Ostseite des Friedhofs wurde von 1889—93 und 1903 nach Wiehls Entwurf der Ehrenfriedhof (Slavín) errichtet, die letzte Ruhestätte vieler großer Geister der tschechischen Nation.

Auf den Grasflächen, wo einst ein ausgebranntes Zeughaus stand, wurden 1948 drei Statuengruppen von Myslbek von der beschädigten Palacký-Brücke aufgestellt. Im Jahre 1978 kamen Přemysl und Libussa als die letzten rekonstruiten Statuen hinzu. Myslbeks Heldengestalten wurden aus der damaligen national-mythologischen Ideenwelt der

Königshofer Handschrift geboren. Lumír mit dem verkörperten Lied entstand 1888, Přemysl und Libussa 1892, Záboj und Slavoj zurückkehrend aus dem siegreichen Kampf 1895 und Ctirad und Šárka 1897. Berauschende poetische Vorstellungen von der ruhmreichen Vergangenheit des Slawentums fanden auf dem Vyšehrad ihre volle Rechtfertigung.

DAS EMMAUSKLOSTER (NA SLOVANECH) 188 — wurde 1347 vom Karl IV für slawische Benediktiner gestiftet, die hier ein einmaliges Zentrum der Bildung und Kunst schufen. Hier entstand 1395 der glagolitische Teil des sogenannten Reimser Evangeliums, auf das die französischen Könige während der Krönungszeremonie ihren Eid ablegten.

In der Zeit der Hussitenkriege wurde hier das einzige tschechische kalixtinische (d. h. utraquistische) Kloster errichtet.

Das im Laufe der Geschichte mehrmals umgebaute Klosterareal mit der Kirche der Hl. Jungfrau Maria wurde im Jahre 1945 durch einen amerikanischen Bombenangriff schwer beschädigt. In der Folgezeit wurde das Bauwerk nach einem Entwurf von F. M. Černý rekonstruiert, 1967 erhielt es zwei auffallend moderne weiße Turmspitzen, die wie Segel oder Flügel zum Himmel streben.

DAS SLAVÍN-TOR 195 — das markanteste Monument des Friedhofs von Vyšehrad stellt an dessen Ostseite Slavín dar, die gemeinsame Ehrengruft vieler verdienter Persönlichkeiten der tschechischen Nation. Der Ausbau erfolgte in den Jahren 1889—90 nach dem Entwurf des Architekten A. Wiehl, die Skulpturendekoration besteht aus 3 Statuen: dem Genius der Nation, der jauchzenden Nation und der trauernden Nation, die von J. Maudr in den Jahren 1892—93 geschaffen wurden. Als erster wurde auf dem Slavín-Friedhof der tschechische Dichter Julius Zeyer im Jahre 1901 begraben. Ihm folgten 53 bedeutende Persönlichkeiten (unter anderem J. V. Myslbek, V. Hynais, E. Destinová, A. Mucha, J. Kubelík, V. Špála). Führende tschechische Architekten und Bildhauer haben die Grabsteine auf diesem Friedhof angefertigt.

DIE ROTUNDE DES HEILIGEN MARTIN AUF DEM VYŠEHRAD 196 — das älteste erhalten gebliebene Monument des Vyšehrad stammt aus der 2. Hälfte des 11. Jahrhunderts. Es verlor nach Errichtung der Vyšehrader Befestigungsanlage an Bedeutung, als die Kapelle in ein Pulvermagazin umwandelt wurde. Im 19. Jahrhundert wurde es als Lager benutzt.

Im Jahre 1878 kaufte das Vyšehrader Kapitel den wertvollen Bau und ließ ihm im gleichen Jahr nach dem Entwurf von Architekt A. Baum renovieren. Das Interieur wurde durch A. Königs und J. Heřmans Wandmalereien ausgeschmückt: F. Sequens schuf das Altarbild. Der Bau wurde im Jahre 1915 und 1969—70 erneut renoviert.

DER KULTURPALAST UND DAS HOTEL FÓRUM 198, 199 — der Bedarf an einem großen Konferenz- und Kulturzentrum in Prag führte 1975 zum Regierungsbeschluß über den Bau des Prager Kulturpalastes. Das riesige monolitische Gebäude in Form eines unregelmäßigen Siebenecks, dessen Veranstaltungen von politischen Versammlungen bis zu Konzerten reichen, wurde 1980 nach einem Projekt des Militärischen Projektinstituts gebaut (Mayer, Ustohal, Vaněk, Karlík). Der Kongreßsaal bietet mehr als 2800 Delegierten — oder Musik- und Theaterliebhabern — Platz.

Auf der gegenüberliegenden Seite aum Ende der 500 m langen Nusler Brücke, die die dicht besiedelte Nusler Talsenke überspannt, ragt das polygonale Hochgebäude des im Jahre 1988 zu Ende gebauten Hotels FORUM empor. Dieses Hochgebäude genauso wie die anderen Wolkenkratzer in der Prager Skyline bieten den Pragern ständig Anlaß zu Diskussionen über ihren architektonischen Wert.

DAS PRAGER AUSSTELLUNGSGELÄNDE 201, 202 — hat seine Dominante im Kongreßpalast, einem Eisenbau von B. Münzberger aus dem Jahre 1891 im Stile des Neubarocks, von 1952—54 neu gestaltet. Das Ausstellungsgelände nimmt einen Teil des einstigen Königlichen Wildgeheges ein. Im Jahre 1891 wurde hier nach einem Projekt von A. Wiehl auf der Gesamtfläche von 300 000 m^2 das Ausstellungsgelände für die Jubiläumslandesausstellung fertiggebaut. An die Ausstellung von 1891 erinnert heute noch der ursprüngliche Ausstellungssaal, in dem die Kunst- und Erinnerungsausstellung stattfand und wo sich heute die Akademie der bildenden Künste befindet. Auf der rechten Seite des Eingangsgeländes befindet sich das Pavillon der Hauptstadt Prag, das heute als Lapidarium des Nationalmuseums dient. Auf dem Ausstellungsgelände ist eine ganze Reihe von anziehenden Pavillons zu sehen (beispielsweise jenes, wo das monumentale Diorama der Schlacht bei Lipany von Marold untergebracht wurde) sowie weitere verschiedene Anziehungspunkte (u. a. die erneuerte Fontäne des Erfinders Fr. Křižík).

DAS SCHLOSS TROJA 203 — im ehemaligen Weinanbaugebiet am nördlichen Rande des Prager Talkessels wurde am Ende des 17. Jh. vom Grafen V. V. von Sternberg (Šternberk) im Stile der italienischen Vorstadtvillen erbaut. An den Projektarbeiten sowie an den eigentlichen Bauarbeiten beteiligten sich D. Orsi de Orsini, S. Carloni, aber auch der hervorragende burgundische Baumeister J. B. Mathey. Die außerordentlich reiche Ausmalung der Innenräume mit Allegorien und Kryptoportraits der Angehörigen der Familie Sternberg stammt von F. und G. F. Marcheti, die Gemälde im Hauptsaal, zu Ehren der Habsburger entworfen, schuf von 1691—97 A. Godyn, ein Maler niederländischer Herkunft. Der ehrgeizige Bauherr verfolgte zielbewußt und hart seine Karriere als Hofbeamter. Sein luxuriöser Landessitz sollte auch bei einem Herrscherbesuch als Erholungsort nach der Jagd dienen. Wohlbedacht war auch die landschaftliche Einbettung des Schlosses: vom Podest der großzügig erbauten Außentreppe mit den Statuen der Gigantomachie von den Dresdner Bildhauern J. J. und P. Heermann aus sieht man in der geraden Achse die Silhouette der Prager Burg.

In dem neu rekonstruierten Schloßgebäude — samt der Replik des ursprünglichen historischen Gartens — installierte die Prager Bildergalerie ihre Sammlungen aus dem 19. Jh.

DAS SCHLOSS ZBRASLAV 204—209 — das am linken Moldauufer malerisch gelegene und von Prag mit dem Dampfer erreichbare Schloß Zbraslav diente als Prälatur der Zistenzienserabtei. Das Bauwerk aus dem Jahre 1739 mit Fresken von V. V. Reiner wurde in den Jahren 1911—12 in ein Schloß umgebaut und gehörte der Familie Bartoň von Dobenín.

Wenzel (Václav) II. stiftete das Kloster Zbraslav bereits im Jahre 1291. In der Abteikirche der Jungfrau Maria wurden der Stifter. der König Wenzel (Václav) III, und die Königin Eliška Přemyslovna beigesetzt. Die hiesigen Äbte schufen die berühmte Zbraslaver Chronik, deren Anfänge bis 1337 reichen.

Das Konventgebäude der Abtei wurde vor 1709 nach einem Entwurf von J. Santini umgebaut und in den Jahren 1724—32 nach F. M. Kaňka fertiggebaut. Die Stuckverzierung stammt von T. Soldati, die wertvollen Freskenmalereien schufen V. V. Reiner und F. X. Palko. Im Jahre 1785 wurde das Kloster aufgelöst und es verfiel allmählich. Im 20. Jh. als die Familie Bartoň von Dobenín das Schloß erwarb, wurden die Innenräume des Schlosses und des Konvents von D. Jurkovič und A. Čenský neu gestaltet. In der gegenwärtigen Zeit sind im Konventgebäude Bildhauersammlungen des 19. und 20. Jh. der Nationalen Galerie Prag untergebracht. Einen wesentlichen Teil dieser Sammlungen bilden Kunstwerke der Künstler der sogenannten Generation des Nationaltheaters, z. B. der Originalentwurf der Triga aus dem Jahre 1873 von B. Schnirch für das Nationaltheater. Besonders hervorgehoben ist auch das Schaffen von J. V. Myslbek, dem ein selbständiger Saal gewidmet ist, genauso wie J. Štursa, der herausragenden Persönlichkeit der tschechischen Bildhauerkunst der ersten drei Jahrzehnte des 20. Jh.

PRAGUE

THE VLTAVA 1, 185 — Springing from the Šumava hills, the 430.2 km long Vltava river with a catchment area of 28.090 square km is a left-bank tributary to the Elbe river near the town of Mělník. Though second in size, the river is, in terms of its importance enhanced by the nation's mythology, the leading stream in Bohemia. In Prague, the Vltava features a considerable width and depth (316 m and up to 3.8 m respectively). It consists of four reservoirs and, articulated into arms, gives rise to several islands (such as Žofínský, Střelecký, Rohanský, and Císařský islands). The river plays a significant role in the picturesque character of Prague's landscape.

PRAGUE CASTLE 2, 6, 46, 99, 180 — Prague Castle was founded after 880 on the Hradčany headland near the Vltava river, becoming the seat of Bohemian princes, transferred from the Levý Hradec castle. The centre of the Bohemian state ruled by the Premyslids was a religious centre as well. The first Christian church of the Virgin Mary was built here in the late 9th century, and St. Vitus rotunda with an Episcopal Palace and St. George monasterial church were founded in the second half of the 10th century. The palace, a residence of Bohemian kings from the 13th century, experienced its greates growth under Emperor Charles IV, who was an ardent and cultured builder. The representative character of Prague Castle was emphasized by a large-scale construction of St. Vitus' Cathedral, launched in 1344 in the French style. In the late 15th century, King Vladislav Jagellonský extended the palace with the Vladislav Hall. During his reign, the well-known tower Daliborka was designed by Ried and built as a part of the late Gothic castle fortifications, bearing the name of Knight Dalibor of Kozojedy, who served his sentence here. His romantic life story was used by Smetana in an opera of his, Dalibor. The White Tower, used as a public prison from 1584, was also a part of the fortification system.

In the 16th century, the Castle's double moat filled in and the second courtyard was established, extended later and rebuilt by Pacassi in 1775. The northern castle wing includes the Spanish Hall with Rudolph's Gallery. The ground floor of the western wing and the stables were turned into the Castle Picture Gallery in 1965. In the south-eastern corner of the courtyard there is the Chapel Holy Cross, designed originally by Anselmo Lurago. After reconstruction, the St. Vitus Treasury was installed here in 1963.

The third castle courtyard, which is the centre of the Castle, includes Renaissance palaces of Kaiser Rudolph II, Maxmilian II and an early Baroque palace of the Queen, whose fronts were restored in a uniform manner by Pacassi in the third quarter of the 18th century. Today, one can find the Office of the President of the Republic here. Its representative entrance, provided with a balcony, is decorated with sculptures created by Francis I. Platzer in 1760—61. This courtyard encircles the Royal palace and St. Vitus' Cathedral and is linked with the courtyard of St. George Square. On the opposite side of the courtyard, we can enter Vikářská (Vicars') street and have a look at a former chapter house of the Dean and a new vicariate, which houses a famous restaurant „Na Vikárce", associated with Svatopluk Čech's literary work.

The Prague Castle area also includes the Powder Tower, sometimes called Mihulka, built in the late 15th century by Ried. Used originally as an artillery tower, the Powder Tower houses an exhibition showing the level of science and culture at the Castle in the 16th and 17th centuries, including a model of the alchemists' workshop.

Prague Castle is encompassed with southern castle gardens, the Paradise garden, and the „Na valech" garden, allowing unique views of Prague's panorama.

FRANTIŠEK ŽENÍŠEK (1849—1916), LIBUSSA AUGURS GLORY OF PRAGUE, 3 — The work of a representative of the first National Theatre generation deals with a mythical character of Czech legends, Princess Libussa and depicts her prophetic vision of the town's glory—the glory of Prague.

OLD TOWN TOWNHALL 4, 105, 107, 114—120, 123 — Rising beautifully on the Old Square, the impressive remnants of the Old Town Townhall witness the significance of the town's self-government dating from 1338. The core of the building, which was rebuilt many times in its history, is Wolflin of Stone's Gothic house, bought later by burghers, who built a tetrahedral tower with a chapel (consecrated in 1381) with a beautifully ornamented bay beside it. The main entrance was topped with a portal in 1470—80, created probably by Matěj Rejsek of Prostějov. The Townhall front on the first floor below the Council Hall was provided with a window bearing an inscription "Praga caput regni" (Prague, the Capital of the Kingdom) and the Old Town emblem of 1475. A famous architect Benedikt Reid is considered responsible for this early Renaissance reconstruction. It was not until the 19th century that the Town Hall was extended and rebuilt. One day before the end of World War II, on 8 May 1945, the northern neo-Gothic part of the Townhall, built by Nobil, was seriously damaged and burnt out. After the rest of this the building was pulled down; any reconstructing and constructing attempts turned out unsuccessful.

The Townhall vestibule shows a mosaic decoration created by a Czech artist of the late 19th and early 20th centuries, Mikoláš Aleš, called "Tribute of Slavs to Prague" (1904). It is a fine-art replica of a speech pronounced by Karel Sladkovský on the occasion of the festive laying of the foundation stone of the National Theatre. It shows Libussa's prophetic vision of a town, "whose glory will reach the stars". The old ceremonial hall, preserved in its original appearance of 1470, is the most valuable historical interior of the Townhall. It is mostly decorated with Brožík's paintings referring to historic events that influenced significantly the rise of the national self-confidence.

PRAGUE'S BRIDGES 5, 98, 156, 178, 184 — In addition to their technical and functional aspects, the bridges have a well-perceptable aesthetic character, following from their designs and decorative elements as well as their harmony with the course, reflexes and moods of the river.

HRADČANY SQUARE 7 — Hradčany Square provides a view of the first, last-built Prague Castle courtyard with an entrance gate. The courtyard was built in the Italian-Viennese neo-Classicist style in 1759—69 according to a project of Pacassi's. The attics of the buildings were equipped with military emblems and Platzer's statues. The courtyard was restored in 1920—22 by Janek and, on a larger scale, in 1979—80.

Behind the entrance gate of the first courtyard lies the Matthias Gate, designed most likely by Filippi in the style of Italian fortification constructions, because it had originally been a part of the wall above the castle moat.

ARCHBISHOP'S PALACE 8 — Closing Hradčany Square before the front of the Prague Castle, the Archbishops' Palace is a most representative building, adapted in the Baroque style and carrying the emblem of Archbishop Antonín Příchovský. The core of the palace was the former Gryspekovský house, bought by Ferdinand I to be used as a seat of the renewed Archbishopric of Prague.

The palace was rebuilt three times—in 1562—64 by Aostalis, in 1669—79 by Mathey, a ward of the archbishop J. B. of Wallenstein coming from France, and, finally, in 1764—65 by Wirch, a leading representative of the Viennese Rococo style. The palace is decorated with Faith and Hope statues made by Seidan in 1880's and works by Francis I. Platzer, who also created the statues at the staircase. The palace houses unique collections as well. The 1599 chapel is decorated with ceiling paintings by D.A. of Květná and, above all, with guilded busts of St. Peter and Paul dating from about 1413. The Throne Hall features a valuable collection of eight tapestries, showing the exotic environment of New India and produced by Neilson's studio in Paris according to drawings of Desportes'. Valuable picture collections include works by Heinsch, Halwachs, Dallinger, and others. A set of portraits of Prague's archbishops is a unique collection too. Applied art collections show, for example, an excellent set of Bohemian cut glass products and a large set of Viennese china. The palace is open to visitors every year on Maundy Thursday.

PRAGUE CASTLE ENTRANCE GATE 9 — The entrance gate on Hradčany Square consists of a stately bar gate and a Rococo fence, dating from the period of Mary Theresa. It is decorated with groups of Wrestling Giants bowls and putts, created by Platzer in 1769. Deteriorating sandstone sculptures, however, had to be replaced with copies in 1912, made by Vosmík and Procházka.

In the background, there is a magnificent pre-Baroque gate, established under Emperor Matthias in 1614. In addition to the Emperor's ranks, there are also emblems of all the countries of the empire on its sides.

PRAGUE CASTLE THIRD COURTYARD 10 — The third courtyard was built after a great fire in 1551, when the remainders of the medieval constructions had been covered with earth. After World War I, a concrete platform paved with granite was built by Plečnik over the archeological finds.

The northern edge of the third courtyard is closed with the southern part of St. Vitus' Cathedral by a tall tower, founded by Peter Parler in 1396. In 1770, the tower was rebuilt in the Renaissance style by Pacassi. The 99.6 m tall tower contains four Renaissance bells, the greatest of which is a 203 cm tall bell called Zikmund. This bell-founding masterpiece in Bohemia was created by T. Jaroš in 1549.

Below the tower, on the right-hand side, there is an arcade-like portico, the so-called Golden Gate, housing a chamber with the coronation jewels of the Kingdom of Bohemia. Its front is decorated with a mosaic work, Last Judgement, created of Bohemian glass by Venetian masters in 1370—71.

The form of the building of the Old Provost's Residence behind a Mrákotín monolith comes from the 17th century. A Romanesque bishop's palace used to stand here before.

ST. GEORGE'S BASILICA 11 — St. George's Basilica is situated on the eastern side of St. George Square and represents the best-preserved Romanesque construction in Prague. The church was founded by Prince Vratislav in 921 and rebuilt into a three-aisle basilica in the period of Abbess Bertha, that is before 1142, after a great fire at Prague Castle. The main front was restored in the Baroque style most probably by Caratti in 1677—78. The architect Kaňka built the Chapel of St. John of Nepomuk in 1718—22, which was decorated with a group of sculptures by Ferdinand M. Brokoff above its entrance. In the 14th century, St. Ludmila's Chapel was built next to the southern basilica tower, dating from the 12th century. The southern edge of the basilica attracts one's attention with its Renaissance column portal, created in Ried of Pískov's workshop around 1500. A Gothic relievo of the dragon-slayer, St. George, was replaced with a copy in 1934. In the remnants of Virgin Mary's Chapel below the southern tower, there are Romanesque decorations, dating from the first half of the 13th century. The basilica, adapted in the Romanesque style at the turn of the 19th and 20th centuries, houses, among others, the tombs of Princes Boleslav II, Oldřich and Vratislav.

The first women's convent in Bohemia of the Benedictine order, established by a sister of Boleslav II, Blessed Mlada, is also a part of the neighbouring built-up area. Rebuilt many times, the convent was abolished in 1782 and soon converted into barracks. In 1962—74, it was made over to the National Gallery of Prague, restored and turned into a gallery of Bohemian Art of the Gothic, Renaissance and Mannerism periods.

ST. VITUS' CATHEDRAL 12, 44 — St. Vitus' Cathedral is Pragues biggest and most important church, housing the coronation jewels of the Kingdom of Bohemia and the relics of Bohemian kings. The cathedral, a significant component of the Hradčany contour, was established by Charles IV in 1344, replacing a Romanesque three-aisle basilica and a rotunda built by St. Wenceslas, the patron of Bohemia, before 935. The construction of a three-aisle cathedral, including a transept, a gallery and a ring of chapels, began, according to the design of Mathias of Arras', a Frenchman. After Mathias' death, Peter Parler, from Gmünd in Swabia, continued the construction, followed by his sons, Wenceslas and John. After the construction of the chancel with chapels was finished and that of the main tower was started (1420), an important Renaissance period began. In 1564, Wohlmut built a tower gallery and a helmet-shaped roof. The Baroque onion-shaped roof was finished in 1770 by Pacassi. The cathedral, only finished completely as late as 1929, experienced a neo-Gothic building period too, which began in 1873. This period yielded a neo-Gothic altar with kings' mausoleum, hewed in marble by Colin in 1566—89. The cathedral's triforium contains 21 busts dating from 1374—85, showing Charles IV and his family, archbishops and the builders of the church. There is a royal vault under the church, where the remnants of a Romanesque rotunda can be found. The chamber with coronation jewels, secured with seven locks, is a most important place. It is St. Wenceslas' crown of 1346 that is considered the most valuable of the coronation jewels.

The chapels of the gallery contain tombs of Czech rulers, created in Parler's foundry in 1370—75. The King's oratory was built in 1493 in a naturalistic design combining the emblems of countries and intertwined branches: Vladislav Jagellonský being the patron.

In the Renaissance period, Wohlmut's organ choir was established, transferred into the transept in 1924. A Baroque tomb of Count Šlik, created by Fischer of Erlach, Kaňka and Brandl in 1723, attracts one's attention too. The statue of the kneeling cardinal Schwarzenberg, made by Myslbek in 1892—95, is a unique work of the modern period. There are a great variety of stained glass windows in the cathedral, coming from the first third of the 20th century and designed by Alfons Mucha, František Kysela, Cyril Bouda and others. The cathedral is a treasury of artistic works ranging from the Romanesque period (the Rhineland, so-called Jerusalem candelabra) to 20th century artifacts.

ST. WENCESLAS' CHAPEL 13 — Designed by Matthias of Arras, the chapel was meant as a counterpart to the Holy Cross Chapel at the Karlštejn castle. It was finished by Peter Parler in 1362—66. It stands on the site of the original grave of a saint of 935, that is at the southern part of the front aisle, and represents the most valuable jewel of peak Gothic in Bohemia. Its bottom part is faced with 1,345 jaspers and amethysts. It is decorated with an excellent Passion Cycle created by an unknown painter in 1372—73 and with paintings by Master of Litoměřice in 1506—1509, showing the legend of St. Wenceslas. The chapel altar includes a Gothic tomb dating from the 14th century. The argillite statue of St. Wenceslas was created by J. Parler in 1373. Small paintings above the altar show Charles IV and his fourth wife, Eliška of Pomerania, Wenceslas IV and Jane of Bavaria. The dominating figures painted above the statue of St. Wenceslas are most probably Vladislav Jagellonský and his wife, Anna de Foi-Candale. Lithurgical objects on the altar, a guilded tabernacle and a chandelier dating from 1912—13 (made by Anýž according to projects by Hilbert, Sucharda and Kryšpín) are Gothic and Renaissance artifacts. Below the chapel window there is a small portal leading to the staircase to the coronation chamber, protecting a set of coronation jewels.

MASTER THEODORIK, ST. POPE, ST. JEROME, ST. AUGUSTINE, AND ST. VITUS 15—17 — These desk paintings were created by an Emperor's painter and the Senior of the Painting Guild of Prague in 1370s to be installed in the court chapel of Charles IV at Karlštejn. A hundred and thirty pictures, hanging in three rows on boarded walls, imply the idea of a universal unity of the heavenly and the earthly worlds. This polyptych is strictly hierarchically arranged. The grandiose above-lifesized figures of the Emperor's treasure guards are a unique example of the feudal system, guaranteed by the monarch, respecting the Victorious Church. The paintings showing Christ's heavenly army witness a medieval worship of saints-martyrs, whose relics are contained in the frames of all the pictures.

Theodorik's softly picturesque form combined with naturalistic modification of a single physiognomic type witnesses advanced creative orientations of this master, admired by the Emperor. His knowledge of both Byzantine and Western, especially Venetian and Bolognan works, seems to be obvious.

MASTER OF TŘEBOŇ, CHRIST ON MOUNT OF OLIVES, CRICIFIXION, LAYING TO REST, AND RESURRECTION 18—21 — These works can be found in the collections of the National Gallery of Prague and come from the altar of the Augustinian Church of St. Giles in the town of Třeboň. The Resurrection desk comes from St. Barbara's Chapel near Třeboň. These desk pictures were created by an anonymous master of the highest world level around 1380. Their sophisticated composition with a fine arabesque of shapes and their deep colour contrasts intensify the fine-art idealism and special mystical ecstasy. The works with lyrical impact anticipate the fine arts around 1400.

VLADISLAV HALL 22 — The Vladislav Hall covers the entire area of the second floor of the Prague Castle Old Palace. The most important state events taking place here, the hall is the most respectable room of the Castle. It was established in 1492—1502 under Vladislav Jagellonský when the royal court had moved from the Old Town to the Prague Castle. Its construction, replacing three Gothic halls dating from the period of Charles IV, was designed by the king's builder B. Ried. The 62 m long, 16 m wide and 13 m high hall was the largest and the most representative secular room of the Central-European late Gothic style. Coronations and meetings of the Estates as well as knights' jousts, making use of the adjacent horsemen stairs, took place in the hall. When the emperor had moved to Vienna, the hall was used as a public meeting place and a marketplace of court stallkeepers. After World War I, the hall was restored in a pious manner by the removal of later decorations.

From the Vladislav Hall one can approach the side wing of the Castle, the so-called Louis Palace, built in the early 16th century.

OLD PARLIAMENT OF PRAGUE CASTLE 23 — The Old Parliament, where the Supreme Court of Bohemia used to sit until 1847 and the representatives of the Bohemian Estates used to assemble, was built in 1559—65 by the Emperor's builder Wohlmut. This representative hall with a reticulated vault was also used for electing kings by the Estates' assemblies until 1857. At present, constitutional documents are signed by the President and festive sittings of the Czech National Council take place here.

ADRIAEN DE VRIES (1546—1626, RUDOLPH II) 24 — Rudolph II (1603), one of the three portraits of the Kaiser painted by de Vries, who was called "the greatest and the first art lover in the world" by a theorist and painter van Mander, belongs to Rudolph's unique collections, the remainder of which can be seen in Prague Castle's Picture Gallery. The Netherlander de Vries was the most prominent sculptor of Rudolph's court. A large number of his works were seized by the Swedish during the siege of Prague in 1648.

ST. GEORGE 25 — The bronze equestrian statue of a legendary dragon-slayer is a copy of a work created by George and Martin of Klausenburg in 1373. Originally, it was installed in the southern part of the Castle courtyard in front of the so-called Maxmilian laboratories. Later, the figures of the horse and the dragon were re-cast partly and, after being damaged in 1562, restored by the metal founder Jaroš. When the third courtyard was being paved, the architect Plečnik designed the plinth of the statue (1928) and also an 18 m tall monolith of Mrákotín granite. The latter was erected on the occasion to the 10th anniversary of the creation of the Republic and in the memory of World War I victims.

TIZIANO VECELLIO (ABOUT 1480/90—1576), YOUNG WOMAN'S TOILET 26 — This work of the greatest representative of Venetian 16th century painting is documented to have been exhibited in the Prague Castle Gallery in 1685. The picture of a strawberry-blonde young woman with toilet requisites, being served admiringly by a young man carrying a turban, is similar in type to a Viennese picture, Gipsy Madonna (around 1510), created in the period of Titian's full admiration for Giorgiono. The Prague painting, created approximately in 1512—15, was made smaller (to 83 times 79 cm) in the second half of the 18th century, probably for the purpose of wall boarding. A precise Renaissance copy (109.2 times 91.3 cm in size) was sold to a private owner at the Christie's auction room in London on 27 November 1957. Other, worse Baroque copies were found by J. Neumann in some private collections (in Toulouse, for example).

The subject of a young woman's toilet can be found in some other modifications, the best-known of which is Titian's work in the Louvre, coming from a collection of Charles I, King of England. The genuineness of the painting in Prague had doubt cast upon it many times in the past. In 1832, the picture was thought to have been painted by Orazio, Titian's son. Later, it was considered a copy.

PETER PAUL RUBENS (1577—1640), MEETING OF OLYMPIAN GODS (DETAIL) 27 — Even this early work of the leading representative of Flemish Baroque features a powerful energy, sensuality and a symphonic stream of multi-layer events, which is typical of Rubens' later work. The painting probably originated in 1602, when Rubens became a court painter of Duke Vinzenzo Gonzaga of Mantua. The picture depicts a meeting of Olympian gods with Jupiter at the head. The patron of firm bonds of matrimony, Hera-Juno, is putting forward her complaint against a light-minded, yet triumphant goddess of love, Aphrodite-Venus, crowned by the Amorettes.

This painting, obviously influenced by G. Roman, is documented to have been a part of the Castle collections in 1685 for the first time, namely as a work by an anonymous master, and then in 1718—37 as a work of Raphael's. Rubens' authorship was briefly mentioned in 1797 and confirmed in 1962 by Neumann.

KAREL ŠKRÉTA (1610—1674), PORTRAIT OF THE DIAMOND-CUTTER DIONYSIUS MISERONI AND HIS FAMILY (DETAIL) 28 — This work, created by a founder of the Czech Baroque painting most likely in 1653, shows a master of a cutting workshop and a custodian of the artistic collections of the Castle, encircled with his family. It was Dionysius Miseroni who kept the Swedes from penetrating into Rudolph's art chamber in 1648. His father, Octavio Miseroni, was called on from Milan to the court of Rudolph II in 1588, appointed court diamond-cutter and awarded a noble attribute in 1608.

JAN KUPECKÝ (1667—1740), ALLEGORY OF PAINTING 29 — The Allegory of Painting, a work of a Czech exile, ranking among the leading European portrait painters of the early 18th century, is a counterpart to the Allegory of Sculpture installed in the National Gallery collections in Prague. The personification of painting as a young lady in a Baroque robe and a laurel wreath of glory on her fair hair is thought to date from the second decade of the 18th century, when the author lived mostly in Vienna.

PETR BRANDL (1668—1735), SELF PORTRAIT 31 — Created in 1697, the painting belongs to the Lobkovic collections and was loaned to the National Gallery of Prague. Authentically, the portrait witnesses a perfect mastering of characteristics and colours of the greatest painter of the top Baroque period in Bohemia, who became famous not only as a portrait painter but especially as a creator of altar paintaings with light dynamics and mythological and genre works.

PAOLO CALIARI, CALLED VERONESE (1528—1588), ST. CATHERINE WITH ANGEL 32 — This work, created by one of the most prominent representatives of Venetian 16th century painting in about 1580, is documented to have been possessed by Gallery No. II of the Prague Castle in 1685 under the name "Saint's Temptation". A false interpretation of the painting may have been deduced from the intimate gesture of the angel. In Neumann's opinion, the saint of Alexandria is depicted as Christ's bride, being revealed her destiny, namely a martyr's death, by a heavenly messenger, as apparent from a palm branch and a sword held by the angel.

LOBKOVIC PALACE AND THE BLACK TOWER 33 — The buildings can be approached by climbing the Old Castle Stairs in the eastern part of the Castle. The Black Tower, established in the second quarter of the 12th century on earlier foundations, was a part of the Romanesque fortification system built during the reign of Prince Soběslav. After a fire in 1538, the tower had to be lowered by one floor, which found its reflection in its name too. Earlier, the tower was called Golden Tower, because its roof was covered with guilded lead plate under Charles IV. Used originally as the eastern Castle gate, the tower was also used as a prison for debtors. In 1230, under Wenceslas I, a new entrance gate was built below the tower. It is adjacent to the Lobkovic (originally Pernštejn) Palace, built by Jaroslav and Vratislav of Pernštejn in 1555—62 and 1570—76. In 1625, the palace was damaged by fire. In 1626, it became a possession of the Lobkovic house and was restored in 1651—68. Ordered by Wenceslas Eusebius of Lobkovic, its reconstruction was designed by Carlo Lurago and decorations were made by Italian stone-cutters G. Galli and G. Pozzo. A stuccoer D. Galli created beautiful stuccoes and V. Hárovník oil paintings on the Main Hall ceiling. Domestic artists participated in the decorating activities too. Small-scale reconstructions were made in the following periods, especially in 1810 and 1861—62. In 1976, the palace was rebuilt to house an exhibition of the Historical and Archeological Department of the National Museum. As a restitution, the palace was returned to the Roudnice branch of the Lobkovic family in 1992.

VIEW OF PRAGUE FROM LOBKOVIC PALACE 34 — Looking from the Lobkovic palace, we are impressed by the unique view of the large Lesser Town enclave of the Wallenstein Palace, covering an area of the former 23 houses with courtyards and gardens, a brick-yard and a town gate. Behind the palace we can find St. Thomas' Church and a monastery, established by Wenceslas II after 1285 to be used by the Augustinians-eremites. The Baroque reconstruction in 1723—31 was designed by an outstanding architect, Kilian I. Dienzenhofer. The church was decorated by leading Bohemian Baroque artists and by Rubens, who created two paintings on the main altar, transferred later into the National Gallery and replaced with copies.

KOLOWRAT PALACE GARDEN 35 — Designed by Palliardi in 1769—89, the garden lies behind the main wing of the Kolowrat Palace and the smaller Černín Palace, which replaced the house of Popel of Lobkovic in 1770. This Rococo terrace-shaped garden with oriental exotic flavour and beauty, includes arbours and staircases with balustrades, leading to a tripartite salla terrena.

ROYAL GARDEN 36 — Arranged in the English style today, the Royal Garden was established by Ferdinand I in 1535 between the Powder Bridge and the Stag Moat, resembling Italian Renaissance gardens. Exotic plants and vine were planted in the garden and a Dutch giardinetto was established in the garden. A variety of constructions, such as an aviary, an orangery, water reservoirs, fountains, and a maze, were established. The garden was re-arranged by Kilian I. Dienzenhofer in 1725—34, which is witnessed by sculptures of lions, vases and allegories, created in Matthias Braun's workshop and installed in the French-like flower area.

HARTIG PALACE GARDEN 37, 50 — Together with other beautiful and picturesque gardens, this garden is situated on the southern slope of the Prague Castle hill. In addition to pleasant walks connected with a wonderful view of Prague, the gardens used to offer impressive cultural performances, in the musical pavilion of the Hartig Palace garden, for example. Designed most likely by Alliprandi in the early 18th century, the pavilion features paintings of castle ruins and stuccoes in its upper hall. In front of the pavilion there are statues of ancient gods, made in A. Braun's worshop around 1735 and transferred from the Štiřín castle garden in 1945.

SINGING FOUNTAIN 38 — Situated in front of the Royal summer residence, the Singing Fountain was cast by a Brno metal founder Jaroš in 1564—68 according to the design by an Italian master Terzio. The fountain stands in the middle of a restored giardinetto, established according to the pattern of the Dutch architect and decorator, V. de Vries. Its name is derived from the sound of water drops falling down a two-layer reservoir, decorated with hunting scenes. The fountain ranks among the most beautiful Renaissance works of its kind North of the Alps.

GREAT BALL-GAME HALL, MATTHIAS BERNARD BRAUN—DAY, NIGHT 39, 40 — The Great Ball-Game Hall was built by Wohlmut and Aostalis in the Royal Garden above the Stag Moat in 1567—69 to be used for the ball games, fashionable at that time. The noble, 60 m long hall with Palladian columns is surfaced with delicate grafitti, representing the allegories of Virtues, Sciences and Elements. Having been abandoned, however, the building was converted into stables in 1723 and a military magazine later. In 1734, allegoric groups of Night and Day, created by Matthias B, Braun's nephew, A. Braun in his uncle's workshop, was installed in front of the Great Ball-Game Hall. The Allegory of Day was destroyed during a bombardment by Prussians in 1757.
The Ball-Game Hall got burnt in 1945, was restored in 1952 and re-adapted in 1971—73. Being equipped with Brussels 17th century tapestries by J. van Leefdael showing Antonius and Cleopatra, the Hall is used for representative purposes at present.

ROYAL SUMMER RESIDENCE (BELVEDER) 41 — Built up in the vicinity of the Prague Castle above the Brusnice stream in 1538—63, the summer residence is a perfect specimen of Italian Renaissance in the Czech countries. Initiated by Ferdinand I, the building was designed by an Italian stone-dresser and architect, della Stella, the architect Tirol and court master-builders, Wohlmut and Aostalis. The Czech Chamber secretary, of Griesbach, was authorized to supervise the construction. Stone-cutting decorations were made in della Stella's workshop (before 1538) and then by other Italian masters. The summer residence was designed for the recreation and pleasure of Queen Ann. It included a rich gallery and a dancing hall, provided with very costly equipment. Belveder and its collections were damaged by the invasion of Swedish troops in 1648. Under Joseph II, the building was devalued by being converted in a laboratory (until 1836). In 1851—65, scenes from Czech history were painted on the walls of the first floor according to the drawings of Ruben's, the Prague Academy director. Having been restored, the summer residence is now used as a gallery.

GOLDEN LANE 42 — Golden Lane is situated behind St. George's Basilica above the Stag Moat. Its tiny houses, painted with festive colours today were inserted in the late 16th century and later in the arches of the Castle's fortification, dating from the reign of the Jagellonský dynasty. They were inhabited by archers, craftsmen and goldbeaters of Rudolph II until 1597. The name of the lane, Zlatnická (Goldsmith's), used from the 1670s, gave rise to a legend that the lane had been occupied by Rudolph's alchemists. In 1952—55, the houses and a roofed gallery, linking three towers and used for transport of prisoners, were restored. An exhibition concerning the history of this popular part of the Castle and book and souvenir shops were established in the renovated houses.

ST. NICHOLAS CHURCH IN LESSER TOWN 43, 59—60, 62, 64, 65 — St. Nicholas Church, a dominant feature of Baroque Prague achitecture is to be found in the middle of the Lesser Town Square, where a Gothic house and butcher's shops used to stand, and adjoins a former Jesuit college at its south side. St. Nicholas' Church was built in 1704—1711 by Christopher Dienzenhofer and in 1732—52 by his son, Kilian I. Dienzenhofer, who built a presbytery and a copula. Dienzenhofer's brother-in-law, Anselmo Lurago, built a slim Rococo belfry in 1751—56, which had been subject to disputes with the Lesser Town community and led to a delay in the construction of the church.
The front of the church, completed in 1710, witnesses an influence of the Roman illusional Baroque style. In addition to the emblem of František Liebštejnský of Kolowraty, the church is decorated with statues of church fathers and an allegory of Theology, created by the sculptor A. Braun before 1735.
The church interior is the most pompous example of the peak of Baroque in Prague. Its frescoes are works of Kracker's and Heger's, the 75 sqm large grandiose chapel was decorated by F. X. Palko. Four larger than life-size wooden stuccoed statues of saints under the copula were made by Platzer in 1752—55, who is also the creator of the copper St. Nicholas statue on the main altar and other works. The church also shows pictures by Škréta, Raab, and Kracker. Wolfgang Amadeus Mozart used to play the organ made by Schwarz in 1745—46.
After the Jesuit order was cancelled by Pope Clement XIV in 1773, St. Nicholas' Church became the Lesser Town parish church.

LORETTO 45 — Built and financed by the Lobkovic dynasty against the stately coulisse of the Černín Palace, the Loretto used to be a pilgrims' place, adjoining the first Capuchin monastery in Bohemia built in 1601. The Loretto's facade is the work of Kilián Ignác Dienzenhofer of 1621—23 and its sculptures, replaced with duplicates today, were created by Quittiner and Kohl. The front of the church culminates in a 1693 tower with chimes by the watchmaker Neumann. Impressive Marian song variations, giving life to the picturesque Hradčany area, are produced by a complex mechanism of small bells cast in Amsterdam. In the very centre of the Loretto there is a Holy Hut (Santa casa), built by the architect Orsi in 1631 and decorated with remarkable stucco relievos created by Italian masters in 1664. They remind us of a legend of the Virgin Mary's house in Nazareth, which was allegedly transferred to the Italian Loretto in the 13th century. Therefore, one can find pictures relating to the Virgin Mary's life and her cedar sculpture inside the hut. Near the east-side ambits there is a church of the Birth of the Lord, built in 1734—35 according to the plans of Aichbauer's and decorated with Reiner's ceiling frescoes.
The Loretto, returned to the Caputchin order, houses a unique collection of treasures. Its treasury includes many goldsmith's works, among which a diamond-set monstrance of 1699 (featuring 6,222 diamonds) is the most valuable exhibit.

PETŘÍN LOOK-OUT TOWER 47 — A 60 m high look-out tower rises on a 318 m high rocky hill (rocks gave the hill its name—petri = rock) to the West of the Lesser Town basin. The construction of the look-out tower, a smaller copy of the Eiffel Tower of Paris, was initiated by the Tourists' Club in connection with the preparations for the Bohemian Jubilee Exposition in 1891.

PETŘÍN OBSERVATORY 48 — Council flats at the Rose Garden on the Petřín hill were converted into an observatory in 1925—30 financed by the Czech Astronomical Society according to the design by J. Veselík. Even today, the observatory satisfies the needs of amateur astronomers and houses a permanent astronomical exposition.

THE STRAHOV MONASTERY 51 — Established by Prince Vladislav II in 1140 at the instance of the Bishop of Olomouc, Jindřich Zdík, the monastery was populated with canonry of the Premonstratensian order, devoted to the dissemination of education and culture. A vast monasterial complex above Prague on the slopes of the Petřín hill includes two churches, a monastery, a monasterial prelacy, libraries and out-buildings. Each was exposed to great changes and building upsets, in the periods of the Hussite movement and the onslaughts of French or Prussian troops in the 18th century in particular. The core of the whole area is the monastery with its library, where the Monument of National Literature was established in 1953. The main entrance to the area is a gate from Pohořelec, built by Anselmo Lurago in 1742. The St. Roch Church, situated to the left of the gate, was built by Rudolph II to express thanks for the averting of plague. Anselmo Lurago took also part in the reconstructions of the abbatial church of the Assumption of Virgin Mary, which included a 12th century Romanesque basilica.
On the main courtyard there is a prelacy dating from the late 16th century, adapted in 1680—99 according to Matheye's and Canevallo's project. The ceiling frescoes were painted by a Premonstratensian, S. Nosecký. The four-wing convent building with Romanesque foundations (after 1142) was rebuilt in the early and peak Baroque periods. Going upstairs, one gets to the monastery itself, built in 1782—84 un-

der the abbot Mayer by an architect Ignác J. Palliardi. The Philosophical and Theological Halls, showing magnificent decorations and unique historical collections, are masterpieces of the monastery. An architecturally arranged garden below the left wing is also a part of the monastery. The monastery was returned to the Premonstratensian order in 1991, who continues the work of the monastery and takes over what remained of its historical and artistic collections.

CHURCH OF THE ASSUMPTION —— The church includes the remnants of a Romanesque rotunda, built in 1182 and extended many times. The current appearance comes from 1745—52, designed by Anselmo Lurago. The church interior has the original three-aisle shape in a Baroque arrangement and is decorated with Palliardi's stuccoes, Kramolín's, Raab's, Neunherz', Palko's, Liška's, and Willmann's paintings based on the Marian legend or St. Norbert's celebration, and Quittainer's sculptures and many others. The chapel ceilings were decorated by a Strahov monk and painter, Nosecký. The altar of St. Ursula's Church contains the relics of St. Norbert, the founder of the Premonstratensian order. There is a Baroque organ in the church, once played by Wolfgang Amadeus Mozart.

THEOLOGICAL HALL 53 — Built by the architect Orsi in 1671—79, the Theological Hall was used originally as a library hall. This is attested to by the theological literature stored in its Baroque cabinets, which includes a section of prohibited books ("libri prohibiti"). The cabinets contain rare illuminated manuscripts, the oldest of which, the Strahov Evangeliary, dates from the 9th century. The Hall, decorated with stuccoes and wall paintings relating to librarianship, by the Premonstratensian painter Nosecký, exhibits 17th century astrological globes, showing the scientific interests of the order members.

PHILOSOPHICAL HALL 54 — Established in 1782—84, in which years the monastery buildings were built by Palliardi, the Philosophical Hall ranks among the most remarkable rooms of the monastery. It was decorated with a unique ceiling paining, "History of Mankind" in 1794, a work of Maulbertsch', the leading representative of Viennese Baroque. Its Baroque walnut cabinets, created by the carpenter Lachhoven, were transferred from a Moravian Premonstratensian monastery in Louka near the town of Znojmo. These cabinets contain books presented to the monastery by Napoleon's wife, Marie Louise, and a glass-cabinet shows a marble bust of the Emperor Francis Joseph I by Lederer.

HVĚZDA (STAR) SUMMER RESIDENCE 55 — The summer residence was built at the south-western end of the deer park Hvězda in Horní Liboc. Established by Emperor Ferdinand I in 1534, the deer park replaced a forest possessed by the Břevnov monastery from the 10th century and was used as a place of recreation and shooting festivals of the kings in the 16th century. The unusual, star-shaped summer house (40 m in diameter) was designed by the Emperor's well-educated son, Archduke Ferdinand, called of Tyrol, who was Vice-Regent in Bohemia. The summer residence was built in 1555—65 by the Prague court's architects, Aostalis and Lucchese, supervised by Tirol and, later, Wohlmut. A. del Pambio, G. Campione and many other Italian masters took part in the rich and fine decorations with motifs from Greek mythology and Greek and Roman history, applying stuccowork in 1556—63 for the first time in Bohemia. The unique character of the whole construction and its decoration followed from the builder's intention — to use the house as a residence for his secret wife, Philippina Welser, who was not allowed to stay at the Castle.
Before the summer residence was decorated with new paintings in the 17th century, the deer park Hvězda, situated at the White Hill, experienced many tragic events in the nation's history. In 1620, the troops of the Estates were defeated by the Catholic League and the Emperor's army. The deer park and the summer house started deteriorating after this White Hill battle, especially owing to enemy troops camping out there in later periods. Under Joseph II, a powder magazine was established in the empty summer residence. The building was not restored until 1918. In 1949—51, the summer house was restored by Janák, to be used as a museum and a memorial to the author of historical novels, Alois Jirásek (1851—1930). In 1964, a museum dedicated to an outstanding Czech painter, Mikoláš Aleš (1852—1913) was opened here.

BŘEVNOV MONASTERY AND ST. MARGARET'T CHURCH 56, 57 — The Břevnov monastery with St. Margaret's Church represents a unique building complex, built in 1708—45 financed by the abbots Zinke and Loebl and designed by Christopher Dienzenhofer and his son, Kilian I. Dienzenhofer. The Monastery replaced a Benedictine monastery, established by the Prague bishop Adalbert and Prince Boleslav II in 993 as the first men's monastery in Bohemia, later destroyed by the Hussites.
The monasterial church is a jewel of Czech architecture with valuable interior decorations and ceiling paintings by Steinfels, dating from 1719—21, and an impressive illusional painting by Hager in 1761. A tomb slab of a Benedictine hermit Vintíř, a Venetian work dating from the 14th century, adjoins the last-named painting. There are such artistic works as paintings by Peter Brandl, sculptures by Jäckl and Prachner. In front of the church chancel there is a crypt dating from the second quarter of the 11th century, which is the most valuable specimen of pre-Romanesque architecture in Bohemia.
The convent and prelacy building, used as a depositary of the State Central Archives until returned to the Benedictine order most recently, is provided with rich fresco decorations. What attracts most attention is the so-called Theresian Hall, decorated with paintings created by a Bavarian painter K. D. Asam in 1727.
There is a Baroque garden behind the monastery, including an abbatial summer-house with a chapel and a fountain, designed by Kilian I. Dienzenhofer. The salla terrena was decorated by a sculptor Prachner in the mid 18th century.

A NIGHT VIEW FROM NERUDA STREET 63 — Culturally, Neruda (Nerudova) street is the most interesting Lesser Town street, descending from Prague Castle to the Lesser Town (Malostranské) Square. Exhibiting mostly Baroque facades decorated with beautiful house signs, the street was named after a poet and journalist, Jan Neruda, who lived in the houses "At Three Black Eagles" and "At Two Suns".

WALLENSTEIN PALACE 66—70, 72—74 — Situated on a rather large area (30, 306 sqm) at the foot of the Hradčany hill, the Wallenstein Palace is the first stately construction of the early Baroque period in the Czech countries. This magnificent residence of Albrecht of Wallenstein was in accordance with the eccentric ambitions of the "general of the Baltic and Oceanic Seas", who, as the general of the Emperor's troops during the Thirty Year War, made an attempt at the king's crown and, after being betrayed, was murdered upon the order of the Emperor.

The palace and its four multi-purpose courtyards were built in 1624—30, designed by a Lombard Spezza, then Sebregondi and from 1626 by a fortification engineer and architect Pieroni. Italian and domestic craftsmen took part in the construction. A Madonna of Val D'Urazzo remained preserved on the palace front as a part of the built-in Trčkovský Palace. A Knights' Hall with marble wainscotting, carried over from the Černín Palace in 1853 covers two floors of the northern wing. The ceiling fresco, showing the Apotheosis of Wallenstein as a God of War, Mars, is a work of del Bianco's, an Italian. The hall is perpendicularly linked with three other halls—the so-called Leather Hall with a ceiling fresco of Pallas Athena painted by Maixner in 1866, the Mirror Hall and Walenstein's alleged workroom.

The palace is suronded with an architecturally imposing garden with a lake, fountains, an aviary for rare birds, stalactite grottoes, and a festive loggia decorated with stuccowork by Italian masters and paintings of del Bianco's based on Vergil's Aeneid (Canto 2, Trojan War). The sculptures, created by a master of Rudolph's era, de Vries, stolen by Swedes in 1648 and installed in the Drootningholm castle gardens, were replaced by duplicates.

Today, the palace is used primarily by the Ministry of Culture.

KOLOVRAT PALACE AND PÁLFFY PALACE 71 — Situated opposite the Wallenstein Palace in the Wallenstein (Valdštejnská) street, the palaces are interlinked with magnificent Rococo terrace-like gardens, ascending as high as to the Hradčany hill. The Kolovrat Palace, today the seat of the Ministry of Culture, was a seat of the Presidium of Czechoslovakia in 1918—38. Hence, difficult negotiations took place in here concerning the Munich agreement and the beginning of the Protectorate. Ordered by the Černín house, the palace itself was designed by Paliardi and built after 1784. In the 19th century, before it was sold to the Kolovrat dynasty, the palace was Alfred von Windischgrätz's residence.

The neigbouring palace was possessed by a mysterious oppressor of Chods, famous from legend, Lomikar—V. M. of Laminger. The palace was extended and rebuilt in 1712 by its new owner, J. J. of Wallenstein. J. J. of Wallenstein was followed by the Fürstenberg dynasty, a member of which, Karel Egon, arranged the first session of the Learned Society of Sciences in 1775 in the palace. In the 19th century, the palace interiors were rebuilt in the neo-Rococo style, and the palace was called after its last owners—the Pálffy family (until 1945).

AERIAL VIEW OF PRESIDIUM AND KRAMÁŘ'S VILLA 75 — The view includes part of the Letná gardens, established in 1859—60, where a pseudo-Baroque state villa, built in 1908—11 for Dr. Kramář and based on the design of Ohmann's, and a large building of the former Straka's Academy can be found. The latter building, arresting one's attention with its copula dating from the period of reconstruction (1893—96) projected by Roštapil, used to be an educational establishment for aristocratic young men, founded in 1710 by Count Straka's Foundation. Today the building houses the Office of the Presidium.

CHARLES BRIDGE 76, 77, 79—81, 93, 100, 101 — Connecting the Old Town and the Lesser Town, Charles Bridge is Prague's most ancient bridge preserved up to this day. Originally, it was called Prague Bridge or Stone Bridge. In 1870, it was named Charles Bridge, because it was founded by Charles IV in 1357 to replace the Judith Bridge, which was built in 1165 and collapsed in 1342. Made of sandstone blocks, the 520 m long and 10 m wide bridge lies on sixteen arches. The construction was supervised by a twenty-seven-year old builder, Peter Parler, and completed as late as the early 15th century. The bridge is a part of the Kings' Route and experienced a lot of dramatic events, in 1648 for example, when it was used by the Swedish Army during their invasion to Prague and partly damaged.

In 1723, the bridge was equiped with oil lighting and in 1866 with gas lighting, using cast-iron Gothic style lamp-posts made in the Komárov foundry.

What impresses most are the decorations, such as the bridge towers, but especially a set of 33 statues and groups of sculpures installed on its parapet. Having been badly affected by the weather, these works are gradually being replaced with copies and installed in the lapidaries of the National Museum and the Museum of the Capital of Prague.

The sculptures represent a wonderful gallery, exhibiting works by outstanding Bohemian artists of 1683—1714, such as Matthias B. Braun, Ferdinand M. Brokoff, Matěj V. Jäckl, J. B. Kohl, and J. O. Mayer. There is a Bruncvík (Brunswick) statue near the Charles Bridge, created by Ludvík Šimek in 1884 and reminding us of the privilege of the Old Town inhabitants to the bridge.

HANAVSKÝ PAVILON 78 — Originally, the pavilion was a cast-iron product of the Prince Hanavský's foundry to be shown at the Bohemian Jubilee Exposition in 1891, designed by Heiser and Hercík. In 1898 it was presented to the community of Prague and assembled in the Letná gardens. Today, a high-quality restaurant is located in this effectively situated neo-Baroque cast-iron construction.

CALVARY GROUP ON CHARLES BRIDGE 82 — In 1657, a guilded bronze group of sculptures, created by Brohn and cast in Dresden, was installed at a Gothic cross, which used to stand here from the 14th century. It follows from a Hebrew inscription around the cross that the means necessary for the creation of the group came from a fine paid by a Jew, who had ridiculed the cross. The statues of the Virgin Mary and St. John Evangelist were made by E. Max in 1861.

LESSER TOWN 83, 84 — Visible from the Lesser Town Tower, built after 1411, The Lesser Town was originally called the New Town and later the Smaller Quarter of Prague. It was founded in 1257 by Přemysl II. Being close to the Prague Castle, this quarter experienced a great upsurge in fortune under Charles IV, who expanded it and encircled it with walls. The proximity of the Prague Castle, however, also had negative political consequences. Almost the whole area of the Lesser Town was destroyed by fire in 1419, being involved in the fight of Prague's inhabitants against the king's troops. A further upward development of the town was slowed down again by a fire in 1541, which demaged the Castle as well. It was in the Baroque period that the town experienced its greatest boom, which is witnessed by a number of magnificent monuments, such as St. Nocholas' Church, Wallenstein, Fürstenberg. Lichtenstein, Nostic, Michna, and Buquoy Palaces. Nevertheless, it is rather in the picturesque composition of beautiful cozy corners and varied nature conditions than in these monuments that the spell of the Lesser Town finds its reflection.

ST. FRANCISCUS-SERAPH'S CHURCH AND CHARLES IV MEMORIAL 86, 94, 97— The church and the memorial are situated on an urbanistically impressive square, surrounded with St. Saviour's (Salvator's) Church and the Colloredo-Mansfeld Palace and situated on the busiest route towards the Charles Bridge. The church was built upon Gothic foundations by Canevallo in 1679—89 according to a design by the Burgundian architect, Jean-Baptiste Mathey, to be used by the Knights of the Cross with a red star. The seat of this only Czech clerical order, established in the mid 13th century, was in the neighbouring monastery. A magnificent copula of the church is decorated with Václav V. Reiner's fresco „Last Judgement", the interiors show wall and suspended paintings by Liška, Willmann and Pirner as well as sculptures by Jäckl and stuccoes of saints by Dresden sculptors J. and K. Süssners. The front of the church is provided with sculptures by Prachner of 1758 and other Czech artists. At the corner, we can find the so-called Vintners' Column Memorial, erected in 1846, with a St. Wenceslas statue, created by Bendl in 1676.

When the terrain of the unique Knights of the Cross (Křižovnické) Square had been conditioned by the Klein Brothers of Wiesenberg company, a neo-Gothic memorial to Emperor Charles IV with allegories of four university colleges was erected in 1849 at the cost of Prague University. It was created in the workshop of a Nürnberg metal founder Burgschmidt according to a model by Hähnel, a sculptor from Dresden.

OLD TOWN BRIDGE TOWER 95, 96 — Enhancing the historical importance of Křižovnické Square, the bridge tower was built on the first pillar of Charles Bridge and designed by Peter Parler. It is considered one of the most beautiful bridge constructions in Europe. Completed in 1391, the tower was not only a part of the bridge, but also a part of the Old Town fortification system. In about 1380, the tower was decorated with top works of Central-European sculpture. Parler's workshop concentrated on rulers and builders of the bridge, Charles IV and Wenceslas IV, protected by the patrons of Bohemia, and emblems of the countries. In 1978, the sculptures were replaced with copies and installed in the National Gallery. In 1621, heads of twelve executed Bohemian noblemen, who had taken part in the revolt of Estates, were exhibited on the tower to remain there for ten years. The sculptures of the western tower side were damaged in 1648, during the invasion of Swedes to Prague. The tower was restored and its roof was completed in 1874—78.

LADISLAV ŠALOUN (1870—1946), MASTER JOHN HUSS MEMORIAL (DETAIL) 102 — The memorial was unveiled on the 6 July 1915, on the occasion of the 500th anniversary of the burning to death of this Czech preacher and reformer in Constance. The enormous size of this multi-figure memorial, created by a representative of the Czech Art Nouveau school of sculpture of stone and bronze, was the subject of many controversies. These concerned the composition, and location of the work in the historical environment of the Old Town Square in front of the Golz-Kinský Palace.

OLD TOWN SQUARE 103, 104, 121, 122, 125, 127, 129 — Called Old Town Square in 1895 (Marketplace, Great Marketplace before), the square is, together with the Prague Castle, the most eventful place in Prague. A vast marketplace of the today's area (about 9,000 sqm) was established here on a crossing of trade paths at the turn of the 11th and 12th centuries. It included a custom-house (Ungelt today) where goods brought to Bohemia used to be unloaded. The square and its Townhall turned into a traditional meeting place used for political and revolutionary events, representative events and repressive acts. On the square, a radical Hussite preacher, John Želivský, was executed in 1422 and the last Hussite captain, John Roháč of Dubá, put to death in 1437. Crosses in the pavement mosaic in front of the eastern Townhall wing remind us of the execution of 27 Bohemian noblemen and burghers, who took part in the Estates revolt. George of Poděbrady was elected King of Bohemia in 1458 in the Townhall's Council Hall. The square saw a rally in 1918, requiring the establishment of an independent republic, and a rally in February 1948, organized by the Communists.

It was also modern architecture that enhanced the representative character of the square with original Gothic and rebuilt houses and the Rococo Golz-Kinský Palace. Let us mention, above all, an Art Nouveau Baroque-like building of the former Prague Municipal Insurance Office, today the seat of the Ministry of Trade and Tourism, designed by architect Polívka and decorated with Ladislav Šaloun's and Bohuslav Schnirch's sculptures. In front of it, there is a sizeable John Huss memorial.

The Old Town Square and the Kings' Route, crossing the square, are the most attractive sights of Prague.

„AT THE MINUTE" HOUSE 106 — Adjacent perpendicularly to the Old Town Townhall, the house has Gothic foundations of the early 15th century. In 1564, it was rebuilt in the Renaissance style. After 1603 and 1610, it was decorated with Renaissance grafiti based on the engravings of Raimondi's and Beham's. In the late 18th century, the house included a chemist's store and was provided with a stone lion at its corner. The grafiti were uncovered in 1905 and restored. Today, the building houses the offices of the Municipal Board.

THE ASTRONOMICAL CLOCK OF THE OLD TOWN 108—113 — In its original shape, this clock was constructed around 1410 by watch-maker Nicholas of Kadaň. The Townhall being rebuilt, the horologe was reconstructed by Master Hanuš. The clock mechanism was updated in 1553—60 and was decorated with statuettes and models in 1659, then in the 18th century and, finally, in 1864. In 1865, a calendar plate featuring Allegories of Months, a work of Josef Mánes' (1820—1871), the leading representative of the Czech 19th century art, was installed. In 1885, the original painting was delivered to the collections of the Museum of the Capital of Prague and replaced by a copy, which got burnt in 1945, together with some carvings. In 1962, a new copy was made by B. Číla. The burnt apostles were replaced with carvings by Vojtěch Sucharda (1884—1972) as early as 1948.

The astronomical clock is one of the most attractive Old Town sights. Its mechanism, moving figures with allegorical, religious and historical associations (memento mori, allusion to Turks' incursions, etc.), is put into operation on the hour every hour.

GOLZ KINSKÝ PALACE AND „AT THE BELL" HOUSE 126— The most beautiful buildings of the Old Town Square are situated in front of the cathedral of the Virgin Mary before Týn (Týn cathedral). After the neo-Baroque facade as removed from the house „At the Bell" (U zvonu), a unique Gothic front from about 1350 was discovered with stone-cutting decorations. A building search of the house interior revealed a chapel with Gothic wall paintings originating in the mid 14th century. The Gallery of Prague now uses the interiors of the reconstructed house for exhibiting contemporary arts.

The neighbouring Rococo Golz-Kinský Palace, possessed by Prince Kinský as early as 1635, got its graceful and impressive appearance in 1755—65, as it was rebuilt by Anselmo Lurago according to the plans of Kilián Ignác Dienzenhofer's. The palace, built up on older, Romanesque foundations, is used by the National Gallery of Prague for exhibitions.

ŠTORCH'S HOUSE 128 — Štorch's house, one of the impressive houses on the eastern edge of the Old Town Square, was built in 1897 according to a project of Ohmann's and Krieghammer's. The neo-Renaissance building of Štorch's publishing house attracts one's attention by its figure paintings created by Novák according to Aleš's drawings, showing St. Wenceslas and the Three Magi. The paintings, damaged in May 1945, were restored by a painter Sembtner.

A VIEW FROM TÝN CATEDRAL TOWER 130—131 — A marvellous three-aisle cathedral, founded in 1365, provides a view of Prague from its eighty-metre high towers, completed as late as the late 16th century.

OLD TOWN ST. NICHOLAS' CATHEDRAL 131 — St. Nicholas' cathedral was built within a Benedictine monastery according to K. I. Dienzenhofer's project in 1732—35. Some more space was considered in the project because of houses situated close to the cathedral's front, which were pulled down later. The sculptures were created by Matthias Braun's nephew, A. Braun, and the copula was painted by Assam. The cathedral being used by the Czechoslovak Church, the equipment was transferred to other Catholic churches.

In 1906, a neo-Baroque fountain with dolphins was created by B. Kříženecký in front of this outstanding monument near the Pařížská Avenue is provided with a sculpture of St. Nicholas by B. Šimonovský, erected in 1906 too.

CAROLINUM 132—134 — Situated in Železná street, leading to the Old Town Square, Carolinum is the central residence of Charles University (Caroline University), founded by Charles IV on 7 April 1348 as one of the university colleges. It was the first college in Central Europe, aimed at raising the then level of education to the most advanced one. The core of the campus under construction was Rothlev's house, obtained by Wenceslas IV and presented to Charles College in 1383, which had resided in a house next to St. Nicholas' Church. The appearance of Carolinum comes from the period of its Baroque reconstruction, completed by Kaňka in 1718. The front looking out into Železná street is provided with a Baroque window, dating from 1687, and a glazed arcade with a ribbed Gothic vault. A wing, built around 1385 and spreading towards the Theatre of the Estates, includes a well-preserved and valuable bay chapel with rich outside decorations. It was restored in 1881 by Mocker and, further, in 1946—75 according to a design by Frágner with the aid of sculptors Makovský, Lidický, Lauda, and Pokorný. The Great Hall, built after 1383, is at it's centre. It was connected with the bay chapel. There is a tapestry of Mrs. Teinizerová's in the front part of the hall, made in 1947 and related to the theme of the Charles University seal made by a sculptor Sychra, namely Charles IV kneeling before St. Wenceslas.

THEATRE OF THE ESTATES 135 — Called Tyl Theatre and Nostic Theater before, the Theatre of the Estates is a neo-Classicist building, built in 1781 financed by Count Francis Nostic according to the design by Haffenecker and expert advice by Count Khünigl. The theatre was rebuilt in 1859, 1881 and 1892 and completely restored in 1980s and early 1990s (finished 1991). The reconstruction also included an operational connection with the Kolowrat Palace, standing opposite the theatre.

Originally, plays performed in the theatre were in German and Italian. In 1787, Mozart's opera Don Giovanni had its first night in the theatre. The composer Carl M. von Weber was opera conductor here in 1813—16. On 21 December 1834 the theatre performed a play of Josef K. Tyl's, „Fidlovačka" (Spring Festival), with music composed by František Škroupa. This play included a song, "Kde domov můj" (Where is My Home), which became the Czechoslovak state anthem in 1918.

NATIONAL MUSEUM 136, 138, 139, 141, 142 — This over 100 m long stately building of the National Museum closes the upper part of Wenceslas Square, where a Horse Gate used to stand. Designed by Prof. Schulz, the building was constructed in 1885—90 to be used as a seat of a museum established by patriotic nobility in 1818 with the aim of promoting cultural and scientific development. The costly, neo-Renaissance building has four wings and two courtyards. Its representative entrance is located on an elevated platform with a fountain and allegoric statues by A. Wagner in 1891—94, representing Bohemia, Moravia and Silesia, and the Elbe and the Vltava rivers. The National Museum statues are an illustrative gallery of Czech fine arts of the late 19th century, competing with works by the master sculptor Schwantaler of Munich. His bronze sculptures of Libussa, Přemysl, Wenceslas and Přemysl II, destined originally for a set of 24 works for the Czech Slavín in Tupadly near Liběchov, were located in the entrance hall, decorated with columns and a representative staircase, covering almost the entire area of the central wing. This wing also shows 16 busts of prominent men, who played a significant role in the history of the National Museum, and 32 medallions of Bohemian kings, created by Popp and Schirch in 1897—99

A square-shaped building of Pantheon, culminating in a copula with 48 busts and statues of the genii of the Czech nation, is a sanctuary of the Czech nation's desires and an expression of its self-confidence. Its historically oriented paintings are by leading representatives of the National Theatre generation, such as Václav Brožík and František Ženíšek. The allegorical decorations below the copula are the works of Vojtěch Hynais', a French-oriented painter of the above mentioned generation.

The National Museum houses departments relating to history and natural sciences as well as a valuable library, containig about one million unique medieval manuscripts.

JOSEF VÁCLAV MYSLBEK (1848–1922), EQUESTRIAN STATUE OF ST. WENCESLAV 137 – The equestrian statue of St. Wenceslas, the patron of Bohemia, is a symbol of the nation's identity and independence. Designed architecturally by Dryák and ornamented by Klouček, the statue was installed in the upper part of Wenceslas Square in 1912–13. It was in 1887 that Myslbek started working on the subject and in 1904 that a plaster model of the final design was made. This noble, neo-Renaissance work and the statues of St. Procope, Blessed Agnes, and St. Ludmila make up a whole. The last statue, St. Adalbert, which had not been completed by Myslbek, was cast in Mašek's workshop. A classically emotive work with animated expressions of its figures was apparently affected by French sculpture.

JUNGMANN SQUARE 140 – The Jungmann Square is a small square near the Wenceslas Square with a statue of a writer and a leading representative of the Czech National Revival, Josef Jungmann. Created according to old drawings of Levý's by Ludvík Šimek in 1872, the statue was installed on a marble plinth, designed by Barvitius in 1878.

PŘÍKOPY 144 – The "Příkopy" (The Moat) zone is one of the busiest business areas of Prague, starting at the bottom part of the Wencslas Square and Můstek with a post-modern ČKD building designed by A. Šrámková. It is the constructivistic buidling of the Children's Store that arrests the greatest attention among the modern structures of the "Na Příkopě" street. On the right-hand side of the street, we can find the oldest department store in Prague, designed by a famous Viennese architect Hansen and built in 1869–71. The Sylva-Taroucco (originally Piccolomini) Palace, built by Kilián Ignác Dienzenhofer and Anselmo Lurago in 1743–51, witnesses the fine aristocratic culture of the Rococo period. The Church of the Holy Cross was built in 1816–24 and its reserved Empire design was the work of J. Fischer. The Slavonic House (Slovanský dům), originally a Baroque palace of the Píchovský family, was rebuilt by Heger in 1798. The most imposing of the banks located in the Příkopy zone is the Investment Bank, built in the neo-Renaissance style in 1894–96 by the arrchitect Polívka and decorated with Mikoláš Aleš's mosaic works and Klouček's and Sucharda's relievos.

WENCESLAS SQUARE 145 – Called originally the Horse Market, Wenceslas Square used to be the main market place of the new Town with a St. Wenceslas statue created by J. Bendl in 1680 (carried over to Vyšehrad in 1879) in its middle. A 750-metre long square is a most important social and business avenue with representative hotels. The upper part of the square is perpendicularly closed with a stately construction of the National Museum (J. Schulz, 1885–90), a homage to knowledge. Myslbek's grandiose memorial with an equestrian statue of St. Wenceslas is an expression of the nation's self-confidence and solace. A wooden theatre, Bouda, used to stand at the opposite, bottom part of the square in 1786–89, housing the first Czech stage. On either side as well as in the middle of the square one can enter the underground railway stations.

POWDER TOWER 146–148 – Built in honour of King Vladislav Jagellonský in 1475 and designed by Matěj Rejsek of Prostějov, the Powder Tower replaced a fortification gate. Wenceslas IV got the Royal Court built in its neighbourhood, used as a royal residence. After being abandoned in 1483, the importance of the Royal Court started to decline Ranking among the most valuable monuments of the late Gothic period, the Tower was used as a powder magazine in the late 17th century. While being besieged by Prussians, the Tower was damaged. In 1875–76, it was rebuilt in the neo-Gothic style by the architect Mocker, being completed with a gallery and a roof. The Tower provides a view of the oldest town quarter, the Old Town, and one of the busiest places in Prague, the Republic Square, including the former Main Custom-House of about 1810, the "At the Hyberns" house (U hybernů), a Capuchin church of St. Joseph, and a modern bank of 1938.

MUNICIPAL HOUSE OF THE CAPITAL OF PRAGUE 149–150 – The Municipal House was built in the Royal Court in 1906–11 according to Balšánek's and Polívka's project. A representative social and cultural centre replaced a seat of Czech kings, of George of Poděbrady in particular, who not only summoned the Czech assemblies here, but also appealed to European kings to unite and maintain peace. Today, concerts, balls and exhibitions take place here and one can find a café, a restaurant, and a wineyard here. The interiors are full of paintings and sculptures by leading Czech artists of the early 20th century such as Alfons Mucha (paintings in the Mayor's Hall), Jan Preisler (paintings in the Palacký Hall), and František Ženíšek (paintings in the Grégr Hall). The ground floor and the restaurant are decorated with Mikoláš Aleš's and Obsovský's paintings. Scultures by Josef V. Myslbek, K. Novák and Ladislav Šaloun can be found in the Smetana Concert Hall and the Rieger Hall.

NATIONAL THEATRE 151–154 – The National Theatre was built by means of public money collections in 1868–81 according to Josef Zítek's project. Once finished, the valuable neo-Renaissance building was destroyed by fire. Its renewal and completion, supervised by the architect Josef Schulz, was finished in 1883, including new interior decorations and a new curtiain made by Vojtěch Hynais. The external decorations of the loggia were created by the painter Tulka, sculptors Wagner, Myslbek, and Schirch. The dominating features of the representative foyer are Mikoláš Aleš's and František Ženíšek's paintings, the latter being the author of the auditorium's ceiling paintings as well. The Royal Box, now the President's Box, is decorated with paintings by Vojtěch Hynais, Václav Brožík, and Julius Mařák. Busts in the foyer remind us of great persons of Czech culture.

While a vast reconstruction in 1977–83, connected with the updating of the technological equipment, the open space between the theatre and St. Ursula's convent was built up. Designed by the architect prager and decorated with glass facint tiles designed by Libenský, a new, seven-storey building and the New Stage of the National Theatre were completed in 1983.

Opposite the historical building of the National Theatre there is a former Lažanský Palace with the Slavia café, built in the French Renaissance style in 1861–63. A leading Czech composer, Bedřich Smetana, lived on the first floor of the count's palace until 1869.

The side wall of the National Theatre enters the Masaryk embankment, featuring a number of representative blocks of flats, provided with historicizing fronts and looking out on the Vltava river and the Slavonic island, called Žofín until 1925.

STŘELECKÝ (SHOOTERS') ISLAND 155 – The name of the island was not chosen at random. Having been joined to the Old and New Towns, the island was used as a training ground of Prague marksmen. In the 16th century, popular shooting games of the inhabitants of Prague were held here, called "bird shooting". In the late 19th century, great rallies took place on the island. In 1882 the island saw the First Sokol rally.

BEDŘICH SMETANA (1824–1884) STATUE, SMETANA MUSEUM AND NOVOTNÝ FOOTBRIDGE 157–158, 179 – Smetana embankment represents the oldest urbanistic solution of this kind in Prague, made by the Dann company in 1841–45 according to the project by Grueber. The blocks of flats were designed by a building director Strobach in 1836. A mill was replaced with a neo-Gothic building of Charles Baths, where a Czech poet and journalist, Karel Havlíček Borovský, lived in 1848. In front of the baths, we can find Novotný footbridge, bearing the name of a descendant of an old millers' family. The buildings of the Old Town mills were built in the neo-Renaissance style of Ulmann's and decorated with Myslbek's sculptures of putts. There is a Water Tower here, built in 1480 and rebuilt many times, after the 1885 fire for the last time. The footbridge is closed with the Smetana museum building, representing the so-called Bohemian Renaissance of 1883 and designed by the architect Wiehl originally for the purpose of Prague water works. Its front is adorned with a grafitto, Fight with Swedes on Charles Bridge in 1648, based on drawings of Ženíšek's. Its niches show paintings of people who gained recognition for defending Prague against the Swedes, created by Šubič according to Aleš's and Koula's drawings. The museum was fouded by the Bedřich Smetana Association in 1936 and houses documents relating to the life and work of this leading Czech composer. In 1984, a statue of Smetana was created by Malejovský and erected in front of the museum.

"AT THE GOLDEN WELL" house 159 – The house is a corner building between Liliová and Karlova streets, the latter being the busiest route, leading from the Old Town towards the Charles Bridge. This Renaissance house, adapted in the Baroque style, attracts one's attention with its stucco relievos of protectors against the plague, St. Sebastian and St. Rochus, created by a sculptor Mayer most probably after 1760, after an epidemic of the plague.

OLD TOWN HOUSE SIGNS 160 — House No. 10 in Týnská street was called "In Hell" in the 17th century. Later it was posseessed by the Kinský family, whose emblem showed three wolf's claws or, more likely, three boar'-s teeth. When the house was rebuilt in the 18th century by the architect Heger, the sign bore three ostrich's feathers.

In addition to their identificating, representative and orientational functions, house signs, which are also associated with the tradition of shop-signs, used to have a symbolic meaning as well. Located not only in the Old Town, but also in the Lesser Town and the Hradčany Town, beautiful house signs tell us many stories of the old Prague.

OLD JEWISH CEMETERY, OLD-NEW SYNAGOGUE 161—164 — They witness a Jewish settlement round the Prague Castle as early as the 10th century. The Jewish community accounted for almost one third of the inhabitants of Prague in the early 18th century. Despite this, a number of pogroms and restrictions made the Jews live in a closed ghetto. When liberation decrees had been issued by Joseph II, the Jewish Town in Prague was called Josefov and, as the fifth town, became an equal town quarter after 1848. Bad hygienic conditions, however, resulted in its demolition around 1900.

It is an old Jewish cemetery that reminds us of the centuries' long Jewish history of Prague. The oldest of about 11 thousand tombstones (lying on up to 12 lower layers) dates from 1439. The mournful spell of this cemetery witnesses a unique history. The tombstones show not only names and birth and death dates, but also social positions and symbols of traditional families, arranged in a princely hierarchy. Names of the dead are often replaced with symbols endowed with special poeticizing meanings. Among the tombstones there is a tomb of a powerful Jewish Mayor and Primate, Mordechaj Maisl († 1601), after which a street of the former ghetto and a synagogue were named. Another well-known tombstone carries a name of Rabbi Löw ben Bezalel, who, as a legend says, created an artificial man—the Golem.

The Jewish Town had the oldest synagogue in Europe, called the Old-New Synagogue, which remained preserved up to now. It was established around 1280 as a two-aisle hall. Its brick gable dates from the 14th century, when a vestibule was built. Since the main aisle was reserved for men only, another building was constructed on the northern side in the18th century to be used by women. The interior shows valuable works of Jewish culture of the 16th—19th centuries.

There is a former ceremony hall near the Old Jewish Cemetery, today housing an exposition, "Children's Drawings from Terezín". The so-called High Synagogue is used as an exhibition hall, showing synagogue textiles. The Pinkas Synagogue is a memorial to victims of Nazism, the Maisl Synagogue exhibits a unique collection of silver and other metal objects. The esoteric spell of the Jewish Town sights is underlined by the Jewish Townhall with a tower and a clock provided with a Hebrew dial.

KAREL HLADÍK (1912—1967), FRANZ KAFKA 165 — A bust decorating a building built in 1902 by Polívka, used originally as a prelacy of the former Benedictine monastery, reminds us of the birthplace of an ingenious writer of Jewish origin, born here in 1883. The bust was created by a representative of the home classical realistic stream, influenced primarily by the contemporary Italian art.

THE CHURCH OF ST. JACOB 166—167 — This church, together with its cloisters, was founded in 1232 by Václav 1st. and is situated in Malá Štupartská street angled opposite to the Ungelt exit.

The front facade is decorated in stucco work by the Italian sculptor O. Most, begun in 1695 and completed when the church was given a baroque character after the fire in 1689.

The church's two alters and ceiling frescoes, by F. M. Wogel, give the interior a rich appearance, and were finished toward the and of reconstruction in the years 1736—39.

A feature of the excellent interior decoration is the painting of such artists as P. Brandle, V. V. Reiner, etc.

A good example of excellent workmanship is the tombstone of the High Chancellor Vratislav of Mitrovic, which is the work of J. B. Fischer of Erlach from the years 1714—16.

THE CHURCH OF ST. HENRY 168 — Situated in Jindřišská street in the New Town, the Gothic church was founded in the second half of the 14th century and includes a Renaissance vestibule, additional Baroque constructions and Baroque interior arrangements. Many tombstones were transferred from an abolished cemetery to the church outer wall. In 1875—79, Mocer re-Gothicized the church. The church interior is decorated with Gothic works (a desk picture of St. Stephen's Madonna from the 15th century, St. Henry statue and others), a variety of Baroque works, created by Czech painters and sculptors in particular, and 19th century works (windows painted according to Sequens in 1891, for example).

The re-Gothicized belfry near the church was built in about 1475. The parish was built in 1386 in the Gothic style.

PRESBYTARY OF THE CHURCH OF OUR LADY OF SNOW 169 — The tallest church in Prague, which was never completed, towers behind the Franciscan parish. It was founded by Charles IV in 1347 as a coronation church used also by the Carmelite order. What has been preserved up to today was built in 1379—97; unfortunately, the original, higher vault had collapsed. The Hussite revolutionary movement considerably affected the history of the church. In 1419, the leader of the poor of Prague, John Želivský, initiated here a march towards the New Town Townhall, resulting in the defenestration of the town councillors, and later seized the church. He preached sermons in this church until executed in 1422. In 1622, the church and the monastery were presented by the Prague archbishop to the Franciscans, who experienced a tragedy here. After the Passau troops invaded Prague in 1611, the poor people, suspecting the monks of having hidden escaping soldiers, broke into the church and murdered all the Franciscan monks.

What attracts one's attention in the church interior is an early Baroque altar, the tallest in Prague, built in 1649—61, when the church was possessed by the Franciscans again. There are also ten statues of Franciscan saints created around 1625, a valuable picture "Annunciattion of Virgin Mary", created by Václav V. Reiner in 1724 and situated on a side altar, and a tin baptismal font of 1449.

ST. GILES' CHURCH 170 — Located between Jilská and Husova streets in the Old Town, St. Giles' Church was built in 1339—71 by Bishop John of Dražice and later by Archbishop Ernest of Pardubice as a three-aisle chapter church. The church was used by John Milíč of Kroměříž for preaching Czech sermons in 1364 and then by the Hussites in 1420. In 1626, the church was donated to the Dominicans by kaiser Ferdinand II, who built a large monastery there. In 1731, the monastery was rebuilt in the Baroque style by the architect Kaňka. Its vault paintings and St. Wenceslas picture were created by Václav V. Reiner, most sculptures by Quittainer and, in 1839—45, by Schwanthaler, a professor of Munich, and carvings by Weiss in 1734—38.

CHURCH OF THE HOLIEST HEART OF THE LORD 171 — Located in the middle of George of Poděbrady Square in Vinohrady, the church was built in 1928—32 according to the design of Plečnik in the style of an ancient Christian temple. The original transformation of the antiquating art finds its reflection in the church's decoration—in Stefan's plastic works above the three portals, in the form of the marble main altar, and in Pešan's sculptures inside the church.

VILLA AMERICA 172 — Called originally Michna summer residence, Villa America is the first work of the leading Baroque architect in Bohemia, Kilian I. Dienzenhofer. The attractive building in today's Ke Karlovu street in the New Town, harmonizing the influence of Viennese monumental constructions by Hildebrandt and French elegance and balance intended by this builder, was built in 1712—20 at the cost of Count Michna of Vacínov. The main hall was decorated with wall paintings by Schor in 1720, showing mythological scenes. The summer residence was surrounded with a garden adorned with vases and groups of Seasons of the Year, created in A. Braun's workshop. This garden was used as a cattle marketplace from the late 18th century. In 1932, the summer residence was purchased by the Antonín Dvořák Association and turned into a museum dedicated to this world-renowned composer.

Called after a pub in the vicinity in the 19th century, Villa America is separated fom the street by a copy of Baroque barred fence. Its wonderful location gets lost among neighbouring higher buildings.

DVOŘÁK'S HALL IN RUDOLPHINUM 174 — Following the National Theatre, Rudolphinum is the second most important neo-Renaissance building designed by Zítek, Schulz and Vejrych in 1876—84. Being a seat of the Czech Philharmony, it is used for concerts and socially important events. The building was named after the Prince Royal, Rudolph.

CLEMENTINUM'S MIRROR HALL 175 — Built by Kaňka in 1724, the Mirror Hall of the former Jesuitical college is a worderfully decorated room, where concerts and exhibitions are held. Rich stuccoes with built-in mirrors are a frame to the ceiling paintings showing scenes from Virgin Mary's life, created probably by Hiebl. The saints' pictures are by Václav V. Reiner. The chapel was abolished in 1784 and restored for some time in 1816. Today it is a part of the National Library.

WOLFGANG AMADEUS MOZART (1756—1791) MEMORIAL AT BERTRAMKA 176, 177 — Bertramka, a provincial manor dating from the 17th century and reconstructed in 1873 for the last time, went down in history as a place of abode of a most prominent composer, Wolfgang A. Mozart. In 1784, a composer František X. Dušek and his wife Josephine, an outstanding singer, bought Bertramka and Mozart used to be their guest when he was in Prague. In 1787, he composed here the best-known opera of his, Don Giovanni, which had its successful first night in the Nostic Theatre.

PAŘÍŽSKÁ AVENUE 181, 182 — Connecting the Old Town Square with Svatopluk Čech Bridge, Pařížská avenue allows an approach to the former Jewish Town, pulled down due to its bad hygienic condition. This broad avenue, called Mikulášská (Nicholas) before, includes representative blocks of flats built mostly in 1901—1906. Behind the Old-New Synagogue, the most significant monument of the former Jewish Town, there is a park area with a bronze statue of Moses made by František Bílek in 1905. The avenue is closed with College of Law of Charles University, built in 1924—27 according to a project by Jan Kotěra of 1914. A large hotel, Intercontinental, was built opposite the College in 1970—74, designed by Filsak, Bubeníček and Švec.

THE ATRIUM HOTEL 182 — Having been completed in 23 months, this construction of Franc', Nováček's, and Fencl's is a hotel with the largest width in Central Europe. Its atrium structure houses 788 rooms providing a total of 1,568 beds. Its restaurant offers international menus as well as a specifically Bohemian cuisine.

VYŠEHRAD CASTLE 187, 189—195 — A famous residence of the first Czech princes, Libussa (Libuše) and the Premyslid dynasty, was established on a rock above the Vltava river probably in the 10th century, following the Prague Castle. Under Vratislav II (1061—92, crowned king in 1085), it became the king's seat and a chapter was founded here in 1070. At the same time, the original wooden castle was replaced by a stone one, and the old churches, destroyed during the Hussite wars, were replaced by new ones.

The present day Vyšehrad is encircled with Baroque walls and bastions, constructed by Italian fortification builders and adapted in 1882. The walls surround the St. Peter and Paul's chapter church of Romanesque origin, rebuilt in the Gothic and Baroque periods and adapted in the neo-Gothic style in 1885—87. Near the church there are remnants of a Romanesque bridge, which was probably a part of the castle fortifications. In front of the church we can find St. Ludmila's chapel. The only Romanesque monument preserved until now at Vyšehrad is St. Martin's rotunda, which may be approached through and entrance gate from the "V pevnosti" street.

The St. Peter and Paul Church faces the main gate of a cemetery, founded around 1890 by Antonín Wiehl to be used as a burying place for merited sons of the nation. The burial ground, proposed by the provost Štulc, was situated in the old parish cemetery of 1660. In 1889—93 and 1903, "Slavin" (Pantheon), a decent burying ground for the nation's most prominent persons, was established in the middle of the eastern side of the cemetery.

Three sculptural groups of Myslbek's were transferred from the damaged Palacký bridge to Vyšehrad lawns, to a place of a burnt-out armoury. The last of the restored groups, "Přemysl and Libuše", was installed in 1978. Myslbek's heros were created to correspond to the national mythological characters of the Královodvorský Manuscript, which was topical at that time. The "Lumír and the Lay" group was created in 1888, "Přemysl and Libuše"' in 1892, "Záboj and Slavoj" (heros returning from a victorious battle) in 1895, and "Ctirad and Šárka" in 1897. Impressive and poetic ideas of the glorious past of Slavs thus realised their importance at Vyšehrad.

"NA SLOVANECH" MONASTERY (EMAUS) 188 — The monastery was established by Charles IV in 1347 as a seat of Slavonic Benedictines, who turned it into a unique centre of education and arts. In 1395, the glagolitic part of the so-called Reims Gospel, used by French kings for taking oaths during coronation after 1546, was created here. During the Hussite wars, the only Czech Caixtin monastery was established here.

The monastery with the Virgin Mary's Church was rebuilt many times and seriously damaged in 1945 by air-raids. Reconstructions began in he post-war years and were completed in 1967, resulting in an up-to-date front and towers designed by the architect Černý.

SLAVÍN GATE 195 — Slavín is the dominant feature of the Vyšehrad cemetery, a common burial place of the most merited representatives of the nation. It was built in 1889—90 according to the project by Wiehl and decorated with sculptures Genius of Homeland, Trimphant Homeland, and Mourning Homeland, created by Maudr in 1892—93. The first person buried in Slavin was a poet, Julius Zeyer, in 1902, who was followed by another 53 personalities (Josef V. Myslbek, Vojtěch Hynais, Emma Destin, Alfons Mucha, Jan Kubelík, Václav Špála, and others). The tombstones at the cemetery were made by leading Czech sculptors and architects.

ST. MARTIN'S ROTUNDA 196 — St. Martin's rotunda is the oldest monument at Vyšehrad preserved up to now, dating from the second half of the 11th century. Being converted into a powder magazine when the Vyšehrad fort had been built, the importance of the rotunda declined. In the 19th century, it was used as a store room. In 1878, however, it was bought by the Vyšehrad chapter and restored according to the project by the architect Baum. Its interior was decorated with wall paintings by König and Heřman and an altar painting by Sequens. Further reconstructions took place in 1915 and 1969—70.

PALACE OF CULTURE AND THE FORUM HOTEL 198, 199 — A need for a social and cultural centre large enough to hold conferences, symposiums and congresses resulted in a governmental decision upon a construction for a Palace of Culture in 1975. A gigantic monoblock of the Palace of Culture in the shape of an irregular heptagon was built according to the project of a team of the Military Design Institute architects (Mayer, Ustohal, Vaněk, and Karlík) and completed in 1980. On the opposite side of the southern part of the Nuselský bridge head, there is the polygonal tower of the Forum hotel. The twenty-seven--storey building was built in 1988 according to a project of Trávníček's.

PRAGUE'S EXHIBITION AREA 201, 202 — The dominant feature of the exhibition area is the Congress Palace, a neo-Baroque iron construction designed by Münzberger in 1891 and reconditioned in 1952—54. The exhibition area is in the former Royal Deer Park. According to Wiehl's project, 300,000 sqm were turned into exhibition groups in 1891 to provide space for the Bohemian Jubilee Exposition. The original exhibition hall of the Artistic and Retrospective Exposition, today the seat of the Academy of Fine Arts, reminds us of the event. To the right of the entrance sector, there is a pavilion of the Capital of Prague, used as a National Museum lapidary. The large exhibition area includes many attractive pavilions (such as Marold's grandiose panorama of the Lipany battle, built in 1898) and sights (a restored fountain, designed by the inventor František Křižík, for example).

TRÓJA MANSION 203 — In the late 17th century, a mansion in the style of Italian suburban villas was built by Count Šternberk in a vine-growing area in the northern part of the Prague basin. Such architects as Orsi de Orsini, Carloni and a famous Burgundian Mathey participated in the project. The interiors were decorated by famous painters: the allegories and crypto-portraits of the Šternberk dynasty were painted by the Marchetis, and the paintings in the Main Hall in honour of the Habsburg dynasty by a Dutch painter Godyn in 1691—97. The count was an ambitious man, attempting the career of a court officer. His country house was intended to be a rest place for the monarch, tired by hunting. The mansion's composition was sophisticated—standing on the outside staircase landing, decorated with Bigantomachia sculptures and works of the Heermanns' of Dresden, and looking straight ahead one can see the silhouette of Prague Castle.

The mansion and its garden have been reconstructed and the interiors now show 19th century picture collections of the Prague Gallery.

ZBRASLAV MANSION 204—209 — Standing majestically on the left Vltava river bank and accessible by steamboat from Prague, the Zbraslav mansion used to be a Cistercian abbey prelacy. It was built in 1739, decorated with frescoes by Václav V. Reiner and turned into a mansion of the Bartoň of Dobenín house in 1911—12.

The Zbraslav monastery was founded by Wenceslas II in 1291, who is buried in the church of the Virgin Mary together with Wenceslas III and Eliška Přemyslovna. The local abbots became famous for their Zbraslav Chronicle, describing events from 1337.

The abbey convent was rebuilt according to the design of Santini's before 1709 and completed by the architect Kaňka in 1724—32. The stucco decorations were created by Soldati and the frescoes by Reiner and Palko. The monastery was abolished in 1785 and started deteriorating. Under the Bartoň house, the interiors of the mansion and the convent were reconstructed by the architects Jurkovič and Čenský. At present, the convent houses the Prague National Gallery sculpture collections of the 19th and 20th centuries.

The exhibition dealing with the National Theatre generation is most important, showing the original project of Bohuslav Schnirch's, the Trigas of 1873 for the National Theatre pylons, installed in 1910—11 according to the revised design by Hallmann, Rous, and Šaloun. A special emphasis is put on the most significant representative of this generation, Josef Václav Myslbek, and the leading sculptor of the first quarter of the 20th century, Jan Štursa. Separate halls show the works of both artists.

PRAGUE

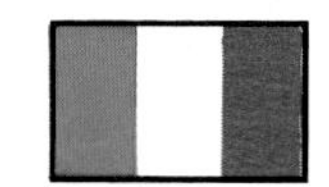

VLTAVA 1, 185 — rivière qui prend sa source dans la région forestière du massif de la Šumava (longueur 430,2 km; bassin 28 090 km²). Affluent du Labe (Elbe), qui la reçoit sur sa rive gauche, près de Mělník. Deuxième cours d'eau de Bohême après le Labe, la Vltava y occupe cependant la première place par son importance et la mythologie nationale dont elle est porteuse. Elle atteint à Prague une largeur de 316 m et une profondeur de 3,8 m. Aménagée par des barrages en quatre cascades, elle comprend nombre de bras et des îfles, dont, à Prague, les îles Žofínský (de Sophie), Střelecký (des Tireurs), Rohanský (des Rohan) et Císařský (de l'Empereur). La Vltava contribue éminement au charme pittoresque de Prague.

LE CHÂTEAU DE PRAGUE 2, 6, 46, 99, 180 — Il a été fondé après l'an 880 sur la hauteur de Hradčany, à proximité du cours de la Vltava, pour devenir le siège des ducs de Bohême, auparavant établis à Levý Hradec. Ce futur centre de l'Etat des Přemyslides était aussi un lieu important de la vie religieuse. Avant la fin du IXe siècle y fut construite une église de la Vierge Marie. La seconde moitié du Xe siècle vit s'élever à proximité du palais ducal la rotonde St-Guy (Svatý Vít), le palais épiscopal et l'église St-Georges. Au XIIIe siècle, le palais ducal devint palais royal, remplissant le rôle de résidence de divers souverains, dont le plus marquant fut l'empereur Charles IV, homme cultivé et grand constructeur. Le prestige de sa résidence impériale s'accrut notament avec la construction de la cathédrale St-Guy, commencée en 1344 et conçue dans l'esprit de modèles français. La fin du XVe siècle fut une autre période importante d'activités architecturales : le roi Vladislav Jagellon agrandit le palais en l'enrichissant de la vaste Salle Vladislav. C'est sous son règne que fut construite, d'après le projet de B. Ried, la célèbre tour dite Daliborka, incorporée aux fortifications de la période du gothique finissant. La tour doit son nom au chevalier Dalibor de Kozojedy, qui y fut emprisonné. Les fortifications comprennent encore une autre tour : la tour Blanche, transformée en prison d'Etat en 1584.

Le comblement de deux fossés dans le deuxième quart du XVIe siècle permit d'aménager la deuxième cour du Château, dont les bâtiments furent successivement achevés ou remaniés d'après les projets de N. Pacassi (travaux achevés en 1775). L'aile nord comprend la Salle espagnole avec la Galerie Rodolphe. Le rez-de-chaussée de l'aile ouest ainsi que les écuries furent aménagés en 1965 pour abriter le musée de peintures du Château. L'angle sud-est de la deuxième cour est occupé par la chapelle de la Sainte-Croix, construite à l'origine d'après un projet d'Anselmo Lurago. Réaménagée en 1963, elle abrite aujourd'hui le Trésor de la cathédrale St-Guy.

La troisième cour constitue le noyau de l'ensemble du Château. Cette partie comprend le palais des empereurs Rodolphe II et Maximilien II, ainsi que le palais de la reine, construit dans le style du premier baroque. Tous ces édifices ont des façades d'aspect untaire, réalisées dans le 3e quart du XVIIIe siècle, d'après les projets de N. Pacassi. C'est là que se trouvent les services de l'Office du président de la République. Surmontée d'un balcon, l'entrée principale s'orne de statues de I. F. Platzer datant de 1760—61. Délimité par le palais royal et la cathédrale St-Guy, cet espace communique avec la place Saint-Georges. En face débouche la rue Vikářská (r. du Vicaire). Là se trouvent l'ancienne maison capitulaire du doyen et la maison vicariale dite nouvelle, où est situé aujourd'hui le restaurant Na Vikářce, lié à l'œuvre littéraire de Svatopluk Čech.

Fait également partie de l'ensemble du Château de Prague la tour Poudrière (appelée aussi Mihulka). Datant de la fin du XVe siècle, cette tour fut, elle aussi, construite par B. Ried. Initialement destinée aux artilleurs, elle abrite aujourd'hui une exposition permanente consacrée aux activités scientifiques et culturelles, telles qu'elles étaient pratiquées au Château durant les XVIe et XVIIe siècles. On peut y voir aussi un atelier d'alchimiste reconstruit. Le Château de Prague est entouré par les jardins du sud, le jardin dit du Paradis (Rajská zahrada) et le jardin des Remparts (zahrada Na valech), d'où l'on a une vue unique sur la ville.

FRANTIŠEK ŽENÍŠEK (1849—1916), LIBUŠE PRÉDISANT LA GLOIRE DE PRAGUE 3 — Œuvre d'un représentant de la première génération dite « du Théâtre national ». Elle nous montre la princesse Libuše, figure centrale des vieilles légendes tchèques, prophétisant la naissance et la gloire d'une grande ville, qui sera Prague.

LE VIEIL HÔTEL DE VILLE 4, 105, 107, 114—120, 123 — En partie mutilé, il se présente encore sur l'une des faces de la place de la Vieille-Ville comme édifice pittoresque et d'une belle allure, qui témoigne de l'existence d'une municipalité autonome et puissante, remontant jusqu'à l'an 1338. A l'origine, il y avait à cet emplacement la maison de style gothique de Wolflin de Kamen. Cette maison fut achetée par les bourgeois, qui la dotèrent d'un beffroi carré (1346) abritant une chapelle à très bel encorbellement (consacrée en 1381). La réalisation du portail de l'entrée principale (mis en place en 1470—80) est atribuée à M. Rejsek de Prostějov. Après 1520, une fenêtre surmontée de l'insription Praga caput regni (Prague, capitale du royaume) et d'un emblème (datant de 1475) de la Vieille-Ville a été ménagée au premier étage de la façade, sous la Salle des Conseils. Ce remaniement dans le style de la Renaissance est généralement attribué au célèbre architecte B. Ried. Les extensions et les transformations de l'hôtel de ville se sont poursuivies jusqu'à XIXe siècle. Le 8 mai 1945, un jour avant la fin de la guerre en Europe, la partie nord de l'édifice (conçue dans le style néo-gothique par P. Nobile) fut gravement endommagée et ravagée par un incendie. Les ruines furent déblayées, mais aucun des projets ultérieurs de recontruction de cette aile ne fut approuvé.

Le vestibule de l'hôtel de ville s'orne d'une mosaïque représentant l'Hommage du monde slave à Prague (1904), œuvre due à Mikuláš Aleš, un classique de l'art tchèque de la fin du XIXe siècle et du début du XXe siècle. Elle constitue une sorte de pendant plastique au discours prononcé par K. Sladkovský lors de la pose de la pierre de fondation du Théâtre national. La mosaïque met en scène Libuše prononçant ses paroles prophétiques sur la ville dont « la gloire atteindra, les étoiles ». Parmi les locaux anciens de l'hôtel de ville, la plus remarquable est certainement la Salle des cérémonies, qui a conservé l'aspect qu'elle avait en 1470. L'intérieur s'orne de tableaux de V. Brožík consacrés à divers événements prospres à influencer et à former la conscience de l'identité nationale.

LES PONTS DE PRAGUE 5, 98, 156, 179, 184 — En plus de leur caractère technique et fonctionnel, ces ouvrages intéressent par leur aspect esthétique, dû non seulement aux lignes de leur construction et aux éléments qui les ornent, mais aussi à leur accord harmonieux avec le cours pittoresque de la rivière, avec ses reflets et ses changements au gré du temps et des saisons.

LA PLACE DE HRADČANY 7 — Elle offre une belle vue sur la première cour du Château royal de Prague et sa porte d'entrée. Chronologiquement la plus récente, cette cour fut réalisée en 1759—69 dans l'esprit du néo-classicisme italo-viennois, d'après un projet de

N. Pacassi. Au-dessus de l'attique ont été placés des emblèmes militaires sculptés et des statues dues au ciseau de I. F. Platzer. La cout fut réaménagée en 1920—22 par P. Janák. D'importants travaux d'aménagement furent également effectués en 1979—80.

En face de la porte d'entrée de la première cour se dresse la porte Mathias, construite sans doute par G. M. Filippi. Ayant fait partie à l'origine des fortifications dominant le fossé d'enceinte du Château, elle est conçue dans l'esprit des architectures militaires italiennes.

LE PALAIS DES ARCHEVÊQUES 8 — Situé à l'extrémité est de la place de Hradčany, devant la façade du Château royal de Prague, il se présente comme un prestigieux édifice signé par le baroque, sur lequel domine l'emblème de l'archevêque Antonín Petr, comte Příchovský. Le palais vit le jour à partir de l'ancienne maison des Gryspek, que l'empereur Ferdinand Ier avait achetée pour en faire le siège de l'archevêché restauré de Prague.

Un premier remaniement, réalisé par O. Aostalis, eut lieu en 1562—64. Une transformation plus radicale se déroula au cours des années 1669 à 1679, sous la conduite du remarquable architecte d'origine française Jean-Baptiste Mathey, amené à Prague par l'archevêque Jan Bedřich (Frédéric) de Vallenstein, son protecteur. C'est l'architecte J. J. Wirch, représentant du style d'orientation viennoise, qui, en 1764—65, devait donner à l'édifice son aspect rococo. Le palais s'orne de statues symbolisant la Foi et l'Espérance, réalisées par T. Seidan dans les années 1880, et de sculptures décoratives dues à I. F. Platzer, que l'on retrouve aussi dans l'escalier. Il possède aussi une collection d'œuvres d'art uniques. La chapelle, qui date de 1599, s'orne de peintures de plafond exécutées par D. Adam de Květná. On peut y admirer aussi les bustes dorés représentant saint Pierre et saint Paul, œuvres réalisées vers 1413. La salle du trône est decorée de huit tapisseries de grand prix sur le thème de la Nouvelle-Inde, réalisées à Paris par l'atelier de tapisseries Neilson, d'après les cartons d'A. Desportes. La collection de tableaux comprend des œuvres de J. J. Heinsch, M. W. Halwachs, F. Dallinger et autres. La série des portraits des archevêques de Prague offre un spectacle unique. Le domaine des métiers d'art est représenté notamment par d'admirables ouvrages en verre de Bohême gravé. Riche également est la collection des porcelaines viennoises. Les intérieurs du palais peuvent être visités chaque année, le jour du jeudi saint.

LA PORTE D'ENTRÉE DU CHÂTEAU DE PRAGUE 9 — De la place de Hradčany, on passe dans l'espace du Château par une monumentale porte grillée, placée au milieu d'une clôture à grilles style rococo, datant de l'époque de Marie-Thérèse. Le décor sculpté comprend deux groupes de Géants se livrant combat, ainsi que des vases et des putti, œuvres réalisées en 1796 par I. F. Platzer. Détériorées par les intempéries, ces sculptures de grès ont été remplacées en 1912 par des copies dues à Č. Vosmík et à A. Procházka.

Au fond domine la porte de pierre pré-baroque, construite en 1614, sous le règne de l'empereur Mathias. Y sont rappelés les titres de l'empereur, encadrés de part et d'autre par les emblèmes des divers pays de l'Empire.

LA TROISIÈME COUR DU CHÂTEAU DE PRAGUE 10 — Elle fut progressivement aménagée après le grand incendie de 1551, suivi du comblement des vestiges des constructions médiévales. Après la Première Guerre mondiale, J. Plečnik conçut un abri de béton pour protéger les fondations mises au jour d'une chapelle et d'une basilique du haut moyen âge et projeta également le dallage de granit.

La partie nord de la troisième cour est délimitée par la face sud de la cathédrale St-Guy et sa grande tour, commencée en 1396 par P. Parler. Cette tour fut dotée plus tard d'un clocher Renaissance, transformé en 1770 d'après un projet de Pacassi. Le clocher de la tour (haute de 99,6 m) contient quatre cloches de l'époque de la Renaissance, dont la plus remarquable est celle de Sigismond (Zikmund), haute de 203 cm, coulée en 1549 par T. Jaroš. C'est la plus grande cloche réalisée en Bohême.

A droite au bas de la tour, se trouve un portique à arcades appelé Porte d'or (Zlatá brána) supportant une petite pièce où sont conservés les joyaux de la Couronne de Bohême. La mosaïque de la partie supérieure du portique représente le Jugement dernier. Elle fut réalisée en 1370—71 en pièces de verre de Bohême par des maîtres artisans de Venise.

Le bâtiment de l'Ancien Prévôté, non loin duquel se dresse un monolithe en granit de Mrákotín (sud-est de la Bohême), a gardé l'aspect que lui donna le XVIIe siècle. A son emplacement se trouvait jadis un palais épiscopal roman.

LA BASILIQUE ST-GEORGES 11 — Formant la face est de la place St-Georges, elle est l'édifice roman le mieux conservé de Prague. Elle fut fondée en 921 par le duc Vratislav. La façade principale fut habillée dans le style baroque en 1677—78, sans doute par F. Caratti. A côté, F. M. Kaňka construisit au cours des années 1718—1722 la chapelle St-Jean-Népomucène (svatý Jan Nepomucký), dont l'entrée est surmontée d'un groupe dû au ciseau de F. M. Brokoff. Au clocher sud de la basilique, datant du milieu du XIIe siècle, fut ajoutée au XIVe siècle la chapelle Ste-Ludmila. Le flanc sud de l'église captive par son portail à colonnes Renaissance, taillé vers 1500 dans l'atelier de B. Ried, originaire de Pístov (ouest de la Bohême). Le relief gothique représentant saint Georges tuant le dragon fut remplacé en 1934 par une copie. Sous la tour sud, dans ce qui reste de la chapelle de la Vierge Marie, est conservée une fresque datant de la première moitié du XIIIe siècle. L'intérieur de la basilique (aménagé dans le style roman à la charnière des XIXe et XXe siècles) abrite, outre les sépultures des ducs Boleslav II et Oldřich, le tombeau du duc Vratislav.

A l'ensemble architectural se rattache le premier couvent féminin de Bohême, couvent qui observait la règle de saint Benoît. Fondé par la bienheureuse Mlada, soeur de Boleslav II, l'édifice du couvent subit plusieurs transformations, pour être finalement désaffecté en 1782 et partiellement transformé en casernes. Remis à la Galerie nationale en 1969, il connut d'importants travaux de réfection et d'aménagement, terminés en 1974. Il abrite maintenant les collections d'art tchèque des périodes du gothique, de la Renaissance, du maniérisme et ba baroque.

LA CATHÉDRALE SAINT-GUY 12, 44 — Le plus grand et le plus important édifice religieux de Prague. C'est là que sont gardés les joyaux de la Couronne de Bohême et que reposent aussi nombre de souverains de Bohême. Elément inséparable de la silhouette de Hradčany, la cathédrale fut fondée par Charles IV en 1344, à l'emplacement d'une basilique à trois nefs et d'une rotonde que saint Venceslas, patron de la Bohême, avait fait construire avant 935. Projetée comme église à trois nefs dotée d'un transept, d'un déambulatoire et d'une couronne de chapelles, la cathédrale fut mise en chantier à partir des plans de l'architecte français Mathieu d'Arras. Après sa mort en 1356, les travaux furent poursuivis sous la conduite de Peter Parler, originaire de Gmünd, en Souabe, relayé plus tard par ses fils Venceslas et Jan. En 1420, alors que le chœur et la chapelle sont achevées et que la tour principale est en construction, s'annonce une nouvelle période: celle de la Renaissance. En 1564, B. Wohlmut réalise le pourtour extérieur en haut de la tour, qu'il coiffe d'un toit pyramidal. L'actuel toit de la tour en bulbe date de 1770, année où il fut achevé par N. Pacassi. La construction de la cathédrale n'a éte terminée qu'en 1929, après avoir connu une étape d'approche néo-gothique, commencée en 1873. C'est de cette période que date l'autel néo-gothique devant lequel se trouve le mausolée royal, taillé dans le marbre par A. Colin, en 1566—89. Le triforium s'orne de 21 bustes réalisés entre 1374 et 1385, représentant Charles IV et les membres de la famille royale, les archevêques et les créateurs de la cathédrale. Au sous-sol, où sont conservés les vestiges d'une rotonde romane, se trouve la crypte royale. Un autre endroit important est la petite chambre où sont gardés les joyaux de la Couronne, pièce fermée à sept serrures. L'objet le plus précieux de ce trésor est la couronne de saint Venceslas, datant de 1346. Les chapelles du déambulatoire contiennent les tombeaux des souverains de Bohême, tombeaux réalisés par l'atelier de Parler en 1370—75. En 1493, sous le règne de Vladislav Jagellon, fut édifié l'oratoire royal, à décor naturaliste de rameaux entrelacés et portant les emblèmes des provinces. La période de la Renaissance se signale par la tribune d'orgue due à Wohlmut, déplacée dans le transept en 1924. Pour ce qui est des éléments baroques du décor, il y a lieu de mentionner notamment le tombeau du comte L. Šlik, œuvre collective de J. E. Fischer von Erlach, F. M.Kaňka et M. Brandl, réalisée en 1723. Un chef-d'œuvre de date plus récente est la statue du cardinal Schwarzenberg priant, réalisée par J. V. Myslbek en 1892—95. Nombreux vitraux des chapelles datent du premier tiers du XXe siècle. Ils ont été exécutés d'après des cartons d'Alfons Mucha, de F. Kysela, de C. Bouda et d'autres artistes. La cathédrale est un trésor où la ferveur des hommes a réuni au fil des siècles de nombreuses œuvres d'art, allant des objets de l'époque romane (le chandelier rhénan, dit de « Jérusalem ») aux réalisations du XXe siècle.

LA CHAPELLE ST-VENCESLAS 13 — dont la construction fut inaugurée par Matthias d'Arras — fut conçue en tant que pendant de la chapelle de la Ste Croix. Elle fut terminée entre 1362 et 1366 par P.

Parler, sur l'emplacement du tombeau primitif du saint (datant de 935), c'est-à-dire dans la partie sud de la nef antérieure. La chapelle compte parmi les joyaux les plus précieux du gothique tchèque culminant ; la partie inférieure est couverte de 1345 jaspes et améthystes. La peinture — de haute valeur artistique — représente le cycle de la Passion, œuvre d'un maître inconnu (des années 1372—73), la partie supérieure, qui est l'œuvre du Maître de Litoměřice (des années 1506—09), illustre la légende de St. Venceslas. L'autel de la chapelle a une tombe du XIVe siècle; la statue de St. Venceslas fut sculptée en marne par P. Parler en 1373. Les petites peintures au-dessus de l'autel représentent Charles IV et sa quatrième femme, Elisabeth de Poméranie, puis on y voit les figures de Venceslas IV et de Jeanne de Bavière. Les figures dominantes peintes au-dessus de la statue de St. Venceslas sont sans doute celles de Vladislas Jagellon et de sa femme Anne de Foi-Candale. Les objets liturgiques sur l'autel ainsi que le tabernacle doré et le lustre datant de 1912—13 (réalisation de F. Anýž d'après les projets de K. Rilbert, S. Sucharda et J. Kryšpín) complètent la suite d'objets gothiques et Renaissance. Sous la fenêtre de la chapelle il y a un petit portail ouvrant sur l'escalier qui conduit dans la chambre de couronnement où est déposé en sûreté l'ensemble de joyaux de couronnement.

MAÎTRE THÉODORIC, SAINT PAPE, SAINT JÉRÔME, SAINT AUGUSTIN, SAINT GUY 14—17 — tableaux sur bois du peintre impérial et représentant de la corporation des peintres de Prague ; créés dans les années 70 du XIVe siècle pour la chapelle de la cour de Charles IV, à Karlštejn. L'unité universelle du monde céleste et terrestre est l'idée que reflètent les 130 tableaux qui revêtent en trois bandes les murs. Ce polyptyque est arrangé de façon strictement hiératique. Les figures des gardiens du trésor impérial, plus grandes que nature et monumentales dans leur conception, sont un exemple unique de l'ordre féodal dont répondait la personne du monarque respectant l'Eglise victorieuse. Les peintures représentant l'armée céleste du Christ témoignent également du culte médiéval des saints — martyres dont les reliques furent placées dans le cadre de chaque tableau.

La douce forme picturale à variations naturalistes d'un même type physionomique démontre l'orientation créatrice avancée de Théodoric, ce maître préféré par l'empereur. La connaissance de la création byzantine aussi bien qu'occidentale (notamment celle de Venise et de Bologne) semble être prouvée.

MAÎTRE DE TŘEBOŇ, LE CHRIST AU MONT DES OLIVIERS, LA CRUCIFIXION, LA MISE AU TOMBEAU, LA RÉSURRECTION 18—21 — ces œuvres exposées à la Galerie nationale de Prague sont originaires de l'autel de l'église augustinienne St-Gilles de Třeboň ; le tableau « La Crucifixion », peint sur bois, provient de la chapelle Ste-Barbe près de Třeboň. Ces peintures sur bois sont l'œuvre d'un maître anonyme de niveau mondial et datent de 1380 environ. La composition compliquée à arabesque raffinée des formes, ainsi que le vif contraste des couleurs intensifient un idéalisme plastique et une extase mystique particulière. Ces œuvres à portée lyrique anticipent sur l'art du beau style d'environ 1400.

LA SALLE VLADISLAS 22 — occupe toute la superficie du second étage du Vieux Palais du Château de Prague. C'est l'espace le plus majestueux du Château ; c'est ici que se déroulent traditionnellement les plus importantes cérémonies d'Etat. La salle fut édifiée sous Vladislas Jagellon, entre 1492 et 1502, après le déplacement de la cour royale de la Vieille Ville au Château. La construction, sur l'emplacement de trois salles gothiques de l'époque de Charles IV, fut entreprise par B. Reit, architecte du roi. On construisit l'espace profane le plus grand et le plus représentatif du gothique tardif en Europe centrale (longueur : 62 m, largeur : 16 m, hauteur : 13 m). Ce fut le lieu de sacres, de réunions de la noblesse, mais aussi (avec l'escalier attenant « des Cavaliers ») de tournois de chevaliers. Après le transfert de la résidence royale à Vienne, la salle servait de lieu de rassemblement de la société, mais aussi de marché aux forains de la cour. Après la 1ère Guerre mondiale, on enleva les peintures tardives et la salle fut restaurée avec soin.

La salle Vladislas donne accès à l'aile latérale du Château, le soi-disant Palais Louis, du commencement du XVIe siècle.

LA VIEILLE SALLE DE DIÈTE DU CHÂTEAU DE PRAGUE 23 — siège, jusqu'à 1847, de la Cour suprême du pays, lieu des états généraux tchèques, elle fut construite par l'architecte impérial B. Wohlmuth dans les années 1559—65. Cet espace représentatif (voûte cintrée à nervures rayonnantes) servait, jusqu' à 1857, aux états généraux lors de l'élection des rois. A l'époque moderne, c'est ici que le Président de la république signe des actes constitutionnels ; exceptionnellement on y voit les séances solennelles du Conseil national tchèque.

ADRIEN DE VRIES (1546—1626), RODOLPHE II 24 — l'un des trois portraits (exécuté en 1603) de l'empereur que le théoricien et peintre Van Mander appela « le plus grand et le premier ami de l'art du monde ». L'œuvre provient des collections exceptionnelles de Rodolphe, collections dont les fragments sont exposés dans la galerie du Château de Prague. Le Hollandais de Vries fut la plus grande personnalité de la cour de Rodolphe en matière de sculpture. Une grande partie de ses œuvres furent emportées par les Suédois lors du siège de Prague en 1648.

ST. GEORGES 25 — la statue équestre en bronze du tueur légendaire de dragon est une copie de l'œuvre des maîtres Georges et Martin de Cluj (Klausenburg), œuvre créée en 1373. Primitivement, elle fut placée dans la partie sud de la cour du Château, devant les soi-disant « cuisines de Maximilien ». Les figures du cheval et du dragon furent plus tard partiellement refondues et, après avoir été endommagées en 1562, restaurées par le fondeur T. Jaroš. En 1928, lors du dallage de la 3e cour, J. Plečnik conçut un socle pour cette statue ; il fit aussi ériger un monolithe de 18 mètres de hauteur, en granit de Mrákotín. L'œuvre fut inaugurée pour le dixième anniversaire de la République et à la mémoire des victimes de la 1ère Guerre mondiale.

TIZIANO VECELLIO (ENV. 1480—1576), LA TOILETTE D'UNE JEUNE FEMME 26 — cette œuvre du plus grand représentant de la peinture de Venise du XVIe siècle fut attestée dans la galerie du Château en 1685. Une jeune femme rousse aux objets de toilette, servie par un jeune admirateur avec turban, est typologiquement proche du tableau de la Vierge tsigane (env. 1510), tableau exécuté dans la période de la pleine admiration de Titien pour Giorgione. La peinture pragoise, créée entre 1515 et 1516, fut, après la deuxième moitié du XVIIIe siècle, réduite aux dimensions de 83 × 79 cm — peut-être pour servir de revêtement. Une copie exacte Renaissance (109,2 × 91,3 cm) fut vendue, le 27 novembre 1957, par la maison londonienne d'enchères Christie, pour une collection privée. D'autres copies, baroques, de moindre valeur, furent enregistrées par J. Neumann dans d'autres collections privées (p. ex. à Toulouse).

Ce thème de la Toilette d'une jeune femme apparaît dans d'autres versions, dont la plus connue est l'œuvre de Titien, œuvre qui provient de la collection de Charles Ier d'Angleterre, et qui se trouve au Louvre. L'originalité de la peinture pragoise fut parfois mise sans doute dans le passé. Dès 1832, le tableau fut attribué au fils de Titien, Orazio ; plus tard, il fut considéré comme copie.

PETRUS PAULUS RUBENS (1577—1640), LE RASSEMBLEMENT DES DIEUX OLYMPIENS (DÉTAIL) 27 — déjà cette œuvre, parmi les premières, du représentant principal du baroque flamand trace la puissance de l'énergie, la sensualité et le courant symphonique des actions à plusieurs couches, dont fourmillent les œuvres de Rubens plus tard. La peinture date probablement de 1602 environ, lorsque Rubens devint peintre officiel de la cour de Vincent Gonzague, duc de Mantoue. La scène représente un rassemblement des Olympiens, Jupiter en tête, lorsque Héra — Junon, protectrice des fermes liens conjugaux, présente sa plainte contre Vénus — Aphrodite, la légère mais triomphante déesse de l'amour, couronnée par de petits amours.

Cette peinture portant le sceau de l'influence de J. Romain, est attestée, pour la première fois, dans les collections du Château, en 1685, en tant qu'œuvre d'un auteur inconnu ; dans les années 1718—37, on l'attribue à Raphaël. L'authenticité de Rubens, brièvement mentionnée en 1797, fut confirmée après 1962 par J. Neumann.

KAREL ŠKRÉTA (1610—1674), PORTRAIT DU TAILLEUR DE PIERRES PRÉCIEUSES DIONYSIUS MISERONI AVEC SA FAMILLE (DÉTAIL) 28 — l'œuvre du fondateur de la peinture baroque tchèque, créée probablement en 1653, montre le chef de l'atelier des tailleurs de pierres et intendant des collections artistiques du Château, dans le cercle de sa famille. C'est justement Dionysius Miseroni qui, en 1648, s'opposa à l'entrée des Suédois dans les collections renommées de la Chambre d'art de Rodolphe. Son père, Octavio Miseroni, avait été appelé en 1588 de Milan à la cour de Rodolphe II, où il fut nommé tailleur officiel de pierres précieuses. En 1608, il obtint son titre de noblesse.

JAN KUPECKÝ (KUPETZKY JOHANNES, 1667–1740), ALLÉGORIE DE LA PEINTURE 29 – œuvre de l'exilé tchèque qui se rangea parmi les portraitistes éminents de l'Europe du début du XVIIIe siècle ; pendant pictural de « l'Allégorie de la sculpture » des collections de la Galerie nationale de Prague. La personnification de la peinture en tant que jeune femme en robe baroque, couronnée de laurier dans sa riche chevelure blonde, est classée dans la deuxième décennie du XVIIIe siècle – période dans laquelle il travailla surtout à Vienne.

PETR BRANDL (1668–1735), AUTOPORTRAIT 31 – provient des collections des Lobkovic, prêtées à la Galerie nationale de Prague; créé en 1697. Témoignage authentique de la maîtrise caractérologique de ce coloriste – le plus grand peintre du baroque culminant en Bohême, qui s'imposa non seulement comme portraitiste mais surtout comme auteur de peintures d'autel d'un dynamisme lumineux, ainsi que d'œuvres mythologiques et de genre.

PAOLO CALIARI, DIT IL VERONESE (1528–1588), STE CATHERINE ET L'ANGE 32 – l'œuvre de l'un des plus grands représentans de la peinture vénitienne du XVIe siècle, créée autour de 1580, attestée dans la 2^e^galerie du Château de Prague dès 1685 sous le titre « Tentation d'une sainte ». L'interprétation erronée du tableau se basait sans doute sur le geste familier de l'ange. Mais d'après J. Neumann, la sainte d'Alexandrie est représentée en tant que fiancée du Christ au moment où le messager céleste lui annonce son sort – le martyre – comme en témoignent le rameau de palmier et l'épée à la main de l'ange.

LE PALAIS LOBKOVIC ET LA TOUR NOIRE 33 – sont accessibles du côté du Vieil escalier dans la partie est du Château. La Tour noire, construite sur des fondations plus anciennes dans le deuxième quart du XIIe siècle, avait fait partie de la fortification romane à l'époque du comte Soběslav Sa dégradation après l'incendie de 1538, lorsque l'on dut enlever un étage, se refléta aussi dans son nom : en effet, auparavant, elle avait été appelée « Tour d'or » – d'après son toit couvert, sous Charles IV, d'une tôle de plomb dorée. Elle servait également de prison pour les débiteurs. Primitivement, elle avait tenu lieu de porte est du Château. Sous Venceslas Ier, après 1230, une nouvelle porte d'entrée fut construite plus bas. La tour est attenante au Palais Lobkovic (originairement Pernštejn), construit par les Pernštejn (Jaroslav et Vratislav) entre 1555 et 62 et puis entre 1570 et 76. En 1625, le bâtiment fut endommagé par un incendie. Une nouvelle reconstruction du palais fut entreprise surtout dans les années 1651–68, sous les Lobkovic, qui devinrent propriétaires du palais en 1626. Václav Eusebius de Lobkovic en confia les projets à C. Lurago, les travaux en pierres furent exécutés par les Italiens G. Galli et G. Pozzo ; le stucateur D. Galli décora le plafond de la salle principale ; F. V. Hárovník y apposa des peintures à l'huile. La décoration fut achevée par des artisans tchèques. Des reconstructions partielles suivirent dans des époques postérieures, notamment en 1810 et dans les années 1861–62. En 1976, de grandes reconstructions furent entreprises dans le palais où l'on avait transféré l'exposition du département historico-archéologique du Musée national. Dans le cadre des restitutions de 1992, le palais redevient propriété de la famille Lobkovic (branche de Roudnice).

LE PANORAMA DE PRAGUE VU DU PALAIS LOBKOVIC 34 – une magnifique vue de la vaste enclave du palais Wallenstein (quartier de la « Petite ville de Prague »), érigé sur l'emplacement de 23 maisons avec des cours et des jardins, d'une briqueterie et d'une porte de la ville. Plus loin se dresse l'église St-Thomas, fondée avec le monastère par Venceslas II, en 1285, pour les ermites augustiniens. C'est l'excellent architecte K. I. Dienzenhofer qui est l'auteur de la reconstruction baroque de 1723–31, conservée jusqu'à nos jours. La décoration pompeuse de l'église est l'œuvre d'éminents représentants tchèques de l'époque baroque, mais pour le maître-autel, on commanda deux œuvres de P. P. Rubens : aujourd'hui, elles sont remplacées par des copies (les originaux ayant été transférés à la Galerie nationale).

LE JARDIN KOLOWRAT 35 – conçu dans les années 1769–89 par I. J. Palliardi, s'étend derrière le bâtiment principal du Palais Kolowrat et le Palais Černín (mineur), érigé en 1770 à la place de l'ancienne maison de Popel de Lobkovic. Le jardin rococo à terrasses, teinté d'exotisme oriental pittoresque, est orné de pavillons et d'escaliers à balustrades conduisant à une « salla terrena » en trois parties.

LE JARDIN ROYAL 36 – à présent aménagé en style anglais, fut fondé en 1535 par Ferdinand Ier dans l'esprit des jardins de la Renaissance italienne, dans l'espace entre le Prašný most (Pont poudrier) et le Jelení příkop (Fossé des cerfs). Il contenait entre autres des plantes exotiques, mais aussi une vigne ; on fonda un « giardinetto » hollandais, et on bâtit de nombreuses constructions, une volière, une orangerie, des bassins d'eau, des fontaines, des jets d'eau, un labyrinthe. Une refonte essentielle eut lieu entre 1725 et 1734 : d'après un projet de K. I. Dienzenhofer, le parterre de fleurs du style français fut complété par des sculptures de lions, de vases et d'allégories provenant de l'atelier de M. B. Braun.

LE JARDIN HARTIG 37,50 – s'étend sur le versant sud du Château de Prague, parmi d'autres jardins d'une beauté et d'un pittoresque extraordinaires. En plus des promenades liées à la vue superbe sur Prague, on présenta ici des productions prenantes – comme p. ex. dans le pavillon de musique du Jardin Hartig. Le bâtiment du premier quart du XVIIIe siècle, attribué à G. B. Alliprandi, a sa salle supérieure ornée de stucs et de peintures de ruines. Devant le pavillon on plaça des sculptures de divinités, œuvres de l'atelier d'A. Braun, datant d'environ 1735 et transférées au Château de Prague, après 1945, des jardins du château de Štiřín.

LA FONTAINE CHANTANTE 38 – qui se trouve devant le Pavillon de plaisance royal, fut coulée entre 1564 et 1568 par le fondeur T. Jaroš de Brno, d'après un plan du maître italien F. Terzio. La fontaine est placée au milieu du « giardinetto » renouvelé, créé d'après un modèle de V. de Vries, architecte et décorateur hollandais. Son nom est dû au bruit des gouttes d'eau tombant de deux étages de la bassine ornée de motifs de chasse. Cette œuvre compte parmi les plus belles réalisations Renaissance de ce genre au Nord des Alpes.

LA GRANDE SALLE DU JEU DE PAUME – MATYÁŠ BERNARD BRAUN – ATELIER – LA NUIT (39, 40) – La grande salle du jeu de paume fut construite dans le Jardin royal au-dessus du Fossé des cerfs par B. Wohlmut et O. Aostalis au cours des années 1567 à 1569 tout d'abord pour satisfaire à la mode des jeux de ballon. La construction noble de la salle (de 60 mètres de longueur) avec des colonnes en style Palladie est recouverte de sgraffites fragiles qui sont des allégories de la Vertu, des Sciences et des Forces naturelles. Le bâtiment abandonné fut transformé en 1723 en écuries et plus tard en entrepôt militaire. Encore en 1734 on installa pourtant devant sa façade un groupe de sculptures provenant de l'atelier de M. B. Braun et créé par son neveu. A. Braun, représentant la Nuit et le Jour. Ce second ouvrage fut détruit pendant le bombardement du Château de Prague par les Prussiens en 1757.

En 1945 la salle du jeu de paume a été détruite par un incendie, mais elle a été réparée en 1952 et remaniée en 1971–1973. De nos jours elle sert à la représentation et on y a installé des tapisseries de Bruxelles provenant de J. van Leefdael qui les créa au XVIIe siècle suivant le thème « Antoine et Cléopâtre ».

LE BELVÉDÈRE ROYAL (41) fut construit près du Château de Prague au-dessus de la vallée de la Brusnice en 1538 à 1563 et c'est un représentant magnifique de l'influence jouée par la Renaissance italienne dans les pays tchèques. La construction à laquelle donna l'impulsion Ferdinand Ier fut réalisée suivant les projets du tailleur de pierres et architecte italien P. de la Stella et ensuite de H. Tirol et de l'architecte de la cour B. Wohlmut et de O. Aostalis. La surveillance des travaux fut confiée au secrétaire de la Chambre tchèque F. de Griesbach. Les riches ornements en pierre furent réalisés par l'atelier de P. de la Stella (jusqu'en 1538) et ensuite par d'autres maîtres italiens. Le Belvédère était destiné au repos et au divertissement de la reine Anne. On y installa une riche galerie, on y aménagea une salle de bal et l'intérieur fut doté d'un équipement onéreux. L'invasion des forces armées suédoises laissa son empreinte aussi sur le Belvédère et les collections qu'il abritait. Sous le règne de Joseph II le bâtiment fut déprécié par sa transformation en laboratoire (jusqu'en 1836). Au cours des années 1851–1865 fut peint sur les murs du premier étage un cycle de thèmes de l'histoire de la Bohême qui furent réalisés suivant les cartons de K. Ruben, directeur de l'Académie de Prague.

LA RUELLE D'OR (42) s'étend derrière le burgraviat du Château au-dessus du Fossé des cerfs. Les petites maisons à façades bigarrées, construites à des époques différentes, commencèrent a être installées dans les arcs des fortifications du Château provenant du temps des Jagellons. Jusqu'en 1597 y vivaient les tireurs du Château, de petits artisans et les batteurs d'or de Rodolphe II. L'appelation « Ruelle des orfèvres » utilisée depuis les années 70 du XVIe siècle devint plus tard à l'origine de la légende qu'à cet endroit vivaient les alchymistes de Rodolphe. Entre les années 1952 et 1955 les petites maisons ont été remaniées en galerie couverte reliant trois tours par laquelle étaient transférés les prisonniers. Dans les petites maisons restaurées fut installée une exposition consacrée à l'histoire de cette partie populaire du Château et on y trouve également des magasins vendant des livres et des cadeaux-souvenirs.

L'ÉGLISE SAINT-NICOLAS DE MALÁ STRANA 43, 59, 60, 62, 64, 65 — Au milieu de la place Malostranská où se trouvait jadis une maison gothique entourée d'étals de viande, se dresse le monument dominant de l'architecture pragoise en style baroque attenant du côté sud à un ancien collège jésuite. La construction de l'église Saint-Nicolas fut réalisée de 1704 à 1711 par K. Diezenhofer venu à Prague en passant par Waldsass; son fils K. I. Dienzenhofer y ajouta le chœur et la coupole. Le beau-frère de Dienzenhofer. A. Lurago, construisit ensuite de 1751 à 1756 un clocher effilé en style rococo, objet primitif d'un litige avec la commune de Malá Strana, qui retarda la construction du complexe religieux. La façade de l'église terminée en 1710 documente l'influence exercée par le baroque romain de l'école illusive. A côté du blason de Fr. Liebstein de Kolowrat on y trouve des statues des Pères de l'Eglise ainsi que des allégories de la Théologie créées par le sculpteur A. Braun avant l'année 1735.

L'espace intérieur de l'église est l'exemple le plus pompeux du baroque culminant à Prague. A la réalisation des fresques participèrent à cet endroit J. L. Kracker et J. Heger et la chapelle monumentale de 75 m² fut décorée par F. X. Palko. Quatre statues en bois plus grandes que nature garnies de stuc et représentant des saints de l'Eglise furent installées au-dessous de la coupole en 1752 à 1755 par I. F. Platzer, auteur d'une statue en cuivre de St. Nicolas située sur l'autel principal et d'autres sculptures. A la décoration pompeuse de l'église contribuent également des tableaux de K. Škréta, I. Raab et J. L. Kracker. De l'orgue construite en 1945 et 1946 par T. Schwarz a joué lors de ses séjours à Prague W. A. Mozart.

Après l'abolition de l'ordre des jésuites par le pape Clément XIV en 1773 l'église Saint-Nicolas devint l'église paroissiale de Malá Strana.

NOTRE-DAME DE LORETTE 45 — construite aux frais de la famille des Lobkowitz en face de la coulisse monumentale du palais Černín aux environs du Château de Prague de 1626 à 1750 était un endroit de pélérinage attenant au premier monastère des capucins construit en Bohême en 1601. La façade de Notre-Dame de Lorette fut réalisée de 1621 à 1623 par K. I. Dienzenhofer et la décoration sculpturale remplacée actuellement par des copies fut l'œuvre de O. F. Quittainer et J. B. Kohl. La façade est dépassée par une tour de l'année 1693 abritant un carillon du maître horloger P. Neumann. Les variations fascinantes des chants de Marie avivant la place pittoresque devant le Château de Prague sont créées par un mécanisme compliqué de cloches coulées à Amsterdam. Au milieu de la cour de Notre-Dame de Lorette se trouve la Santa casa construite par l'architecte C. B. Orsi en 1631 et garnie de reliefs attrayants en stuc provenant de maîtres italiens et datant de l'année 1664. On voulut rappeler la légende sur la maison de la Vierge Marie construite à Nazareth qui aurait été transportée au XIIIe siècle par des anges à la Lorette italienne. C'est pourquoi on trouve à l'intérieur de la construction des tableaux représentant la vie de la Sainte Vierge et sa statue en bois de cèdre. A côté des cloîtres situés à l'est de la construction fut construite en 1734 et 1735 une église de la Nativité utilisant les plans de J. J. Aichbauer et ornée de fresques de V. V. Reiner.

Notre-Dame de Lorette rendue récemment au monastère des capucins abrite une richesse exceptionnelle de collections. Dans la châsse renfermant des bijoux d'un prix inestimable se trouvent surtout des ouvrages d'orfèvres parmi lesquels figure une monstrance en diamants de 1699 (avec 6 222 diamants), la plus précieuse de tout le trésor.

LA TOUR DE PETŘÍN 47, — haute de 60 mètres, se dresse sur une pente rocheuse (qui lui donna son nom « peri » = pierre) et qui se trouve à 318 mètres au-dessus du bassin de Malá Strana du côté ouest. La tour fut construite comme copie réduite de la tour Eiffel de Paris sur l'initiative du Club des touristes à l'occasion de la préparation de l'Exposition nationale de 1891.

L'OBSERVATOIRE ASTRONOMIQUE DE PETŘÍN 48 — fut construit au bout d'une roseraie entre 1925 et 1930 sur l'emplacement de la maison municipale primitive aux frais de l'Association astronomique tchèque (suivant le projet de J. Veselík). Il est toujours encore utilisé aux travaux astronomiques amateurs et abrite en outre une exposition astronomique permanente.

LE MONASTÈRE DE STRAHOV 51 — fut fondé par le prince Vladislav II en 1140 sur l'initiative de l'évêque d'Olomouc Jindřich Zdík. On y installa des chanoines du clergé régulier de l'ordre des prémontrés s'occupant de l'éducation et de la diffusion de l'instruction. Le complexe majestueux du monastère se dressant au-dessus de la ville de Prague sur la pente de Petřín englobe deux églises, un monastère, la résidence du prélat, des bibliotèques et des cours de ferme. Les différents bâtiments connurent plusieurs transformations et changements de la construction, notamment pendant le mouvement hussite et les attaques des armées françaises ou prussiennes au XVIIIe siècle. Le noyau de tout le complexe est formé par le monastère avec sa bibliothèque où a été installé en 1953 le Musée de la littérature nationale. L'entrée principale dans le complexe est assurée par la grande porte de Pohořelec construite en 1742 par A. Lurago. La petite église Saint-Roche située à gauche fut construite aux frais de Rodolphe II comme remerciement de l'écartement de la peste. A. Lurago participa également au remaniement de l'église abbatiale de l'Assomption de la Sainte Vierge qui renferme dans son noyau la basilique romane primitive du XIIe siècle. Sur la cour principale se trouve le bâtiment majestueux de la résidence du prélat de la deuxième moitié du XVIe siècle qui fut remaniée suivant le projet de J. B. Mathey et M. A. Canevallo. Les fresques sur le plafond furent peintes par le prémontré S. Nosecký.
Le bâtiment à 4 ailes du couvent de la fondation romane (après l'année 1142) fut remanié en style baroque primitif et culminant. Par l'escalier ajouté on peut accéder au bâtiment du couvent construit aux temps de l'abbé V. Mayer par l'architecte I. P. Palliardi de 1782 à 1784. L'orgueil de ce bâtiment est la Salle philosophique et théologique richement décorée et rappelant la richesse des collections historiques. De l'aire du monastère fait partie un jardin architectoniquement aménagé au-dessus de l'aile sud. Le monastère a été rendu en 1991 à l'ordre des prémontrés qui a renoué avec l'activité interrompue et a repris dans ses mains les torses des fonds historiques et artistiques.

L'ÉGLISE DE L'ASSOMPTION 52 — avec des vestiges d'une rotonde romane terminée en 1182 et souvent complétée permet de se faire une image de la construction réalisée par A. Lurago en 1745—1752. L'intérieur de l'église conserva sa disposition romane primitive à trois nefs en style baroque avec des stucs de K. A. Palliardi, des tableaux sur le thème de la légende de la Vierge Marie ou des célébrations de saint Norbert de J. Kramolin, I. Raab, V. Neunherze, F. X. Palko, I. K. Liška et M. Villiams et des sculptures de J. A. Quittainer, etc. A la réalisation des peintures sur le plafond participa le religieux et peintre S. Nosecký. Dans la chapelle de sainte Ursule sont disposés sur l'autel les reliques de saint Norbert, fondateur de l'ordre des prémontrés. Parmi les curiosités culturelles figurent les orgues baroques sur lesquelles avait joué W. A. Mozart.

LA SALLE THÉOLOGIQUE 53 construite de 1671—1679 par l'architecte G. D. Orsi fut utilisée primitivement comme salle de lecture. On y trouve toujours encore dans des armoires baroques une littérature théologique y compris la section des livres prohibés. Dans les vitrines sont disposés des manuscrits enluminés précieux dont le plus ancien, l'Evangéliaire de Strahov, date du IXe siècle. Dans l'espace de la salle décorée de stucs et de peintures murales consacrés à la bibliothéconomie et provenant du peintre et prémontré S. Nosecký sont installés des globes célestes du XVIIe siècle documentant les intérêts scientifiques des membres de l'ordre.

LA SALLE PHILOSOPHIQUE 54 — datant de l'époqe de la construction de monastères par I. J. Palliardi de 1782 à 1984 se range indiscutablement parmi les espaces les plus remarquables du monastère. En 1794 elle fut décorée d'un plafond unique en son genre, l'Histoire de l'humanité, du représentant éminent du rococo viennois, P. Maulbertsch. Les armoires en bois de noyer créées en style baroque par le menuisier J. Lachhoven furent transportés à cet endroit du monastère des prémontrés moraves situé à Louka près de Znojmo. Dans une vitrine est installé le buste en marbre de l'empereur François 1er créee par F. X. Lederer et dans les armoires se trouvent encore de nos jours des livres donnés su monastère par l'épouse de Napoléon, Marie Louise.

LE PAVILLON DE CHASSE HVĚZDA (ETOILE) — 55 — fut construit au bout sud-ouest de la chasse gardée de même nom s'étendant à Horní Liboc où se trouvait auparavant une forêt appartenant depuis le Xe siècle au monastère de Břevnov. La réserve de chasse fondée par l'empereur Ferdinand 1er 1534 devint au XVIe siècle un endroit de passe-temps du roi et de fêtes de tireurs. L'auteur du projet du pavillon de chasse peu commun avec plan en étoile (de 40 mètres de diamètre) fut le fils érudit de l'empereur, l'archiduc Ferdinand, dit des Tyrols, gouverneur royal en Bohême. La construction du pavillon de chasse fut réalisée de 1555—1565 par les architectes de la cour royale G. M. Aostalis et G. Lucchese travaillant sous la surveillance de H. Tirol et plus tard de B. Wohlmut. La décoration riche et fine ayant pour thèmes la mythologie grecque ainsi que l'histoire grecque et romaine, fut créée avec la participation d'A. del Pambia, G. Campion et d'autres maîtres italiers mettant en valeur de 1556 à 1563 pour la première fois en Bohême des décorations en stuc d'un niveau remarquable. Le caractère exceptionnel de toute la construction et de sa décoration fut dicté également par l'intention du maître d'œuvre qui voulait y installer Philippine Welser qu'il épousa en secret et qui n'avait pas le droit de séjourner au Château.

Avant les nouvelles phases — à savoir la décoration picturale de la 2e moitié du XVIIe siècle — la réserve de chasse Hvězda située audessous de la Montagne blanche, devint un endroit important de l'histoire nationale mouvementée. En 1620 s'y déroula une bataille sanglante qui finit par la défaite des armées des états luttant contre la ligue catholique et l'armée impériale. A partir de la bataille de la Montagne blanche, la réserve de chasse Hvězda avec son pavillon commença à se dégrader surtout lorsqu'on se mit à y installer les camps militaires des armées ennemies. Sous le règne de Joseph II fut installée dans le pavillon abandonné une poudrière. La construction a été remaniée après l'année 1918 et adaptée entre les années 1949 et 1951 comme musée. En 1951 on y a installé le monument de l'écrivain tchèque A. Jirásek, auteur de romans historiques (1851—1930). En 1964 y a été ouvert le musée du peintre tchèque célèbre, M. Aleš (1852—1913).

LE MONASTÈRE DE BŘEVNOV AVEC L'ÉGLISE SAINTE-MARGUERITE 56, 57 — représente un complexe architectural exceptionnel, construit entre 1708 et 1745 aux frais des abbés O. Zinke et B. Loebl suivant le projet de K. Dienzenhofer et de son fils K. I. Dienzenhofer. Cette construction fut réalisée sur l'emplacement du monastère des bénédictins détruit et paralysé par les Hussites qui fut fondé par l'évêque de Prague Adalbert et le prince Boleslav II, en 993, comme premier monastère pour hommes en Bohême.

L'église du monastère est un bijou de l'architecture tchèque ayant une décoration intérieure également précieuse — sur le fond des peintures sur le plafond de J. J. Steinfels créées de 1719 à 1721 se font valoir les peintures illusionnantes de J. Hager datant de l'année 1761. A l'église fut annexée un ouvrage vénitien du début du XIV siècle, une plaque tombale de l'ermite bénedictin Vintíř. Parmi les ouvrages artistiques on remarque des tableaux de P. Brandl et des statues de M. V. Jäckel et de R. Prachner. Au-dessous du choeur de l'église fut découvert le vestige le plus précieux de l'architecture préromane tchèque, une crypte datant du deuxième trimestre du XIe siècle.

Le bâtiment du couvent et la résidence du prélat ayant servi jusqu'à leur restitution à l'ordre des bénédictions comme depôt des Archives d'Etat centraux sont richement décorés de fresques. Particulièrement intéressant est notamment la Salla dite de Thérèse avec des peintures de l'artiste bavarois K. D. Asam datant de l'année 1727.

Derrière le monastère s'étend un jardin baroque avec le pavillon de plaisance abbatial Vojtěška construit suivant un projet de K. I. Dienzenhofer, une chapelle et une source. La salla terrena fut décorée au milieu du XVIe siècle par le sculpteur R. Prachner.

LA VUE NOCTURNE DE LA RUE NERUDOVÁ 63 — permet de suivre la communication culturellement la plus intéressante de Malá Strana descendant du Château de Prague jusqu'à la place Malostranská. La rue riche en façades baroques avec des enseignes pittoresques de différentes maisons doit son nom au poète et journaliste J. Neruda qui y vivait dans les maisons « Chez trois aigles » et « Aux deux soleils ».

LE PALAIS DE WALLENSTEIN 66—70, 72—74 — construit sur une surface anormale (30 306 m^2) sous la pente de Hradčany représente la première construction monumentale du premier baroque édifiée en Bohéme. Cette résidence pompeuse d'Albrecht von Wallenstein répondait à l'ambition excentrique du « général des mers Baltiques et de 1'Oceán » qui tenta de s'emparer au cours de la guerre de Trente ans, en tant que généralissime, des armes impériales, et de la couronne royale et fut bientôt démasqué et liquidé sur l'ordre de l'empereur.

La construction datant des années 1624—1630 avec ses quatre cours à usage multiple fut réalisée suivant les projets de A. Spezza de Lombardie, après lui ceusæ de N. Sebregondi et finalement, après l'année 1626, ceux de l'ingénieur des fortifications et architecte G. Peroni. A la constrution du palais contribuèrent des artisans italiens et locaux. Dans la façade du palais resta conservé un tableau de la Vierge Marie de Val d'Urazzo faisant partie du palais Trčka incorporé. Deux étages de la partie nord de la construction sont traversés par la Salle représentative des Chevaliers avec un chambranle en marbre amené en 1853 du Palais des Černín. Le plafond représentant l'apothéose de Wallenstein en tant que dieu de la guerre Mars est l'œuvre de l'Ialien B. del Bianco. A la salle sont perpendiculairement raccordés trois espaces, à savoir la Salle de cuir avec un plafond représentant Pallas Athéna et créé par P. Maixner en 1866, la Salle des glaces et le cabinet de travail prétendu de Wallenstein.

Le palais est entouré d'un beau jardin avec un étang, des fontaines, une volière pour oiseaux rares, des grottes avec des concrétions calcaires et une loggia représentative avec des stucs de maîtres italiens et des peintures de B. del Bianco influencées par l'Enéide de Vergile (2e chant consacré à la guerre de Troie). La décoration sculpturale créée par le maître rodolphin A. del Vriese, volée en 1648 par les Suédois et installée dans le jardin du palais Drootningholm fut remplacée par des reproductions.

Actuellement le palais sert surtout aux besoins du ministère de la Culture.

LE PALAIS DES KOLOWRAT ET LE PALAIS DES PÁLFFY 71 — situés en face du palais Wallenstein dans la rue Wallenstein sont raccordés par des jardins magnifiques en terrasse du style rococo montant vers la pente de Hradčany. Le palais des Kolowrat, utilisé actuellement comme siège du ministère de la Culture, a été en 1918—1938 le siège de la présidence du gouvernement de la Tchécoslovaquie. Ce fut pour cette raison que s'y sont deroulés les entretiens néfastes concernant Munich et la création du Protectorat Böhmen und Mähren. Le palais lui-même fut construit après l'année 1784 par N. Palliardi à la demande de la famille des Černín. Au XIXe siècle, avant l'achat du palais par la famille des Kolowrat, il servait de résidence à A. Windischgrätz.

Le palais voisin était de 1660 à 1689 la propriété de l'oppresseur obscur des Chods, rentré dans les légendes, V. M. Laminger. La construction fut élargie et remaniée en 1712 par son nouveau propriétaire, J. J. von Wallenstein. Sa famille y fut remplacée plus tard par celle des Fürstenberg et l'un de ses membres, Charles Egon, organisa en 1775 dans le palais la première Séance de la Société savante des sciences. Au XIX siècle on réaménagea l'intérieur du palais en style néorococo et il reçut le nom des Pálffy d'après ses derniers propriétaires (jusqu'en 1945).

LA VUE AÉRIENNE SUR LE SIÈGE DE LA PRÉSIDENCE DU GOUVERNEMENT ET LA VILLA DE K. KRAMÁŘ 75 — permet de contempler le bord du parc de Letná aménagé en 1859—1860 où a été construite en 1908—1911 une villa d'Etat pseudobaroque destinée au dr. K. Kramář et réalisée suivant un projet de B. Ohmann ainsi que le vaste xomplexe de l'ancienne Académie Straka. Dans ce complexe avec une coupole expressive créée pendant la reconstruction des années 1893—1896 suivant un projet de V. Roštapil fut installée une école pour les enfants des familles nobles, financée en 1710 de la donation de J. P. comte Straka. Actuellement se trouve dans le bâtiment le Bureau de la présidence du gouvernement.

LE PONT CHARLES 76, 77, 79—81, 87—93, 100 ET 101 — qui raccorde la Vieille Ville au quartier Malá Strana est le pont le plus ancien conservé à Prague jusqu'à nos jours. Primitivement on l'appelait pont de Prague ou pont de pierres et en 1870 il reçut le nom de l'empereur Charles, car il fut fondé par Charles IV à l'emplacement de l'ancien pont Judith créé déjà en 1165 qui s'écroula plus tard. Le pont en pierres de grès reposant sur 16 arches a 520 mètres de longueur et

10 mètres de largeur. Sa construction fut dirigée par l'architecte P. Parlér, âgé alors de 27 ans et ne fut terminée qu'au début du XVe siècle. Ce pont par lequel passait la „route royale" connut également des événements mouvementés, notamment en 1648 où les Suédois le franchirent en attaquant Prague et démolirent praratiellement sa décoration.

En 1723 on installa sur le pont un système d'éclairage avec des lampes à huile et en 1866 on le remplaça par un éclairage au gaz utilisant des candélabres en fonte fournis par les Fonderies de Komárov et formant un élémant gothisant.

On est toujours impressionné surtout par la décoration du pont formée par ses tours et surtout par 33 statues et groupes de sculptures installés graduellement sur la balustrade. Ces ouvrages soumis à influence néfaste des intempéries sont remplacés successivement par des reproductions et les originaux sont déposés au lapidaire du Musée national ou au Musée de la Ville de Prague.

Les ouvrages sculpturaux forment une galerie magnifique glorifiant la création des représentants éminents de la culture tchèque surtout entre les années 1683 et 1714: M. B. Braun, J. Brokoff, F. M. Brokoff, M. V. Jäckel, J. B. Kohl ou J. O. Mayer.

Juste à côté du pont Charles se trouve une statue du héros Bruncvík créée en 1884 par L. Šimek et rappelant les droits exclusifs des habitants de la Vieille Ville au pont.

LE PAVILLON DE PLAISANCE HANAVSKÝ 78 — créé primitivement comme objet d'exposition en fonte fabriqué par les fonderies de V. prince Hanavský pour l'Exposition nationale de 1891 suivant les projets de Heizer et Herčík, fut donné en 1898 à la commune de Prague et installé sur la plaine de Letná. Actuellement se trouve dans cette construction en fonte bien placée en style néobaroque un restaurant de luxe.

LE GROUPE DE SCULPTURES SUR LE PONT CHARLES (DÉTAIL) 82 — Il se trouvait à l'endroit où une croix gothique fut dressée depuis le XIVe siècle. Une partie dorée coulée en bronze à Dresden, due à N. Brohn, y fut placée en 1657. De l'inscription hébraïque contournant la croix résulte qu'elle y fut faite avec l'argent payé comme amende par un Juif qui s'était moqué de cette croix. Les statues de la Sainte Vierge et du Saint-Jean Evangéliste furent sculptées en 1861 par E. Max.

LE QUARTIER DE MALÁ STRANA, LITTÉRALEMENT « LE PETIT CÔTÈ » (MAIS ON TRADUIT AUSSI PAR « PETITE VILLE » OU DE PRÉFÉRENCE PETIT QUARTIER) 83, 84 — qu'on peut embrasser (en majeure partie) d'un coup d'œil du haut de la Tour de Malá Strana, construite après 1411. Il s'appelait à l'origine Ville Neuve de Prague et plus tard Ville Mineure de Prague. Il fut créé en 1257 sous l'impulsion du roi Přemysl Ottokar II. Au voisinage du Château, ce quartier connut un grand essor, sous le règne du roi Charles IV. qui le fit élargir et fortifier. La proximité du Château eut aussi des conséquences politiques négatives. En 1419, au cours des combats des Pragois contre des soldats royaux, le Quartier de Malá Strana brûla presque entièrement. De même, l'incendie de 1541 qui endommagea même le Château, freina d'une façon désagréable le nouveau développement du quartier. Le quartier connut le plus grand essor à l'époque du baroque ce qui est prouvé par les monuments historiques bien conservés — l'Eglise Saint-Nicolas, les Palais de Wallenstein, de Fürstenberg, de Lichtenstein, de Nostic, de Michna, de Buquoy etc. Néanmoins la magie principale de Malá Strana ne se reflète pas dans ces monuments mais plutôt dans la constellation pittoresque de ce quartiers avec des coins ravissants qui résultent même des conditions naturelles.

L'EGLISE SAINT-FRANÇOIS SÉRAPHIN ET LA STATUE DU ROI CHARLES IV. 86, 94, 97 — Elles se trouvent sur la route la plus animée menant vers le Pont Charles, sur une place impressionnante du point de vue de l'urbanisme, place fermée par l'Eglise de jésuites Saint-Sauveur et par le Palais de Colloredo-Mansfeld. L'Eglise fut bâtie sur la fondation gothique par D. Canavall dans les années 1679—89 d'après des plans de l'architecte J. B. Mathey de Bourgogne pour l'ordre des Croisés à étoile rouge. L'unique ordre religieux tchèque, créé au milieu du XIIIe siècle avait son siège dans le couvent adjacent. Dans la coupole splendide de l'église, il y a une fresque de V. V. Reiner « Le Dernier Jugement ». l'intérieur de l'église est parachevé par les peintures murales et les peintures suspendues de J. K. Liška, M. Willmann et M. Pirner ainsi que les sculptures de M. V. Jäckl et les statues de saints en stuc, œuvres des sculpteurs J. et K. Süssner. La façade est ornée de statues de R. Prachner de 1758 et d'autres auteurs tchèques. A son angle, la soi-disant colonne des vignerons fut construite en 1846 avec la statue de Saint-Venceslas, due à J. Bendl de 1676.

Après l'aménagement du terrain par les frères Klein de Vizenberk, le monument néo-gothique représentant l'empereur Charles IV avec les allégories des quatre facultés universitaires fut construit en 1849, aux frais de l'Université de Prague, dans cet espace de la Place des Croisés. Il fut créé dans l'atelier du fondeur D. J. Burgschmidt de Nüremberg d'après un projet du sculpteur A. Hähnel de Dresden.

LA TOUR DE LA VIEILLE VILLE, 95, 96 — La tour qui représente le summum de l'importance historique de la Place des Croisés fut construite sur le premier pilier du Pont Charles d'après un projet de P. Parlér. La Tour du Pont qui compte parmi les plus belles œuvres de ce genre en Europe, fut terminée vers 1391, non seulement comme partie du pont mais aussi comme partie intégrante des remparts de la Vieille Ville de Prague. Son unique décoration sculpturale considérée comme une des œuvres du sommet de la sculpture de l'Europe centrale, est née vers 1380, avant l'achèvement de la Tour. L'atelier de P. Parlér concentra son attention sur les souverains, sur les constructeurs du pont, sur Charles IV et Venceslas IV comme patrons du pays tchèque, et sur les symboles des pays. Les statues furent remplacées par des copies et les originaux ont été placés à la Galerie Nationale, en 1978. En 1621, les douze têtes décapitées des seigneurs tchèques participant à la résistance des nobles furent exposées sur la tour et y restèrent dix ans entiers. La décoration plastique du côté ouest de la tour souffrit en 1648, au cours du siège de Prague par les Suèdois. La restauration et son achèvement furent effectués dans les années 1874—78.

LADISLAV ŠALOUN (1870—1946), LE MONUMENT DU MAÎTRE JAN HUS (DÉTAIL) 102 — Le monument fut inauguré le jour du 500ème anniversaire du supplice sur le bûcher de l'orateur et réformateur tchèque à Constance le 6 juillet 1415. L'étendue imposante du monument en pierre et en bronze représentant plusieurs statues construites par un des principaux représentants de la sculpture tchèque de l'art nouveau fit l'objet de nombreuses discussions. Les discussions concernaient la composition et l'emplacement de l'œuvre dans le milieu historique de la Place de la Vieille Ville devant le Palais de Golz-Kinský.

LA PLACE DE LA VIEILLE VILLE 103, 104, 121, 122, 125, 127, 129 — Elle perte son nom à partir de 1895 /à partir du XIVe siècle Tržiště (Marché), Velké Tržiště (Grand Marché), Rynk (Petite Place), Velký rynk (Grande Place)./ Avec le Château de Prague, elle compte parmi les endroits qui cinnurent les événements historiques les plus mouvementés à Prague. Déjà à la charnière du XIème et XIIème siècles, le carrefour des routes des marchands formait un vaste marché avec une surface de la place actuelle de 9000 m^2 environ. La douane, l'actuel Ungelt, où on étalait la marchandise importée en Bohême, faisait partie de la Place. La Place avec l'Hôtel de Ville sont devenus aussi le lieu de rassemblement traditionnel à l'occasion des événements politiques et révolutionnaires, des actes représentatifs et des représailles. En 1422, dans la cour de l'Hôtel de Ville fut exécuté le prédicateur radical hussite Jean Želivský. En 1437, le dernier chef hussite Jean Roháč de Dubá fut exécuté sut la Place de la Vieille Ville. Les croix dans la mosaïque du pavé devant l'aile est de l'Hôtel de Ville rappellent aussi l'exécution de 27 nobles et seigneurs tchèques. En 1458, dans la salle de conseil, Jiří (Georges) de Poděbrady fut élu roi tchèque. En 1918, une manifestation importante pour la création de la république autonome y a eu lieu. Une autre manifestation initiée par les communistes y a eu lieu en février 1948.

Les contructions nouvelles le mieux représentées par le bâtiment de l'art nouveau reconstruit en style baroque décoré par les sculpteurs L. Šaloun, F. Procházka et B. Schnirch de l'ancienne Maison d'Assurance de la Ville de Prague, due à l'architecte O. Polívka, et servant actuellement au ministère du Commerce et du Tourisme, et contribuèrent par le monument immense de Maître Jean Huss à la représentativité de la Place avec des maisons gothiques originales et des maisons reconstruites et avec le Palais de Golz-Kinský en style rococo.

La Place de la Vieille Ville et la Route Royale qui la traverse comptent parmi les parties de Prague les plus recherchées par les touristes.

LA MAISON « A LA MINUTE » 106 — contiguë perpendiculairement à la maison municipale de la Vieille Ville; elle a un noyau gothique du début du XVe siècle. Sa reconstruction en style Renaissance fut réalisée après 1564. Les sgraffites de Renaissance faits d'après des gravures de M. Raimondi et H. S. Beham furent criés après 1603 et 1610. A la fin du siècle, quand il y avait là une pharmacie, une statue de lion en pierre fut placée à l'angle. Les sgraffites renouvelés plus tard furent de nouveau dégagés seulement en 1905. Aujourd'hui, des bureaux de la municipalité se trouvent dans cette maison.

L'HORLOGE DE LA VIEILLE VILLE 108—113 — L'horloge dans sa forme originale fut construite vers 1410 par l'horloger Mikuláš de Kodaň. Sa reconstruction avec des aménagements constructifs plus pompeux de l'Hôtel de Ville furent effectués par le Maître Hanuš nommé « de la Rose ». Le mécanisme de l'horloge fut amélioré dans les années 1553—60; les plastiques furent réalisées en 1659, puis au XVIIIe siècle et en 1864. La peinture de la plaque avec le calendrier de l'horloge et les allégories des Mois fut réalisée en 1865 par J. Mánes (1820—1871), le principal représentant de l'art national du XIXe siècle. L'original de cette peinture fut transféré dans les collections du Musée de la Ville de Prague et remplacé par une copie déjà en 1659. La copie et une partie de la décoration en bois ont brûlé en 1945. En 1962, elle a été remplacée par une copie de B. Číla. Les sculptures des apôtres sur bois furent effectuées par le sculpteur V. Suchard (1884—1972) déjà en 1948.

L'horloge compte parmi les principales attractions touristiques de la Vieille Ville: le mécanisme des figures mobiles ayant des liaisons allégoriques, religieuses et historiques (memento mori, allusion aux conquêtes des Turcs etc.) se met en marche toutes les heures.

L'EGLISE SAINT-NICOLAS DE LA VIEILLE VILLE 124 — fut construite à côté du monastère des Bénédictins d'après un projet de K. I. Dienzenhofer dans les années 1732—35.

LA PALAIS GOLZ-KINSKÝ ET LA MAISON « CHEZ LA CLOCHE » 126 — sont les plus beaux bâtiments sur la Place de la Vieille Ville placés devant Notre-Dame de Týn. En dégageant le crépi néobaroque sur la maison « Chez la Cloche » on a découvert une façade unique gothique conservée avec la décoration en pierre de 1350 environ. Pendant l'inspection de l'intérieur de la maison on a découvert une chapelle avec des fresques gothiques de la moitié du XIVe siècle. A l'intérieur de la maison restaurée des expositions d'art nouveau sont organisées par la Galerie de la ville de Prague. Le bâtiment contigu rococo du Palais Golz-Kinský, appartenant au comte R. Kinský déjà en 1635 fut reconstruit dans sa forme gracieuse et impressionnante dans les années 1755—65 par A. Laurag d'après des projets de K. I. Dienzenhofer. Le Palais construit sur la place de l'ancienne construction romane est utilisé par la Galerie Nationale de Prague pour ses expositions.

LA MAISON DE ŠTORCH 128 — une des maisons de la rangée impressionnante sur la partie est de la Place de la Vieille Ville fut construite en 1897, d'après un projet des architectes B. Ohmann et R. Krieghammer. La maison néo-renaissance de la maison d'édition de Štorch retient l'attention par la peinture figurative de L. Novák d'après des cartons de M. Aleš, représentant Saint-Venceslas et Les Trois Mages. La peinture abîmée en mai 1945 fut renouvelée par le peintre F. Sembtner.

LA VUE DE LA TOUR DE NOTRE-DAME DE TÝN 130—131 — cette excellente construction gothique à trois nefs fondée en 1365, représente une vue des tours d'une hauteur de 80 mètres, terminées seulement au début du XVIe siècle.

LE CAROLINUM 132—134 — représente le bâtiment central de l'Université Charles fondée par Charles IV le 7 avril 1348 qui fut à l'origine un des collèges universitaires dans la rue Železná, débouchant sur la Place de la Vieille Ville. Il s'agissait de la première école supérieure en Europe centrale ayant pour but d'amener la culture locale au niveau le plus haut. La maison de Rothlev acquise par Venceslas IV qui en fit cadeau en 1383 au collège universitaire Charles, étant placée jusqu'à ce temps dans une maison près de l'église Saint-Nicolas, représente la base d'un complexe de constructions. L'aspect extérieur du Carolinum provient surtout de la reconstruction baroque terminée en 1718 par F. M. Kaňka. Au front de la rue Železná se trouvent une fenêtre baroque datant de 1687 et des arcades vitrées avec une voûte gothique nervurée. L'annexe construite en direction du Théâtre Stavovské datant de l'époque de 1358 environ a conservé une chapelle précieuse avec un encorbellement à riche décoration externe. Sa restauration fut effectuée par J. Mocker en 1881; d'autres transformations et arrangemets ont été faits entre 1946—75 d'après un projet de J. Fragner avec la participation des sculpteurs V. Makovský, K. Lidický, J. Lauda et K. Pokorný.

Une grande aula reconstruite et bâtie déjà après 1383 représente le noyau du bâtiment. Une chapelle avec un encorbellement y fut annexée. Au front de l'aula se trouve une tapisserie de M. Teinitzerová de 1947. Elle s'inspire du sujet représenté sur le cachet de l'Université Charles avec la statue de Charles IV agenouillé devant Saint-Venceslas, créé par le sculpteur V. Sychra.

LE THÉÂTRE STAVOVSKÉ 135 — appelé auparavant Théâtre de Tyl et à l'origine Théâtre de Nostic — représente un bâtiment néoclassique construit aux frais du comte F. A. Nostic en 1781, d'après un projet de A. Haffenecker et avec le concours spécial du comte K. H. Khünigl. Les transformations et aménagements de ce bâtiment se succédèrent en 1859, 1881 et 1892. Une restauration générale étundue fut terminée en 1991. Une partie intégrante de la restauration était le raccordement de service au Palais Kolowrat situé en face.

A l'origine les pièces étaient jouées au Théâtre en allemand et en italien. En 1787, la première de l'opéra Don Giovanni de Mozart y fut exécutée. Le compositeur C. M. von Weber était chef de l'opéra dans les années 1813—16. La pièce « Fidlovačka » de Tyl avec la musique de F. Škroupa y fut jouée le 21 décembre 1834. La chanson « Où est ma patrie », devenue hymne tchécoslovaque à partir de 1918 retentit, pour la première fois dans cette première.

LE MUSÉE NATIONAL 136, 138, 139, 141, 142 — situé sur une place occupée auparavant par La Porte Cochère, représente un bâtiment long de plus de 100 mètres et fermant d'une façon imposante la partie supérieure de la Place Venceslas. Le bâtiment fut construit dans les années 1885—90, d'après un projet du Professeur J. Schulz pour les besoins du musée fondé en 1818 par les nobles qui suivaient des buts culturels et scientifiques avec un principe de patriotisme du pays.

La construction néo-renaissance créée à grands frais possède quatre ailes et deux cours. L'entrée représentative s'effectue par la rampe avec une fontaine et des statues représentant les allégories de la Bohême, de la Moravie et de la Silésie et les rivières l'Elbe et la Vltava, dues à A. Wagner des années 1891—94. La décoration sculpturale du bâtiment représente une collection bien ordonnée des créations plastiques tchèques de ce type de la fin du XIXe siècle, en concurrence avec l'œuvre du sculpteur L. Schwanthaler de Munich. Ses sculptures en bronze représentant la princesse Libuše, le prince Přemysl, les rois Venceslas et Ottokar Přemysl II commandées à l'origine pour l'ensemble de 24 sculptures destinées au Slavín tchèque à la ville de Tupadla près de Liběchov furent placées dans le hall d'entrée avec des piliers. Le hall est raccorde à l'escalier représentatif ayant les dimensions de presqu'e une aile centrale entière du bâtiment. L'escalier est complété par des statues représentant 16 torses d'hommes qui ont mérité du musée et 32 médaillons des rois tchèques, dus à A. Popp et B. Schnirch des années 1897—99.

La construction carrée du Panthéon avec une coupole accompagnée de 48 bustes et statues des grands esprits de la nation tchèque représente le sanctuaire des désirs nationaux tchèques et de la conscience manifestée. Les tableaux avec des sujets historiques ont été crées par des peintres de premier ordre de la génération du Théâtre National, V. Brožík et F. Ženíšek; les panneaux décoratifs allégoriques au-dessous de la coupole sont dus à V. Hynais, peintre de cette génération orienté vers la France.

Les sections histoire et sciences-naturelles et la bibliothèque précieuse comprenant un fonds d'un million de livres avec des manuscrits uniques moyen-âgeux se trouvent dans le bâtiment du musée.

JOSEF VÁCLAV MYSLBEK (1848—1922), STATUE ÉQUESTRE DE SAINT-VENCESLAS 137 — La statue du patron du pays tchèque est aussi le symbole de l'identité nationale et de l'indépendance de la nation. L'œuvre a été placée dans la partie supérieure de la Place Venceslas d'après un projet architectonique de A. Dryák avec la décoration ornementale de C. Klouček dans les années 1912—13. Myslbek commença à développer le sujet en 1887. Le modèle de l'œuvre finale en plâtre a été terminé en 1904. Cette œuvre sublime d'une conception néo-renaissance fait un ensemble avec les statues de Saint-Prokop, de la bienheureuse Agnès et de Sainte-Ludmila. La dernière statue représentant Saint Adalbert n'a pas été achevée par Myslbek. Elle a été fondue dans l'atelier de Mašek et mise à sa place en 1924. L'œuvre ressentie d'une façon classique avec l'air intelligent des figures, révèle l'orientation vers la création antérieure française.

LA PLACE JUNGMANN 140 — se trouve près de la Place Venceslas. Avec une sensibilité urbaniste, la statue de J. Jungmann, écrivain et représentant principal du renouveau littéraire tchèque, est installée sur cette la place pas très grande. L'œuvre sculpturale de L. Šimek de 1872 faite d'après une esquisse plus ancienne de V. Levý fut installée sur un piédestal en marbre dû à Barvitius en 1878.

LA RUE DES FOSSÉS (PŘÍKOPY) 144 — représente une des parties commerciales les plus animées, renouant avec le bout inférieur de la Place Venceslas et Můstek avec le bâtiment post-moderne construit pour ČKD dû à A. Šrámková. Parmi les constructions nouvelles sur la rue des Fossés (Příkopy), c'est le bâtiment du constructivisme de La Maison des enfants de 1928 qui attire l'attention. Le grand magasin le plus ancien de Prague, construit par Th. Hansen, architecte célèbre de Vienne, dans les années 1869—71, se trouve à droite. Le Palais Sylva-Tarouccovský (à l'origine Piccolominiovský) construit dans les années 1743—51 par K. I. Dienzenhofer et A. Lurage est une preuve de la culture aristocratique raffinée de l'époque du rococo. La construction sobre en style empire de l'Eglise de la Sainte-Croix des années 1816—24 fut proposée par J. Fischer. La Maison des Slaves, à l'origine palais baroque des Příchovští fut aménagée par F. Heger en 1798. Parmi les banques placées sur la rue des Fossés (Příkopy), la plus impressionnante est celle des investissements, construite avec l'esprit de néo-renaissance par O. Polívka dans les années 1894—96 et décorée avec les mosaïques de M. Aleš et les reliefs de C. Klouček et S. Sucharda.

LA PLACE VENCESLAS 145 — appelée à l'origine Le Marché aux chevaux était le marché principal de la Ville Neuve. La statue de Saint-Venceslas due à J. J. Bendl de 1680 (déplacée à Vyšehrad en 1879) se dressait à l'époque au centre du Marché. La place, dont la longueur est de 750 mètres, représente avec ses hôtels somptueux le plus important boulevard social et commercial. La partie supérieure de la place est perpendiculairement renfermée par la construction imposante du Musée National (J. Schulz, 1885—90), qui représente un hommage au savoir et aux connaissances auxquels le musée doit servir. Un monument imposant comprenant la statue équestre de Saint-Venceslas, dû à Myslbek, exprime la conscience et l'espoir national. En face, dans la partie inférieure il y avait dans les années 1786—89 le théâtre en bois Bouda où se trouvait la première scène tchèque. Les accès au métro se trouvent dans les deux parties opposées de la place ainsi qu'au centre de la place.

LA TOUR POUDRIÈRE 146—148 — qui fut construite en l'honneur du roi Vladislav Jagellonský en 1475 est une œuvre de M. Rejsek de Prostějov. Elle fut construite sur la place d'une ancienne grande porte des remparts. Dans son voisinage, Venceslas IV fit construire la Cour Royale comme résidence du souverain. Après son évacuation en 1483, l'importance de ce lieu commença à diminuer. La Tour qui est comptée parmi les monuments les plus précieux du gothique tardif servit comme dépôt de poudre déjà à la fin du XVIIe siècle. Pendant le siège des Prussiens, la construction fut endommagée. Sa reconstruction néo-gothique est une œuvre de l'architecte J. Mocker des années 1875—76 qui construisit en plus le pourtour et le toit. De la tour nous avons une vue sur le plus ancien quartier de la Vieille Ville ainsi que sur une des places animées de Prague — la Place de la République avec le bâtiment de l'ancienne douane principale, 1810 env., avec la Maison « Chez les hybern », l'Eglise des capucins Saint-Joseph et la construction moderne d'une banque de 1938.

LA MAISON MUNICIPALE DE LA VILLE DE PRAGUE 149, 150 — fut construite sur la place de la Cour Royale dans les années 1906—11 d'après des projets de A. Balšánek et O. Polívka. Là, où il y avait jadis le siège des rois tchèques et surtout de Georges de Poděbrady qui y convoqua les Etats généraux tchèques et qui lança de là des appels de paix et de réunification aux souverains européens, se trouve aujourd'hui un centre représentatif culturel et social. On y organise des concerts, bals, expositions. Il y a un café, un restaurant et un bar. Les locaux ont une riche décoration sculpturale et picturale due aux artistes tchèques les plus connus du début du XXe siècle: dans la salle du maire il y a une peinture de A. Mucha, dans la salle de Palacký une peinture de J. Preisler; la salle de Grégr est décorée par la peinture de F. Ženíšek. Le souterrain et le restaurant sont décorés par des tableaux de M. Aleš et J. Obrovský. Les sculpteurs J. V. Myslbek, K. Novák et L. Šaloun sont représentés dans la salle Smetana et dans le petit salon Rieger.

LE THÉÂTRE NATIONAL 151—154 — fut construit grâce à des collectes dans les années 1868—81, d'après un projet de l'architecte J. Zítek. La construction précieuse néo-renaissance fut aussitôt après l'achèvement ravagée par l'incendie. Sa reconstruction et son achèvement par l'architecte J. Schulz furent terminés en 1883, avec une nouvelle décoration interne et avec un rideau effectué par V. Hynais. Le peintre J. Tulka participa à la décoration externe de la loggia. Les sculptures proviennent surtout de A. Wagner, J. V. Myslbek et B. Schnirch. Les tableaux à lunettes de M. Aleš et de F. Ženíšek, qui est aussi l'auteur de la peinture du plafond de la salle, dominent le foyer représentatif du théâtre. La loge royale, actuellement présidentielle, est décorée par les peintures de V. Hynais, V. Brožík, et J. Mařák. Les nombreuses sculptures dans le foyer représentent les torses des géants de la culture tchèque.

Pendant la reconstruction importante et la modernisation technique du théâtre dans les années 1977—83, une construction a été bâtie entre le théâtre et le Couvent des ursulines. Ce bâtiment nouveau de sept étages et la Nouvelle Scène du Théâtre National ont été achevés en 1983, d'après un projet de l'architecte K. Prager avec l'utilisation de revêtements en verre de S. Libenský.

En face du Théâtre National historique, il y a le Palais Lažanský avec la cafétéria Slavia qui fut construit dans le style de la renaissance française dans les années 1861—63. Jusqu'à 1869, B. Smetana, un des compositeurs tchèques les plus importants vécut au premier étage du palais du comte.

La partie latérale du Théâtre National ainsi qu'une rangée représentative d'immeubles avec des façades historiques longent le quai Masaryk. D'ici il y a une vue sur la Vltava et sur l'île des Slaves nommée jusqu'à 1925 Žofín.

L'ILE DE TIR 155 — Le nom de l'île n'est pas fortuit. Après 1472, l'île fut attribuée à la Vieille Ville et à la Ville Neuve. Elle devint terrain d'entraînement des tireurs pragois. Au XVIe siècle, des jeux de tir préférés par les Pragois, appelés « tir sur un oiseau » y avaient lieu. A la fin du siècle s'y déroulaient aussi des meetings du peuple. En 1882, la lère fête fédérale des Sokols y eut lieu.

LA STATUE DE BEDŘICH SMETANA (1824—1884), LE MUSÉE SMETANA ET LA PASSERELLE DE NOVOTNÝ 157—158, 179 — Le Quai Smetana est une preuve de la plus vieille solution urbaniste pragoise de ce type, ayant été effectuée par la maison V. Lanna dans les années 1841—45 d'après un projet de B. Grueber. La construction principale des immeubles fut projetée par le directeur des constructions Strobach déjà en 1836. Sur la place de l'ancien moulin, fut construit un bâtiment néo-gothique des Bains Charles dans lequel K. H. Borovský, poète et journaliste tchèque vécut en 1848. Devant les Bains du quai sort la passerelle de Novotný de 1879, nommée d'après un descendant d'une vieille famille meunière. Les bâtiments des moulins de la Vieille Ville ont un caractère néo-renaissance dans le style de I. Ulmann et sont décorés par des putti de J. V. Myslbek. La tour d'eau construite en 1489 et reconstruite plusieurs fois, dernièrement après l'incendie de 1885, se dresse ici. La passerelle de Novotný est close par le bâtiment du musée Smetana justifiant la prétendue renaissance tchèque de 1883. Elle fut projetée par l'architecte A. Wiehl à l' origine pour le château d'eau de la ville de Prague. La façade de la construction est couverte par le sgraffite « La Lutte avec les Suédois sur le Pont Charles en 1648 » d'après des cartons de F. Ženíšek. Dans les niches, il y a des figures des personnes méritant de la sauvegarde de Prague devant les Suédois, comme elles furent exécutées par J. Šubič d'après des projets de M. Aleš et J. Koula. En 1936, la société de Smetana y fond un musée et y concentra la documentation sur la vie et sur la création de ce principal compositeur tchèque dont la statue, due à J. Malejovský, a été installée devant le bâtiment en 1984.

LA MAISON « AU PUITS D'OR » 159 — représente un bâtiment à l'angle des rues Liliova et Karlova formant des artères de communication importantes menant vers le Pont Charles. Ce sont les reliefs en stuc des protecteurs devant la peste Saint-Sébastien et Saint-Roch, faits par le sculpteur J. O. Mayer après l'épidémie de la peste probablement vers 1700, placés sur cette maison de renaissance aménagée en style baroque, qui attirent l'attention.

LES ENSEIGNES SUR LES MAISONS DE LA VIEILLE VILLE 160 — Dans la rue de Týn No 10, elle indique la maison qui au XVIIe siècle portait le nom « En enfer ». La maison appartenait plus tard problement à la famille Kinský ayant sur son blason trois griffes de loup ou plutôt trois dents de sanglier. Après la reconstruction de la maison au XVIIIe siècle par l'architecte F. Heger, l'enseigne fut repeinte en trois plumes d'autruche.

L'importance des enseignes sur les maisons liées à la tradition des enseignes en dehors du but d'identification, de représentation et d'orientation, avait aussi un sens symbolique évident. Les charmants signes placés sur les maisons racontent des histoires de la ville de Prague, non seulement de la Vieille Ville, mais aussi des coins pittoresques du Petit Quartier, de Hradčany etc.

LE VIEUX CIMETIÈRE JUIF, LA VIEILLE-NOUVELLE SYNAGOGUE 161—164 — sont des preuves du peuplement juif dans le bourg au pied du château, déjà au Xe siècle. Au début du XVIIIe siècle, le bourg juif représentait à Prague presque un tiers de la population. Néanmoins, on remarqua toute une série de pogromes et de restrictions forçant les Juifs à vivre presque sans exception dans un ghetto clos. Après la publication des decrets de libéralisation de l'empereur Joseph II, la Ville Juive de Prague fut nommée Josefov et ne devint le cinquième quartier pragois avec les mêmes droits qu'après 1848. Ses conditions hygiéniques insatisfaisantes menèrent à son assainissement vers 1900.

Le vieux Cimetière Juif, où la plus vieille pierre tombale conservée date de 1439, rappelle l'histoire juive pragoise de longs siècles. La magie élégiaque de ce cimetière avec approximativement 11 mille pierres tombales (sous lesquelles il y a jusqu'à 12 couches de cimetière), représente un prix historique unique. Les tombeaux désignent non seulement les noms et les dates des défunts mais aussi leur position dans la société avec des symboles des familles traditionnelles formant depuis longtemps une hiérarchie sacerdotale. Les noms des défunts sont souvent indiqués par un symbole de remplacement, ayant une expression poétique spéciale. Parmi les monuments funéraires, il y a un tombeau conservé du maire important et primat de la Ville Juive M. Mordechaj Maisl (mort en 1601). Une rue au milieu du ghetto ancien et une des synagogues furent nommées d'après lui. Le nom de J. Löwe ben Bezalel sur une autre pierre tombale recherchée est lié à une légende suggestive. D'après la légende, Golem, un personnage artificiel, fait par ce célèbre rabbin Löwe, sortit de son atelier.

La plus ancienne synagogue en Europe — nommée La Vieille-Nouvelle — appartenant à la Ville Juive s'est conservée. Elle fut construite vers 1280 comme salle à deux nefs. Le pignon en brique est du XIVe siècle, du temps de la construction du vestibule. Comme l'espace principal n'était destiné qu'aux hommes, une annexe pour les femmes fut construite sur la partie nord au XVIIIe siècle. L'intérieur de la synagogue donne des preuves valables de la culture juive surtout du XVIe au XIXe siècles.

A côté du vieux Cimetière Juif, il y a une ancienne salle de cérémonie qui est utilisée aujourd'hui pour l'exposition des Dessins des enfants de Terezín. La soi-disant Haute synagogue où il y des tissus de synagogue est utilisée aux expositions. La Synagogue de Pinkas est un monument des victimes du nazisme. Dans la Synagogue de Maisel il y a une exposition d'une collection unique d'objets en argent et d'autres objets métalliques. La magie ésotérique des monuments de la Ville Juive est complétée par la Mairie Juive avec une tour et une horloge avec un cadran hébraïque.

KAREL HLADÍK (1912—1967), FRANZ KAFKA 165 — le buste sur le bâtiment construit en 1902 par O. Polívka à l'endroit où une prélature de l'ancien couvent des bénédictins placée auparavant, rappelle qu'un écrivain génial d'origine juive y nacquit en 1883. L'œuvre fut faite par un représentant de la création réaliste classique du pays s'acquittant des impulsions de la plastique italienne contemporaine.

L'EGLISE SAINT-JACOB 166—167 — avec un couvent, disposée dans la rue Petite Štupartská de biais contre la sortie d'Ungelt fut fondée par Venceslas Ier en 1232. La façade est décorée par une œuvre de stuc du sculpteur italien O. Most du 1695 faite pendant la reconstruction de l'église en style baroque, après l'incendie de 1689. A l'intérieur de l'église avec 21 autels, il y a des fresques de plafond impressionnantes dues à F. M. Vogel et effectuées à l'achèvement de la reconstruction dans les années 1736—39. Les tableaux de P. Brandl, V. V. Reiner etc. font partie intégrante de la décoration. Le monument funéraire du grand chancelier J. V. comte Vratislav de Mitrovic, œuvre de J. B. Fischer d'Erlach des années 1714—16, se fait remarquer par sa qualité.

L'EGLISE SAINT-HENRI 168 — dans la rue Jindřišská dans la Ville Neuve représente une construction gothique fondée dans la deuxième moitié du XIVe siècle, un vestibule Renaissance, avec des annexes et des aménagements intérieurs baroques. Une série de pierres tombales du cimetière supprimé, fut transférée sur la partie externe de l'église. Le renouvellement de l'église en style gothique fait par Mocker fut réalisé dans les années 1875—79. Son riche équipement intérieur compte des objets historiques de l'époque du gothique (par ex. le tableau de la Madone Sainte-Etienne du XVe siècle, la statue de Saint-Henri etc.), et une série d'œuvres d'art baroques provenant surtout des peintres et sculpteurs tchèques créées jusqu'au XIXe siècle (par ex. les fenêtres peintes d'après un projet de F. Sequens de 1891).

Le clocher renouvelé en style gothique dans la proximité de l'église fut construit déjà vers 1475. La cure fondée en 1386 est d'origine gothique.

LE PRESBYTERE DE NOTRE-DAME-DE-NEIGES 169 — la plus grande église à Prague terminée se dresse derrière la cure des franciscains sur la place Jungmannova. Elle fut fondée comme église de couronnement par Charles IV en 1347 et servit en même temps à l'ordre des carmes. La construction du chœur qui est restée bien conservée, date des années 1379—97 car la voûte à l'origine plus haute s'écroula avant cette date. L'ultérieur mouvement révolutionnaire des hussites toucha l'histoire de l'église d'une façon importante. J. Želivský, chef des miséreux de la ville de Prague, devant l'église dont il s' empara plus tard, provoqua une marche vers l'Hôtel de Ville de la Ville Neuve où fut effectuée la défenestration des échevins. Il prêcha dans l'église jusqu'à son exécution en 1422. L'archevêque pragois fit cadeau de l'église et du couvent aux franciscains dont la vie connut un épisode tragique. En 1611, lors de l'incursion des armées de Pasov à Prague, les pauvres gens soupçonnant les franciscains d'avoir caché les soldats s'enfuyant pénétrèrent dans le couvent et massacrèrent tous les franciscains.

A l'intérieur de l'église ce trouve le plus haut autel du premier baroque à Prague construit pendant une nouvelle installation des franciscains dans les années 1649—61 attirant l' attention. L'aménagement précieux de l'intérieur de l'église où il y a 10 statues des saints franciscains placées aux murs, de l'époque vers 1625, est formé par ex. par le tableau de « L'Annonciation de la Sainte Vierge », de V. V. Reiner de 1724 placé sur l'autel latéral ou par les fonts baptismaux en étain de 1449.

L'EGLISE SAINT-GILLES 170 — située dans la Vieille Ville entre les rues Jilská et Husova d'aujourd'hui, fut construite dans les années 1339—71 par l'évêque Jean de Dražice et puis par l'archevêque Arnošt de Pardubice comme église capitulaire à trois nefs. J. Milíč de Kroměříž y prêcha en tchèque en 1364. Dans cet esprit, l'église servait aux hussites. Contrairement à cela, l'empereur Ferdinand II la donna en 1626 aux dominicains qui y annexèrent un vaste couvent. En 1731, ils effectuèrent un renouvellement dans le style baroque auquel participa F. M. Kaňka. La peinture sur les voûtes et le tableau de Saint-Venceslas sont l'œuvre de V. V. Reiner, la décoration sculpturale principale fut effectuée par J. A. Quittainer et dans les années 1839—45 par le professeur L. Schwanthaler de Munich. F. I. Weis créa les sculptures sur bois dans les années 1734—38.

L'EGLISE DU SACRÉ-CŒUR 171 — fut construite dans les années 1928—32 d'après un projet de J. Plečnik à la façon de l'église du christianisme primitif et placée au centre de la vaste Place Georges de Poděbrady à Vinohrady. Une transformation originale de l'art dans l'esprit de l'antiquité se projette dans la décoration, dans les plastiques de B. Stefan au-dessus des trois portails de l'église et dans l'autel principal en marbre ainsi que dans la décoration intérieure, due à D. Pešan.

LA VILLA AMÉRIQUE 172 — appelée à l'origine Pavillon d'été de Michna, est la première construction du tout premier créateur de l'architecture baroque en Bohême K. I. Dienzenhofer. Une construction ravissante se trouvant aujourd'hui dans la rue Ke Karlovu dans la Ville Neuve unissant l'influence de la création monumentale viennoise de L. Hildebrandt à l'élégance et a la proportionnalité françaises fut bâtie dans les années 1712—20 aux frais du comte J. V. Michna de Vacínov. La salle principale fut décorée par une peinture murale sur le sujet des légendes mythologiques, œuvre de J. F. Sochor. Le Pavillon fut entouré par un jardin décoré des vases et des groupes de Quatre Saisons provenant de l'atelier de A. Braun. A partir de la fin du XVIIIe siècle, les marchés des bestiaux y avaient lieu. En 1932, le Pavillon a été acheté par la Société de A. Dvořák. Le musée de ce compositeur mondialement connu, installé par la Société s'y trouve jusqu' aujourd'hui.

La Villa Amérique nommée au XIXe siècle d'après l'auberge située à proximité, est séparée de la rue par une copie de grilles baroques. L'emplacement charmant de la construction est étouffé aujourd'hui par les constructions dominantes situées à proximité.

LA SALLE DVOŘÁK AU RUDOLPHINUM 174 — Comme siège de la Philharmonie Tchèque, la salle est utilisée pour les concerts et d'autres événements importants. Après le Théâtre National, ce sont les constructions néo-renaissance les plus importantes, créée par les architectes J. Zítek, J. Schulz et V. Vejrych aux années 1876—84. Le bâtiment fut nommé en l'honneur du Prince héritier Rodolphe.

LA SALLE DES GLACES AU CLÉMENTINUM 175 — bâtie en 1724 par F. M. Kaňka comme partie intégrante du collège de jésuites est un endroit décoré d'une façon superbe où on organise des concerts et des expositions. Les riches stucs dans lesquels on logea des glaces, forment le cadre des peintures de plafond avec le sujet de la vie de la Sainte Vierge, effectuées probablement par J. Hiebl. Les tableaux des saints furent faits par V. V. Reiner. La chapelle fut supprimée en 1784 et brièvement ouverte en 1816. Aujourd'hui, elle fait partie de la Bibliothèque Nationale.

LE MUSÉE WOLFGANG AMADEUS MOZART (1756—1791) DANS LA VILLA BERTRAMKA 176, 177 — A l'origine du XVIIe siècle et reconstruite pour la dernière fois en 1873, la villa Bertramka représentant une propriété faubourienne s'inscrivit dans l'histoire culturelle de Prague comme lieu où séjournait W. A. Mozart, un des tous premiers génies de musique. Puis, après 1784, quand le compositeur Fr. X. Dušek avec sa femme Josephine, excellente cantatrice, achetèrent Bertramka, Mozart fut leur hôte au cours de ses séjours à Prague. En 1787, il y composa Don Giovanni son opéra le plus connu, dont la première au Théâtre Nostic eut un succès extraordinaire.

L'AVENUE DE PARIS (PAŘÍŽSKÁ TŘÍDA) 181, 182 — reliant La Place de la Vieille Ville au Pont Sv. Čech assure en même temps l'accès aux restes de la Ville Juive, démolie pendant l'assainissement. Cette large avenue appelée à l'époque De Nicolas (Mikulášská), est composée d'immeubles représentatifs construits en majorité dans les années 1901—1906. Derrière le monument historique le plus important de l'ancienne Ville Juive, La Vieille-Nouvelle Synagogue, il y a un espace vide avec la statue en bronze de Moïse, créée par F. Bílek en 1905. Au bout de l'avenue, se trouve le bâtiment de la Faculté de Droit de l'Université Charles, construit dans les années 1924—27 d'après un projet de J. Kotěra de 1914. En biais en face, le complexe étendu de l'hôtel Intercontinental fut construit dans les années 1970—74 d'après un projet de K. Filsak, K. Bubeníček et Švec.

L'HÔTEL ATRIUM 182 — la construction de Franc, Nováček et Fencl achevée en 23 mois en juin 1990, représente la plus grande construction d'hôtel en Europe centrale. La construction du type d'atrium comporte 788 chambres avec 1568 lits. Le restaurant offre des plats des cuisines internationales et une cuisine spéciale tchèque.

VYŠEHRAD 187, 189—191 — siège légendaire des plus anciens princes tchèques, de Libuše et des Přemyslides, fut fondé après le Château de Prague, vers le Xe siècle sur le rocher de Vyšehrad au-dessus de la Vltava. Sous le règne du prince Vratislav II (1061—92, couronné roi en 1085), y fut transféré le siège du souverain . En 1070, fut fondé auprès du siège le chapitre de l'Eglise. En même temps le château en bois fut reconstruit en château en pierre. Auprès du château, de nouvelles églises furent fondées qui furent par suite détruites pendant les mouvements révolutionnaires hussites.

Vyšehrad d'aujourd'hui est bastionné et entouré de murailles baroques construites par des constructeurs italiens spécialistes de forteresses et aménagées en 1882. Les murailles entourent l'église capitulaire de Saint-Pierre et Saint-Paul qui est d'origine romane, reconstruite à l'époque du gothique et aussi du baroque et aménagée d'une façon néo-gothique dans les années 1885—87. A proximité de l'église, il y a des restes d'un pont roman qui fut probablement partie intégrante des fortifications du palais. En face de l'église se trouve une petite chapelle de Sainte-Ludmila. Parmi les monuments de Vyšehrad, une rotonde romane originale nommée Saint-Martin, vers laquelle on arrive par la porte d'entrée de la rue Dans la forteresse (V pevnosti), resta conservée.

En face de la façade de l'Eglise de Saint-Pierre et Saint-Paul il y a la porte principale du cimetière construit vers 1890 par A. Wiehl comme nécropole des fils méritants de la nation. Un projet imposé par le prévôt V. Štulc fut effectué sur la place du cimetière paroissial de 1660. Le Slavín, respectable mausolée des grands esprits et héros de la Patrie fut construit au centre de la partie est du cimetière, d'après des projets de Wiehl dans les années 1889—93 et en 1903.

Les trois groupes de sculptures dus à Myslbek provenant du pont Palacký endommagé, furent placées en 1948 sur les surfaces herbeuses à la place du dépôt d'armes brûlé. En 1978, le dernier groupe de sculptures renové — de Přemysl et Libuše — y fut introduit. Les statues des héros furent faites d'après un sujet national-mythologique du Manuscrit Královodvorský, actuel à l'époque. Lumír avec la Chanson furent effectués en 1888, Přemysl et Libuše en 1892, Záboj et Slavoj revenant du combat victorieux en 1895 et Ctirad et Šárka en 1897. Les images poétiques et enivrantes du passé illustre des Slaves trouvèrent leur justification à Vyšehrad.

LE COUVENT D'EMAÜS (EMAUSY, NA SLOVANECH) 188 — fondé en 1347 par Charles IV pour les bénédictins slaves qui y créèrent un centre unique du savoir et de l'art. C'est ici que nacquit 1395 la partie glagolitique pour le soi-disant Evangile de Reims, servant d'accompagnement du serment du couronnement des rois français, après 1546. Au cours des guerres hussites, l'unique couvent des calixtins tchèque y fut établi. L'aire du couvent successivement reconstruite avec l'église de Notre-Dame ont été gravement endommagés par le bombardement en 1945. Des reconstructions ont eu lieu dans les années suivantes. En 1967, la nouvelle construction des façades et des tours a été effectuée d'après un projet de F. M. Černý.

PORTE DU SLAVÍN 195 — C'est le Slavín, mausolée commun des représentants les plus importants de la nation, se trouvant dans la partie est de Vyšehrad, qui domine le cimetière de Vyšehrad. La construction de ce monument fut effectuée dans les années 1889—90 d'après un projet de l'architecte A. Wiehl. La décoration sculpturale représentant « Le Génie de la Patrie », « La Patrie se réjouissant » et « La Patrie en chagrin » fut faite par J. Maudr dans les années 1892—93. C'est le poète J. Zayer qui a été enterré le premier à Slavín et après lui 53 personnalités importantes (entre autres J. V. Myslbek, V. Hynais, E. Destinová, A. Mucha, J. Kubelík, V. Špála). Les pierres tombales dans ce cimetière sont dues aux meilleurs sculpteurs et architectes tchèques.

LA ROTONDE SAINT MARTIN 196 — le plus ancien monument bien conservé de Vyšehrad, datant de la seconde moitié du XIe siècle. Son importance diminua après la construction de la forteresse de Vyšehrad, quand la chapelle fut transformée en poudrière. Au XIXe siècle, elle fut utilisée comme dépôt. En 1878 le chapitre de Vyšehrad acheta toutefois cette construction précieuse et en 1878, il la fit renouveler d'après un projet de l'architecte A. Baum. L'intérieur fut complété par la peinture murale de A. König et J. Heřman. La peinture de l'autel est due à F. Sequens. La construction a été de nouveau restaurée en 1915 et dans les années 1969—70.

LE PALAIS DE LA CULTURE ET L'HÔTEL FORUM 198, 199 — En 1975, le besoin d'avoir un important centre culturel et social, avec possibilité d'organiser des conférences, des colloques et des congrès, a mené le gouvernement à faire construire un Palais de la Culture. La construction du monobloc gigantesque du Palais de la Culture a été achevée en 1980 sur un plan d'un heptagone irrégulier d'après un projet des auteurs de l'Institut militaire des projets d'urbanisme (J. Majer, V. Ustohal, A. Vaněk, J. Karlík). La tour polygonale de l'hôtel Forum se dresse en face du Palais de la Culture, au bout sud du pont de Nusle. La construction qui compte 27 étages a été terminée en 1988 d'après un projet de J. Trávníček.

LE PARC DES EXPOSITIONS DE PRAGUE 201, 202 — c'est le Palais des Congrès, une construction néo-baroque en fer due à B. Münzberger de 1891 et aménagée de nouveau dans les années 1952—54, qui forme la dominante du Parc. Le parc des expositions occupe la surface de l'ancienne Réserve Royale peuplée de gibier. En 1891, le Palais des expositions (un projet de A. Wiehl) pour l'Exposition anniversaire du pays fut achevé sur la superficie de 300.000 m^2. La salle ancienne des expositions artistique et retrospective à gauche où siège aujourd'hui l'Académie des arts plastiques reste comme souvenir de l'Exposition anniversaire du pays. Le Pavillon de Prague qui sert aujourd'hui comme lapidaire du Musée National, se trouve à droite de l'entrée. Toute une série de pavillons attractifs (par ex. pour l'exposition du « Panorama monumental de la bataille à Lipany » de Marold de 1898) et d'autres attraits (par ex. la fontaine renouvelée de l'inventeur Fr. Křižík) se trouvent sur la grande superficie du Parc des expositions.

LE CHÂTEAU DE TROJA 203 — fut construit à la fin du XVIIe siècle à la façon des villas italiennes du faubourg dans la région des vignes à l'orée nord du bassin pragois par le comte V. V. de Šternberk. D. Orsini de Orsini et S. Carloni et l'architecte éminent de Bourgogne J. B. Mathey participèrent au projet et à la construction. La décoration des espaces intérieurs exceptionnellement riche, avec les allégories et cryptoportraits des membres de la famille Šternberk, fut effectuée par F. et G. F. Marcheti. Les peintures de la salle principale qui représentent l'honneur de la dynastie des Habsbourgs furent effectuées par A. Godyn, peintre d'origine néerlandaise, dans les années 1691—97. (Le constructeur ambitieux fit franchement la carrière d'employé de la Cour). Sa confortable résidence de campagne devait servir aussi comme lieu de repos du souverain après la chasse au cours de ses visites attendues. La composition du château était bien réfléchie: La silhouette du Château de Prague est nettement visible dans l'axe droit du palier de l'escalier magnifiquement conçu avec les statues de Gigantomachie, œuvre de J. J. et P. Heermann de Dresden.

En 1989, la Galerie de Prague a installé des collections de tableaux du XIXe siècle dans le bâtiment du château reconstruit — avec la réplique du jardin historique de l'époque.

LE CHÂTEAU DE ZBRASLAV 204—209 — servant de prélature de l'abbaye des cisterciens se dresse d'une façon représentative sur la rive gauche de la rivière Vltava, navigable de Prague. Le bâtiment de 1739 avec les fresques de V. V. Reiner a été reconstruit en château appartenant à la famille Bartoň de Dobenín, dans les années 1911—12.

Le couvent de Zbraslav fut fondé par Venceslas II déjà en 1291. Son fondateur et après lui Venceslas III et Elisabeth des Přemyslides sont enterrés à l'Eglise abbatiale de Notre-Dame. La Chronique célèbre de Zbraslav remontant vers 1337 est une œuvre des abbés d'ici.

Le bâtiment du couvent de l'abbaye a été reconstruit avant 1709, d'après un projet de J. Santini. Dans les années 1724—32, il fut achevé d'après un projet de F. M. Kaňka. La décoration en stuc est due à T. Soldati. V. V. Reiner et F. X. Palko achevèrent les peintures en fresque de qualité. En 1785, le couvent fut supprimé et tomba en ruines. Dans la période des Bartoň de Dobenín, les intérieurs du château et du couvent furent aménagés de nouveau par D. Jurkovič et A. Čenský. Actuellement, les collections de sculptures des XIXe et XXe siècles appartenant à la Galerie Nationale de Prague sont installées dans le bâtiment du couvent.

Le chapitre consacré à la génération du Théâtre National forme une partie importante: par ex. on rappelle le projet original des pylônes du Théâtre National de B. Schnirch et Triga de 1873, dont l'installation a été effectuée dans les années 1910—11, d'après un projet remanié de E. Hallmann, S. Rous et L. Šalamoun. Un accent spécial est mis sur la création de J. V. Myslbek, le plus important représentant de cette génération à qui est consacrée une salle de même qu'à J. Štursa, le chef de file des sculpteurs créant au premier quart du XXe siècle.

PRAGA

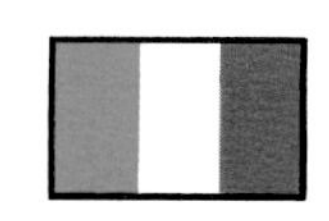

MOLDAVA 1, 185 — con le sorgenti che si trovano nelle foreste di Šumava (la sua lunghezza è di 430,2 km, il suo bacino fluviale di 28.090 km), essa è l'affluente sinistro del fiume Elba presso Mělník. Anche se, rispetto alla sua grandezza, la Moldava occupa il secondo posto, per la sua importanza potenziata dalla mitologia nazionale essa occupa il primo posto in Boemia. A Praga raggiunge larghezza e profondità notevoli (larghezza 316, profondità fino ai 3,8 m). Si divide in quattro bacini e i suoi bracci formano alcune isole (per es. Žofínský, Střelecký, Rohanský, Císařský). In modo rilevante prende parte alla ricchezza di colori del paesaggio praghese.

IL CASTELLO DI PRAGA 2, 6, 46, 99, 180 — fu costruito sulla lingua di terra nelle vicinanze del fiume Moldava dopo il 880, quando la sede dei principi cechi fu portata qui da Levý Hradec. Il centro nascente dello stato ceco governato dal casato dei Premyslidi diventava pure un centro degli avvenimenti eclesiastici. La prima chiesa cristiana della Vergine Maria fu costruita prima della fine del IX secolo; nella seconda metà del X secolo, nelle vicinanze del palazzo del principe, fu costruita la rotonda di San Vito con il palazzo vescovile e la chiesa monastica di San Giorgio. Il palazzo, dal XIII secolo reale, adempiva alla funzione residenziale del sovrano, e la sua ascesa culminò ai tempi dell'imperatore Carlo IV, costruttore zelante e coltivato. La rappresentatività della sede imperiale promosse in particolare un'ampia costruzione della cattedrale di San Vito, iniziata nel 1344 nello spirito degli esempi francesi. Un'imponente attività urbanistica si registrò verso la fine del XV secolo, quando il re Vladislao Jagellone decise di ampliare il palazzo costruendo la Sala di Vladislao. Sotto il suo governo, secondo il progetto di B. Ried, inserita nelle fortificazioni tardo gotiche del castello, fu costruita la famosa Torre Daliborka, chiamata secondo il cavaliere Dalibor di Kozojedy, il quale fu detenuto proprio qui. La sua avventura romantica divenne tema per l'opera Dalibor di Smetana. Alle fortificazioni apparteneva pure la Torre Bianca, dal 1584 prigione dello Stato.

Dopo l'interramento del duplice fossato nel secondo venticinquennio del XVI secolo avvenne la costruzione del secondo cortile del Castello, gradualmente completato e ulteriormente ristrutturato secondo il progetto di N. Pacassi entro l'anno 1775. L'ala settentrionale contiene la Sala Spagnola con la Galleria di Rodolfo. La parte del pianterreno nell'ala occidentale, assieme ai maneggi, nel 1965 fu ristrutturata e adattata alla pinacoteca del castello. All'angolo sud-est del cortile si trova la cappella della Santa Croce, originariamente costruita secondo il progetto di A. Lurago. Nel 1963, in seguito alla ristrutturazione, qui fu trasferito il tesoro di San Vito.

Il terzo cortile del Castello che forma il nucleo dell'area, comprende il palazzo rinascimentale dell'imperatore Rodolfo II, dell'imperatore Massimiliano II, e il palazzo primo barocco della regina, che hanno l'aspetto unitario delle facciate, eseguito secondo il progetto di N. Pacassi nel terzo venticinquennio del XVIII secolo. Qui si trovano gli uffici della Cancelleria del presidente della Repubblica. L'ingresso di rappresentanza con il balcone è decorato con le statue di I. F. Platzer degli anni 1760—61. Il cortile è chiuso dal palazzo reale e dalla cattedrale di San Vito e si collega con la piazza di San Giorgio. Dall'altro lato vi sfocia la via Vikářská con l'ex edificio capitolare del decano e con il nuovo vicariato, in cui oggi si trova il famoso ristorante Na Vikárce, legato all'opera letteraria di Sv. Čech.

All'area del Castello di Praga appartiene anche la cosiddetta Torre delle Polveri risalente alla fine del XV secolo, ora chiamata Torre Mihulka, costruita da B. Ried. In questa torre, che dapprincipio serviva da bastione d'artiglieria, è ospitata un'esposizione dedicata alla scienza e alla cultura coltivate al Castello nei secoli XVI e XVIII, non manca nemmeno un modello dell'officina alchimica.

Il Castello di Praga è circondato dai giardini meridionali Rajská zahrada e Na valech, che offrono, tra l'altro, vedute singolari sul panorama di Praga.

FRANTIŠEK ŽENÍŠEK (1849—1916), LIBUSSA PREDICE LA GLORIA A PRAGA; 3 — è l'opera del personaggio appartenente alla prima generazione del Teatro Nazionale. Essa riflette la figura leggendaria delle fiabe boeme, la sacerdotessa Libussa che in maniera profetica vede la futura gloria della città — Praga.

IL MUNICIPIO DELLA CITTÀ VECCHIA 4, 105, 107, 114–120, 123 — il cui torso che colpisce l'occhio si erge in alto in maniera pittorica al lato della Piazza della Città Vecchia, è la dimostrazione dell'esistenza di un'importante amministrazione cittadina le cui radici risalgono al 1338. Il nucleo del fabbricato parecchie volte ristrutturato fu la casa gotica di Wolflin od Kamene. La casa fu comprata dai cittadini, i quali le aggiunsero nel 1364 una torre quadrilatero con la cappella (consacrata nel 1381) con un balcone chiuso meravigliosamente decorato. A M. Rejsek di Prostějov viene attribuito il portale decorativo dell'ingresso principale, risalente agli anni 1470–80. Sulla facciata del municipio, a livello del primo piano, proprio sotto la sala del consiglio comunale e verso la parte estesa dell'edificio (del bottegaio Kříž), dopo l'anno 1520 fu collocata la finestra portante l'iscrizione Praga caput regni — Praga capo del regno e l'emblema della Città Vecchia del 1475. La ristrutturazione in stile del primo rinascimento viene attribuita al celebre B. Ried. L'ampliamento e altre ristrutturazioni del municipio avvennero poi nel XIX secolo. Il giorno precedente la conclusione della seconda guerra mondiale, quindi l'8 maggio 1945, fu gravemente danneggiato e incendiato il tratto nord del fabbricato, costruito da P. Nobile. Dopo la demolizione dei resti del fabbricato si registrarono i tentativi miranti alla ricostruzione o alla nuova costruzione del tratto, e furono pure banditi concorsi, ma senza successo.

Nel vestibolo del municipio ci sono le decorazioni a mosaico del classico dell'arte ceca della fine del XIX e degli inizi del XX secolo, M. Aleš: esse rappresentano l'Omaggio del mondo Slavo dato a Praga (1904). Si tratta di una replica espressiva al discorso tenuto da K. Sladkovský durante la posa della prima pietra al nascente Teatro Nazionale. Fu fatto cenno infatti alla visione profetica di Libussa di una città «la cui gloria toccherà le stelle». All'interno del municipio bisogna ricordare l'antica sala di cerimonie, conservatasi nell'aspetto originario del 1470. L'interno è decorato con le pitture di V. Brožík che si orientano verso gli atti storici, che in maniera sostanziale influirono sulla formazione della autocoscienza nazionale.

PONTI DI PRAGA 5, 98, 156, 178, 184 — oltre all'impostazione tecnica e funzionale hanno un carattere estetico chiaramente comprensibile, che scaturisce non soltanto dalle componenti edile e decorativa, ma anche dall'armonia unita al carattere pittoreo del flusso del fiume, ai suoi riflessi e ai suoi umori naturali.

HRADČANSKÉ NÁMĚSTÍ 7 — offre la veduta del primo, il più recente cortile del Castello di Praga e del suo portone d'ingresso. Il cortile fu costruito nello spirito del neoclassicismo italo-viennese negli anni 1759–69, secondo il progetto dell'architetto N. Pacassi. Sull'attico degli edifici sono collocati emblemi militari e le statue di I. F. Platzer. La ristrutturazione del cortile fu eseguita tra gli anni 1920–22 da P. Janák, il successivo adattamento avvenne negli anni 1979–80.

Di fronte al portone del primo cortile si trova la Porta di Mattia costruita probabilmente da G. M. Filippi, che ricorda le fortificazioni italiane: infatti la porta faceva parte delle fortificazioni sopra il fossato del castello.

PALAZZO ARCIVESCOVILE 8 — che chiude la piazza Hradčanské náměstí di fronte alla facciata del Castello di Praga, rivela un edificio di rappresentanza ristrutturato in stile barocco e porta l'emblema dominante dell'arcivescovo Antonín Příchovský. Alla base del palazzo servì la casa Gryspek, acquistata da Ferdinando I per la sede dell'arcivescovado di Praga allora rinnovato.

Negli anni 1562–64 ci fu la ristrutturazione di O. Aostalis. Un'altra ristrutturazione vigorosa fu eseguita tra il 1669 e il 1679 dal favorito dell'arcivescovo J. B. di Valdštejn, J. B. Mathey, architetto di origini francesi. L'aspetto finale in stile rococò lo impresse all'edificio negli anni 1764–65 J. J. Wirch, rappresentante principale dello stile orientato a Vienna. Il palazzo è decorato con le statue che rappresentano la Fede e la Speranza, eseguite da T. Seidan negli anni Ottanta del XIX secolo; i resti delle decorazioni scultoree sono di I. F. Platzer, le cui statue si trovano tuttora anche all'interno della scalinata. Il palazzo comprende anche una collezione singolare. Nella cappella risalente al 1599, decorata con i dipinti al soffitto per opera di D. A. di Květná, eccellono le buste dorate dei Santi Pietro e Paolo risalenti agli anni attorno al 1413. Nella Sala del Trono si trova la collezione di otto tappezzerie con temi esotici di Nuove Indie, eseguite nello studio di Neilson a Parigi secondo i cartoni di A. Desportes. Nella collezione dei quadri si trovano le opere di J. J. Heinsch, M. V. Halwachs, F. Dalfinger e di altri. Singolare è la successione dei ritratti degli arcivescovi di Praga. Nella collezione dell'arte artigianale eccelle l'esposizione del vetro tagliato di Boemia e della porcellana di Vienna. L'arredamento del palazzo si può vedere ogni anno nel giorno del Giovedì santo.

PORTONE D'INGRESSO DEL CASTELLO DI PRAGA 9 — da parte della piazza Hradčanské náměstí è formato dalla cancellata monumentale inserita nella balaustrata rococò risalente ai tempi di Maria Teresa. La decorazione è formata dal gruppo dei Giganti in lotta, dai vasi e putti, eseguiti nel 1769 da I. F. Platzer. Le sculture in pietra arenaria fatiscenti nel 1912 furono però sostituite dalle copie eseguite da Č. Vosmík e da A. Procházka.

Sullo sfondo domina la porta in pietra pre-barocca, costruita ai tempi dell'imperatore Mattia nel 1614. Ai lati, accanto alle designazioni dei gradi dell'imperatore, ci sono pure emblemi dei singoli paesi dell'impero.

IL TERZO CORTILE DEL CASTELLO DI PRAGA 10 — fu costruito gradualmente dopo il grande incendio del 1551, in seguito al quale furono interrati i residui delle costruzioni medioevali. Dopo la prima guerra mondiale J. Plečnik fece progetto per una costruzione in calcestruzzo e per il pavimento in granito per coprire i ritrovamenti archeologici.

Il lato settentrionale del terzo cortile si chiude con la parte meridionale della cattedrale di San Vito per mezzo di una torre costruita da P. Parléř nel 1396. La successiva torre in stile rinascimentale fu ristrutturata nel 1770 secondo il progetto di N. Pacassi. Nella torre alta 99,6 m si trovano quattro campane rinascimentali, tra le quali per la sua altezza di 203 cm eccelle la campana Zikmund. Quest'opera più grande del settore in Boemia la fece T. Jaroš nel 1549.

A destra sotto la torre si trova un porticato ad arcate, la cosiddetta Porta d'oro, nella quale si trovano i gioielli d'incoronazione del regno di Boemia. Sulla sua fronte si trova il mosaico Giudizio universale, eseguito tra gli anni 1370–71 dai maestri di Venezia con l'uso del vetro boemo.

L'edificio della Prepositura Vecchia che si trova dietro l'obelisco, fatto di un monolito di Mrákotín, ha l'aspetto risalente al XVII secolo. Al suo posto si trovava il palazzo vescovile romanico.

BASILICA DI SAN GIORGIO 11 — che forma il lato est della piazza di San Giorgio, è costruzione romanica più conservata di Praga. La chiesa fu fondata nel 921 dal principe Vratislao, però l'aspetto di una basilica a tre navate risale al tempo della badessa Berta, quindi prima del 1142, quando il Castello fu distrutto dall'incendio. La facciata principale è trasformata in stile barocco — probabilmente da F. Caratti tra il 1677 e 1678. Oltre questo F. M. Kaňka negli anni 1718–22 aggiunse la cappella di San Giovanni Nepomuceno che fu completata dal gruppo di statue di F. M. Brokoff che si trovano sopra l'ingresso. Alla torre sud della basilica risalente alla metà del XII secolo, nel XIV secolo fu aggiunta la cappella di Santa Ludmilla. Nel lato sud della basilica attira l'attenzione il portale rinascimentale a colonne, scolpito nella bottega di B. Ried di Pístov attorno al 1500. Il rilievo gotico di San Giorgio mentre uccide il drago, nel 1934 fu sostituito da una copia. Sotto la torre meridionale, nei resti della cappella della Vergine Maria sono conservate pitture romaniche risalenti alla prima metà del XIII secolo. All'interno della basilica, adattata in stile romanico a cavallo dei secoli XIX e XX, si trovano i monumenti sepolcrali dei principi Boleslao II e Oldřich nonché la tomba del principe Vratislao.

Fa parte del complesso edilizio adiacente anche il primo chiostro ceco della regola di San Benedetto: il convento fu fondato dalla sorella del principe Boleslao II, beata Mlada. Il convento ricostruito a più riprese fu abolito nel 1782 e presto fu trasformato in caserma. Negli anni 1962–74 fu concesso alla Galleria Nazionale di Praga e in seguito alla ristrutturazione vi fu allestita l'esposizione dell'arte ceca dei periodi gotico, rinascimento e manierismo.

LA CATTEDRALE DI SAN VITO 12, 44— è la chiesa più grande e più importante di Praga, nella quale sono depositati i gioielli d'incoronazione del Regno di Boemia. Qui riposano pure i resti mortali di sovrani cechi. La cattedrale, che in maniera espressiva completa la siluetta di Hradčany, fu fondata da Carlo IV nel 1344 sul posto di una basilica romanica a tre navate e di una rotonda precedente, quest'ultima costruita da San Venceslao, patrono della Boemia, prima del 935. La cattedrale a tre navate, con una navata trasversale, il deambulatorio e una corona di cappelle, fu costruita dapprincipio dal francese Mathieu de Arras, mentre dopo la sua morte nel 1356 i lavori furono proseguiti da Petr Parléř di Gmünd in Svevia. Gli successero i figli Václav e Jan. Terminata la costruzione del coro con le cappelle si passò ai lavori sul campanile principale che furono conclusi nel 1420; importante è il periodo successivo: nel 1564 l'architetto B. Wolmut costruì il deambulatorio sulla torre campanaria ed elmi. Il tetto barocco a cipolla fu terminato nel 1770 da N. Pacassi. La cattedrale fu completata solo nel 1929: la fase finale ebbe cioè la sua tappa neogotica iniziata nel 1873. Da quel periodo proviene pure l'altare neogotico, davanti al quale si trova il mausoleo reale, scolpito in marmo da A. Colin negli anni 1566—89. Nel triforio della chiesa si trovano 21 busti risalenti agli anni 1374—85 che raffigurano Carlo IV e la famiglia reale, arcivescovi e costruttori della cattedrale. Nei sotterranei dove sono conservati i resti della rotonda romanica, si trova il mausoleo reale. Il luogo importante è la camera che custodisce i gioielli di incoronazione, chiusa con sette serrature. Tra i tesori d'incoronazione più preziosi figura la corona di San Venceslao dell'anno 1346. Nelle cappelle del deambulatorio della cattedrale si trovano le tombe dei sovrani boemi, eseguite nella bottega di Parléř tra gli anni 1370—75. Durante il governo di Vladislao Jagellone, esattamente nel 1493, fu costruito l'oratorio reale con l'ornamento naturalistico che raffigura rami intrecciati e gli emblemi delle regioni. L'epoca rinascimentale è documentata dal coro con l'organo, costruito da Wohlmut. Il coro fu trasferito nella navata trasversale nel 1924. Tra le decorazioni barocche della cattedrale risalta soprattutto la tomba del conte L. Šlik, eseguita in comune da J. E. Fischerm di Erlach, F. M. Kaňka e M. Brandl nel 1723. Alle opere eccezionali del tempo moderno appartiene la statua del cardinale B. Schwarzenberg inginocchiato, scolpita da J. V. Myslbek tra il 1892 e il 1895. Dal primo venticinquennio del 20° secolo proviene la serie di finestre colorate nelle singole cappelle, seguite secondo i cartoni di A. Mucha, F. Kysela, C. Bouda. La cattedrale rappresenta tesoro delle opere artistiche, nell'ampiezza dal periodo romanico (renano, il cosiddetto candelabro di Gerusalemme) fino agli artefatti del 20° secolo.

LA CAPPELLA DI SAN VENCESLAO 13 — la cui costruzione fu iniziata da Mathieu de Arras, fu concepita come riscontro della Cappella della Santa Croce di Karlštejn. La costruzione fu terminata da P. Parléř negli anni 1362—66 sul posto del sepolcro originario del santo, dell'anno 935, quindi nei pressi del lato sud della navata anteriore. La cappella appartenente ai gioielli principali del gotico ceco è rivestita in basso con 1345 giaspidi e ametisti. Le pitture di altissimo livello rappresentano il ciclo della Passione, e furono eseguite da un maestro sconosciuto tra gli ani 1372—73. Nella parte superiore le pitture sono opera del Maestro di Litoměřice degli anni 1506—1509 e rippresentano la leggenda di San Venceslao. L'altare della cappella ha una tomba gotica del XIV secolo, mentre la statua in marna di San Venceslao fu scolpita da J. Parléř nel 1373. Le pitture più piccole sopra l'altare rappresentano Carlo IV e la sua quarta consorte, Elisa di Pomerania, ci sono quindi le figure di Venceslao IV e di Giovanna di Baviera. Le figure dominanti dipinte sopra la statua di San Venceslao rappresentano probabilmente Vladislao Jagellone e la sua consorte Anna de Foi-Candale. Gli oggetti liturgici sull'altare, così come il tabernacolo dorato e il lampadario degli anni 1912—13 (eseguito da F. Anýž in base ai progetti di K. Hilbert, G. Sucharda e J. Kryšpín) completano la successione degli artefatti gotici e rinascimentali. Sotto la finestra della cappella si trova un piccolo portale conducente alla scalinata della sala d'incoronazione, in cui è depositata la collezione dei gioielli dell'incoronazione che qui si trovano al sicuro.

MAESTRO TEODORICO, SAN PAPA, SAN GIROLAMO, SANT'AGOSTINO, SAN VITO 14—17 — le pitture su tavola del pittore imperiale ed esponente della corporazione dei pittori praghesi furono eseguite negli anni Settanta del XIV secolo e destinate per la cappella della corte di Carlo IV a Karlštejn. L'idea dell'unità universale dei mondi celeste e terrestre rispecchia 130 quadri, dislocati in tre fasce delle pareti intavolate. Questo polittico ha una precisa composizione ieratica. Le figure dei custodi del tesoro imperiale più grandi del naturale e viste in maniera monumentale, rappresentano un esempio singolare dell'ordinamento feudale, garantito dalla personalità del sovrano che rispetta la Chiesa vincente. Le pitture rappresentano l'esercito celeste di Cristo e documentano il culto medioevale dei santi — martiri, le cui reliquie sono inserite nelle cornici di ogni quadro.

La forma finemente pittorica di Teodorico con la riproduzione alternata di un tipo fisionomico documenta l'orientamento creativo maturo del maestro preferito dall'imperatore. La conoscenza delle creazioni bizantine così come di quelle occidentali, nominatamente delle creazioni di Venezia e di Bologna, è più che evidente.

MAESTRO DI TŘEBOŇ, CRISTO SUL MONTE DEGLI OLIVI, LA CROCIFISSIONE, LA DEPOSIZIONE NEL SEPOLCRO, LA RESURREZIONE 18—21 — le opere rappresentate nelle collezioni della Galleria Nazionale a Praga provengono dall'altare della chiesa degli Agostiniani dedicata a Sant'Egidio a Třeboň, la tavola con la crocifissione proviene dalla cappella di Santa Barbara nei pressi di Třeboň. Le pitture su tavole furono fatte da un maestro anonimo a livello mondiale attorno all'anno 1380. La composizione complessa con l'arabesco di fini forme e il contrasto carico di colori ridimensionano l'idealismo e una particolare estasi mistica. Le opere di contenuti lirici precorrono l'arte del periodo all'incirca il 1400.

LA SALA DI VLADISLAO 22 — comprende la posizione dell'intero secondo piano del Palazzo Vecchio del Castello di Praga. Essa occupa gli spazi più dignitosi del Castello, poiché qui si svolgono tradizionalmente i più importanti atti di Stato. La sala fu costruita ai tempi di Vladislao Jagellone tra gli anni 1492—1502, dopo il trasferimento della sede della corte reale dalla Città Vecchia al Castello. La costruzione nel posto delle tre sale gotiche del tempo di Carlo IV fu progettata dall'architetto reale B. Ried. Così fu costruito lo spazio borghese più grande e più rappresentativo del tardo gotico centroeuropeo (lunghezza 62 m, larghezza 16 m, altezza 13 m). Qui avvenivano le incoronazioni nonché le assemblee degli Stati, ma anche tornei cavallereschi, ai quali serviva la Scalinata dei cavalieri. Dopo il trasferimento della residenza imperiale a Vienna la sala veniva adibita per varie assemblee pubbliche, qui avvenivano pure i mercati dei bottegai della corte. La sala fu ristrutturata con devozione dopo la prima guerra mondiale, allorché furono eliminate le pitture più tardive.

Dalla Sala di Vladislao si accede nell'ala laterale del Castello, nel cosiddetto Palazzo di Lodovico, risalente agli inizi del XVI secolo.

L'ANTICA SALA DELLA DIETA AL CASTELLO DI PRAGA 23 — nella quale fino al 1847 svolgeva le sedute il tribunale supremo del paese e dove si radunavano i rappresentanti degli Stati cechi, fu costruita negli anni 1559—65 dall'architetto imperiale B. Wohlmut. La sala di rappresentanza con la volta a rete rotatoria fu usata fino al 1857 per le riunioni degli Stati riguardanti l'elezione del re. All'epoca moderna qui il presidente della Repubblica firma i documenti costituzionali, eccezionalmente qui avvengono le riunioni del Consiglio nazionale ceco.

ADRIAEN DE VRIES (1546—1626), RODOLFO II 24 — uno dei tre ritratti che de Vries fece all'imperatore (del 1603), che il pittore e teorico Van Mander denominò «il più grande e il primo amico dell'arte nel mondo», proviene dalle collezioni singolari di Rodolfo, i cui resti sono esposti nella pinacoteca del Castello di Praga. L'olandese De Vries fu la maggiore personalità della scultura alla corte rodolfina. Una grande parte delle sue opere fu compresa nel bottino che le truppe svedesi si portarono da Praga durante l'assedio del 1648.

SAN GIORGIO 25 — la statua equestre in bronzo del leggendario uccisore del drago è la copia dell'opera eseguita dai maestri Jiří e Martin di Klausenburg nel 1373. All'origine essa era collocata nella parte meridionale del cortile del castello, di fronte alle cosiddette cucine di Massimiliano. Le figure del cavallo e del drago furono più tardi fuse e dopo il danneggiamento avvenuto nel 1562 riparate dal fonditore T. Jaroš. Lo zoccolo della statua al momento della pavimentazione del terzo cortile lo progettò nel 1928 J. Plečnik; quest'ultimo progettò pure l'obelisco alto 18 m, fatto di un monolite del granito di Mrákotín. Esso fu eretto in occasione del decimo anniversario della Repubblica Cecoslovacca e in memoria delle vittime della prima guerra mondiale.

TIZIANO VECELLIO (cca. 1480/90 — 1576), TOILETTE DELLA GIOVANE DONNA 26 — quest'opera del più grande rappresentante della pittura veneziana del XVI secolo fu documentata nella pinacoteca del castello nel 1685. Una giovane donna con i capelli rossicci con i bisogni di toilette, servita con l'ammirazione da un giovane con il turbante, s'assomiglia tipicamente al quadro viennese della Madonna zingara (attorno al 1510), dipinta nel periodo in cui Tiziano ammirava pienamente Giorgione. La pittura praghese realizzata attorno agli anni 1512—15, probabilmente verso la metà del XVIII secolo fu ridotta, forse per motivi di intavolatura (a 83×79 cm). Una precisa copia rinascimentale del quadro (con le dimensioni di 109,2×91,3 cm) fu venduta (il 27 novembre 1957) ad un collezionista privato all'asta nella casa Christe a Londra. Altre copie barocche di qualità minore furono registrate da J. Neumann in altre collezioni private (per es. a Toulouse).

Il tema Toilette della giovane donna appare anche in altre versioni, la più nota delle quali è l'opera di Tiziano a Louvre, che proviene dalla collezione di Carlo I, re d'Inghilterra. L'autenticità della pittura di Praga nel passato veniva messa in dubbio. Già nel 1832 l'opera veniva attribuita ad Orazio, figlio di Tiziano, più tardi si pensava ad una copia.

PETRUS PAULUS RUBENS (1577—1640), L'ASSEMBLEA DEGLI DEI SULL'OLIMPO (dettaglio) 27 — già quest'opera nascente del principale rappresentante del barocco fiammingo imposta l'imponente energia, la sensualità e il flusso sinfonico degli avvenimenti a più strati, di cui più tardi abbondano i lavori di Rubens. La pittura fu eseguita probabilmente attorno al 1602, quando Rubens divenne pittore di corte del duca di Mantova Vincenzo Gonzaga. Il quadro riprende l'assemblea degli abitanti dell'Olimpo con a capo Giove, al momento in cui Era — Giunone, custode di solidi legami matrimoniali, presenta la propria lamentela nei confronti di Venere — Afrodite, spensierata ma trionfante dea dell'amore, incoronata di amoretti.

La pittura, che porta il sigillo dell'influenza di G. Romano, nelle collezioni del Castello è confermata per la prima volta nel 1685 in quanto opera di un anonimo, mentre negli anni 1718—37 essa viene collegata con il nome di Raffaello. Il nome di Rubens in quanto autore del quadro viene fatto brevemente nel 1797: l'autenticità della sua opera fu confermata dopo il 1962 da J. Neumann.

KAREL ŠKRÉTA (1610—1674), RITRATTO DEL TAGLIATORE DI PIETRE PREZIOSE DIONISIO MISERONI E DELLA SUA FAMIGLIA (dettaglio) 28 — l'opera della personalità del fondatore della pittura barocca ceca risalente probabilmente al 1653, riprende il capo della bottega degli arrotini e amministratore delle collezioni artistiche del Castello, assieme alla sua famiglia. Fu proprio Dionisius Miseroni ad impedire nel 1648 l'entrata dei soldati svedesi nei locali delle famose collezioni della Kunstkammer rodolfina. Suo padre Ottavio Miseroni nel 1588 fu chiamato da Milano alla corte di Rodolfo II, dove fu nominato tagliatore della corte di pietre preziose e nel 1608 ottenne il titolo di nobile.

JAN KUPECKÝ (KUPEZKY JOHANNES, 1667—1740), ALLEGORIA DELLA PITTURA 29 — l'opera di questo esule ceco inseritosi tra i principali ritrattisti europei dell'inizio del XVIII secolo, è la pittura rispondente all'Allegoria della scultura che si trova nelle collezioni della Galleria Nazionale di Praga. La personificazione pittorica di una giovane donna con un vestito barocco e con la corona d'alloro sui suoi ricchi fulvi capelli, viene collocata nel secondo decennio del XVIII secolo, quando l'autore operava a Vienna.

PETR BRANDL (1668—1735), AUTORITRATTO 31 — il quadro fu dipinto nel 1697 e proviene dalle collezioni del casato Lobkovic, ora imprestato alla Galleria Nazionale di Praga. Il quadro documenta con veridicità le capacità caratteristiche e coloristiche del più grande pittore del barocco culminante in Boemia, che entrò nella subcoscienza non solo come portretista, ma soprattutto come creatore di tele degli altari con luci dinamiche, nonché di opere con temi mitologici e di determinato genere.

PAOLO CALIARI, DETTO VERONESE (1528—1588), SANTA CATERINA CON L'ANGELO 32 — l'opera di uno dei maggiori rappresentanti della pittura veneziana del XVI secolo, eseguita attorno all'anno 1580, è documentata nella II galleria del Castello di Praga già nel 1685 sotto la denominazione Tentazione della Santa. L'interpretazione erronea del quadro proviene probablimente dal gesto famigliare dell'angelo. Secondo J. Neumann, la santa di Alessandria viene però dipinta in quanto la sposa di Cristo al momento, in cui il messaggero divino le rivela la sua sorte, quindi la morte di martire, come ne accenna il ramoscello di palma e la spada nella mano dell'angelo.

IL PALAZZO LOBKOVIC E LA TORRE NERA 33 — sono accessibili dalla Antica Scala del Castello nella zona est. La Torre Nera, costruita sulle fondamenta più antiche nel secondo venticinquennio del XII secolo, faceva parte delle fortificazioni romaniche dei tempi del principe Soběslao. Il suo degrado dopo l'incendio del 1538, quando la torre dovette essere ridotta di un piano, si proiettò anche nella sua denominazione. Prima cioè la torre veniva detta „D'oro" — secondo il tetto coperto di lamiera dorata in piombo ai tempi di Carlo IV. La torre era usata anche come prigione per i debitori. Alle origini serviva come porta orientale del castello. Ai tempi di Venceslao I, dopo il 1230, sotto di essa fu costruita una nuova porta d'ingresso, attigua al Palazzo Lobkovic, prima Palazzo Pernštejn, costruito da Jaroslav e Vratislav di Pernštejn nelle epoche 1555—62 e 1570—76. L'edificio nel 1625 fu danneggiato a causa dell' incendio. La nuova ricostruzione del palazzo avvenne in particolare tra il 1651 e il 1668, quando la sua proprietà dal 1626 passò ai nobili Lobkovic. Václav Eusebius di Lobkovic commissionò il progetto a C. Lurago: gli scalpellini italiani G. Galli e G. Pozzo eseguirono lavori in pietra, lo stuccatore. D. Galli decorò il soffitto della sala principale, mentre F. V. Hárovník qui eseguì le pitture ad olio. La decorazione fu completata da artigiani locali. Le ristrutturazioni parziali avvennero anche nei periodi più tardivi, in particolare nel 1810 e 1861—62. Nel 1976 iniziò la ricostruzione del palazzo e vi fu collocata un'esposizione storico archeologica del Museo Nazionale. Il palazzo, nell' ambito delle restituzioni, nel 1992 fu riconsegnato al ramo di Roudnice della famiglia Lobkovic.

PANORAMA DI PRAGA DAL PALAZZO LOBKOVIC 34 — coglie una veduta singolare dell'ampia isola di Malá Strana con al centro Palazzo Valdštejn, costruito sull'area di 23 case con i cortili e con i giardini, di una fornace e della porta cittadina. Dietro il palazzo si erge la chiesa di San Tommaso, fondata assieme al convento da Venceslao II nel 1285 per l'ordine degli Agostiniani-eremiti. L'autore della ristrutturazione barocca tuttora conservata degli anni 1723—31 fu l'importante architetto F. I. Dienzenhofer. La decorazione sfarzosa della chiesa è dovuta agli artisti principali cechi del periodo barocco; per l'altare maggiore furono commissionate due opere di P. P. Rubens, oggi documentate da rispettive copie (gli originali furono trasferiti nella Galleria Nazionale).

IL GIARDINO KOLOWRAT 35 — progettato negli anni 1769—89 da I. J. Palliardi, si stende dietro l'edificio principale del Palazzo Kolowrat e dietro il palazzo più piccolo Černín, costruito nel 1770 sul posto dell'ex casa della famiglia Popel di Lobkovic. Il giardino rococò a terrazzi, con le sfumature dell' esotica orientale e dell' aspetto pittorico, contiene le pergole e le scalinate con le balaustrate conducenti verso le sale terrene in tre parti.

IL GIARDINO REALE 36 — oggi in stile inglese, fu fondato nel 1535 da Ferdinando I nello spirito dei giardini rinascimentali italiani nell'area tra il Ponte delle Polveri e il Fossato dei Cervi. Vi si coltivavano molte piante esotiche ma anche l'uva, c'era pure un giardinetto olandese. Furono eseguite qui numerose costruzioni, posto per gli uccelatori, serbatoi di acqua, fontane e getti d'acqua, labirinti. La ristrutturazione fondamentale fu eseguita su progetto di K. I. Dienzenhofer tra il 1725 e il 1734, quando il pianterreno floreale di stile francese fu completato di sculture di leoni, di vasi e di allegorie provenienti dalla bottega di M. B. Braun.

IL GIARDINO HARTIG 37,50 — si stende sui pendii meridionali del Castello di Praga in mezzo ad altri giardini di singolare bellezza e amenità. Oltre alle passeggiate unite alle vedute meravigliose del panorama di Praga, qui si offrivano anche interessanti produzioni culturali, come per esempio nel padiglione di musica nel Giardino Hartig. La costruzione risalente al primo venticinquennio del XVIII secolo, attribuita a G. B. Alliprandi, ha la sala superiore decorata con le pitture che raffigurano i ruderi, e con gli stucchi. Davanti al padiglione furono collocate le sculture delle divinità antiche, provenienti dalla bottega di A. Braun e fatte attorno al 1735: esse furono trasferite nei giardini del Castello di Praga dopo il 1945 dalla villa di Štiřín.

LA FONTANA CANTANTE 38 — che si trova davanti al Belvedere reale, fu colata negli anni 1564—68 dal fonditore di Brno, T. Jaroš, in base al progetto del maestro italiano F. Terzio. La fontana si trova in mezzo al giardinetto rinnovato, eseguito secondo il campionario dell'architetto e decoratore olandese V. de Vries. Il suo nome proviene dal suono delle gocce d'acqua che cadono dal serbatoio a due piani decorato con motivi di caccia. La fontana è considerata una delle più belle opere rinascimentali di questo tipo a nord delle Alpi.

LA GRANDE SALA DELLA PALLA
MATYÁŠ BERNARD BRAUN — BOTTEGA, LA NOTTE 39, 40 — la Grande Sala della Palla fu costruita nel Giardino reale sopra il Fossato dei Cervi da B. Wohlmut e O. Aostalis tra il 1567 e il 1569, dapprincipio per la moda dei giochi con la palla. Gentile costruzione

a sala (lunga 60 m) con le colonne palladiane è coperta di fragili graffiti, allegorie delle Virtù, delle Scienze e degli Elementi. Il locale abbandonato nel 1723 fu trasformato in stalle per cavalli, più tardi nel deposito militare. Ancora nel 1734 però davanti alla facciata fu collocato un gruppo di statue proveniente dalla bottega di M. B. Braun, eseguito dal suo nipote A. Braun: si trattava dell'allegoria Notte e Giorno. Questa seconda opera fu distrutta durante il bombardamento prussiano del Castello di Praga nel 1757.

Nel 1945 la Sala della Palla fu incendiata, ma nel 1952 fu ricostruita e negli anni 1971—73 fu riadattata. Al momento attuale serve per scopi di rappresentanza, per cui qui furono trasferite tappezzerie di Bruxelles fatte da J. van Leefdael nel XVII secolo che raffigurano Antonio e Cleopatra.

IL BELVEDERE REALE 41 — costruito nelle vicinanze del Castello di Praga, sopra la valle del fiume Brusnice, negli anni 1538—63, documenta eminentemente l'influenza del rinascimento italiano sui paesi cechi. La costruzione stimolata da Ferdinando I proseguiva secondo il progetto dello scalpellino italiano ed architetto P. della Stella, e quindi di H. Tirol, dell' architetto della corte B. Wohlmut, O. Aostalis. La sopraintendenza alla costruzione fu assegnata al segretario della Camera ceca, F. di Griesbach. La ricca decorazione in pietra fu eseguita dalla bottega di P. della Stella (fino all'anno 1538) e in seguito da altri maestri italiani. Il Belvedere era destinato al riposo e ai divertimenti della regina Anna. Vi sorse una ricca galleria, fu costruita la sala da ballo, i locali possedevano costose decorazioni. L'incursione delle truppe svedesi nel 1648 colpì sia il Belvedere che le sue collezioni. Ai tempi di Giuseppe II il fabbricato fu svalorizzato essendo trasformato in un laboratorio (così rimase fino al 1836). Negli anni 1851—65 sulle pareti del primo piano fu dipinto un ciclo di temi riguardanti la storia della Boemia, in base ai cartoni del direttore dell'Accademia praghese, K. Ruben. Al momento attuale il Belvedere, dopo i restauri eseguiti da P. Janák, serve ai fini espositivi.

IL VICOLO DELL'ORO 42 — passa dietro la casa del burgravio del Castello, sopra il Fossato dei Cervi. Le odierne casine pittoresche in miniatura erano man mano inserite nelle volte delle fortificazioni del castello, a cominciare dal XVI secolo, periodo dei Jagelloni. Fino al 1597 qui abitavano i tiratori del castello, piccoli artigiani e orafi di Rodolfo II. Secondo il nome del vicolo „Degli orafi" — usato fino agli anni Settanta del XVII secolo — nacque più tardi la leggenda che vuole la via abitata dagli alchimisti. Tra gli anni 1952—55 le casette furono ristrutturate, come pure il corridoio coperto che collega le tre torri, attraverso il quale venivano portati i prigionieri. Nelle casette restaurate fu allestita l'esposizione sulla storia di questa parte popolare del Castello, ci sono poi i negozi di libri e di souvenirs.

LA CHIESA DI SAN NICOLA A MALÁ STRANA 43, 59—60, 62, 64, 65 — In mezzo alla piazza Malostranské náměstí, dove prima stava una casa gotica e nelle sue vicinanze si trovavano botteghe di macellai, c'è la dominante del barocco praghese, che al lato sud è adiacente all'ex-collegio dei Gesuiti. La costruzione della chiesa di San Nicola ebbe luogo tra gli anni 1704—11 e fu diretta da K. Dienzenhofer, architetto venuto a Praga attraverso Waldsaxen; il suo figlio K. I. Dienzenhofer terminò negli anni 1732—52 il presbiterio con la cupola. Il cognato di Dienzenhofer, A. Lurago, negli anni 1751—56 aggiunse una snella torre campanaria in stile rococò, fulcro originario della contesa con il comune di Malá Strana, che aveva ritardato l'inizio dei lavori di costruzione del complesso chiesastico. La facciata della chiesa terminata nel 1710 rivela l'influenza del barocco romano di orientamento illusorio. Acanto all'emblema di Fr. Liebštejnský di Kolowrat si trovano le statue dei Padri della Chiesa e quindi le allegorie di Teologia, realizzate dallo scultore A. Braun prima del 1735.

L'interno della chiesa è l'esempio fastoso più evidente del barocco culminante di Praga. Negli affreschi si avvicendarono J. L. Kracker e J. Heger, la capella monumentale con le dimensioni 75 m^2 fu decorata da F. X. Palko. Quattro statue in legno stuccate, nella grandezza oltre al naturale, che rappresentano Padri della Chiesa e che si trovano sotto la cupola, furono create negli anni 1752—55 da J. F. Platzer, autore pure della statua in rame di San Nicola sull'altare principale e di altre statue. Fanno parte delle decorazioni sontuose della chiesa anche i quadri di K. Škréta, I. Raab, J. L. Kracker. L'organo installato tra il 1745 e 1746 da T. Schwarz, suonava durante i suoi soggiorni a Praga W. A. Mozart.

Dopo lo scioglimento della Compagnia di Gesù per ordine del papa Clemente XIV nel 1773, la chiesa di San Nicola diventò chiesa parrocchiale di Malá Strana.

LORETA 45 — costruita a spese della famiglia Lobkovic si trova di fronte al panorama monumentale del Palazzo Černín a Hradčany. La costruzione risale agli anni 1626—1750. La chiesa diventò presto luogo di pellegrinaggio. Essa è adiacente al primo convento dei Padri Cappuccini in Boemia che fu costruito nel 1601. La facciata della chiesa di Loreto — Loreta la costruì tra gli anni 1621—23 K. I. Dienzenhofer, mentre la decorazione scultorea — oggi sostituita con le copie — la eseguirono O. F. Quittainer e J. B. Kohl. La facciata fu resa più alta a causa della torre del 1693 che contiene un carillon di campane costruito dall'orologiaio. P Neumann. Le variazioni musicali delle canzoni affascinanti ravvivano la piccola piazza di Hradčany e creano un'atmosfera gioievole a causa del complesso meccanismo di campane fuse ad Amsterdam. Al centro del cortile si trova la Santa Casa, costruita dall'architetto G. B. Orsi nel 1631, coperta di espressivi rilievi a stucco eseguiti dai maestri italiani nel 1664. Vi si ricorda la leggenda sulla casa della Vergine Maria che da Nazaret, nel XIII secolo, sarebbe stata trasportata dagli angeli a Loreto in Italia. Per questo, all'interno della casa ci sono pitture relative alla vita della Vergine Maria e la sua statua del legno di cedro. Vicino al chiostro al lato est del fabbricato si trova la chiesa della Nascita del Signore, costruita tra gli anni 1734—35 secondo il progetto di J. J. Aichbauer, con gli affreschi del soffitto da V. V. Reiner.

Loreta, restituita al convento dei Padri Cappuccini, offre una ricchezza singolare nelle sue collezioni. Nel tesoro con cimeli di ingente valore si trovano opere in oro, tra cui spicca un ostensorio di diamanti del 1699 (con 6.222 diamanti!).

LA TORRE DI PETŘÍN 47 — alta 60 m si erge in alto sul pendio roccioso (di qui la sua denominazione: petri — roccia), che sale all'altezza di 318 m ad ovest dal bacino di Malá Strana. La costruzione della torre, copia ridotta della Torre Eiffel di Parigi, fu promossa dal Club turistico in occasione dei preparativi all'Esposizione giubilare territoriale nel 1891.

L'OSSERVATORIO ASTRONOMICO DI PETŘÍN 48 — che si trova al termine del giardino delle rose, fu costruito tra gli anni 1925—30 con la trasformazione della casa comunale a spese della Società astronomica ceca (progettista J. Veselík). Fino ad oggi serve ai bisogni dell'attività degli astronomi dilettanti e nel contempo vi è collocata un'esposizione astronomica permanente.

IL CONVENTO DI STRAHOV 51 — fondato dal principe Vladislao II nel 1140 su stimolo del vescovo di Olomouc Jindřich Zdík, fu dato all'ordine dei canonici regolari dell'Ordine Premonstratese, i cui membri si impegnavano nel settore educazione e nella promozione della civilizzazione. L'esteso complesso del convento situato sopra Praga, sul pendio di Petřín, comprende due chiese, un convento, una prelatura del convento, le biblioteche e fattorie. Singoli stabili passarono attraverso numerose trasformazioni spesso anche complesse, e attraverso cambiamenti edilizi, in particolare ai tempi del movimento ussita e durante gli attacchi delle truppe francesi o prussiane nel XVIII secolo. Al centro dell'intera area si trova il convento con la biblioteca, dove, nel 1953, fu installato il Monumento di letteratura nazionale. L'ingresso principale nell'area conduce attraverso la porta dalla parte di Pohořelec: la porta stessa fu costruita nel 1742 da A. Lurago. La chiesetta di San Rocco al lato sinistro fu costruita a spese di Rodolfo II, come ringraziamento per lo scongiuramento della peste. A. Lurago prese parte anche alle ricostruzioni della chiesa abaziale dedicata all'Assunzione della Vergine Maria, nel cui nucleo è contenuta anche la basilica romanica originaria del XII secolo. Sul cortile principale si trova l'edificio della prelatura della seconda metà del XVI secolo, ristrutturato negli anni 1680—99, secondo il progetto di J. B. Mathey e M. A. Canevalle. Gli affreschi del soffitto furono dipinti dal premonstratese S. Nosecký. L'edificio del convento a quattro ali di origini romaniche (dopo il 1142) fu ricostruito nei primo barocco e poi nel barocco culminante. Attraverso la scalinata annessa si accede nell'edificio del convento costruito ai tempi dell'abate V. Mayer, dall'architetto I. P. Palliardi negli anni 1782—84. Il vanto del fabbricato sono le sale Teologica e Filosofica con ricche decorazioni, che rievocano la singolare ricchezza di collezioni storiche. Fa parte dell'area anche il giardino architettonicamente adattato sotto l'ala del sud. Nel 1991 il convento fu restituito all'Ordine dei Premonstratesi, il quale ripristina l'attività interrotta e prende in custodia ciò che rimane delle collezioni storiche e artistiche.

LA CHIESA DELL' ASSUNZIONE DELLA VERGINE MARIA 52 — comprendente i resti della rotonda romanica risalente al

1182 e parecchie volte ricostruita, oggi si presenta in veste impressale da A. Lurago negli anni 1745—52. L'interno della chiesa ha una disposizione originaria conservatasi: ci sono tre navate romaniche con i ritocchi barocchi, con gli stucchi di K. A. Palliardi e con le pitture sui temi delle leggende mariane oppure delle celebrazioni in onore di San Norberto, eseguite da J. Kramolín, I. Raab, V. Neunherz, F. X. Palka, J. K. Liška, M. Willmann, con le opere scultoree di J. A. Quittainer e di altri. Le pitture dei soffitti delle cappelle provengono tra l'altro dal pittore del convento di Strahov, S. Nosecký, membro dell'Ordine dei Premonstratesi. Nella cappella di Sant'Orsola sull'altare si trovano le reliquie di San Norberto, fondatore dell'Ordine dei Premonstratesi. Tra le curiosità culturali figura l'organo barocco della chiesa che a suo tempo suonava W. A. Mozart.

SALA TEOLOGICA 53 — costruita negli anni 1671—79 dall'architetto G. D. Orsi, originariamente serviva come sala della biblioteca. Da quel tempo nelle librerie barocche si mantiene la letteratura teologica, compreso il reparto dei libri proibiti («libri prohibiti»). Nelle vetrine sono depositati rari manoscritti con miniature, il più antico dei quali, evangeliario di Strahov, risale al IX secolo. Nell'area della sala, decorata con stucchi e pitture murali sul tema bibliofilia dal pittore premonstratese S. Nosecký, sono collocati globi astrologici del XVII secolo che documentano gli interessi scientifici dei membri dell'ordine.

SALA FILOSOFICA 54 — risalente all'epoca della costruzione degli edifici del monastero da parte di I. J. Palliardi negli anni 1782—84, appartiene agli ambienti più interessanti del monastero. Nel 1794 essa fu decorata con la pittura straordinaria sul soffitto che rappresenta la Storia dell'umanità e che fu eseguita da F. Maulbertsch, principale rappresentante del rococò viennese. Le librerie barocche in noce, eseguite dal falegname J. Lachhoven, furono trasportate qui dal monastero premonstratese di Louka u Znojma. Nella vetrina è collocato il busto in marmo dell'imperatore Francesco I fatto da F. X. Lederer, nelle librerie sono sonservati libri, che aveva donato al monastero la consorte di Napoleone, Maria Luisa.

IL BELVEDERE HVĚZDA 55 — fu costruito all'estremità sud-ovest dell'omonima riserva di caccia a Horní Liboc, nei posti dove c'era prima una foresta, che dal X secolo apparteneva al monastero di Břevnov. La riserva di caccia fondata dall'imperatore Ferdinando I nel 1534, nel XVI secolo fu luogo di divertimenti reali e di festività dei tiratori. L'autore del progetto di questo insolito belvedere con la pianta a stella (del diametro di 40 m) fu il dotto figlio dell'imperatore, arciduca Ferdinando detto Tirolese, allora vicegerente imperiale in Boemia. La costruzione del belvedere negli anni 1555—65 la eseguirono gli architetti della corte reale di Praga, G. M. Aostalis e G. Lucchese, sotto la soprintendenza di H. Tirol e, più tardi, di B. Wohlmut. La decorazione ricca e fine sui temi tratti dalla mitologia greca e dalla storia greca e romana, nasceva alla presenza di A. del Pambio, C. Campione e di altri maestri italiani, che negli anni 1556—63 per la prima volta eseguivano gli stucchi in Boemia a livello eccezionale. La singolarità dell'intera costruzione e le sue decorazioni erano date anche con l'intenzione dell'architetto di portare qui la sua moglie segreta Filipina Welser, che non poteva soggiornare al Castello.

Prima che si giungesse alle fasi successive — quindi alle decorazioni pittoriche della seconda metà del XVII secolo — la riserva di caccia Hvězda situata sotto la Montagna Bianca divenne luogo tragico della storia nazionale. Qui, nel 1620, avvenne la sconfitta sanguinosa degli eserciti degli Stati cechi da parte della Lega cattolica e dell'esercito imperiale. Da questa battaglia della Montagna Bianca la riserva di caccia e il belvedere cominciarono a deteriorare, anche perché nei periodi successivi qui si accampavano gli eserciti nemici. Ai tempi di Giuseppe II nel belvedere fu istituita la polveriera. Alla ricostruzione dell'edificio si giunse soltanto dopo il 1918; negli anni 1949—51, su progetto di P. Janák, il belvedere fu adattato a scopi museali. Nel 1951 qui fu allestito il museo dello scrittore di romanzi storici A. Jirásek (1851—1930). Nel 1964 iniziò la propria attività il museo del noto pittore ceco M. Aleš (1852—1913).

IL MONASTERO DI BŘEVNOV CON LA CHIESA DI SANTA MARGHERITA 56, 57 — rappresenta un complesso edile singolare, costruito tra gli anni 1708—45, a spese degli abati O. Zinke e B. Loebl, secondo il progetto di K. Dienzenhofer e del suo figlio K. I. Dienzenhofer. La costruzione avvenne sul posto del monastero dei Benedettini precedente, distruito e ridotto all'inerzia dagli ussiti, fondato dal vescovo di Praga Adalberto e dal principe Boleslao II nel 993, primo monastero di religiosi in Boemia.

La chiesa del monastero è il gioiello dell'architettura ceca con la decorazione interna adeguata; sullo sfondo delle pitture sul soffitto risaltano quelle di J. J. Steinfels degli anni 1719—21 e lo stesso vale per la pittura illusoria molto efficace di J. Hager dell'anno 1761. Alla chiesa è aggiunto un lavoro tipo veneziano degli inizi del XIV secolo, e cioè la lapide sepolcrale dell'eremita benedettino, beato Vintíř. Tra le opere artistiche risaltano i quadri di P. Brandl, le statue di M. V. Jäckl e R. Prachner. Sotto il coro è stata scoperta la cripta del secondo venticinquennio dell' XI secolo, monumento più prezioso dell'architettura preromanica boema.

L'edificio del convento e della prelatura, che prima della restituzione recente all'Ordine dei Padri Benedettini svolgeva la funzione di deposito dell'Archivio centrale statale, contiene gli affreschi veramente ricchi. Ammirevole è soprattutto la cosiddetta Sala Teresiana con le pitture dell'artista bavarese K. D. Asam risalenti al 1727.

Dietro il monastero si trova il giardino barocco con il belvedere abbaziale Vojtěška, costruito secondo il progetto di K. L. Dienzenhofer, con la cappella e la sorgente dell'acqua. La sala terrena la decorò verso la metà del XVIII secolo lo scultore R. Prachner.

VEDUTA NOTTURNA DALLA VIA NERUDOVA 63 — mette in evidenza la comunicazione più interessante dal punto di vista culturale di Malá Strana, che scende dal Castello di Praga verso la piazza Malostranské náměstí. La via con le facciate prevalentemente barocche, caratteristiche per i segni e simboli delle singole case, è stata denominata secondo il nome del poeta e giornalista J. Neruda, il quale abitava nelle case Alle tre aquile nere e Ai due soli.

PALAZZO VALDŠTEJN 66—70, 72—74 — disteso su un'area insolitamente grande (30.306 m^2) sotto il pendio di Hradčany, rappresenta la prima costruzione monumentale del primo barocco in Boemia. Questa grandiosa sede di Albrecht di Valdštejn rispondeva a suo tempo alle ambizioni eccentriche del «generale del Mar Baltico e dell'Oceano», il quale nel corso della Guerra dei trent'anni, in quanto generalissimo degli eserciti imperiali tese la mano verso la corona del regno ed essendo tradito fu, su ordine dell'imperatore, eliminato in maniera violenta.

La costruzione degli anni 1624—30 contenente quattro cortili di svariato uso fu progettata dal lombardo A. Apezza, poi da N. Sebregondi, ed infine dal 1626 dall'ingegnere per le fortificazioni e architetto G. Pieroni. Alla costruzione presero parte artigiani italiani e locali. Sulla facciata del palazzo è conservata l'immagine della Madonna di Val D'Urazzo, facente parte del palazzo Trčka inserito nella costruzione. Attraverso due piani della parte settentrionale del fabbricato passa la Sala dei cavalieri con il rivestimento in marmo trasportato qui dal Palazzo Černín nel 1853. L'affresco del soffitto che raffigura l'apoteosi di Valdštejn in quanto dio della guerra Marte, fu eseguito dall'italiano B. del Bianco. Verticalmente alla sala sono accostati tre altri locali: la cosiddetta Sala del cuoio con la pittura di Pallade Atena di P. Meixner del 1866 sul soffitto, la Sala degli specchi e il presunto studio di Valdštejn.

Il palazzo è circondato da un giardino monumentale con un laghetto, le fontane, l'uccelliera per gli uccelli esotici, le grotte con le stalactiti, le logge solenni con gli stucchi dei maestri italiani e con le pitture di B. del Bianco, tratte dall'Eneide di Virgilio (canto 2 sulla guerra di Troia). La decorazione scultorea eseguita dal maestro A. de Vries ai tempi di Rodolfo II, rubata nel 1648 dagli svedesi e collocata nei giardini della villa di Drootningholm, fu sostituita con le copie.

Il palazzo oggi serve in prevalenza ai bisogni del Ministero della cultura.

PALAZZO KOLOWRAT E PALAZZO PÁLFFY 71 — situati al lato opposto del Palazzo Valdštejn, nella via Valdštejnská ulice, sono collegati con ameni giardini in stile rococò, disposti a terrazzi, che salgono verso il pendio di Hradčany. Il Palazzo Kolowrat in cui oggi risiede il Ministero della cultura, negli anni 1918—38 fu sede della presidenza del governo cecoslovacco. Per questo motivo qui si svolsero tragiche trattative riguardanti il Patto di Monaco e l'inizio del Protettorato. La costruzione del palazzo per opera di N. Palliardi dopo l'anno 1784, fu commissionata dai signori Černín. Nel XIX secolo il palazzo fu acquistato dai Kolowrat e vi risiedette A. Windischgrätz.

Il palazzo adiacente negli anni 1660—89 apparteneva al losco figuro Lomikar, realmente V. M. di Laminger, entrato nelle leggende come oppressore dell'etnia ceca dei Chodi. L'ampliamento del fabbricato e la sua ristrutturazione avvennero nel 1712, quando la proprietà era di J. J. di Valdštejn. Questa famiglia poi fu sostituita con quella dei Fürstenberg, alla quale apparteneva Karel Egon, il quale nel 1775 organizzò nel palazzo la prima seduta della Dotta società delle scienze. Nel XIX secolo l'interno del palazzo fu nuovamente ristrutturato in stile neorococò e fino al 1945 qui risiedette la famiglia feudale dei Pálffy (di qui la denominazione attuale del palazzo).

VEDUTA AEREA DELL'EDIFICIO DELLA PRESIDENZA DEL GOVERNO E DELLA VILLA KRAMÁŘ 75 — coglie l'estremità del parco Letenské sady, fatto tra il 1859 e il 1860. Qui negli anni 1908—11 venne costruita una villa di stato, villa pseudobaronale, per il dottor Kramář, secondo il progetto di B. Ohmann, e inoltre un'ampio fabbricato dell'Accademia Straka. In questo edificio con una cupola caratteristica — che risale alla ristrutturazione degli anni 1893—96 operata in base al progetto di V. Roštapil — era collocata la scuola per i figli dei nobili. Essa fu fondata nel 1710 a spese della fondazione J. P. conte Straka. Oggi qui risiede l'Ufficio della Presidenza del governo.

IL PONTE CARLO 76, 77, 79—81, 87—93, 100, 104 — che collega la Città Vecchia e la Malá Strana è il ponte più antico conservatosi a Praga. Agli inizi veniva chiamato Praghese oppure Di pietra, nel 1870 ricevette il nome Carlo, dato che fu fondato da Carlo IV nel 1357, sul posto del Ponte Giuditta ormai crollato, costruito nel 1165. Il ponte, costruito di blocchi di pietra arenaria, che poggia su sedici archi, è lungo 520 m a largo 10 m. La costruzione fu diretta dal ventisettenne Petr Parléř; la costruzione fu terminata solo agli inizi del XV secolo. Il ponte, sul quale passava la Via reale, vide anche avvenimenti tragici, in particolare nel 1648, quando fu preso d'attaco dalle truppe svedesi che cercavano di entrare a Praga: allora furono danneggiate pure le sue decorazioni.

Sul ponte nel 1723 fu installata l'illuminazione ad olio, nel 1866 vi fu portata l'illuminazione a gas con l'utilizzo di candelabri in ghisa piuttosto gotici, prodotti nelle fonderie di Komárov.

Il ponte è imponente con le sue decorazioni, tra l'altro con le torri e in particolare con il complesso di 33 statue o gruppi di statue, che man mano venivano installate sulle spallette. Queste opere soggiacenti agli influssi esterni non favorevoli, sono sostituite con le copie, mentre gli originali sono trasferiti nei lapidari del Museo Nazionale oppure del Museo della capitale Praga.

Le sculture rappresentano una meravigliosa galleria che documenta le creazioni di importanti rappresentanti della cultura ceca tra gli anni 1683—1714: M. B. Braun, J. Brokoff, F. M. Brokoff, M. V. Jäckel, J. B. Kohl oppure J. O. Mayer.

Nei pressi del Ponte Carlo si trova la statua di Bruncvík di L. Šimek del 1884, che ricorda i diritti e privilegi posseduti dagli abitanti della Città Vecchia nei riguardi del ponte.

IL PADIGLIONE HANAVSKÝ 78 — costruito originariamente come fabbricato in ghisa delle fonderie del principe V. Hanavský, per l'Esposizione giubilare territoriale del 1891, secondo il progetto di Heiser e Hercík. Nel 1898 esso fu donato al comune di Praga e quindi fu montato a Letná. Oggi in questo fabbricato di ghisa, in stile neobarocco, collocato in una posizione meravigliosa, esiste un ristorante di ottimo livello.

GRUPPO SCULTOREO IL CALVARIO SUL PONTE CARLO (dettaglio) 82 — si trova sul posto, dove dal XIV secolo era collocata una croce gotica. Nel 1657 qui fu collocato il corpo in bronzo dorato di N. Brohn, fuso a Dresda. Dall'iscrizione in ebraico attorno alla croce risulta che la spesa fu fatta con la multa pagata da un Ebreo, il quale aveva deriso la croce. Le statue della Vergine Maria e di San Giovanni Evangelista furono scolpite da E. Max nel 1861.

MALÁ STRANA 83, 84 — in gran parte visibile dalla Torre di Malá Strana risalente al periodo successivo l'anno 1411, agli inizi veniva chiamata Nuova, e più tardi Città Minore di Praga. La sua fondazione avvenne nel 1257 su proposta di Premysl Ottocaro II. Essendo vicino al Castello di Praga il quartiere registrò un notevole sviluppo ai tempi di Carlo IV, il quale la ampliò e la fortificò con le mura. La vicinanza con il Castello aveva però anche aspetti politici negativi. Nel 1419, nello scontro dei praghesi con le truppe del re, il quartiere Malá Strana fu distrutto dall'incendio. Analogamente l'incendio del 1541 danneggiò il quartiere e il Castello, e causò che Malá Strana fu ostacolata nel suo crescente sviluppo. La sua più grande prosperità fu raggiunta nel periodo del barocco, realtà confermata tra l'altro dalle costruzioni monumentali, some cono la chiesa di San Nicola, il Palazzo Valdštejn, i palazzi Fürstenberk, Lichtenštejn, Nostic, Michna, Buquoy, ecc. Cionostante il miraggio principale di Malá Strana non si riflette solo nei monumenti suddetti, bensí piuttosto nella costellazione pittorica del quartiere con i suoi ameni recessi, datigli attraverso le sue condizioni naturali.

LA CHIESA DI SAN FRANCESCO SERAFICO CON IL MONUMENTO A CARLO IV 86, 94, 97 — nella piazza con una soluzione dal punto di vista urbanistico attraente, chiusa con la chiesa dei Gesuiti dedicata a San Salvatore, e con il Palazzo Colloredo-Mansfeld, sul tracciato di una comunicazione molto viva conducente al Ponte Carlo, si trova la chiesa suddetta, costruita sulle fondamenta gotiche da D. Canevalle tra agli anni 1679—89, secondo i progetti dell'architetto della Borgogna J. B. Mathey per l'ordine dei Cavalieri con la stella rossa. Questo ordine religioso, unico del suo stampo esistente in Boemia, fondato nel XIII secolo, aveva la sua sede nel convento adiacente. Nella cupola meravigliosa vediamo l'affresco di V. V. Reiner raffigurante il Giudizio universale, l'interno della chiesa è completato da pitture sospese di J. K. Liška, M. Willmann e M. Pirner, nonché da opere scultoree di M. V. Jäckl, mentre gli stucchi con le figure dei santi provengono dagli scultori di Dresda J. e K. Süssner. La facciata della chiesa è abbellita con le statue di R. Prachner del 1758 e di altri autori cechi. All'angolo si trova la cosiddetta Colonna dei vignaiuoli del 1846 con la statua di San Venceslao, eseguita da J. Bendl nel 1676.

Nell'area signolare della Piazza del Crociati (Křižovnické náměstí), dopo le rifiniture del suo terreno, la ditta Fratelli Klein di Víznberk nel 1849, a spese dell'Università di Praga, costruì il monumento neogotico all'imperatore Carlo IV con le allegorie di quattro facoltà dell'università. Esso fu eseguito nella bottega del fonditore di Norimberga D. J. Burgschmidt, secondo il modello dello scultore di Dresda A. Hähnel.

LA TORRE DEL PONTE DELLA CITTÀ VECCHIA 95, 96 — con la quale culmina l'importanza della Piazza dei Crociati, fu edificata sul primo pilastro del Ponte Carlo, secondo il progetto di P. Parléř. La torre, considerata una delle più belle opere di questo tipo in Europa, fu completata attorno al 1391 non soltanto come una parte del ponte, ma anche come una parte delle fortificazioni della Città Vecchia di Praga. Prima della sua rifinitura, attorno al 1380, nascevano le sue singolari decorazioni scultoree, considerate opera più valida della scultura centroeuropea. La bottega di P. Parléř si concentrò sulle personalità dei sovrani e dei costruttori del ponte, quindi di Carlo IV e Venceslao IV, sotto la protezione dei patroni dei Paesi cechi, e sugli emblemi dei singoli territori. Nel 1978 le statue furono levate e sostituite con le copie: le statue originarie sono collocate nella Galleria Nazionale. Nel 1621 sulla torre furono appese le teste di dodici feudali cechi, giustiziati perché avevano partecipato alla resistenza capeggiata dagli Stati della Boemia contro gli Asburgo; le teste rimasero lì per interi dieci anni. Le decorazioni scultoree dalla parte ovest della torre furono dannaggiate nel 1648, durante gli attacchi delle truppe svedesi in cerca di conquistare Praga. I restauri sostanziali e le rifiniture del tetto avvennero tra gli anni 1974—78.

LADISLAV ŠALOUN (1870—1946) — MONUMENTO AL MAESTRO JAN HUS (dettaglio) 102 — fu scoperto in occasione del 5° centenario della morte sul rogo del predicatore ceco e riformatore, avvenuta a Costanza il 6 luglio 1415. L'estensione monumentale dell'opera in pietra e in bronzo comprendente numerose figure, eseguita da uno dei principali rappresentanti dell'arte scultorea ceca di stile liberty, fu oggetto di numerose critiche riguardanti la composizione e la collocazione del monumento nell'ambiente storico della Piazza della Città Vecchia, di fronte al palazzo Goltz-Kinský.

LA PIAZZA DELLA CITTÀ VECCHIA 103, 104, 121, 122, 125, 127, 129 — che ottenne la propria denominazione a cominiciare dal 1895 (dal XIV secolo si chiamava Il Mercato, Il grande Mercato, Piazza, Grande Piazza), accanto al Castello di Praga figura tra i posti che videro i più commoventi avvenimenti storici a Praga. Già a cavallo dei secoli XI e XII qui c'era un crocevia delle strade commerciali e quindi si formò anche un'ampio mercato, nelle dimensioni dell'attuale piazza (circa 9.000 m^2). Vi era aggiunta la dogana, l'odierna Ungelt, dove veniva scaricata la merce portata in Boemia. La piazza con il municipio divenne tradizionalmente luogo di assemblee durante vari moti politici e rivoluzionari, durante gli atti di rappresentanza, nonché al momento delle repressioni. Nel 1422, nel cortile del municipio, fu giustiziato il predicatore radicale ussita J. Želivský, nel 1437 in piazza fu giustiziato l'ultimo capitano ussita Jan Roháč di Dubá. L'esecuzione capitale di 27 signori e cittadini cechi, i quali presero parte all'insurrezione degli Stati, è ricordata da una croce inserita nel mosaico della pavimentazione davanti all'ala est del municipio. Nella sua Sala del consiglio, nel 1458, fu eletto a re di Boemia Giorgio di Poděbrady. Nel 1918 qui si tenne un'importante manifestazione a favore della Repubblica Cecoslovacca indipendente, un'altra manifestazione promossa dai comunisti avvenne qui in febbraio del 1948.

Alla rappresentatività della piazza con le sue case originariamente gotiche e poi ricostruite, con il palazzo rococò Goltz-Kinský, aveva contribuito anche l'edilizia moderna, realtà confermata meglio dall'edificio barocco tendente allo stile liberty delle Assicurazioni della città di Praga, costruito su progetto dell'architetto O. Polívka, oggi sede del Ministero ceco del commercio e del turismo — con le decorazioni scultoree —, di L. Šaloun, F. Procházka e B. Schnirch, espresse nell'esteso monumento di grandi dimensioni al maestro Jan Hus.

La Piazza della Città Vecchia e la Via reale che la attraversa, sono luoghi di Praga maggiormente ricercati dai turisti.

CASA AL MINUTO 106 — adiacente verticalmente all'edificio municipale della Città Vecchia, ha un nucleo gotico risalente agli inizi del XV secolo. La sua ristrutturazione rinascimentale avvenne dopo il 1564, i graffiti rinascimentali eseguiti in base alle incisioni di N. Raimondi e H. S. Beham, nascevano dopo il 1603 e 1610. Verso la fine del XVIII secolo, quando qui c'era una farmacia, all'angolo fu messa la statua in pietra di un leone. Alla scoperta di graffiti più tardi rinnovati di giunse solo nel 1905. Nell'edificio al momento attuale si trovano uffici del municipio.

L'OROLOGIO DELLA CITTÀ VECCHIA 108—113 — L'orologio nel suo aspetto originario fu messo insieme nel 1410 dall'orologiaio Mikuláš di Kadaň, la sua ricostruzione in occasione della ristrutturazione del Municipio fu eseguita dal maestro Hanuš detto di Rosa. Il complesso meccanismo fu perfezionato tra agli anni 1553—60; le statue furono fatte nel 1659, poi nel XVIII secolo e nel 1864. Le pitture delle tavole del calendario dell'orologio con allegorie di dodici mesi fece nel 1865 il principale rappresentante dell'arte nazionale ceca del XIX secolo, J. Mánes (1820—1871). L'originale di questa pittura fu trasferito già nel 1885 nel Museo nazionale della capitale Praga e sostituito con una copia che bruciò assieme ad una parte delle decorazioni in legno nel 1945. Nel 1962 essa fu sostituita da una copia eseguita da B. Číla, le scultore in legno degli Apostoli furono eseguite già nel 1948 dallo scultore V. Sucharda (1884—1972).

L'orologio appartiene alle maggiori attrazioni turistiche della Città Vecchia: ogni ora viene messo in moto il meccanismo con le figure che si muovono, con riferimenti allegorici, religiosi e storici (memento mori, allusioni alle espansioni turche, ecc.)

LA CHIESA DI SAN NICOLA NELLA CITTÀ VECCHIA 124 — fu costruita presso un monastero benedettino secondo il progetto di K. I. Dienzenhofer negli anni 1732—35.

IL PALLAZZO GOLZ-KINSKÝ E LA CASA ALLA CAMPANA 126 — in Piazza della Città Vecchia sono i fabbricati più belli tra quelli che si trovano davanti alle chiesa della Vergine Maria di Týn. Quando è stato tolto l'intonaco neobarocco dalla casa Alla Campana, è apparsa una facciata gotica singolare del tutto conservata e risalente al 1350, contenente decorazioni in pietra. Durante le indagini edilizie della casa è stata accertata l'esistenza di una cappella con pitture murali gotiche della metà del XIV secolo. Nei locali interni della casa restaurata la Galleria della capitale Praga allestisce le esposizioni dell'arte contemporanea.

Il fabbricato adiacente è il palazzo Golz-Kinský, che dal 1635 appartiene al principe R. Kinský: nel suo aspetto grazioso ed effettivo lo ristrutturò negli anni 1755—65 A. Lurago, secondo il progetto di K. I. Dienzenhofer. Il palazzo che si trova sul posto di un'edificio romanico più antico viene utilizzato dalla Galleria Nazionale di Praga per le proprie esposizioni.

LA CASA ŠTORCH 128 — si trova nell'affascinante serie di case che si trovano al lato est della Piazza della Città Vecchia. Fu costruita nel 1897 secondo il progetto di B. Ohmann e R. Krieghammer. La casa Štorch in stile neorinascimentale ospita la casa editrice omonima che attira l'attenzione con la pittura di L. Novák secondo i cartoni di M. Aleš, che riprende la figura di San Venceslao e dei Re magi. Le pitture danneggiate nel maggio 1945 furono restaurate dal pittore F. Sembtner.

VEDUTA DALLA TORRE DELLA CHIESA DI TÝN 130—131 — le costruzioni gotiche eccezionali a tre navate, risalenti al 1365, vi si presentano dall'altezza della torre di ottanta metri. Le torri furono completate solo all'inizio del XVI secolo.

IL KAROLINUM 132—134 — che si trova nella via Železná e che a sua volta sbocca in Piazza della Città Vecchia, è l'edificio centrale dell'Università Carlo, fondata da Carlo IV il 7 aprile 1348, alle origini uno dei collegi universitari. Fu la prima università in Europa centrale, il cui scopo fu quello di promuovere la civiltà locale portandola su un livello più alto. La base del complesso universitario nascente fu la Casa Rothlev, acquistata da Venceslao IV e donata nel 1383 al Collegio Carlo, situato fino a quel momento nella casa adiacente alla chiesa di San Nicola. L'aspetto esterno del Karolinum proviene dalla ristrutturazione barocca eseguita e conclusa nel 1718 da F. M. Kaňka. Sulla facciata della via Železná è una finestra barocca del 1687 e una loggia a vetro con la volta gotica con nervatura. Il fabbricato annesso risalente all'anno 1385 in direzione del Teatro degli Stati, comprende una capella preziosa con balconi ancora conservata, con le decorazioni esterne molto ricche. La ristrutturazione avvenne nel 1881 per opera di J. Mocker; altri interventi ebbero luogo negli anni 1946—75 secondo il progetto di J. Frégner, con la partecipazione degli scultori V. Makovský, K. Lidický, J. Lauda e K. Pokorný.

Al centro del fabbricato si trova l'aula magna costruita già dopo l'anno 1383. Ad essa fu poi aggiunta la cappella con i balconi. Sulla fronte dell'aula si trova la tappizzeria di M. Teinitzerová del 1947, che parte dal tema rilevato sul sigillo dell'Università Carlo eseguito dallo scultore V. Suchra: vi si trova la figura di Carlo IV in ginocchio davanti a San Venceslao.

IL TEATRO DEGLI STATI 135 — prima chiamato Teatro Tyl e alle origini Teatro Nostic — è un edificio neoclassicista, costruito a spese del conte F. A. Nostic nel 1781, secondo il progetto di A. Haffenecker e in cooperazione specializzata con il conte K. H. Khünigl. Negli anni 1859, 1881 e 1892 man mano venivano eseguite ristrutturazioni e ritocchi, ma la più ampia e generale ristrutturazione fu conclusa nel 1991. La ristrutturazione comprende anche il Palazzo Kolowrat che sta di fronte.

Alle origini le lingue usate nel teatro erano il tedesco e l'italiano. Nel 1787 qui fu presentata per la prima volta l'opera Don Giovanni di Mozart. Negli anni 1813—16 era a capo dell'opera il compositore C. M. von Weber. Il 21 dicembre 1834 qui fu presentato lo spettacolo Fidlovačka con la musica di F. Škroupa. Nella prima rappresentazione per la prima volta fu cantata la canzone Dov'è la mia patria, che dal 1918 è l'inno nazionale cecoslovacco.

IL MUSEO NAZIONALE 136, 138, 139, 141, 142 — che si trova al posto dell'allora Porta dei Cavalli, rappresenta l'edificio lungo oltre 100 metri. Esso, in maniera imposante chiude la parte superiore della Piazza Venceslao. La costruzione fu realizzata negli anni 1885—90 in base al progetto del prof. J. Schulz per scopi museali. Il museo fu fondato nel 1818 sotto l'impulso del patriottismo ceco dai signori nobili, che perseguivano fini culturali e scientifici.

Il fabbricato neorinascimentale che costò parecchio, è composto di quattro ali con due cortili. L'ingresso di rappresentanza si trova sulla rampa con una fontana con le statue allegoriche di A. Wagner degli anni 1891—94, che rappresentano le allegorie Boemia, Moravia e Slesia, nonché i fiumi Elba e Moldava. La decorazione scultorea dell'edificio intero è rappresentata da una rassegna dell'arte creativa ceca dell'XI secolo, in concorrrenza con l'opera dello scultore di Monaco L. Schwanthaler. Le sue statue in bronzo di Libussa, Přemysl, Venceslao e Přemysl II, originariamente commissionate per il complesso di 24 statue destinate per il centro slavo ceco, „Český Slavín" di Tupadla presso Liběchov, furono collocate nella sala d'ingresso con le colonne, alla quale si unisce la scalinata rappresentativa nell'ampiezza della quasi intera ala centrale dell'edificio. L'area è completata dalle statue di A. Popp e B. Schnirch degli anni 1897—99, che rappresentano 16 buste di uomini che portano maggiori meriti per il costruendo museo, e 32 medaglioni dei re boemi.

Il sacrario dei desideri nazionali cechi e la sua coscienza manifestata all'esterno sono reppresentati nel Pantheon, chiuso con la cupola con 48 busti e statue dei grandi personaggi della nazione ceca. I quadri orientati verso la storia furono eseguiti dai principali pittori della generazione vissuta alla fondazione del Teatro Nazionale, quindi da V. Brožík e F. Ženíšek; i riempimenti decorativi allegorici sotto la cupola sono opera del pittore della stessa generazione con orientamenti verso la Francia, V. Hynais.

Nel museo si trovano reparti orientati alla storia e alle scienze naturali nonché una preziosa biblioteca contenente collezioni di circa un milione di unità con singolari manoscritti medioevali.

JOSEF VÁCLAV MYSLBEK (1848—1922), LA STATUA EQUESTRE DI SAN VENCESLAO 137 — patrono della terra boema, simbolo della sua autonomia e protettore dell'indipendenza nazionale. La collocazione dell'opera nella parte superiore della Piazza Venceslao risale agli anni 1912—13, sue basi architettoniche di A. Dryák e con le decorazioni ornamentali di C. Klouček. Myslbek cominciò ad elaborare questo tema già nel 1887, il modello in gesso dell'opera intera fu completato nel 1904. Il gentile lavoro neorinascimentale forma un'insieme con le statue di San Procopio, Sant'Agnese e Santa Ludmilla. Nel 1924 fu messa a posto l'ultima statua, quella di Sant'Adalberto, da Myslbek non terminata, fusa nella bottega di B. Mašek. L'opera sentita in maniera classica con le espressioni dell'animo delle singole figure, ci fa capire l'orientamento alla creazione francese precedente.

LA PIAZZA JUNGMANN 140 — nell'ambito della quelle, con un preciso sentimento urbanistico, è collocata la statua dello scrittore e del principale rappresentante del rinascimento letterario ceco J. Jungmann, si trova nelle immediate vicinanze con la Piazza Venceslao. L'opera scultorea di L. Šimek dell'anno 1872, fatta secondo il progetto più vecchio di V. Levý, fu collocata sullo zoccolo in marmo, secondo il piano di A. Barvitius del 1878.

PŘÍKOPY 144 — rappresenta una delle parti più animate di Praga, che si allaccia all'estremità inferiore della Piazza Venceslao e a Můstek con la sua moderna construzione di A. Šrámková, fatta per la ditta ČKD. Příkop con le sue moderne case è interessante anche per il suo edificio orientato al construttivismo, quale è la Casa del bambino (Dětský dům) risalente al 1928. Al lato destro si trova il grande negozio più vecchio di Praga, costruito dal celebre architetto di Vienna Th. Hansen tra gli anni 1869—71. La cultura aristocratica raffinata del periodo rococò è documentata nel palazzo Sylva-Tarouccà (originariamente palazzo Piccolomini), costruito tra il 1743—51 da K. I. Dienzenhofer e A. Lurago. La parca costruzione in stile impero della chiesa di Santa Croce risalente agli anni 1816—24 fu progettata da J. Fischer. La Casa Slava (Slovanský dům), originariamente il palazzo barocco Příchovský, fu ritoccata da F. Heger nel 1798. A Příkopy troviamo pure numerose banche, la più bella delle quali è quella degli investimenti, costruita nello spirito neorinascimentale da O. Polívka negli anni 1894—96, decorata con i mosaici di Aleš e con i rilievi di C. Klouček e S. Sucharda.

PIAZZA VENCESLAO 145 — originariamente chiamata Piazza dei cavalli (Koňský trh) era infatti mercato principale della Città Nuova, al centro del quale era situata la statua di San Venceslao, scolpita da J. Bendl nel 1680 (nel 1879 fu trasferita a Vyšehrad). La piazza è lunga 750 m e rappresenta il più importante boulevard sociale e commerciale e comprende anche vari alberghi di rappresentanza. La parte superiore della piazza è chiusa frontalmente dal Museo Nazionale (J. Schulz, 1885—90), edificio che rappresenta un omaggio alla scienza e alla conoscenza, realtà alle quali il museo è destinato a servire. L'espressione della coscienza nazionale e della consolazione è pure la monumentale statua equestre di San Venceslao. Alla parte opposta, quindi nella piazza inferiore, negli anni 1786—89 era situato il teatro costruito di legno, la cosiddetta Bouda (Baracca): era la prima scena ceca della città. Alle estremità nonché al centro della piazza si trovano le stazioni della locale metropolitana.

LA TORRE DELLE POLVERI 146—148 — costruita per onorare il re Vladislao Jagellone nel 1475, è opera di M. Rejsek di Prostějov, al posto di una porta più vecchia delle mura cittadine. Nelle sue vicinanze il re Venceslao IV fece costruire la Corte reale, come residenza del sovrano. Dopo la sua liquidazione nel 1483 l'importanza del luogo cominciò a calare. La torre stessa, inserita tra i monumenti più validi del tardo gotico, già verso la fine del XVII secolo serviva da deposito della polvere da sparo. Durante l'assedio prussiano la costruzione fu danneggiata. Il suo rimaneggiamento neogotico è opera dell'architetto J. Mocker degli anni 1875—76: quest'ultimo aggiunse ancora il deambulatorio e il tetto. Dalla torre si offre la veduta del quartiere cittadino più antico, la Città Vecchia, ma anche di uno dei luoghi animati di Praga, Piazza della Republica (Náměstí Republiky) con l'ex-vecchia dogana (attorno al 1810), con la casa U hybernů, con la chiesa di San Giuseppe appartenente ai Cappuccini, ed infine con l'edificio della banca costruita nel 1938.

LA CASA COMUNALE DELLA CAPITALE PRAGA 149, 150 — fu costruita sul luogo della corte del re negli anni 1906—11 secondo il progetto di A. Balšánek e O. Polívka. Là, dove si trovava la sede dei re boemi, in particolare di Giorgio di Poděbrady, che riuniva qui non solo la dieta di Boemia, ma che da questo posto invitava i sovrani europei alla pace e all'unificazione, si trova oggi un centro di rappresentanza della società e della cultura. Qui si organizzano concerti, balli, esposizioni, c'è una caffetteria, un ristorante, una taverna. I locali interni posseggono una ricca decorazione pittorica e scultorea, eseguita dai principali artisti dell'inizio del XX secolo: nella Sala del primo sindaco si trovano le pitture di A. Mucha, nella Sala Palacký quelle di J. Preisler, la Sala Grégr quindi porta le pitture di Ženíšek. Il pianterreno e il ristorante sono adornati di pitture di M. Aleš e J. Obsovský. Gli scultori J. V. Myslbek, K. Novák, e L. Šaloun sono rappresentati nella Sala Smetana e nel Salotto Rieger.

IL TEATRO NAZIONALE 151—154 — fu costruito con la raccolta svoltasi in tutta la nazione tra gli anni 1868—71, secondo la proposta dell'architetto J. Zítek. Il fabbricato di grande valore, costruito in stile neorinascimentale, poco dopo il termine dei lavori fu distrutto dall'incendio. La sua ricostruzione e il suo compimento per opera dell'architetto J. Schulz furono terminati nel 1883 comprese le decorazioni interne e l'allestimento del sipario che fu eseguito da V. Hynais. La decorazione esterna del loggione proviene in parte dal pittore J. Tulka, le opere scultoree provegono soprattutto da A. Wagner e da J. V. Myslbek, nonché da B. Schnirch. Nel foyer di rappresentanza dominano le pitture a lunette di M. Aleš e F. Ženíšek, quest'ultimo è pure autore delle pitture del soffitto nella sala spettatori. Il loggione reale, ora presidenziale è adornato di pitture eseguite da V. Hynais, V. Brožík e J. Mařák. Numerose statue nel foyer ritraggono busti dei grandi personaggi della cultura ceca.

Nel corso delle ampie ricostruzioni del teatro negli anni 1977—83, unite all'ammodernamento degli impianti tecnici, è stato costruito un nuovo edificio tra il teatro e il convento di Santa Ursula. Il nuovo fabbricato a sette piani nonché la Nuova scena del Teatro Nazionale, furono completati nel 1983, secondo il progetto dell'architetto K. Prager con l'utilizzo dei rivestimenti in vetro di S. Libenský.

Di fronte all'edificio storico del Teatro Nazionale si trova l'ex palazzo Lažanský con la caffetteria Slavia: l'edificio fu costruito in stile del rinascimento francese negli anni 1861—63. Nel primo piano del palazzo dei conti visse fino al 1869 il principale compositore della musica ceca, B. Smetana.

La parete laterale del Teatro Nazionale guarda il lungofiume Masaryk, via che registra numerosi caseggiati d'affitto con le facciate storicizzanti e con la veduta della Moldava, dell'isola Slovanský ostrov che dal 1925 viene denominato Žofín.

L'ISOLA STŘELECKÝ OSTROV 155 — Il nome dell'isola non è casuale. Quando nell'anno 1472 essa fu presa in possesso dalle Città Vecchia e Nuova, diventò luogo di esercitazione dei tiratori praghesi. Nel XVI secolo qui ebbero luogo giochi preferiti dai Praghesi, che si denominavano „tiri su uccello". Verso la fine del XIX secolo qui avvenivano le riunioni popolari e nel 1882 qui ebbe luogo la prima manifestazione dell'organizzazione sportiva Sokol.

LA STATUA DI BEDŘICH SMETANA (1824-1884, IL MUSEO SMETANA E LA PASSERELLA NOVOTNÝ 157—158, 179 — il lungofiume Smetana rivela la soluzione urbanistica più antica di questo tipo, eseguita dalla ditta V. Banna negli anni 1841—45 secondo il progetto di B. Grueber. La costruzione principale delle case d'affitto fu progettata dal direttore edile Strobach già nel 1836. Sul posto dell'ex mulino fu costruito l'edificio neogotico delle Terme Carlo, dove nel 1848 abitava il noto poeta e giornalista ceco, K. H. Borovský. Davanti alle terme, a partire dal lungofiume, devia la Passerella Novotný risalente all'anno 1879, denominata secondo il discendente dell'antica famiglia dei mugnai. Gli edifici dei mulini della Città Vecchia portano l'aspetto neorinascimentale nello stile di I. Ulmann, e sono decorati con le statue di putti eseguite da J. V. Myslbek. Qui si alza verso il cielo anche la torre della centrale idraulica costruita nel 1480, che fu parecchie volte ricostruita, ultimamente dopo l'incendio del 1885. La passerella si conclude con l'edificio che ospita il Museo Smetana, che documenta il cosiddetto rinascimento ceco dell'anno 1883. Il caseggiato fu progettato dall'architetto A. Wiehl, originariamente per la centrale idrica di Praga. La facciata dell'edificio ci fa vedere il graffito La lotta con gli Svedesi sul Ponte Carlo del 1648, che fu eseguito secondo i cartoni di F. Ženíšek. Nelle nicchie sono raffigurate persone che si sono rese meritevoli per la difesa di Praga di fronte agli Svedesi. la realizzazione è di J. Šubič in base ai progetti di M. Aleš e di J. Koula. Il Museo invece fu fondato dalla Società B. Smetana nel 1936: qui furono concentrati i documenti sulla vita e sull' opera di questo principale compositore musicale ceco, la cui statua di J. Malejovský, nel 1984 fu collocata davanti all'edificio.

LA CASA AL POZZO D'ORO 159 — è l'edificio che forma l'angolo tra le vie Liliová e Karlova; quest'ultima è un'arteria importante che porta dalla Città Vecchia al Ponte Carlo. Su questo edificio rinascimentale, ristrutturato in stile barocco, attirano l'attenzione i rilievi dei Santi Sebastiano e Rocco, protettori davanti alla peste. I rilievi furono fatti dallo scultore J. O. Mayer, probabilmente dopo l'epidemia della peste del 1700.

LE INSEGNE DELLE CASE DELLA CITTA VECCHIA 160 — nella via Týnská, al num. 10, l'insegna ci indica la casa che nel XVII secolo si chiamava Nell'inferno. Più tardi la casa probabilmente passò nella proprietà dei conti Kinský, che avevano nel loro emblema tre branche di lupo, oppure piuttosto tre denti di cinghiale. Dopo la ristrutturazione della casa nel XVIII secolo da parte dell'architetto F. Heger, l'insegna è stata trasformata in tre penne di struzzo.

Il senso delle insegne sulle case, che avevano una certa correlazione anche alla tradizione dei simboli familiari, oltre ai fini di identificazione, di rappresentanza e di orientamento, era anche evidentemente simbolico. Amene insegne delle case sono inserite anche negli episodi della vecchia Praga, non solo della Città Vecchia, ma anche nei recessi di Malá Strana, Hradčany, e via dicendo.

IL VECCHIO CIMITERO EBRAICO SINAGOGA VECCHIA-NUOVA 161—164 — documentano l'insediamento ebraico, registrato nel sobborgo del Castello di Praga già nel X secolo. All'inizio del XVIII secolo la comunità ebraica a Praga rappresentava quasi un terzo della popolazione intera. Ciononostante qui fu registrata tutta una serie dei pogrom e delle limitazioni, che costringevano gli Ebrei a vivere quasi senza eccezioni nel ghetto chiuso in se stesso. Dopo i decreti liberalizzanti di Giuseppe II, la Città Ebraica di Praga cominciò a denominarsi Josefov, che dopo il 1848 divenne quinto quartiere di Praga del tutto equo con gli altri. Ma le condizioni igieniche malsane, dovute al sovrappopolamento, portarono alla demolizione e alla ricostruzione attorno al 1900.

I lunghi secoli della storia ebraica di Praga sono ricordati dal Vecchio cimetero ebraico, dove la più antica lapide sepolcrale risale all'anno 1439. L'incanto elegiaco del cimitero contenente circa 11 mila lapidi sepolcrali (sotto le quali si nascondono 12 strati di tombe) ha un valore storico eccezionale. Le lapidi ricordano non solo i nomi e i dati dei defunti, ma anche la loro posizione sociale, con i simboli tradizionali delle famiglie che da sempre formavano la gerarchia sacerdotale. I nomi dei defunti sono spesso designati con un simbolo sostitutivo che ha l'espressione poetica speciale. Tra le lapidi è conservata la tomba del sindaco e primate della Città ebraica, M. Mordechaj Maisl († 1601), il cui nome porta una via al centro del ghetto, nonché una delle sinagoghe. Una leggenda suggestiva è legata al nome di un'altra lapide sepolcrale, appartenente a Löw ben Bezalel. Dalla bottega di questo famoso rabbino Löw uscì — almeno secondo la leggenda— l'uomo artificiale chiamato Golem.

La Città Ebraica conserva intatta anche la più antica sinagoga in Europa chiamata Vecchia-Nuova. Essa fu costruita attorno all'anno 1280, come una sala a due navate. Il frontone in mattoni nasconde i prodromi del XIV secolo. Dato che lo spazio principale era destinato per soli uomini, nel XVIII secolo al lato settentrionale della sinagoga fu aggiunta una saletta per donne. L'interno della sinagoga mette in rilievo preziosi cimeli della cultura ebraica dal XVI al XIX secolo.

Presso il Vecchio cimitero Ebraico si trova l'ex sala delle cerimonie che oggi serve come l'Esposizione delle pitture dei bambini a Terezín. Come area espositiva serve pure la cosiddetta Sinagoga Alta, in cui si trovano tessuti sacri di varie sinagoghe. La sinagoga Pinkas è trasformata in monumento che ricorda le vittime del nazismo, mentre nella Sinagoga Maisel è esposta una collezione singolare di oggetti in argento e in altri metalli. Il miraggio esoterico dei monumenti della Città Ebraica è completato dal Municipio Ebraico con la torre e l'orologio con il quadrante ebraico.

KAREL HLADÍK (1912—1967), FRANZ KAFKA 165 — il busto che si trova sull'edificio costruito nel 1902 da O. Polívka, — nel luogo in cui prima si trovava la prelatura del monastero dei Benedettini — ricorda che qui, nel 1883, nacque lo scrittore geniale di origini ebraiche. L'opera fu eseguita dal rappresentante dello stile classico realista che adottava in particolare stimoli dell'arte scultorea contemporanea italiana.

CHIESA DI SAN GIACOMO 166, 167 — in via Malá Štupartská, trasversalmente rispetto all'uscita da Ungelt, fu fondata asieme al convento da Venceslao I nel 1232. La facciata è abbellita di nitidi lavori di stucco, realizzati dallo scultore italiano. O. Most nel 1695, nel corso della ristrutturazione barocca della chiesa in seguito all'incendio del 1689. All'interno della chiesa, assieme ai ventuno altari, colpiscono in maniera impresionante le pitture di F. M. Vogel, risalenti al completamento della ristrutturazione negli anni 1736—39. Fanno parte dell'eccezionale decorazione i quadri di P. Brandl, V. V. Reiner, e di altri. Un'opera eccezionale è pure il monumento sepolcrale del cancelliere supremo, Sua Altezza conte Vratislav di Mitrovice, opera di J. B. Fischer di Erlach degli anni 1714—16.

LA CHIESA DI SANT'ENRICO 168 — si trova nella via Jindřišská nella Città Nuova; è una costruzione in stile gotico risalente alla seconda metà del XIV secolo, con il prodomo rinascimentale e con fabbricati annessi in stile barocco, compresi i ritocchi interni, pure in stile barocco. All'esterno della chiesa sono state trasferite numerose lapidi sepolcrali provenienti dal cimitero che è stato soppresso. Negli anni 1875—79 Mocker ritoccò la chiesa in stile gotico; infatti il ricco arredamento interno contiene cimeli a cominciare dal periodo gotico (per es. la pittura su tavola della Madonna da Santo Stefano del XV secolo, la statua di Sant'Enrico, ed altri), attraverso tutta una serie di arte barocca proveniente da pittori e scultori cechi, fino alle opere del XIX secolo (per es. le finestre colorate dell'anno 1891 eseguite secondo il progetto di F. Sequens).

La torre campanaria ritoccata nello stile gotico, che si trova nei pressi della chiesa, fu costruita già attorno al 1475. Di origini gotiche è pure la casa parrocchiale fondata nel 1386.

IL PRESBITERIO DELLA CHIESA DELLA VERGINE MARIA DELLE NEVI 169 — dietro la casa parrocchiale dei Padri Francescani in Piazza Jungmanovo náměstí si erge in alto la più alta costruzione chiesastica di Praga, mai finita. Fu fondata da Carlo IV nel 1347 come chiesa dell'incoronazione e nel contempo al servizio dei carmelitani. La costruzione del presbiterio, che si è conservata, proviene dagli anni 1379—97, poiché la volta originaria, più alta, è crollata nel tempo precedente. Il successivo movimento rivoluzionario ussita colpì decisamente la storia della chiesa. Il capo del proletariato praghese, predicatore J. Želivský, nel 1419 convinse davanti alla chiesa — che in seguito occupò — il popolo ad andare in corteo verso il municipio della Città Nuova, dove avvenne la defenestrazione dei consiglieri. Nella chiesa poi predicava fino alla sua morte violenta nel 1422. Nel 1606 l'arcivescovo di Praga donò la chiesa assieme al convento ai Padri Francescani, la cui opera qui registrò un episodio tragico. Nel 1611, durante l'incursione delle truppe di Passau a Praga, il proletariato, incolpando i religiosi di aver nascosto i soldati di Passau, s'intruse nel convento e uccise tutti i francescani ivi presenti.

All'interno della chiesa attira l'attenzione l'altare del primo barocco, il più alto di Praga, fatto costruire dai Francescani dopo il loro rientro nel convento negli anni 1649—61. Tra gli arredamenti preziosi all'interno della chiesa, in cui attorno alle pareti sono collocate dieci statue dei santi dell'Ordine francescano risalenti al periodo attorno al 1625, si trova per es. il quadro dell'Annunciazione alla Vergine Maria di V. V. Reiner del 1724: si trova su un altare laterale. Da vedere è anche il battistero in stagno del 1449.

CHIESA DI SANT'EGIDIO 170 — situata tra le vie odierne Jilská e Husova, nella Città Vecchia, fu costruita negli anni 1339—71 per opera del vescovo Jan di Dražice, quindi dell'arcivescovo Arnošt di Pardubice, come chiesa capitolare a tre navate. Nel 1364 qui predicava in lingua ceca J. Milíč di Kroměříž. Nello spirito di questa tradizione la chiesa nel 1420 serviva agli ussiti. Al contrario, nel 1626 l'imperatore Ferdinando II la donò ai domenicani, i quali le aggiunsero un ampio chiostro. Nel 1731 essa subì trasformazioni di stile barocco con la partecipazione dell'architetto F. M. Kaňka. I dipinti sulle volte e il quadro di San Venceslao furono eseguiti da V. V. Reiner, le principali decorazioni scultoree furono eseguite da J. A. Quittainer e negli anni 1839—45 dal professore di Monaco L. Schwanthaler; i lavori scultorei in legno furono eseguiti in prevalenza da F. I. Weis negli anni 1734—38.

CHIESA DEL SACRO SUORE DEL SIGNORE 171 — fu costruita negli anni 1928—32 secondo il progetto di J. Plečnik a modo di una chiesa paleocristiana. Si trova al centro della piazza assai ampia Giorgio di Poděbrady a Vinohrady. Nelle decorazioni, nelle statue di B. Stefan situate sopra i tre portali della chiesa, nonché nella modellazione dell'altare maggiore in marmo e nelle decorazioni scultoree interne di D. Pešan si riflette la trasformazione originale dell'arte antica.

VILLA AMERIKA 172 — agli inizi chiamata Belvedere Michna, è la prima costruzione di uno dei principali creatori dell'architettura barocca in Boemia, K. I. Dienzenhofer. La costruzione incantevole che si trova nell'odierna via Ke Karlovu nella Città Nuova, mette in armonia l'influenza dell'opera monumentale viennese di L. Hildebrand e l'eleganza francese e il senso di misuratezza perseguite da questo architetto. Essa risale agli anni 1712—20 e fu costruita a spese del conte J. V. Michna di Vacínov. La sala principale nel 1720 fu abbellita con le pitture murali di J. F. Schor tratte dalle mitologie. Il belvedere era attorniato da un giardino decorato con vasi e gruppi di statue raffiguranti le stagioni, provenienti dalla bottega di A. Braun. Nel giardino dalla fine del XVIII secolo si faceva il mercato del bestiame. Nel 1932 il belvedere fu acquistato dalla Società A. Dvořák. Fino ai giorni nostri qui si trova il museo di questo famoso compositore; l'installazione fu realizzata per opera della Società suddetta.

La Villa America, la cui denominazione proviene dal XIX secolo secondo un'osteria poco distante, è separata dalla via con la copia della cancellata barocca. La posizione incantevole della costruzione oggi si perde tra gli edifici più alti del quartiere.

LA SALA DVOŘÁK DI RUDOLFINUM 174 — è il fabbricato neorinascimentale più in vista dopo il Teatro Nazionale; il progetto lo fecero architetti J. Zítek, e J. Vejrych e la costruzione fu realizzata negli anni 1876—84. L'edificio odierno serve alla Filarmonica ceca per i concerti e per altri avvenimenti solenni. Lo stabile ebbe la denominazione per rendere omaggio al principe Rodolfo.

LA SALA DEGLI SPECCHNI DEL CLEMENTINUM 175 — completata nel 1724 da F. M. Kaňka come parte dell'ex-collegio dei Gesuiti, è uno spazio riccamente decorato, in cui avvengono concerti e esposizioni. Ricchi stucchi, nei quali sono inseriti riempimenti a specchio, formano il quadro alle pitture del soffitto che riproducono la vita della Vergine Maria: l'opera è probabilmente di J. Hiebl. Le pitture dei santi sono di V. V. Reiner. La cappella fu soppressa nel 1784, nel 1816 fu per breve tempo ripristinata. Oggi fa parte della Biblioteca Nazionale.

IL MONUMENTO A WOLFGANG AMADEUS MOZART (1756—1791) A BERTRAMKA 176, 177 — Bertramka, fattoria agricola davanti alle porte della città con le origini nel XVII secolo e ultimamente ristrutturata nel 1873, s'iscrisse nella storia culturale di Praga come luogo, in cui aveva soggiornatto uno dei maggiori geni della musica, W. A. Mozart. Dopo l'acquisto di Bertramka nel 1784 da parte del compositore Fr. X. Dušek e della sua consorte Josefina, ottima cantante, Mozart divenne loro ospite durante i suoi soggiorni a Praga. Nel 1787 qui compose la sua opera più nota, Don Giovanni, la cui prima presentazione nel Teatro Nostic ebbe un successo straordinario.

IL VIALE PAŘÍŽSKÁ TŘÍDA 181, 182 — collega la Piazza della Città Vecchia e il ponte Sv. Čech, e nel contempo è la via d'accesso al torso dell'ex- Città Ebraica, rasa al suolo durante la demolizione. Quest'ampio viale, prima denominato via Mikulášská, è formato dalle case d'affitto veramente rappresentative, costruite in gran parte negli anni 1901—1906. Il monumento più importante dell'ex Città Ebraica, la sinagoga Vecchia-Nuova, e nelle sue vicinanze in un parco si trova la statua in bronzo di Mosè, fatta da F. Bílek nel 1905. In fondo della via si trova l'edificio della Facoltà di giurisprudenza dell'Università Carlo, costruito tra gli anni 1924—27, secondo il progetto di J. Kotěra del 1914. Trasversalmente rispetto all'edificio negli anni 1970—74 fu costruito un ampio complesso dell'albergo Intercontinental, secondo il progetto di K. Filsak, K. Bubeníček e Švec.

L'ALBERGO ATRIUM 182 — costruzione di Franc, Nováček e Fencl fu terminata entro 23 mesi in giugno 1990; rientra tra gli alberghi più ampi dell'Europa centrale. Lo stabile tipo atrio possiede 788 camere con 1.568 posti-letto. Il ristorante offre piatti della cucina internazionale ma un menù particolare è formato pure dalla cucina ceca.

VYŠEHRAD 187, 189—191 — sede leggendaria degli antichi principi boemi, Libussa e altri Premyslidi, fu costruita sulla roccia di Vyšehrad, che si erge a picco sopra il fiume Moldava, dopo la fondazione del Castello di Praga, probabilmente nel X secolo. Ai tempi del Principe Vratislao II (1061—92, nel 1085 fu incoronato re) la sede del sovrano fu trasferita a Vyšehrad e accanto ad essa, nel 1070, fu istituito lì anche il capitolo. Nel contempo il castello di legno fu trasformato in costruzioni in pietra, furono costruite nuove chiese. Queste ultime furono distrutte ai tempi del movimento rivoluzionario ussita.

Oggi Vyšehrad è attorniato da fortificazioni e bastioni barocchi, costruiti da costruttori italiani specializzati nelle fortificazioni: la loro ricostruzione avvenne nel 1882. Le mura circondano la chiesa capitolare dei Santi Pietro e Paolo di origini romaniche: essa fu ricostruita nei periodi gotico e barocco, ultimamente in stile neogotico negli anni 1885—87. Nei pressi della chiesa si trovano i resti di un ponte romanico, che probabilmente faceva parte delle fortificazioni del palazzo originario. Di fronte alla chiesa c'è la cappella di Santa Ludmilla. Tra i cimeli di Vyšehrad resta conservata la rotonda romanica originaria di San Martino, alla quale si accede attraverso la porta d'ingresso dalla via V pevnosti.

Di tronte alla facciata della chiesa dei Santi Pietro e Paolo si trova la porta principale del cimitero, costruito attorno al 1890 da A. Wiehl per la sepoltura dei figli emeriti della nazione ceca. Il progetto, promosso dal prevosto V. Štulc, fu realizzato nel luogo del cimitero parrocchiale del 1660. Al centro della parte orientale del cimitero negli anni 1889—93 e nel 1903 fu costruito, in base al progetto di Wiehl, il cosiddetto Slavín, degno luogo di sepoltura dei grandi figli della nazione.

Negli spazi verdi, nei luoghi in cui c'era la caserma dei vigili del fuoco alquanto diroccata, nel 1948 furono collocati tre gruppi di statue di Myslbek, provenienti dal ponte Palacký danneggiato: nel 1978 qui fu collocato il gruppo di statue ricostruito, che raffigura Přemysl e Libussa. Le figure eroiche di Myslbek furono eseguite in base ai temi attuali mitologico-nazionali contenuti nel manoscritto di Králův Dvůr. Lumír con la Canzone fu scolpito nel 1888, Přemysl e Libussa nel 1892, Záboj con Slavoj mentre tornano dal combattimento conclusosi con la loro vittoria, nonché Ctirad e Šárka furono scolpiti nel 1897. Le immagini inebrianti e poetiche sul glorioso passato degli Slavi, trovarono a Vyšehrad la loro giustificazione.

IL MONASTERO NA SLOVANECH (EMAUZY) 188 — fu fondato da Carlo IV per i Benedettini slavi, i quali fecero qui un centro singolare di civilizzazione e arte. Qui, nel 1395, nacque la cosiddetta parte glagolica dell'Evangeliario di Rheims, sul quale dopo il 1546 i re della Francia facevano il giuramento durante l'incoronazione. Nel corso delle guerre ussite qui fu istituito l'unico convento ceco degli utraquisti.

L'area del monastero gradualmente ricostruita e comprendente la chiesa della Vergine Maria, fu seriamente danneggiata durante i bombardamenti nel 1945. Negli anni successivi si svolse la ricostruzione dei fabbricati, e nel 1967 furono terminati i lavori di ricostruzione della facciata e delle torri, secondo il progetto di F. M. Černý.

LA PORTA DI SLAVÍN 195 — la dominante del cimitero di Vyšehrad al lato orientale è Slavín, mausoleo comune dei rappresentanti più emeriti della nazione. La costruzione avvenne negli anni 1889—90, secondo il progetto dell'architetto A. Wiehl, mentre la decorazione scultorea, che rappresenta il Genio della Patria, la Patria esultante e la Patria afflitta, fu eseguita tra il 1892 e il 1893 da J. Maudr. Come primo fu seppellito a Slavín lo scrittore J. Zeyer nel 1901 e successivamente altre 53 importanti personalità (tra l'altro J. V. Myslbek, V. Hynais, E. Destinová, A. Mucha, J. Kubelík, V. Špála). Le lapidi sepolcrali al cimitero sono state eseguite da principali scultori ed architetti cechi.

LA ROTONDA DI SAN MARTINO 196 — il monumento più antico tuttora conservato a Vyšehrad, proveniente dalla seconda metà dell' XI secolo. La sua importanza fu degradata dopo la costruzione della fortezza di Vyšehrad, quando cioè la cappella fu trasformata in polveriera. Nel XIX secolo essa fu trasformata in deposito. Nel 1878 la rotonda preziosa fu acquistata dal capitolo di Vyšehrad che la fece restaurare secondo il progetto di A. Baum. L'interno fu completato con le pitture parietali di A. König e J. Heřman. Il quadro dell'altare fu dipinto da F. Sequens. La costruzione fu ristrutturata nuovamente nel 1915 e poi tra il 1969 e il 1970.

IL PALAZZO DELLA CULTURA E L'ALBERGO FÓRUM 198, 199 — il bisogno di un centro socio-culturale più ampio con la possibilità di organizzare le conferenze, i simposi, i congressi, condusse nel 1975 alla decisione del governo di costruire il Palazzo della cultura. L'enorme monoblocco del Palazzo della cultura su pianta di un irregolare ettagono fu terminato nel 1980, secondo il progetto elaborato dal collettivo di autori dell'Istituto militare per la progettazione (J. Mayer, V. Ustohal, A. Vaněk, J. Karlík). Dal lato opposto del ponte di Nusle si erge in alto l'edificio poligonale in forma di torre: è l'albergo Fórum. I lavori di costruzione dell'albergo, che conta 27 piani, furono terminati nel 1988 secondo il progetto di J. Trávníček.

LE ESPOSIZIONI DI PRAGA 201, 202 — trovano la propria dominante nel Palazzo dei Congressi, costruzione neobarocca in ferro, realizzata da B. Münzberger nel 1891, ristrutturata negli anni 1952—54. L'area delle esposizioni occupa una parte dell'ex Riserva reale, in cui si cacciavano vari animali. Nel 1891, su progetto di A. Wiehl, su un'area di 300.000 m^2, furono costruiti padiglioni per la Esposizione giubilare territoriale. La ricorda tuttora la sala espositiva originaria che comprendeva oggetti artistici e le produzioni del passato. Essa si trova al lato sinistro, dove oggi è l'Accademia di arti espressive. Al lato destro della parte d'ingresso si trova il padiglione della capitale Praga che oggi serve da lapidario al Museo Nazionale. Su ampie aree delle esposizioni vediamo una serie di padiglioni interessanti (per es. quello che contiene il panorama monumentale della battaglia di Lipany, che fece Marold nel 1898), nonché altri cimeli che attirano la nostra attenzione (per es. la rinnovata fontana dell'inventore Fr. Křižík).

LA VILLA TRÓJA 203 — alle estremità settentrionali della vallata praghese, nella zona caratteristica per numerosi vigneti, il conte V. V. di Šternberk, verso la fine del XVII secolo, fece costruire una villa seguendo l'esempio delle ville suburbane italiane. Alla realizzazione del progetto e all'esecuzione della costruzione presero parte D. Orsi de Orsini, S. Carloni, ma anche l'importante architetto della Borgogna, J. B. Mathey. Le pitture eccezionalmente ricche dei locali interni con le allegorie e i criptoritratti dei membri della famiglia Šternberk le fecero F. e G. F. Marcheti; le pitture della sala principale, che rendono l'onore agli Asburgo, furono eseguite negli anni 1691—97 dal pittore di origini olandesi, A. Godyn. Il signore ambizioso perseguiva senza tergiversazioni la carriera dell'impiegato della corte. La sua sede confortevole di campagna doveva servire anche durante la visita del sovrano, in quanto luogo di riposo e di caccia. Ben ideata era anche la composizione della villa: dal pianerottolo della scalinata esterna concepita in maniera alquanto grandiosa, con le statue di Gigantomachia — opera di J. J. e P. Heermann di Dresda —, ci si trovava in asse diretta con la siluetta del Castello di Praga.

Nella villa recentemente restaurata — con la riproduzione del giardino storico originario — la Galleria della capitale Praga nel 1989 installò le collezioni dei quadri del XIX secolo.

LA VILLA DI ZBRASLAV 204—209 — luogo di rappresentanza che si erge sulla riva sinistra del fiume Moldava, dove i turisti possono giungere da Praga anche utilizzando il vaporetto, serviva da prelatura dell'Abazia cistercense. La costruzione del 1739 con gli affreschi di V. V. Reiner, negli anni 1911—12 fu ristrutturata in una villa appartenente alla famiglia Bartoň di Dobenín.

Il convento di Zbraslav fu fondato da Venceslao II nel 1291. Nella chiesa abaziale dedicata alla Vergine Maria furono seppelliti il fondatore, dopo di lui Venceslao III e Elisa dei Premyslidi, madre di Carlo IV. Gli abati di Zbraslav scrissero la nota Cronaca di Zbraslav che va fino all'anno 1337.

L'edificio conventuale dell'abazia fu ristrutturato nel 1709, secondo il progetto di J. Santini e negli anni 1724—32 i lavori furono conclusi secondo il progetto di M. Kaňka. Le decorazioni a base di stucchi furono eseguite da T. Soldati; V. V. Reiner e F. X. Palko completarono gli affreschi in maniera eccellente. Nel 1785 il convento fu soppresso e quindi fu esposto al degrado. Nell'era della famiglia Bartoň di Dobenín l'interno della villa e del convento furono ristrutturati per opera di D. Jurkovič e A. Čenský. Al momento attuale nell'edificio del convento sono installate le collezioni scultoree del XIX e XX secolo, appartenenti alla Galleria Nazionale di Praga.

Un capitolo importante è dedicato alla generazione degli artisti legati al Teatro Nazionale: basta ricordare per es. il progetto originario di B. Schnirch, Trighe, dell'anno 1873 per i piloni del Teatro Nazionale, la cui dislocazione avvenne negli anni 1910—11, secondo il progetto ritoccato di E. Hallmann, S. Rous e L. Šaloun. L'accento particolare è dato all'opera del maggiore rappresentante di questa generazione, J. V. Myslbek, al quale è dedicata la sala separata, così come a J. Štursa, personalità scultorea eccezionale del primo venticinquennio del XX secolo.

PRAHA

Fotografie Miroslav Krob a Miroslav Krob mladší
Průvodní text PhDr. Marie Mžyková, CSc.
Anglický překlad PhDr. Monika Navrátilová
a Petr Nitsche
Německý překlad Gabriela Cinková
a PhDr. Pavel Cink
Francouzský překlad PhDr. Magda Procházková,
PhDr. Oldřich Kulík, PhDr. Otomar Radina,
JUDr. Emil Fiala a PhDr. Anna Krejzová, CSc.
Italský překlad Jaroslav Kunčík
Grafická úprava, návrh obálky a vazby
akad. malířka Dana Krobová
Vydalo nakladatelství KVARTA Praha 1992
jako svou 21. publikaci
Vydání 1.
Vytiskla SVOBODA, grafické závody,
akciová společnost, Praha

ISBN 80-85570-10-6